murach's
Modern
JavaScript

Mary Delamater

BEGINNER TO PRO

murach's
Modern
JavaScript

Mary Delamater

MIKE MURACH & ASSOCIATES, INC.

3730 W Swift Ave. • Fresno, CA 93722
www.murach.com • murachbooks@murach.com

Editorial team

Author:	Mary Delamater
Writer/Editor:	Joel Murach
Editors:	Anne Boehm
	Lisa Cooper
	Scott McCoy
Production:	Juliette Baylon

Murach also has books on these subjects:

Web development

HTML and CSS
PHP and MySQL
ASP.NET Core MVC

Programming languages

Python
Java
C#
C++

Databases

MySQL
SQL Server
Oracle SQL and PL/SQL

Data analysis

R for Data Analysis
Python for Data Analysis

For more on Murach books, please visit us at www.murach.com

10 9 8 7 6 5 4 3 2 1
ISBN: 978-1-943873-14-2

Contents

Expanded contents

viii   *Expanded contents*

Chapter 6   How to script the DOM

Chapter 7   How to test and debug an app

Section 2 Master the essential skills

Chapter 8   How to work with dates, times, and timers

Section 3   More skills as you need them

Resources

Introduction

According to StackOverflow's 2023 Developer Survey, JavaScript is the most popular language in the world. That's because JavaScript provides the functionality for a web page. As a result, it's a critical part of most websites, from the smallest personal sites to the largest commercial sites. That's why every web developer should know how to use JavaScript.

In the old days, JavaScript was hard to learn due to some quirks in its early versions that caused great confusion. But now, with this book, you can skip the old features and jump straight to the latest features and best practices of modern JavaScript. This makes it easier than ever to learn how to use JavaScript.

Who this book is for

The only prerequisite for this book is a basic understanding of HTML and CSS. After that, this book works if you're a web designer who has no programming experience. But it also works if you're a programmer who has experience with a language like Python, PHP, Java, or C#. Either way, when you finish this book, you'll have the JavaScript skills that you'll need on the job.

5 reasons why you'll love this book

- It doesn't waste your time by explaining old JavaScript features. Instead, it presents the most current features and best practices of modern JavaScript.

- It presents hundreds of examples that range from the simple to the complex. That way, you can quickly get the idea of how a feature works from the simple examples and also see how the feature is used in the real world from the more complex ones.

- The exercises at the end of each chapter provide a way for you to gain valuable hands-on experience without extra busywork.

- All of the information is presented in *paired pages*, with the essential syntax, guidelines, and examples on the right page and clear explanations on the left page. This helps you learn faster by reading less.

- The paired-pages format is ideal for reference when you need to refresh your memory about how to do something.

What you'll learn in this book

This book is divided into three sections. Each section takes you to a new level of expertise.

Section 1 presents a seven-chapter course in JavaScript that gets you started fast. This section works for programming novices as well as experienced programmers because it lets you set your own pace. If you're a beginner, you can read the book carefully and do all the exercises. If you have some experience, you can focus on the differences between JavaScript and the other languages that you've used. When you finish this section, you'll be able to write, test, and debug JavaScript apps of your own.

Section 2 presents the rest of the essential skills that every professional JavaScript programmer should have. This includes validating data, saving data in the browser, and working with dates, times, and timers. In addition, this section shows how to get started with object-oriented programming by creating your own objects and by using ES modules.

Section 3 presents more skills that you can learn as you need them. To start, it shows how to use Ajax to asynchronously update a web page with data from a web server, without reloading the entire page. In addition, it shows how to use Node.js to create a web-based API that runs on a server. Finally, it shows how to work with the Canvas API to create drawings and animations.

Recommended software for this book

To develop JavaScript apps, you can use any text editor. However, we recommend Visual Studio Code (VS Code) because it has many powerful features that can help you develop apps more quickly and with fewer errors.

In addition, we recommend using Google Chrome to do the primary testing for the JavaScript for a web page. That's because Chrome provides excellent developer tools for debugging your JavaScript apps.

Finally, we recommend using Node.js to run JavaScript on a server. That's because it's widely used and provides many powerful features.

All of this software can be downloaded for free from the internet. In addition, appendixes A (Windows) and B (macOS) provide complete instructions for installing it.

What you can download from our website

You can download all the files for this book from our website. These files include:

- the apps presented in this book
- the starting points for the exercises presented at the end of each chapter
- the solutions to those exercises

Appendixes A (Windows) and B (macOS) provide complete instructions for installing these items on your computer.

A companion HTML and CSS book

Besides JavaScript, the best web developers also master HTML and CSS. If you need to brush up on your HTML and CSS, *Murach's HTML and CSS* is the perfect companion to this JavaScript book. With both books at your side, you'll be on your way to developing web pages like a pro.

Support materials for instructors and trainers

If you're a college instructor or corporate trainer who would like to use this book for a course, we offer support materials that will help you set up and run your course as effectively as possible. These materials include instructional objectives, test banks, projects, case studies, and PowerPoint slides.

To learn more, please visit www.murachforinstructors.com if you're an instructor. If you're a trainer, please visit www.murach.com and click on the *Courseware for Trainers* link, or contact Kelly at 1-800-221-5528 or kelly@murach.com.

Please let us know how this book works for you

When we started this book, our goal was to make it as easy as possible for you to master JavaScript. Now, we hope we have succeeded, and we wish you all the best with your JavaScript programming. If you have any comments, we would love to hear from you.

Mary Delamater, Author
maryd@techknowsolve.com

Joel Murach, Editor
joel@murach.com

Section 1

Get started fast

This section presents the skills you need to get started fast with JavaScript. To start, it shows how to use the popular Visual Studio Code text editor to develop your first JavaScript apps. Then, it teaches all of the JavaScript coding skills you need to create an app that modifies the elements of a web page, a common use of JavaScript. When you're done, you'll be able to code, test, and debug basic JavaScript apps.

1

How to code and run your first apps

This chapter assumes that you know how to use HTML and CSS to provide the content and formatting for a web page. As a result, it begins with the background concepts, terms, and skills you need to begin adding JavaScript to provide the functionality for a web page. Then, it presents a quick tutorial on how to use the popular Visual Studio Code text editor to develop your first JavaScript apps. Finally, it shows the code for a JavaScript app that validates the data the user enters on a web page.

If you have some programming experience, you're probably already familiar with many of the concepts and skills presented in this chapter and can go through it quickly. If you're new to programming, though, you'll want to take the time you need to understand the concepts and skills this chapter presents. Then, you can gain some hands-on experience by doing the exercises at the end of the chapter.

An introduction to web apps and JavaScript

A *web app* consists of many components that work together to bring the app to the web browser on your computer or mobile device. This book assumes that you already know how to use HTML to define the content for a web page and CSS to format a web page. Now, it shows how to use JavaScript to add functionality to a web page.

How JavaScript is used for client-side processing

A web app consists of clients and servers. The *clients* are the computers and mobile devices that use the web app. They access web pages through a *web browser* (or just *browser*). The *servers* are powerful computers that typically run at a remote location. They store the files and databases that make up a web app, and they run any code for the web app that's stored on the server.

To start, the web browser builds a request for the web page and sends it to the web server as shown by the diagram in figure 1-1. This request is known as an *HTTP request* because it is formatted using *HyperText Transfer Protocol* (*HTTP*).

When the web server receives the HTTP request, it reads the request and returns an appropriate *HTTP response*. If the browser has requested a web page, the HTTP response typically contains the HTML, CSS, and JavaScript for the page.

When the browser receives the HTTP response, it *renders* (translates) the HTML, CSS, and JavaScript and displays the web page to the user. If the user requests another page, either by clicking a link or typing another web address into the browser, the process begins again. A process that begins with the client making a request and ends with a server returning a response is called a *round trip*.

A *dynamic web page* changes depending on various factors, including the parameters stored in the HTTP request. If, for example, the user has entered data into a form, the HTTP request includes that data as parameters. Then, the web server typically uses an *application server* to process the data in the HTTP request. This may include using *SQL (Structured Query Language)* to get data from a database that's running on a *database server*. Since this processing is done on the server, it's known as *server-side processing*.

On the other hand, a web browser runs on a client device. As a result, when a web browser processes the JavaScript in an HTTP response, it's known as *client-side processing*. Client-side processing works because all modern browsers have a *JavaScript engine* that can run JavaScript. This takes some of the processing burden off the server, which can make an app more efficient. In addition, this limits the number of round trips required by an app, which makes the app more responsive.

An HTTP request and response for a dynamic web page

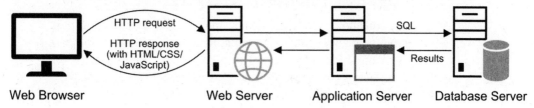

Web Browser   Web Server   Application Server   Database Server

Description

- The internet uses *HTTP (HyperText Transfer Protocol)* to send requests for web pages and to return responses that include the HTML, CSS, and JavaScript for a web page.

- Most web pages available from the internet are *dynamic web pages* that change depending on parameters in the HTTP request that's sent by the web browser.

- When a web server receives an HTTP request for a web page, it can pass the request on to an *application server* that runs code to process the request. Since this processing happens on a server, it's known as *server-side processing*.

- If an application server needs to work with a database, it can use a language known as *SQL (Structured Query Language)* to work with a database that's running on a *database server*.

- The *JavaScript engine* of a web browser runs the JavaScript for a web page.

- Since the web browser runs on a client device, JavaScript running in the web browser is known as *client-side processing*.

- Because JavaScript runs on the client, not the server, it can process the web page without requiring a trip back to the server. This helps a web app run more efficiently.

Figure 1-1   How JavaScript is used for client-side processing

ECMAScript version history

In 1996, an internet company named Netscape released JavaScript as part of its web browser, Netscape Navigator. After that, Microsoft released a competing scripting language named JScript as part of its web browser, Internet Explorer (IE). Eventually, Netscape gave JavaScript to Ecma International, originally known as the European Computer Manufacturers Association (ECMA), to develop a standard. That standard is called *ECMAScript (ES),* and the first version was released in June 1997. Since then, many versions have been released, as shown in figure 1-2.

JavaScript is based on the ECMAScript specification. Over the years, there have been many changes to this specification, with varying degrees of compliance by the various web browsers. Today, most modern browsers, including Chrome, Edge, Safari, Firefox, and Opera, support the newest features of ECMAScript.

In June 2015 the sixth version of the ECMAScript specification was released. At the same time, the committee in charge of the specification changed how it would release new versions going forward. Instead of having a set specification that they would release when all the features were completed, they moved to yearly releases of features that had been approved to that point. Thus, the version released in 2015 was officially named ECMAScript 2015, although you'll often see it referred to as ES6. After that, the versions are usually referred to by the year, such as ECMAScript 2023, or ES2023.

ES5 and ES6 represented significant updates to the ECMAScript specification that helped to usher in the era of modern JavaScript. Since then, each new version has built upon the previous version by adding new features and improving existing features. In this book, you'll learn how to use the most useful features of the modern versions of JavaScript.

Although the latest versions of most modern browsers support the ECMAScript specification, the support by earlier versions of these browsers, or by other legacy browsers, may be spottier. If you want a web app to run in web browsers that don't support the newest ECMAScript features, you may need to make some adjustments to the app. To start, you can follow the link in this figure to view a browser compatibility table. This allows you to check which ECMAScript features are supported by each browser. Then, you can modify the web app so it only uses features that are supported by the browsers you want the app to run in.

ECMAScript version history

Version	AKA	Release date
1		June 1997
2		June 1998
3	ES3	December 1999
4		Abandoned (never released)
5	ES5	December 2009
5.1		June 2011
2015	ES2015, ES6	June 2015
2016	ES2016, ES7	June 2016
...	...	...
2022	ES2022, ES13	June 2022
2023	ES2023, ES14	June 2023

A browser compatibility table

https://compat-table.github.io/compat-table/es2016plus/

Description

- In the early days of web programming, different browsers used different versions of JavaScript. To resolve this issue, Ecma International developed a standard for JavaScript that's known as *ECMAScript*.

- The newest features of ECMAScript are supported by the latest versions of most modern browsers for desktop computers and mobile devices. These web browsers include Chrome, Edge, Safari, Firefox, Opera, and others.

- If you need to support older browsers, you can use the URL shown above to determine which features are supported by which browsers.

Figure 1-2   ECMAScript version history

How to use VS Code to work with existing web apps

HTML, CSS, and JavaScript files are stored as text. As a result, you can use any text editor to work with the files for a web app. For this book, we recommend Visual Studio Code (VS Code), a popular text editor that's available for free and runs on Windows, macOS, and Linux. This text editor provides all the features you need to work efficiently and productively. To learn how to install VS Code, you can refer to appendix A (Windows) or B (macOS).

For this chapter, we used the VS Code color theme named Light to give the text editor a white background. However, VS Code's default theme is named Dark. As you might expect, it gives the text editor a dark background. If you want to change the default theme on your system, you can select File→ Preferences→Theme→Color Theme. Then, you can select the color theme you want.

To get started with VS Code, this chapter begins by showing you how to work with existing apps like the ones included in the download for this book. In particular, it shows how to work with the folders and files of an existing app so you can run it and manage its files.

How to work with folders

To work with a web app in VS Code, you can start by opening the folder that contains all of the subfolders and files for the app as described in figure 1-3. After you open the folder for an app, it's subfolders and files are displayed in the Explorer window on the left side of VS Code's main window.

To make it easier to work with the apps for this book, we recommend that you use VS Code to open the folder that contains all of the apps as shown by the dialog in this figure. After you do that, VS Code displays all of the chapter folders in the Explorer window on the left side of the main VS Code window.

When you're done working with a folder, you can close it as shown in this figure. Or, if you open another folder, it closes the folder that's currently open before it opens the new folder.

This figure also shows how to add, rename, and delete folders. To do that, you right-click the appropriate folder. Then, you select the item you want from the resulting menu.

The dialog for choosing a folder in VS Code

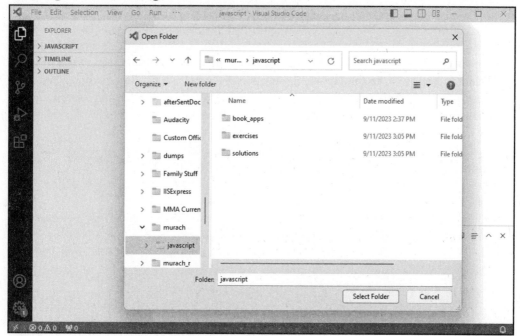

How to open or close a folder

- To open a folder, select File→Open Folder and use the resulting dialog to select the folder.
- To close a folder, select File→Close Folder.

How to add, rename, or delete a folder

- To add a folder, right-click a folder in the Explorer window and select New Folder. Then, enter a name for the folder.
- To rename a folder, right-click it and select Rename. Then, edit the name.
- To delete a folder, right-click it and select Delete.

Description

- Visual Studio Code (VS Code) is a text editor that you can use to work with a variety of file types, including HTML, CSS, and JavaScript.
- To make it easy to navigate to and switch between files, you can open a folder that contains the project or projects you want to work with.
- The files for this book are stored in this folder:

  `Documents\murach\javascript`

- When you open one of the folders for this book, a popup may be displayed asking if you trust the authors of the files in the folder. If so, you can click the Yes button. You'll want to be careful when opening files from other sources, though.

Figure 1-3   How to work with folders

How to work with files

Figure 1-4 presents several techniques that you can use to work with files in VS Code. To start, you can display the file you want to work with by expanding the folder that it's in. To do that, you can click the > symbol to the left of the folder to expand it. In this figure, the Explorer window shows that the book_ apps, ch01, and email_list folders have all been expanded. This displays the four files for the Email List app that are presented at the end of this chapter.

After you display a file in the Explorer window, you can double-click it to open it in a tab in the editor. This is referred to as Standard mode. In this mode, the tab for the file displays the file name in normal font style. In this figure, the first tab displays the file named email_list.js in Standard mode. If you want to keep a file open for a while, you can use this mode.

On the other hand, if you only want to preview a file, you can click it once instead of double-clicking it. This displays the file in Preview mode. In this mode, the tab displays the name of the file in italics. In this figure, the second tab displays the file named index.html file in Preview Mode. Then, if you click the name of a different file, VS Code loads that file in the same tab.

Note that when you open or preview a file, it's displayed in the Open Editors list at the top of the Explorer window. This list helps you keep track of which files have changes that haven't been saved.

When two or more files are displayed in an editor, you can switch between them by clicking the tab for the file you want to display. In this figure, for example, you could switch to the email_list.js file by clicking its tab.

VS Code provides several ways to close or save a file. The easiest way to close a single file is to press Ctrl+W (Windows) or Command+W (macOS), and the easiest way to save a file is to press Ctrl+S (Windows) or Command+S (macOS). You can also save or close all open files by selecting menu items as described in this figure.

VS Code also provides several ways to add, rename, or delete a file. When you add a new file, you must include an extension (.html, .css, or .js) depending on whether you want to add an HTML, CSS, or JavaScript file. Then, VS Code can adjust its editor to work with the syntax for that type of file.

When you add a new file, VS Code doesn't generate any code for it. Because of that, you have to enter all of the code yourself. Another option, though, is to copy code from another file and paste it into the new file. Then, you can modify that code so it's right for the new file.

VS Code with files in Standard and Preview mode

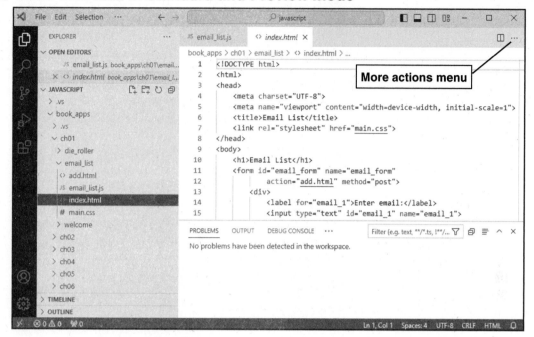

How to preview or open a file

- To preview a file, click it in the Explorer window. This displays the file in a tab with the name of the file in italics. This indicates that the file is in Preview Mode. If you open or preview another file, VS Code reuses the tab.
- To open a file, double-click it in the Explorer window. This displays the file in a tab with the name of the file in normal font style. This indicates that the file is in Standard Mode.
- To display a file that's already open, click its tab.

How to close or save a file

- To close a file, click the X in the upper right corner of the tab for the file or press Ctrl+W.
- To save a file, select File→Save (Ctrl+S).
- To close all open files, click the More Actions menu (the three horizontal dots at the right side of the editor window) and select Close All.
- To save all open files, select File→Save All.

How to add, rename, or delete a file

- To add a new file to a folder, right-click the folder in the Explorer window and select New File. When you name the file, be sure to include an extension.
- To rename a file, right-click it and select Rename.
- To delete a file, right-click it and select Delete.

Figure 1-4   How to work with files

How to install the Open in Browser extension

As you develop web apps, you need to open the HTML files for the app in one or more browsers. Unfortunately, VS Code doesn't provide a built-in way to do that. As a result, we recommend installing an extension to VS Code that makes it easy to open HTML files in a browser. One popular extension is Open in Browser from TechER, and figure 1-5 shows how to install it.

To start, you click the Extensions icon in the left sidebar. Then, VS Code displays the Extensions window in the left sidebar instead of the Explorer window. This window lists any extensions that are already installed as well as any recommended extensions.

To find the Open in Browser extension, you can type "open in browser" in the text box at the top of the Extensions window. When you do, VS Code displays several extensions with that name or a similar name. Because of that, you should make sure to install the one developed by TechER.

To install this extension, click the Install button for it in the Extensions window. Once you've done that, you can open an HTML file in a browser directly from VS Code as shown in the next figure.

If you want to learn more about an extension, you can click it in the Extensions window. Then, VS Code displays more information about the extension in the main window, including buttons that let you disable or uninstall an installed extension.

VS Code after the Open in Browser extension has been installed

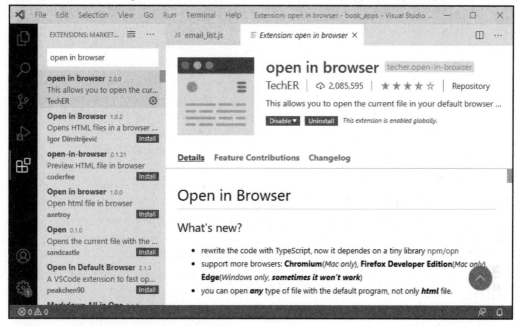

How to install the Open in Browser extension

1. Click the Extensions icon (⬛) in the left sidebar.

2. Enter "open in browser" in the text box at the top of the Extensions window to filter the available extensions.

3. Click the Install button for the Open in Browser extension from TechER.

Description

- By default, VS Code doesn't provide a way to open an HTML file in a browser so you can test the JavaScript code it uses.

- To make it easier to open an HTML file in a browser, you can install an extension to VS Code. One popular extension is the Open in Browser extension developed by TechER, but other extensions are available.

Figure 1-5   How to install the Open in Browser extension

How to run an app

Figure 1-6 shows how to run a web app. To do that, you open the file that contains the HTML for the first page of the app. For example, to run the Email List app that's shown in this chapter, you open its index.html file to display that page in the browser.

If you installed the Open in Browser extension as shown in the previous figure, you can open the index.html file by right-clicking it and selecting the Open in Default Browser option. This opens the HTML file in your default browser, which is usually what you want. Or, if the index.html file is already open in the text editor, you can press Alt+B to open it in your default browser.

However, if you want to open the HTML file in a different browser, you can right-click the HTML file and select Open in Other Browser. This displays a list of the other browsers that are installed on your computer. Then, you can select a browser to display the file in that browser. Note that this may not work for the Edge browser on your system, though.

Another way to open an HTML file is to right-click it and select Reveal in File Explorer (Windows) or Reveal in Finder (macOS). This starts File Explorer or Finder and displays the folder that contains the file. Then, you can double-click the file to open it.

The Email List app shown in this figure uses JavaScript to check that the email addresses entered by the user match. If they do, the web page sends the entries to the web server for server-side processing. If they don't, the JavaScript displays messages so the user can correct the entries.

How to open an HTML file using the Open in Browser extension

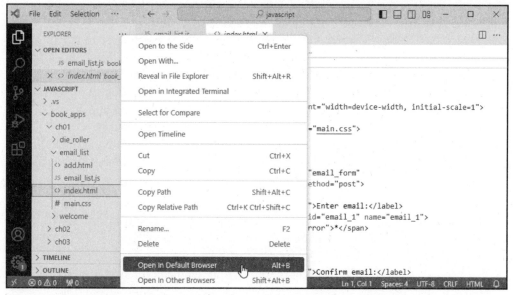

The web page in Chrome

Description

- If you installed the Open in Browser extension as shown in the previous figure, you can open an HTML file by right-clicking the file in the Explorer window and selecting Open in Default Browser to open the file in your default browser.

- If you select Open in Other Browsers when you're using the Open in Browser extension, you can select the browser in which you want the file to be opened. However, note that this may not work for Edge.

- You can also use the extension's shortcut keys shown in the menu above to perform these operations.

- If you haven't installed the Open in Browser extension, you can right-click the file in the Explorer window and select Reveal in File Explorer (Windows) to display it in File Explorer or Reveal in Finder (macOS) to display it in Finder. Then, you can double-click the file to open it.

Figure 1-6   How to run an app

How to use VS Code to develop new web apps

Now that you know how to use VS Code to work with an existing JavaScript app, you're ready to learn how to use it to develop your first new JavaScript app. As you review these skills, don't worry if you don't understand exactly how the code that's presented works. For now, what's important is that you understand how to use VS Code to run apps that use HTML, CSS, and JavaScript.

How to create and run an app

Figure 1-7 begins by showing the code for a simple JavaScript app that displays a dialog that says, "Hi!". The code for this app is stored in an HTML file that defines a simple web page.

At the end of the <body> element, this code includes a <script> element that contains some JavaScript. Within the <script> element, the first line is a *comment* that describes what the code does but is ignored by the JavaScript engine. Then, the second line is a *statement* that calls a *method* named alert() that displays a dialog like the one shown in this figure. JavaScript provides many built-in methods that perform various tasks, and the alert() method is one of them.

To use VS Code to create and run this app, you can use the procedure shown in this figure. As you enter the code, VS Code typically uses a feature called IntelliSense to help you as described in the next figure. When you're done entering the code, make sure to save the HTML file. Otherwise, the browser won't use the correct code when you run the app.

An app that displays a dialog

```html
<!DOCTYPE html>
<html>
    <head>
        <title>Welcome</title>
    </head>
    <body>
        <h1>Welcome to Modern JavaScript</h1>
        <script>
            // call a method that displays a dialog
            alert("Hi!");
        </script>
    </body>
</html>
```

The browser and the dialog

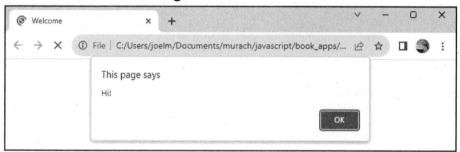

How to create and run an app

1. Create a folder for the app.
2. Within that folder, create an HTML file for the app.
3. Enter HTML and JavaScript code into the HTML file.
4. Save the HTML file.
5. Press Alt+B to run the HTML file in the default browser.

Description

*   In an HTML file, you can use a <script> element to include JavaScript. This can be referred to as *embedded JavaScript*.

*   Within a <script> element, you can use two forward slashes (*//*) to add a *comment* that's ignored when the JavaScript is executed. Comments are often used to describe code.

*   Within a <script> element, you can add one or more JavaScript *statements*. A statement performs a task and typically ends with a semicolon (*;*), though that isn't required.

*   JavaScript provides many built-in *methods* that you can use to perform various tasks. This example uses a method named alert() to display a message.

Figure 1-7   How to create and run an app

How to enter and edit code

Figure 1-8 shows how to edit HTML, CSS, or JavaScript with VS Code. When you open a file with an html, css, or js extension, VS Code knows what type of file you're working with. As a result, it can use color to highlight the syntax components.

As you enter code, VS Code uses a feature called IntelliSense to display completion lists that can help you complete the code you're entering. The list that's displayed depends on the code that you've entered, and it can help you avoid introducing errors into your code.

To illustrate, the example in this figure shows the completion list that's displayed when you type "al". This displays the rest of the name of the built-in alert() method. When a completion list is displayed, you can insert the highlighted item by pressing Enter. If you want to change the highlighted item, you can use the Up and Down arrow keys to move the highlight up or down in the list. Then, you can press Enter to insert the highlighted item.

Although the example shows how to use completion lists with JavaScript, this also works with HTML and CSS. If, for example, you type "<sc" in an HTML document, VS Code presents a list of the elements that start with the letters sc. Then, when you finish entering the opening tag for the element, VS Code adds the closing tag.

Similarly, if you start to enter the name of an element for a CSS style rule, VS Code presents a list of the elements with the letters you enter. If you enter one or more letters to start a property declaration, VS Code presents a list of the properties that start with those letters. And if you start an entry for a property value, VS Code presents a list of values.

As you edit the code for a web page, you can open its HTML file to make sure the code still works correctly. Before you do that, you should save any changes you've made to that file and its related files. That's because the browser only uses the saved changes. One way to be sure you've saved all the changes for an app is to check the Open Editors list. This list indicates how many unsaved files you have open, and it displays a gray dot to the left of the files with changes.

Each time you open an HTML file, a new browser tab is typically opened. Although this works, it can clutter your browser with many versions of the same web page. To avoid that, you can open the HTML file in a browser just once. Then, after you make changes in VS Code, you can save the changes, switch to the browser, and click the Reload or Refresh button in the browser to reload the file with the changes. That way, you use the same browser tab each time you test the app.

The code editor with a completion list

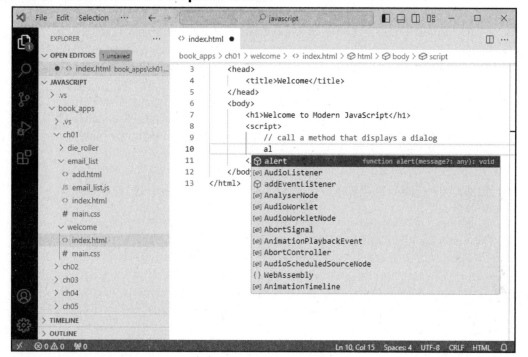

Description

- VS Code provides features like IntelliSense and syntax highlighting that help you enter and edit code.

- IntelliSense displays completion lists for things like keywords, variables, properties, methods, and functions as you type so you can enter them correctly.

- To insert an item from a completion list, use the arrow keys to highlight the item and press Tab or Enter.

- If you enter an opening parenthesis or brace, the closing parenthesis or brace is added automatically.

- If you enter an opening HTML element, the closing element is added automatically.

- After you save the code, you can test it by opening the HTML file. This typically opens another browser tab, or in some cases, another browser window. If the HTML file is already open in a browser, another option is to switch to the browser and click its Reload or Refresh button.

Figure 1-8   How to enter and edit code

How to find and fix syntax errors

As you enter and edit code, it's inevitable that you will make a mistake that results in a *syntax error*. A syntax error occurs when the code violates one of the rules of the JavaScript language. Fortunately, VS Code can help you find and fix syntax errors.

If VS Code detects a syntax error as you type, it displays a red wavy line under the error as shown in figure 1-9. Here, the semicolon after the statement is underlined because the message "Hi!" begins with a double quote but doesn't end with one. To display the description of an error, you can hover the mouse over the red wavy underline. In this figure, the message says, "Unterminated string literal". This indicates that the closing double quote for the message is missing.

You can also open the Problems window to display a list of all the errors. Then, you can click on an error to jump to the line of code that caused the error.

The Explorer window also indicates if a file contains errors. To do that, it displays the name of the folder and subfolders that contain the file in red, and it displays a red dot to the right of those folders and subfolders. In addition, it displays the number of errors to the right of the file name.

The Problems window with an error displayed

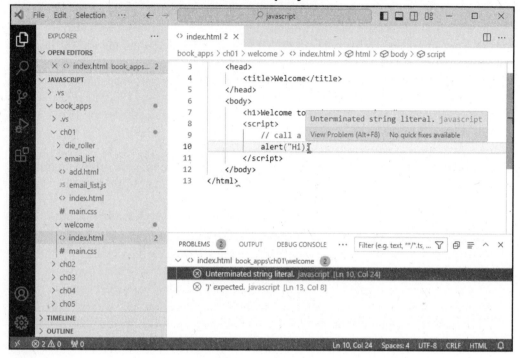

Description

- A *syntax error* violates the rules of the JavaScript language and can be detected before the code is executed.

- If VS Code detects a syntax error, it underlines it with a red wavy line.

- To get the description for an error, hover the mouse over the red wavy line.

- To see all the errors in a file, you can display the Problems window (View→Problems). Then, you can click on an error to take you to it in the file.

Figure 1-9   How to find and fix syntax errors

The Die Roller app

Figure 1-10 shows a JavaScript app that simulates the roll of a six-sided die. This app contains two files: an HTML file named index.html and a CSS file named main.css.

The HTML file begins by using a <link> element to identify the external style sheet for the web page. An *external style sheet* is simply a file that stores the CSS that formats the HTML. When you store CSS in an external file like this, it separates the content (HTML) from the formatting (CSS). That makes it easy to use the same styles for two or more pages.

Here, the external style sheet is named main.css. Since this file only contains basic CSS, it isn't shown in this figure. However, if you want to review it, it's available from the download for this book.

Within the <body> element, an <h1> element contains a <script> element that executes some JavaScript code. After the <h1> element, a <p> element displays some text that indicates that you can click Reload to roll again.

The <script> element contains three JavaScript statements. This figure provides a brief description of the JavaScript that's used by these three statements. In short, the first statement gets a random decimal number between 0 and 6. The second statement rounds that decimal number up to the nearest integer to get an integer from 1 to 6. And the third statement sends some text to the web page that says, "Die Roll: " followed by the integer.

Since this <script> element is coded within the <h1> element, this provides the text for the <h1> element. And since the browser runs this JavaScript each time it loads the page, you can roll the die again by clicking the browser's Reload button.

Although you should understand the HTML presented in this figure, don't worry if you don't understand the JavaScript code contained in the <script> element. You'll learn more about how this code works as you progress through this book.

An app that simulates the roll of a die

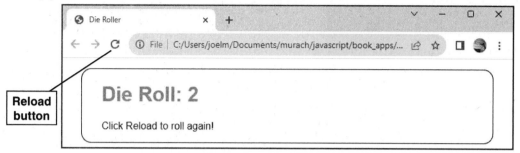

The code for the index.html file

```html
<!DOCTYPE html>
<html>
    <head>
        <title>Die Roller</title>
        <link rel="stylesheet" href="main.css">
    </head>
    <body>
        <h1>
            <script>
                // get a random number between 0 and 6
                const randNum = Math.random() * 6;

                // round up to get a number from 1 to 6.
                const dieRoll = Math.ceil(randNum);

                // write some text and the number to the web page
                document.write("Die Roll: " + dieRoll);
            </script>
        </h1>
        <p>Click Reload to roll again!</p>
    </body>
</html>
```

A brief description of the JavaScript

- The const keyword declares a *constant* that stores a value that can't be changed.
- The assignment operator (=) assigns a value.
- The Math.random() method returns a random decimal number between 0 and 1.
- The multiplication operator (*) multiplies two numbers.
- The Math.ceil() method rounds a decimal number up to the nearest integer.
- The document.write() method writes text to the web page.
- Double quotes identify a string of text.
- The concatenation operator (+) combines text with a number.

Description

- When coding an HTML page, you can use a <link> element to specify an *external style sheet*, which is a file that stores the CSS that formats the HTML elements.

Figure 1-10   The Die Roller app

How to test a web app

Now that you know how to use VS Code, you're almost ready to start learning the JavaScript language. But first, you should know about two more skills that can be helpful when working with JavaScript.

How to use a browser to run an app

When developing simple web apps like the ones shown in this book, you can usually use files that are available from the local file system. Then, you can use VS Code to run the app in a browser as shown earlier in this chapter.

However, you can also run the app in a browser without using VS Code. To do that, you can use the first two techniques shown in figure 1-11. First, you can use File Explorer (Windows) or Finder (macOS) to find the HTML file for the app and then double-click the file. This runs the app in the default browser for your operating system. Second, if you're viewing a web page that has links, you can click a link that requests another page.

After a web app has been uploaded to a web server, you can run the app in a browser by using the next two techniques shown in this figure. First, you can enter the address of the web page into your browser. Second, you can click a link that requests another page. For example, you might search the internet to find the app. Then, you can click a link in the search results to run the app.

To specify the address for a web page, you can enter a *URL* (*Uniform Resource Locator*). A URL consists of four components. First, the protocol is typically HTTP (Hypertext Transfer Protocol) or HTTPS (Hypertext Transfer Protocol Secure). If you omit the protocol, your browser will use whichever protocol is set as its default.

Second, the domain name identifies the web server for the HTTP request. The web browser uses this name to look up the address of the web server for the domain. Although you can't omit the domain name, you can often omit the "www." from the domain name.

Third, the path lists the folders on the server that contain the file. Forward slashes are used to separate the names in the path and to represent the server's top-level folder at the start of the path. In this example, the path is "/shop-books/".

Fourth, the filename specifies the name of the file. In this example, the filename is index.html. If you omit the filename, the web server searches for a default filename in the path. This default filename depends on the web server, but it's typically index.html, default.htm, or both.

An app that's stored on the local file system

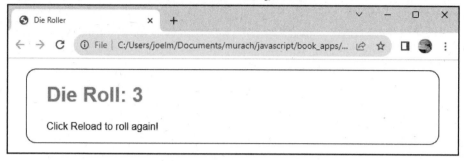

Two ways to run an app from the file system

- Use File Explorer (Windows) or Finder (macOS) to find the HTML file. Then, double-click it.
- Click a link in the current web page to load the next web page.

Two ways to run an app from a web server

- Enter the URL of the web page into the browser's address bar.
- Click a link in the current web page to load the next web page.

The components of a URL

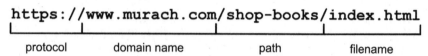

What happens if you omit parts of a URL

- If you omit the protocol, the browser uses the default of http:// or https://.
- If you omit the filename, the browser uses the default document name for the web server, typically index.html, default.htm, or some variation.

Description

- Before an app is deployed to a web server, you can run it from the file system.
- Appendixes A (Windows) and B (macOS) show how to use the http-server module as a web server that you can use to test all of the apps presented in this book.

Figure 1-11   How to use a browser to run an app

How to use your browser to find and fix runtime errors

Although VS Code can help you find errors in your code, it only identifies syntax errors that occur before you run an app. However, most modern browsers, including Chrome, can help you find *runtime errors* that occur when you run an app. As a result, if you run an app and it doesn't run or stops running, you can use Chrome to help find the runtime error. This can help you determine the cause of the error, which is the first step towards fixing the error.

As figure 1-12 shows, if a JavaScript app doesn't run or stops running, you can start looking for an error by opening the *developer tools*. Although there are several ways to do that, the easiest way in most browsers, including Chrome, Firefox, and Edge, is to press F12. That's why the developer tools are often referred to as the *F12 tools*.

After opening the developer tools, you typically open the Console panel to see if there's an error message. In this figure, the Console panel shows a message for an error that occurred when the user started the Die Roller app and the web page didn't display the <h1> element that shows the die roll.

If you click the link to the right of the error message, the browser displays the Sources panel and highlights the JavaScript statement that caused the error. In this case, the code that calls a method named ceiling() is highlighted because a method with that name doesn't exist. That's because this method is actually named ceil(), not ceiling().

In this figure, the Sources panel doesn't show the Debugging pane that's typically displayed as part of the panel. If you're not using this pane, you can close it by clicking the Hide Debugger button in the Sources panel. To redisplay it, you can click the Show Debugger button.

The Console panel with an error displayed

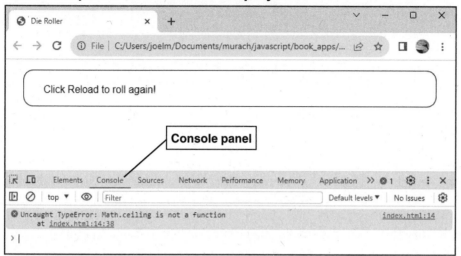

The Sources panel after the link in the Console panel has been clicked

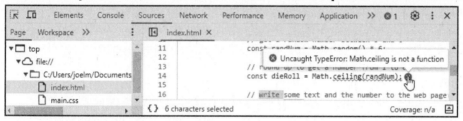

How to use the developer tools

- To open or close the developer tools in your browser, press F12 or look up the specific shortcut key for your browser of choice.
- To change where the developer tools are displayed, click the More Actions menu (three vertical dots) and select a Dock Side item.
- To display a panel, click its tab.

How to get more information about an error

1. In the Console panel, click the link to the right of the error message that indicates the line number that caused the error. This will open the Sources panel and display the statement that caused the error.
2. Hover your cursor over the red X to view the error message.

Description

- A *runtime error* occurs when you run an app and a statement can't be executed.
- The *developer tools* provided by Chrome and other browsers provide some excellent debugging features that can help you find and fix runtime errors.
- Because you typically start the developer tools by pressing the F12 key, these tools are often referred to as the *F12 tools*.

Figure 1-12   How to use your browser to find and fix runtime errors

The components of a web app

When you develop a JavaScript app, you use HTML to define the content and structure of the page, you use CSS to format that content, and you use JavaScript to provide the behavior of the page. This is illustrated by the Email List app presented in the next three figures.

The HTML

HyperText Markup Language (*HTML*) defines the content and structure of a web page. Figure 1-13 starts by showing the user interface that's defined by the HTML for the Email List app before the CSS is applied.

This book assumes that you are already familiar with HTML, but here are a few highlights. First, note that this document starts with a DOCTYPE declaration that declares that it is an HTML document.

Second, in the <head> element, a <meta> element specifies that UTF-8 is the character encoding that's used for the page. After that, another <meta> element sets the viewport to help the page display properly on mobile devices. Then, a <title> element contains the text that's displayed in the browser's tab. Finally, a <link> element indicates that the CSS for the web app is stored in an external style sheet named main.css.

Third, within the <body> element, the page uses <h1>, <form>, <div>, <label>, <input>, and <span> elements. In addition, the <body> element ends with a <script> element. Although a <script> element can also be coded in the <head> element, it's considered a best practice to code <script> elements at the end of the <body> element. That way, the browser loads the HTML before it loads the JavaScript that provides the behavior for the HTML.

In this case, the JavaScript is stored in an external file named email_list.js. The JavaScript in this file performs the operations required by the page. When you store JavaScript in an external file like this, it separates the JavaScript from the HTML and makes it easier to reuse the code in other pages or apps.

In practice, developers often use the terms *elements* and *tags* interchangeably. In this book, we usually use the term *element*, but we occasionally use the term *tag*, especially when referring to an opening tag like <h1> or a closing tag like </h1>.

The web page before the CSS is applied

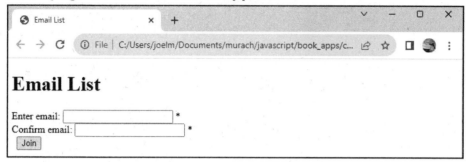

The HTML

```
<!DOCTYPE html>
<html>
<head>
    <meta charset="UTF-8">
    <meta name="viewport" content="width=device-width, initial-scale=1">
    <title>Email List</title>
    <link rel="stylesheet" href="main.css">
</head>
<body>
    <h1>Email List</h1>
    <form id="email_form" name="email_form"
          action="add.html" method="post">
        <div>
            <label for="email_1">Enter email:</label>
            <input type="text" id="email_1" name="email_1">
            <span id="email_1_error">*</span>
        </div>

        <div>
            <label for="email_2">Confirm email:</label>
            <input type="text" id="email_2" name="email_2">
            <span id="email_2_error">*</span>
        </div>

        <div>
            <label> </label>
            <input type="submit" id="join_button" value="Join">
        </div>
    </form>
    <script src="email_list.js"></script>
</body>
</html>
```

Description

- *HTML* (*HyperText Markup Language*) defines the structure and content of a web page.
- The <link> element specifies an external style sheet named main.css.
- The <script> element specifies an *external JavaScript file* named email_list.js.
- The id attributes specify unique names that JavaScript uses to get the HTML elements.

Figure 1-13   The HTML for a web app

The CSS

Cascading Style Sheets (*CSS*) provide a way to separate the formatting of a web page from its content and structure. Figure 1-14 shows the CSS that formats the HTML in the previous figure.

Again, this book assumes that you are already familiar with CSS, but here are a few highlights of what this CSS does. First, the style rule for the <body> element sets the font for the entire document, centers the body in the browser window, sets the width of the body to 600 pixels, puts space between the contents and the borders, puts a black border around the body, and curves the corners of the border. This CSS is typical for most of the apps in this book.

Similarly, the style rules for the <h1>, <div>, <label>, <input>, and <span> elements provide formatting for those elements. For example, the style rule for the <h1> element sets the font color to cornflower blue, and the style rule for the <div> element adds some space after each <div> element.

The style rule for the <label> elements formats each label as an inline block. That way, this rule can specify a width for a label and display a label on the same line as other elements. Then, this style rule sets the width of each label and right aligns its text.

The style rule for the <input> elements sets the left margin so there's space between the labels and the text boxes. It also sets the right margin so there's space between the text boxes and <span> elements.

Last, the style rule for the <span> elements sets the text color to red. That's because the Email List app uses these elements to display validation messages. However, when the browser loads the Email List app for the first time, these elements only contain asterisks (*) to indicate that a field is required.

The web page after the CSS is applied

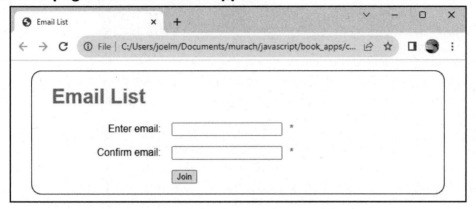

The CSS

```css
body {
    font-family: Arial, Helvetica, sans-serif;
    margin: 1em auto;
    width: 600px;
    padding: 0 2em 0;
    border: 1px solid black;
    border-radius: 1em;
}
h1 {
    color: cornflowerblue;
}
div {
    margin-bottom: 1em;
}
label {
    display: inline-block;
    width: 11em;
    text-align: right;
}
input {
    margin-left: 1em;
    margin-right: 0.5em;
}
span {
    color: red;
}
```

Description

- *Cascading Style Sheets* (*CSS*) specify the fonts, colors, borders, spacing, and layouts of web pages.

Figure 1-14   The CSS for a web app

The JavaScript

Figure 1-15 shows how the Email List app looks in a browser if the JavaScript determines that the two emails in the text boxes don't match after the user clicks the Join button. This shows that the app displays error messages to the right of a text box if it contains an invalid entry. In other words, the JavaScript actually changes the contents of the two <span> elements that are displayed to the right of the two text boxes.

When JavaScript changes the HTML for a page, it is changing the *Document Object Model* (or *DOM*) that's created by the browser when it loads the web page. The DOM represents all of the elements and attributes in the HTML. Then, when JavaScript changes any aspect of the DOM, the browser immediately displays the change. This is known as *DOM scripting* and it's one of the main uses of JavaScript.

The JavaScript for the Email List app may seem daunting at first, but don't worry if you don't yet understand this code. The next six chapters show how to write code like this. For now, you can read the comments that describe what the statements do to get a general idea of how it works.

To start, the code begins with the "use strict" directive that enables strict mode. This mode helps you write safer, cleaner code. As a result, it's generally considered a best practice for modern JavaScript.

After the strict mode directive, this code defines a function named getElement(). A *function* uses braces ({}) to define a block of code that performs a task. The getElement() function accepts a CSS selector as a parameter, gets the first element from the DOM that matches that selector, and returns that element.

After the getElement() function, the code defines a second function named joinButtonClick(). This function contains the code that's executed when the user clicks the Join button. To start, this function uses the getElement() function to get the values from the two text boxes, and it assigns these values to two constants named email1 and email2.

After getting the user entries, this code uses two if-else statements to check if those entries are valid. If the user has entered some text for the first text box and that text matches the text entered in the second text box, this app considers the user entries to be valid. In that case, the browser submits the data to the server.

However, if the user hasn't entered any text for the first text box or that text doesn't match the text in the second text box, the user entries are invalid. In that case, the code in the first two if-else statements replaces the * in the appropriate <span> element with an appropriate error message. Then, the third if statement prevents the browser from submitting the form to the server.

After the two functions, the code executes a complex statement that runs a block of code after the DOM has been loaded. This block of code contains a single statement that attaches the click event for the Join button to the joinButtonClick() function. To do that, this code uses the getElement() function to get the HTML element for the Join button. Then, it specifies that the joinButtonClick() function should be run if the user clicks the Join button.

The web page with JavaScript for data validation

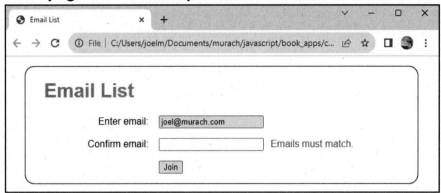

The JavaScript

```javascript
"use strict";

// define a function that gets an HTML element
function getElement(selector) {
    return document.querySelector(selector);
}

// define a function that handles the click event of the Join button
function joinButtonClick(event) {
    // get user entries from text boxes
    const email1 = getElement("#email_1").value;
    const email2 = getElement("#email_2").value;

    // check user entries
    let invalid = false;
    if (email1 == "") {
        getElement("#email_1_error").textContent = "Email is required.";
        invalid = true;
    } else {
        getElement("#email_1_error").textContent = "";
    }

    if (email1 != email2) {
        getElement("#email_2_error").textContent = "Emails must match.";
        invalid = true;
    } else {
        getElement("#email_2_error").textContent = "";
    }

    // cancel form submit if any user entries are invalid
    if (invalid) {
        event.preventDefault();
    }
};

// add code that's run when the web page is loaded
document.addEventListener("DOMContentLoaded", () => {

    // specify the function that's run when the Join button is clicked
    getElement("#join_button").addEventListener("click", joinButtonClick);
});
```

Figure 1-15   The JavaScript for a web app

Perspective

This chapter has presented the background concepts and terms that you need for using JavaScript in your web apps. More importantly, it has shown some practical skills for using Visual Studio Code to develop web apps, and it has shown how to use browser development tools to find and fix errors.

Terms

HTTP (HyperText Transfer Protocol)
dynamic web page
application server
server-side processing
SQL (Structured Query Language)
database server
JavaScript engine
client-side processing
web app
client
web browser
server
HTTP request
HTTP response
render a web page
round trip
dynamic web page
ECMAScript
embedded JavaScript

comment
statement
method
syntax error
constant
external style sheet
URL (Uniform Resource Locator)
runtime error
developer tools
F12 tools
HTML (HyperText Markup
    Language)
HTML element
HTML tag
external JavaScript file
Cascading Style Sheets (CSS)
Document Object Model (DOM)
DOM scripting
function

Before you do the exercises for this book...

Before you do the exercises for this book, you should download and install VS Code and the Chrome browser as well as the apps for this book as described in appendix A (Windows) or B (macOS).

Exercise 1-1   Open and run the Email List app

This exercise gets you started with VS Code by having you open and run the Email List app that's described in this chapter.

Open the folders for this book

1. Start VS Code.

2. Open this folder:

    murach/javascript/book_apps

    This displays the chapter folders within the book_apps folder in the Explorer window.

3. Open this folder:

    murach/javascript/exercises

    This displays the chapter folders within the exercises folder. Note that this closes the book_apps folder.

4. Open this folder:

    murach/javascript

    This displays the book_apps, exercises, and solutions folders in the Explorer window, and you can expand all of these folders.

Run the Email List app

5. Install the Open in Browser extension as described in this chapter.

6. In the Explorer window, expand this folder:

    book_apps/ch01/email_list

    This should display the files for the Email List app.

7. Click the file named index.html to preview its code. Do the same for the files named main.css and email_list.js.

8. Right-click the file named index.html, and select Open in Default Browser. This should open the index.html file in your default browser.

9. Switch back to VS Code. If you have another browser installed, right-click the index.html file again and select Open in Other Browsers. Then, click the name of the other browser to open the file in that browser. But remember that, at the time of this writing, this may not work for Edge.

Exercise 1-2   Create the Welcome app

This exercise has you create the Welcome app from scratch. In addition, it shows how to find and fix syntax errors.

Create the folder and files for this app

1. Start VS Code. If it isn't already open, open the murach/javascript folder.

2. Expand this folder:

    `exercises/ch01`

3. Right-click on the folder and select New Folder. Then, enter the name "welcome" for the folder.

4. Right-click the welcome folder and select New File. Then, enter the name index.html for the file.

5. Right-click the welcome folder and select New File. Then, enter the name main.css for the file.

Add the HTML

6. Click the tab for the index.html file to display the file, and enter all the HTML shown in figure 1-7 except for the <script> element. As you type this code, use code completion to help you enter the opening and closing tags for these elements.

7. When you enter the <title> element, misspell "title" in the opening tag. Note that VS Code uses a red wavy underline to mark the error.

8. Fix this error, and notice that the red wavy underline goes away.

9. Press Alt+B to run the app in your default browser, and make sure the <h1> element is displayed correctly.

Add the CSS

10. Open the main.css file for the Email List app, and copy its code. Then, display the tab for the main.css file for the Welcome app, and paste the code into that file.

11. Within the <head> element of the index.html file, add a <link> element that links to the styles stored in the main.css file.

12. Run the app to make sure it uses the formatting specified in the main.css file.

Add the JavaScript

13. In the <body> element of the index.html file, add a <script> element.

14. Within the <script> element, add a JavaScript statement that displays a dialog that says "Hi" followed by your name.

15. Run the app to make sure that the dialog is displayed correctly.

Exercise 1-3   Edit the Die Roller app

This exercise has you modify the Die Roller app that's described in this chapter. In addition, it shows how to find and fix runtime errors.

Run the Die Roller app

1. Use File Explorer (Windows) or Finder (macOS) to navigate to this folder:

   `exercises/ch01/die_roller`

2. Double-click on the index.html file to run the Die Roller app in your operating system's default web browser.

3. Click the Reload button several times to roll the die several times.

Introduce an error and fix it

4. Start VS Code.

5. Expand this folder:

   `exercises/ch01/die_roller`

6. Open the index.html file.

7. Edit the code that calls the Math.random() method so it attempts to call the Math.ran() method.

8. Run the app and note that the die roll no longer appears.

9. In the browser, press F12 to open the developer tools. Make sure that the Console tab is selected, and then view the error. The error message should give you an idea of why the code is incorrect and what you can do to fix it.

10. Click the link to the right of the error message to display the statement that caused the error in the Sources panel.

11. Switch to VS Code, and then fix the error by changing Math.ran() to Math.random() and save your changes.

12. Switch to the browser, and then click the Reload button to confirm that the app is working correctly.

Modify the app

13. In the index.html file, change the first JavaScript statement so it gets a random number between 0 and 8.

14. Adjust the related comment so it matches the new code.

15. Save your changes to the HTML file.

16. Switch to the browser, and then click the Reload button multiple times until you confirm that you can now roll up to an 8.

2

How to get started with JavaScript

The goal of this chapter is to get you off to a good start with JavaScript, especially if you're new to programming. If you have experience with another language, you can decide how rapidly you move through this chapter. Otherwise, you can read slowly and carefully, test the code as you go, and do each of the exercises at the end of this chapter to be sure you understand the material before moving on.

How to get started

The next few figures show how to get started with writing JavaScript code. To do that, they present the rules, or *syntax*, that you must follow as you write JavaScript. If you don't adhere to these rules, your browser won't be able to interpret and execute your code.

An introduction to coding statements

The first example in figure 2-1 shows some JavaScript that's coded within the <script> element of an HTML file. This JavaScript includes the "use strict" directive and three statements.

A *directive* tells the JavaScript engine how to interpret and compile your code. Because of this, it's always coded before any statements. In the download for this book, most of the apps contain a directive to use *strict mode*. However, due to space considerations, we don't always show this directive in the book.

It's considered a best practice to enable strict mode because it prevents certain "bad" coding practices, such as using a variable without declaring it. This helps you write safer and more secure code, especially when you are still new to programming. As a result, when writing new JavaScript code, you should always code the "use strict" directive before the statements that you want it to apply to.

In contrast to a directive, a *statement* tells JavaScript to perform a task. In the first example, for instance, the first statement assigns a value of 6 to a variable named miles. Then, the second statement performs a calculation that converts miles to kilometers and assigns the result to a variable named kilometers. Finally, the third statement uses a method named alert() to display the dialog with the values of the miles and kilometers variables.

When you write JavaScript, it's considered a good practice to code a semicolon (;) after each directive or statement. This isn't required for some statements, but it makes the code easier to read by clearly identifying the end of each statement.

In addition, you need to know that JavaScript is *case-sensitive*. This means that uppercase and lowercase letters are not the same. As a result, you must use the exact case for your code to work correctly. For instance, the statement in the second example fails because Alert() is not the same as alert(), and there is no method named Alert().

Finally, you need to know that JavaScript ignores extra whitespace in statements. *Whitespace* includes spaces, tabs, and new line characters. By ignoring whitespace, JavaScript lets you break long statements into multiple lines so they're easier to read. For instance, the third example is easier to read than the fourth example because it uses whitespace.

A script that contains a directive and three statements

```
<!DOCTYPE html>
<html>
    <body>
        <script>
            "use strict";

            let miles = 6;
            let kilometers = miles * 1.60934;
            alert(miles + " miles is " + kilometers + " km.");
        </script>
    </body>
</html>
```

The dialog displayed by these statements

```
This page says

6 miles is 9.65604 km.


                                    OK
```

Code that doesn't work due to incorrect case

```
Alert("Hi");      // Alert is not the same as alert - doesn't run
```

Use whitespace to make code easy to read

```
if (kilometers > 10) {
    alert("Long");
} else {
    alert("Short");
}
```

Without whitespace, code becomes hard to read

```
if(kilometers>10){alert("Long");}else{alert("Short");}
```

Description

- A *directive* specifies how the JavaScript engine should interpret code.

- To enable strict mode, you can include the "use strict" directive at the top of a script. When JavaScript is in *strict mode*, it disallows certain JavaScript features and coding practices that are considered unsafe. This helps you write safer, cleaner code.

- A *statement* performs a task.

- It's considered a good practice to code a semicolon (;) after each directive or statement.

- JavaScript is *case-sensitive*, which means that you must use the exact case for the code to work correctly.

- *Whitespace* refers to the spaces, tab characters, and return characters in the code, and it is ignored by the JavaScript engine.

Figure 2-1   An introduction to coding statements

How to code comments

Comments let you add descriptive notes to your code that are ignored by the JavaScript engine. Later, these comments can help you or someone else understand the code.

The example in figure 2-2 shows how comments can be used to describe or explain portions of code. At the start of the script, a *block comment* describes what the code does. This kind of comment starts with **/*** and ends with ***/**. When the app runs, the JavaScript engine ignores everything that's coded between the start and end of a block comment.

On the other hand, a *single-line comment* starts with **//** and continues to the end of the line. In this example, the first four single-line comments are coded on their own line and describe the statement that comes after them. By contrast, the last two single-line comments describe the code that comes before them on the same line.

When testing an app, comments can be useful for disabling a portion of code. To do that, you can enclose the code in a block comment so that it's ignored when the app runs. This is known as *commenting out* a portion of code. Later, after you test the rest of the code, you can enable the code that has been commented out by removing the characters that start and end the block comment. This can be referred to as *uncommenting* code.

If you're using VS Code, you can quickly comment out and uncomment lines of code using either single-line comments or a block comment. To do that, you highlight the lines and then select Edit→Toggle Line Comment or Edit→Toggle Block Comment. Then, if the lines of code are commented, they're uncommented, and vice versa.

When should you use comments to describe or explain code? Generally, if you think a comment would be useful, you should add one. For example, you'll want to use comments for any code that's complicated enough that you can't tell at a glance what it does. This will save time for anyone who has to maintain the code later. On the other hand, you shouldn't use comments to explain code that's easy to understand. That means that you have to strike a balance between adding too many comments and not adding enough.

Note, however, that the examples in this book often include more comments than you typically need. That's because these are instructional examples and the comments are meant to help you understand them.

A final thought on comments: If you change the way your code works, make sure you change the corresponding comments as well. Comments that don't accurately describe your code make the code more difficult to maintain later.

HTML that includes JavaScript with comments

```
<!DOCTYPE html>
<html>
    <body>
        <script>
            /*
            This code is designed to show how to use simple
            JavaScript statements and comments. It was written
            by Joel Murach in 2024.
            */

            // enable strict mode
            "use strict";

            // set the number of miles
            let miles = 6;

            // calculate kilometers from miles
            let kilometers = miles * 1.60934;

            // display the result of the calculation
            alert(miles + " miles is " + kilometers + " km. ");

            if (kilometers > 10) {   // greater than 10
                alert("Long");
            } else {                 // 10 or less
                alert("Short");
            }
        </script>
    </body>
</html>
```

Guidelines for using comments

- Use comments to describe portions of code that are hard to understand.
- Don't use comments unnecessarily.
- If you update your code, update the comments at the same time.

Description

- *Block comments* begin with **/*** and end with ***/**. Anything between the two symbols is ignored by JavaScript.
- *Single-line comments* begin with two forward slashes (**//**) and continue to the end of the line. Anything on the same line after the slashes is ignored by JavaScript.
- During development and testing, comments can be used to *comment out* (disable) portions of code.
- In VS Code, you can quickly comment and uncomment lines of code by highlighting them and then selecting Edit→Toggle Block Comment or Edit→Toggle Line Comment.

Figure 2-2   How to code comments

Three primitive data types

JavaScript provides seven *primitive data types* that specify the type of data for a value. The table at the top of figure 2-3 summarizes three of those data types.

The *number data type* represents a number, which can be an integer or a decimal. *Integers* are whole numbers, and *decimals* are numbers that have one or more digits after the decimal. Numbers may be positive or negative, as indicated by a positive or negative sign. If the sign is omitted, the default is positive.

This figure presents several examples of number values. The fifth value shows that you can include an underscore as a separator for long numbers. Here, the integer 1000000 includes two underscores. These separators are ignored by the JavaScript engine, but they make the number more readable to the human eye.

Regardless of whether a number is an integer or a decimal value, all values with the number data type are stored internally by JavaScript as *floating-point numbers*. A floating-point number can store very large and very small values, but it has a limited number of *significant digits*. To express the value of a floating-point number, you use *floating-point notation*. This notation consists of the significant digits for the number, followed by the letter e and a power of 10 that indicates how many places the decimal point should be moved to the left or right. For example, -3.7e-9 is equal to 0.0000000037, and 3.7e9 is equal to 3,700,000,000.

Although you generally don't need to understand how JavaScript stores numbers, some circumstances require you to understand how floating-point numbers work. In particular, you should know that floating-point numbers can be imprecise when representing the results of some arithmetic operations. In addition, floating-point numbers have a limit to the size of the numbers they can store. If you store a number that's too large, JavaScript converts it to Infinity. Similarly, if you store a number that's too small, JavaScript converts it to -Infinity. Infinity and -Infinity are properties of the global object. You'll learn more about properties and the global object later in this chapter.

The *string data type* stores a string of characters, or just *string* for short. In other words, it stores text. To code a string, you enclose zero or more characters within single or double quotation marks (quotes). However, you must close the string with the same type of quotation mark that you used to start it. If you code two quotation marks in a row without anything between them, the result is called an *empty string*.

The *Boolean data type* stores a value of true or false. To represent Boolean data, you code the *true* or *false* keyword with no quotation marks. This data type can be used to represent one of two states, such as true/false, yes/no, on/off, and so on.

Three primitive data types

Data type	Description
Number	An integer or a decimal value that can start with a positive or negative sign.
String	A string of characters (text).
Boolean	A true or false value.

Number values

```
15                 // an integer
-21                // a negative integer
21.5               // a decimal value
-124.82            // a negative decimal value
1_000_000          // a number that uses separators for readability
-3.7e-9            // floating-point notation for -0.0000000037
Infinity           // a number that's too large to be stored
-Infinity          // a number that's too small to be stored
```

String values

```
"JavaScript"       // a string with double quotes
'String Data'      // a string with single quotes
""                 // an empty string
```

Boolean values

```
true               // equivalent to true, yes, or on
false              // equivalent to false, no, or off
```

Description

- All values in JavaScript have a *primitive data type*, such as number, string, or Boolean.

- A number value can be an *integer*, which is a whole number, or a *decimal*, which can have one or more decimal positions.

- All values with the number type are stored as floating-point numbers. A *floating-point number* provides for very large and very small numbers, but with a limited number of *significant digits*.

- Floating-point numbers can't represent the exact value of some decimals, which can affect some types of numerical calculations and comparisons.

- If a number value is too large or too small to be stored as a floating-point number, it's converted to either Infinity or -Infinity respectively.

- A *string* stores zero or more characters and is typically coded within double quotes or single quotes. The string must start and end with the same type of quotation mark.

- An *empty string* is a string that contains no characters. It's entered by typing two quotation marks with nothing between them.

- A *Boolean value* can only be true or false.

- When you code a value, it's referred to as a *literal value*, or *literal*. To code a numeric literal, you code the number. To code a string literal, you enclose the characters in single or double quotes. To code a Boolean literal, you use the *true* or *false* keyword.

Figure 2-3   Three primitive data types

How to declare and initialize variables

A *variable* stores a value that can change as the app executes. To create, or *declare*, a variable in JavaScript, you code the *let* keyword followed by the name that you want to use for the variable. JavaScript also provides an older keyword, *var*, that you can use to declare and initialize variables. However, for modern JavaScript, it's considered a best practice to use the *let* keyword.

When you declare a variable, it's considered a best practice to also assign an initial value to it. To *initialize* a variable, you code an equal sign (the *assignment operator*) and a value after the variable name. The value that you assign to a variable determines its data type.

In the first example in figure 2-4, the first two statements show how to declare a variable and initialize it with a numeric value. To do that, these statements assign a *numeric literal* to the variable. Here, the first statement declares a variable named count and assigns an integer value of 1 to it. The second statement declares a variable named subtotal and assigns a decimal value of 74.95 to it.

The third, fourth, and fifth statements show how to declare a variable and initialize it with a string. To do that, these statements assign a *string literal* to the variable. A string literal consists of zero or more characters that are enclosed in single or double quotes. The third statement, for example, declares a variable named name and assigns a value of "Joseph" to it. The fourth statement declares a variable named postalCode and assigns a value of "95073" to it. This shows that a string can contain numbers. And the fifth statement is an empty string that doesn't include any characters between the quotes.

The sixth statement shows how to declare a variable and initialize it with a Boolean value. To do that, you assign the *true* or *false* keyword to the variable. Here, the sixth statement assigns a value of false to a variable named isValid.

The seventh statement shows that, in addition to assigning a literal value to a variable, you can assign the value of another variable to it. In this case, it assigns the value of the subtotal variable created by the second statement to a variable named total.

The eighth statement shows that you can declare and initialize two or more variables in a single statement. To do that, you code *let* followed by the variable name, an equal sign, and a value for each variable, separated by commas.

Once a variable is initialized, you can use the assignment operator to assign a new value to it as shown in the second example. If the new value is a different data type, the data type of the variable changes.

The table in this figure presents two more primitive data types, undefined and null. Both of these data types represent the absence of a value. However, as the table indicates, they are used differently than the other primitive data types.

If you declare a variable without initializing it as shown in the third example, JavaScript initializes the variable as *undefined*. However, it's generally a good practice to initialize your variables when you declare them. This is because uninitialized variables are a frequent source of bugs. Instead, you can assign *null*, as shown in the last example. This indicates that the value of a variable has

Declare and initialize a variable

```
let count = 1;                // integer value of 1
let subtotal = 74.95;         // decimal value of 74.95

let name = "Joseph";          // string value of "Joseph"
let postalCode = "95073";     // string value of "95073"
let email = "";               // empty string

let isValid = false;          // Boolean value of false

let total = subtotal;         // assigns value of subtotal variable
let x = 0, y = 0;             // declares and initializes 2 variables
```

Reassign the value of a variable

```
let count = 1;                // value of count is 1
count = 10;                   // value of count is now 10
```

Two primitive data types that indicate the absence of a value

Data type	Description
undefined	Assigned by JavaScript to indicate a variable has not been initialized.
null	Assigned by a programmer to indicate the intentional absence of a value.

An uninitialized variable

```
let message;                  // message is undefined - poor practice
```

Indicate that a variable is intentionally set to no value

```
let message = null;           // message is null - good practice
```

Description

- A *variable* stores a value that can vary as the code is executed.

- To create, or *declare*, a variable, code the *let* keyword and a variable name. To assign an initial value to, or *initialize*, a variable, use the *assignment operator* (=).

- In older code, you may see variables declared with the *var* keyword. This keyword was superseded by *let* in 2015 and should generally be avoided in new code.

- The data type of a variable is determined by the value that's assigned to it.

- You can use commas to declare more than one variable in a single statement.

- After you initialize a variable, you can assign a new value to it. If the data type of the new value is different, the data type of the variable changes.

- If you don't initialize a variable, JavaScript assigns *undefined* to the variable. Not initializing a variable is usually considered a poor coding practice.

- If you want to indicate the absence of a value, it's considered a best practice to initialize a variable with *null*. Then, you can assign a value to the variable later.

Figure 2-4   How to declare and initialize variables

intentionally not been set by the programmer because the value is unknown, unavailable, or not applicable.

How to declare and initialize constants

A *constant* stores a value that remains constant and cannot change once it's been initialized. To declare and initialize a constant, you use the same syntax you do to declare and initialize a variable, except that you use the *const* keyword instead of the *let* keyword.

The first example in figure 2-5 shows statements that work like the ones presented in the previous figure. However, these statements use the *const* keyword to declare constants instead of using the *let* keyword to declare variables. More specifically, the first two statements show how to declare a constant and initialize it with a numeric value. The third, fourth, and fifth statements show how to declare a constant and initialize it with a string. The sixth statement shows how to declare a variable and initialize it with a Boolean value. The seventh statement shows that you can assign the value of another variable or constant. And the eighth statement shows that you can declare and initialize two or more constants in a single statement.

The second example shows that you can't reassign the value of a constant. If you attempt to do this, a runtime error occurs and JavaScript displays an error message like the one shown in this figure.

The third example shows that you must initialize a constant when you declare it. If you don't, JavaScript displays a syntax error. Then, if you run the code without fixing the error, a runtime error occurs and JavaScript displays an error message like the one shown in this figure.

Many JavaScript programmers consider it a best practice to use constants instead of variables unless they're certain they will need to change a value. If you use constants and you try to change a constant's value, JavaScript alerts you by throwing the error shown here. Then, you can evaluate your code and decide if you do in fact need to change that value. If so, you can change the constant to a variable by changing the *const* keyword to *let*.

Declare and initialize a constant

```
const months = 12;              // integer value of 12
const pi = 3.14;                // decimal value of 3.14

const firstName = "Mary";       // string value of "Mary"
const postalCode = "95073";     // string value of "95073"
const message = "";             // empty string

const isValid = true;           // Boolean value of true

const grandTotal = subtotal;    // assigns value of subtotal variable
const min = 0, max = 100;       // declares and initializes 2 constants
```

Code that fails when you assign a new value to a constant

```
const count = 1;      // value of count is 1
count = 10;           // TypeError: Assignment to constant variable.
```

Code that fails when you don't initialize a constant

```
const count;          // SyntaxError: Missing initializer in const declaration
```

Description

- A *constant* stores a value that remains constant as the code executes.
- The syntax for declaring and initializing a constant is the same as the syntax for declaring and initializing a variable, except that you use the *const* keyword, not the *let* keyword.
- Once a constant is declared and initialized, you can't assign a new value to it.
- JavaScript forces you to initialize a constant when you declare it.

Figure 2-5   How to declare and initialize constants

Rules and recommendations for naming variables and constants

When you declare a variable or constant, you name it so you can refer to it in your JavaScript code. Figure 2-6 presents some rules and recommendations for naming variables and constants in JavaScript.

When naming a variable or constant, the name can't be the same as any of the JavaScript *reserved words* (also known as *keywords*). That's because these words are reserved for use within the JavaScript language. A list of these words is shown at the bottom of this figure.

In addition, you should use meaningful names. That means that it should be easy to tell what a name refers to and easy to remember how to spell the name. To create names like that, you should avoid abbreviations. If, for example, you abbreviate the name for monthly investment as mon_inv, it will be hard later to tell what it refers to and remember how you spelled it. But if you spell it out as monthly_investment, both problems are solved.

If you do use abbreviations, you should use them consistently. For example, if you use num as an abbreviation for number in one part of your code, you should use that abbreviation consistently throughout your code.

Similarly, you should avoid abbreviations unless you're sure the abbreviation will be widely understood. For example, mpg is a common abbreviation for miles per gallon, but cpm could stand for several different things and should be spelled out.

To create a name that has more than one word in it, many JavaScript programmers use *camel case*. With this convention, the first letter of each word is uppercase except for the first word. For example, monthlyInvestment and taxRate use camel case.

An alternative naming convention is *snake case*. With this convention, all the words in the name are lower case and separated by underscore characters. For example, monthly_investment and tax_rate use snake case.

If the standards in your organization specify one of these conventions, you should follow it. Otherwise, you can use whichever convention you prefer. Just make sure to use the convention you choose consistently.

This book uses snake case for ids and class names in HTML and camel case for most JavaScript names. That way, it's easy for you to tell if the names are for HTML or JavaScript.

Note that if you use either camel case or snake case, your variable and constant names will start with a lowercase letter. You should know, though, that you can also start variable and constant names with a capital letter. By convention, however, these names aren't capitalized by most JavaScript programmers.

Rules for naming variables and constants

- Names can only contain letters, numbers, the underscore, and the dollar sign.
- Names can't start with a number.
- Names are case-sensitive.
- Names can be any length.
- Names can't be the same as *reserved words*.
- Avoid using global properties and methods as names.

Valid names in JavaScript

```
subtotal              index_1              $
taxRate               calculate_click      $log
```

Camel case versus snake case

```
taxRate               tax_rate
calculateClick        calculate_click
emailAddress          email_address
futureValue           future_value
```

Naming recommendations

- Use meaningful names. That way, your names aren't likely to be reserved words or global properties or methods.
- Be consistent. Either use camel case (taxRate) or snake case (tax_rate) to name variables and constants.
- If you use snake case, use lowercase for all letters.
- Always start variable and constant names with a lowercase letter.

Reserved words in JavaScript

```
abstract        else            instanceof      switch
arguments       enum            int             synchronized
boolean         eval            interface       this
break           export          let             throw
byte            extends         long            throws
case            false           native          transient
catch           final           new             true
char            finally         null            try
class           float           package         typeof
const           for             private         var
continue        function        protected       void
debugger        goto            public          volatile
default         if              return          while
delete          implements      short           with
do              import          static          yield
double          in              super
```

Description

- With *camel case*, all of the words within a name except the first word start with capital letters. With *snake case*, all words are lower case and separated by underscores.

Figure 2-6   Rules and recommendations for naming variables and constants

How to work with numbers

In the preceding figures, you learned how to declare variables and constants and assign values to them. Now, you'll learn some skills for working with numbers, including how to use them in expressions. An *expression* uses *operators* to perform operations on values.

How to code arithmetic expressions

An *arithmetic expression* can be as simple as a single value or it can be a series of operations that result in a single value. The first table in figure 2-7 presents JavaScript operators for coding arithmetic expressions. The first six *arithmetic operators* operate on two *operands*, as shown in the first group of examples. Of these operators, the first four are common to most programming languages and provide for addition, subtraction, multiplication, and division.

The modulus operator calculates the remainder when the left value is divided by the right value. For example, 13 % 4 means the remainder of 13 / 4. Since 13 / 4 is 3 with a remainder of 1, 1 is the result of the expression.

The exponentiation operator raises the left value to the power of the right value. For example, 2 ** 3 means 2 raised to the power of 3, or 2 * 2 * 2. The result of this expression is 8.

The increment and decrement operators operate on a single operand. These operators add or subtract 1 from a variable, as shown by the second example. Here, these operators are coded after the variable name. However, they can also be coded before a variable name, and that can affect the result.

If you code the increment operator after a variable, the increment operation happens after the statement executes. For example:

```
let counter = 0;
alert(counter++);   // displays 0 then increments counter
alert(counter);     // displays 1
```

However, if you move the increment operator before the variable, the increment operation happens before the statement uses the variable. For example:

```
let counter = 0;
alert(++counter);   // increments counter then displays 1
alert(counter);     // displays 1
```

When an expression includes two or more operators, the *order of precedence* determines the order in which the operators are applied, as summarized in the second table. For instance, all multiplication and division operations are done from left to right before any addition and subtraction operations are done.

If the default order of precedence doesn't work for your calculation, you can use parentheses to override the default order. Then, JavaScript executes the expressions in the innermost sets of parentheses first, followed by the expressions in the next sets of parentheses, and so on. This is typical of all programming languages, as well as basic algebra. The last group of examples in this figure shows how this works.

JavaScript's arithmetic operators

Operator	Name	Description
+	Addition	Adds two operands.
−	Subtraction	Subtracts the right operand from the left operand.
*	Multiplication	Multiplies two operands.
/	Division	Divides the right operand into the left operand.
%	Modulus	Divides the right operand into the left operand and returns the remainder.
**	Exponentiation	Returns the value of the left operand raised to the power of the right operand.
++	Increment	Adds 1 to the operand.
−−	Decrement	Subtracts 1 from the operand.

Expressions that perform simple arithmetic operations

```
5 + 7          // 12
5 - 12         // -7
6 * 7          // 42
13 / 4         // 3.25
13 % 4         // 1
2 ** 3         // 8
```

Statements that increment and decrement a variable

```
let counter = 0;   // counter = 0
counter++;         // counter = 1
counter--;         // counter = 0
```

The order of precedence for arithmetic operations

Order	Operators	Direction	Description
1	++	Left to right	Increment operator
2	−−	Left to right	Decrement operator
3	* / %	Left to right	Multiplication, division, modulus
4	+ −	Left to right	Addition, subtraction

Expressions that work with the order of precedence

```
3 + 4 * 5       // 23 (the multiplication is done first)
(3 + 4) * 5     // 35 (the addition is done first)
13 % 4 + 9      // 10 (the modulus is done first)
13 % (4 + 9)    // 0  (the addition is done first)
```

Description

- An *arithmetic expression* consists of one or more *operands* that are operated upon by *arithmetic operators*.

- An arithmetic expression is evaluated based on the *order of precedence* of the operators. To override the order of precedence, you can use parentheses.

Figure 2-7   How to code arithmetic expressions

How to use arithmetic expressions in statements

Now that you know how to code arithmetic expressions, figure 2-8 shows how to use these expressions as you code an *assignment statement* that assigns a value or the result of an expression to a constant or variable. Here, the first two examples show how you can use the multiplication and addition operators in JavaScript statements.

This is followed by a table that presents three of the *compound assignment operators*. These operators provide a shorthand way to code common assignment statements. For instance, the **+=** operator modifies the value of the variable on the left of the operator by adding the value of the expression on the right to that variable. When you use this operator, the variable on the left must already exist and have a value assigned to it.

The other two operators in this table work similarly. The **-=** operator subtracts the result of the expression on the right from the variable on the left, and the ***=** operator multiplies the variable on the left by the result of the expression on the right. The third example shows how these operators work.

The fourth example shows three ways to increment a variable by adding 1 to it. Here, the first statement assigns a value of 1 to a variable named counter. The second statement uses an arithmetic expression to add 1 to the counter. To do that, it codes the variable name on both sides of the **=** operator. The third statement uses the **+=** operator to add one to the counter. Since this statement doesn't need to include the variable name on both sides of the **=** operator, it's more concise. And the fourth statement uses the **++** operator to add one to the counter, which is even more concise. However, it only works for adding 1 to a variable, while the other two techniques can be used to add any value to a variable.

Statements that calculate sales tax

```
const subtotal = 200;
const taxPercent = .05;
const taxAmount = subtotal * taxPercent;      // 10
const total = subtotal + taxAmount;           // 210
```

Statements that calculate the perimeter of a rectangle

```
const width = 4.25;
const length = 8.5;
const perimeter = (2 * width) + (2 * length)      // (8.5 + 17) = 25.5
```

The most useful compound assignment operators

Operator	Description
+=	Adds the result of the expression on the right to the variable on the left.
-=	Subtracts the result of the expression on the right from the variable on the left.
*=	Multiplies the variable value by the result of the expression on the right.

Statements that use the compound assignment operators

```
let subtotal = 74.95;
subtotal += 20.00;                // subtotal = 94.95

let counter = 10;
counter -= 1;                     // counter = 9

let price = 100;
price *= .8;                      // price = 80
```

Three ways to increment a variable named counter by 1

```
let counter = 1;                  // counter = 1
counter = counter + 1;            // counter = 2
counter += 1;                     // counter = 3
counter++;                        // counter = 4
```

Description

- Besides the assignment operator (=), JavaScript provides the *compound assignment operators*. These operators are a shorthand way to code common assignment operations.

- When you use a compound assignment operator, the variable on the left must already exist and have been assigned a value.

Figure 2-8   How to use arithmetic expressions in statements

How to use the console to test expressions and statements

When you're getting started with JavaScript, it's often helpful to use the Console panel, or browser console, to test expressions and statements. For example, you can use the browser console to test the code examples that are presented in this chapter.

Figure 2-9 shows the Console panel of the Chrome browser. To open this panel, you can press F12 to open the developer tools. This also works in most other modern browsers such as Edge, Firefox, and Safari.

Before you display the developer tools, you may want to display a blank web page. That way, the console will be empty when you display it. To display a blank web page, you can enter about:blank in your browser's address bar.

Once you've opened the developer tools, you may need to click the Console tab to display the console. Then, you can type any valid JavaScript expression or statement at the prompt and press Enter. If the expression or statement returns a value, the console displays the value below the expression or statement.

If the expression or statement doesn't return a value, the console displays a value of undefined. In this figure, the statement that declares a variable named counter and initializes it to 0 doesn't return a value. As a result, the console displays undefined below this statement.

When you're using the console, any variable or constant that you declare remains active for the current session. This is true even if you close the developer tools and later open them again. In this figure, for instance, the counter variable is active and so it can be incremented. To view the value of a variable or constant, you can type its name at the prompt and press Enter.

You can also scroll through previous entries by using the up and down arrow keys. Then, you can modify entries if desired and run them again. In addition, you can right-click the console and select "Clear console" to clear the console. When you do that, any variables or constants that are active remain active. For example, if the console displayed in this figure is cleared, the counter variable is still active. In other words, clearing the console clears the visible text but doesn't remove any active variables or constants.

***

If you're new to programming, this is a good time to open the browser console and run some of the expressions and statements that this chapter has presented so far. Then, when you feel comfortable working with the browser console, you might want to enter and run some expressions and statements of your own. This is a great way to reinforce what you've learned so far and to gain some hands-on experience with the browser console. You'll also get the chance to work with the browser console in exercise 2-1 at the end of this chapter.

Chrome's browser console with expressions and statements

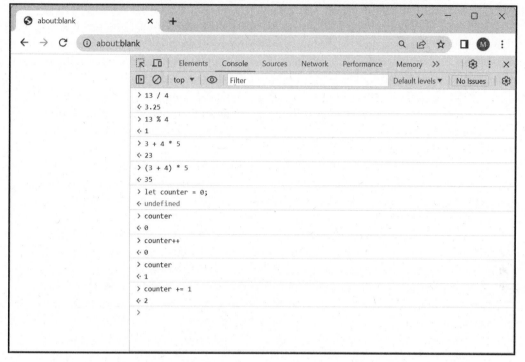

Description

- You can use the browser console in most modern browsers to test expressions and statements quickly and easily.

- To display the console in Chrome, press F12 or Ctrl+Shift+I to open the developer tools. Then, click on the Console tab.

- To be sure that the console is empty when you display the developer tools, you can enter about:blank in the browser's address bar to display a blank web page.

- To test a statement or expression, type it at the prompt and press Enter. If the statement or expression returns a value, the console displays that value. Otherwise, it displays undefined.

- Any constants or variables that are declared remain active for the current session. As a result, you can view the value of a variable by typing its name and pressing Enter.

- To scroll through previous entries, you can press the up and down arrow keys one or more times. This displays the entry. If you want to run an entry again, press Enter.

- To clear the browser console, right-click on it and select "Clear console".

Figure 2-9   How to use the console to test expressions and statements

How to display data in the console

When you create scripts that contain multiple JavaScript statements, it's often helpful to test those statements to make sure they're working correctly. To do that, you can use the built-in *console object* that's automatically available to your code.

The console object contains several methods for communicating with a browser's console. A *method* performs an action that's related to its object. For example, figure 2-10 shows how to use the log() method of the console object to display data in the console.

To execute the log() method, you *call* it by coding the name of the console object, a *dot operator* (period), the name of the method, and a set of parentheses. Within the parentheses, you code a *parameter* that specifies the data that's passed to the method.

In this figure, the first code example contains four statements that perform a calculation, along with three statements that use the log() method of the console object to display data in the console. Here, the first statement that uses the log() method displays a string that indicates that the script is starting. Then, the next two statements that use the log() method display the values for the taxAmount and total constants.

After running a script that uses the log() method to display data, you can open the browser console to view the data. In this figure, the first line in the console shows that the script started successfully. Then, the next two lines show that the script calculated the tax amount and total correctly.

When you code the name of the console object, you must use all lowercase letters. However, some built-in object names may capitalize the first letter. For example, the Math object described later in this chapter starts with a capital letter. Because JavaScript is case-sensitive, you'll want to be sure you use the correct capitalization for the object you're working with.

How to use the typeof operator

From time to time, you may also need to check the data type of a variable or constant. To do that, you can code the typeof operator before the name of a variable or constant. In this figure, the second code example begins with three statements that declare constants. Then, it continues with three statements that use the log() method with the typeof operator to display the data types for each of the constants. This shows that the first constant is the string type, the second is the number type, and the third is the Boolean type.

A method of the console object that displays data

Method	Description
`log(data)`	Displays the specified data in the console.

Display some data in the console

```
console.log("Starting script...")

const subtotal = 200;
const taxPercent = .05;
const taxAmount = subtotal * taxPercent;
console.log(taxAmount);

const total = subtotal + taxAmount;
console.log(total);
```

The data displayed in the console

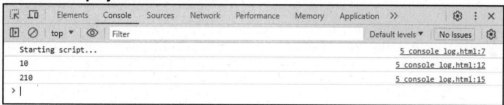

The syntax of the typeof operator

```
typeof operand
```

Check the type of a value

```
const productName = "Hammer";
const price = 11.99;
const inStock = true;

console.log(typeof productName);    // string
console.log(typeof price);          // number
console.log(typeof inStock);        // boolean
```

Description

- JavaScript provides a built-in *console object* that you can use to communicate with the console.

- An *object* can contain one or more methods. A *method* performs an action that's related to the object.

- To execute a method, you *call* it from an object. To do that, you typically code the name of the object, the *dot operator* (`.`), the name of the method, and a set of parentheses. Within the parentheses, you can code zero or more *parameters*, separated by commas, that specify the data to pass to the method.

- You can use the typeof operator to display the data type of a variable or constant.

Figure 2-10   How to display data in the console and use the typeof operator

How to fix a precision problem

Because JavaScript stores numbers as floating-point values, the results of arithmetic operations aren't always precise. The first example in figure 2-11 illustrates this problem. Here, the salesTax result should be 7.495, but is 7.495000000000001 instead. Although this result is extremely close to 7.495, it isn't equal to 7.495, which could lead to errors when comparing two values for equality.

To fix this problem, you can use the toFixed() method of the Number object and the Number() function as shown in this figure. To start, you can use the toFixed() method to round a number to the specified number of decimal places and convert it to a string. For instance, the second example shows how to use the toFixed() method to round a number value of 6.250001 to two decimal places. This rounds the number to 6.25 and returns a string of "6.25". Note that if the number of decimal places isn't specified, the toFixed() method rounds the number to the nearest integer before converting it to a string.

The toFixed() method is available from a Number object. However, you can call it from a number that's stored as the number type. Although primitive data types like the number type don't provide methods, you can call methods from them because JavaScript automatically converts them to a corresponding object before calling the method. As a result, you can call any method of a Number object from a primitive number value.

Since the toFixed() method returns the rounded number as a string, you need to convert it back to a number if you want to use it in another arithmetic operation. To do that, you can use the Number() function. For instance, the second example shows how to convert a string of "6.25" back to a number value of 6.25.

The Number() function is one of the built-in functions available from JavaScript. Like a method, a *function* accepts parameters and performs an action. However, a function isn't related to an object. As a result, you don't need to call a function from an object.

The third example shows how to fix the precision problem from the first example. Here, the toFixed() method rounds the sales tax to two decimal places and returns a string. Then, the Number() function converts that string back to a number so you can use the result in another arithmetic operation. Finally, the last statement adds the sales tax to the subtotal. If this example didn't convert the sales tax back to a number, this final calculation wouldn't work correctly.

The last example shows how you can accomplish the same thing by combining the two statements that call the toFixed() method and the Number() function into a single statement. To do that, you embed the toFixed() method as the parameter of the Number() function. Then, the result of the toFixed() method is passed to Number() function.

A method of the Number object that converts a number to a string

Method	Description
`toFixed(n)`	Rounds a number to n decimal places and converts it to a string. If n is omitted, the default is 0 decimal places.

A function that converts data to a number

Function	Description
`Number(data)`	Converts the specified data to a number.

An arithmetic result that isn't precise

```
const subtotal = 74.95;                  // subtotal = 74.95
const salesTax = subtotal * .1;          // salesTax = 7.495000000000001
const total = subtotal + salesTax;       // total = 82.44500000000001
```

How to use the toFixed() method and the Number() function

```
const num1 = 6.250001;                   // num1 = 6.250001
const numStr = num1.toFixed(2);          // numStr = "6.25"
const num2 = Number(numStr);             // num2 = 6.25
```

A result that's rounded to be precise

```
const subtotal = 74.95;                  // subtotal = 74.95
let salesTax = subtotal * .1;            // salesTax = 7.495000000000001
salesTax = salesTax.toFixed(2);          // salesTax = "7.50"
salesTax = Number(salesTax);             // salesTax = 7.5
const total = subtotal + salesTax;       // total = 82.45
```

A more concise way to code the previous example

```
const subtotal = 74.95;                  // subtotal = 74.95
let salesTax = subtotal * .1;            // salesTax = 7.495000000000001
salesTax = Number(salesTax.toFixed(2));  // salesTax = 7.5
const total = subtotal + salesTax;       // total = 82.45
```

Description

- Because numbers are stored internally as floating-point values, the results of arithmetic operations aren't always precise. To fix this issue, you can use the toFixed() method of the Number object and the Number() function.

- A *function* performs an action much like a method. However, a function isn't related to an object.

- The Number() function is a built-in function that's provided by JavaScript.

- Primitive data types do not have methods or properties, but they can use the methods of objects that correspond to them. That's because, when you call a method from a primitive type, JavaScript automatically converts the value to this corresponding object so it can call the method.

- To make your code concise, you can embed one method or function as the parameter of another method or function. For instance, you can code the toFixed() method as the parameter for the Number() function.

Figure 2-11   How to fix a precision problem with numbers

How to use the Math object

Figure 2-12 shows how to use one property and some methods of the Math object. While a method performs an action that's related to the object, a *property* stores data that's related to the object. For example, the PI property of the Math object stores the value of a mathematical constant.

The first example shows how to round decimal values to integers. Here, the first four statements use the round() method to round the decimal number to the nearest integer. If the decimal number is exactly halfway between two integers, the round() method rounds up, even for negative numbers. That's why the third statement rounds -3.5 up to -3, not down to -4.

The remaining statements in the first example show how to use the floor(), ceil(), and trunc() methods. The floor() method always rounds a fractional value down (towards the "floor"). The ceil() method always rounds a fractional value up (towards the "ceiling"). And the trunc() method doesn't do any rounding at all. Instead, it truncates, or removes, the fractional part of the number.

The second example shows how to use the pow() method to raise a value to the specified power. In addition, it shows how to use the sqrt() method to get the square root of a value.

The third example shows how to use the min() and max() methods. Although the methods shown here supply a list of just two parameters, you can use as many parameters as needed. Then, these methods find the minimum or maximum value in the list.

The fourth example shows how to calculate the area of a circle whose radius is 3. To do that, this example uses the PI property, which contains the value of π, and the pow() method. Here, you can see that you access the value of a property by coding the object name, followed by a dot operator and the name of the property. Although this example uses the pow() method, it could also have used the exponentiation operator like this:

```
Math.PI * 3 ** 2
```

The fifth example shows how to generate a random number between 1 and 10. The first statement uses the random() method to get a random decimal value between 0 and 1, and then multiplies that number by 10. Then, the second statement uses the ceil() method to round the decimal value up to the nearest integer.

The sixth example shows how to round to a specified number of decimal places instead of rounding to an integer. To do that, you can multiply the number by a multiple of 10. Then, you can round that number and divide the rounded number by that same multiple of 10. For instance, to round a number to 2 decimal places, you multiply the number by 100, round it, and then divide the result by 100. The two statements in this example are similar to using the toFixed() method to round a number to 2 or 3 decimal places. However, the values returned by this example are numbers, not strings.

The Math object also provides many trigonometric and logarithmic methods. If you have the appropriate mathematical background, you should be able to use these methods too.

One property and some methods of the Math object

Property	Description
`PI`	Returns 3.141592653589793.

Method	Description
`round(x)`	Rounds x up or down to the closest integer value.
`ceil(x)`	Rounds x up (towards the ceiling) to the closest integer value.
`floor(x)`	Rounds x down (towards the floor) to the closest integer value.
`trunc(x)`	Truncates x so it has no decimal.
`pow(x, power)`	Raises x to the specified power.
`sqrt(x)`	Returns the square root of x.
`min(x1, x2, ...)`	Returns the smallest value from the list of parameters.
`max(x1, x2, ...)`	Returns the largest value from the list of parameters.
`random()`	Returns a random decimal between 0 and 1.

Round decimal values to integers

```
Math.round(12.5)      // 13
Math.round(-3.4)      // -3
Math.round(-3.5)      // -3
Math.round(-3.51)     // -4

Math.floor(12.5)      // 12
Math.ceil(12.5)       // 13
Math.trunc(12.5)      // 12
Math.floor(-3.4)      // -4
Math.ceil(-3.4)       // -3
```

Work with powers and square roots

```
Math.pow(2, 3)        // 8 (same as 2 ** 3)
Math.sqrt(16)         // 4
```

Get the minimum and maximum values

```
Math.max(12.5, -3.4)  // 12.5
Math.min(12.5, -3.4)  // -3.4
```

Calculate the area of a circle that has a radius of 3

```
const area = Math.PI * Math.pow(3, 2);  // area is 28.274333882308138
```

Generate a random number between 1 and 10

```
const randNum = Math.random() * 10;     // get a random num between 0 and 10
const randInt = Math.ceil(randNum);     // round up to nearest integer
```

Round numbers to 2 and 3 decimal places

```
const dec2 = Math.round(3.14159 * 100) / 100;    // dec2 is 3.14
const dec3 = Math.round(3.14159 * 1000) / 1000;  // dec3 is 3.142
```

Description

- A *property* stores data that's related to an object. To access the value of a property, you typically code the name of the object, followed by the dot operator and the name of the property.

Figure 2-12   How to use the Math object

How to work with strings

So far, this chapter has presented some basic skills for working with numbers. Now, the next two figures present some basic skills for working with strings.

How to join strings

Figure 2-13 shows how to *concatenate*, or *join*, two or more strings. This adds one string to the end of another string.

To join strings, you can use the + sign as a *concatenation operator*. In this figure, the first example assigns string literals to the constants named firstName and lastName. Then, the second example creates a *string expression* by joining lastName, a string literal that consists of a comma and a space, and firstName. The result of this string expression is

```
Hopper, Grace
```

which is assigned to a constant named name.

The third example shows how the += operator can be used to get the same result. When you're working with strings, this operator appends the string on the right to the end of the string on the left.

The fourth example shows how to join strings by using a *template literal*. A template literal is a string literal that functions as a template. To code a template literal, you enclose a string literal in tick marks (` `` `) rather than single or double quotes. Then, you embed constants, variables, or expressions within the template literal. To do that, you enclose the embedded constant, variable, or expression within braces ({}) that are preceded by a dollar sign ($). In this example, the lastName and firstName constants are embedded within a template literal that also contains a comma and a space.

The fifth example defines three constants to be used by the last two examples. Three different types of data have been assigned to these constants. The greeting constant is a string, the price constant is a number, and the isValid constant is a Boolean. The last two examples show how to join these three constants with some string literals. This shows that JavaScript converts other data types to strings when you attempt to join them to a string.

In addition, these examples show how to code string expressions that span multiple lines. When you use the + operator, you need to code it at the end of each line that continues to a new line. However, when you use a template literal, you can just press Enter to start a new line. In that case, the line break and any other whitespace are included in the resulting string. Although this may not matter if you output the string as HTML, it can cause formatting issues if you use a method like the alert() method to display the string in a dialog.

When you need to join a string, the technique you use is mostly a matter of personal preference. In general, you should use the technique that yields the most readable and maintainable code.

The concatenation operators for strings

Operator	Description
+	Joins two strings.
+=	Appends one string to the end of another string.

Constants for the next three examples

```
const firstName = "Grace";
const lastName = "Hopper";
```

Use the + operator

```
const name = lastName + ", " + firstName;          // name is "Hopper, Grace"
```

Use the += operator

```
let name = lastName;                               // name is "Hopper"
name += ", ";                                      // name is "Hopper, "
name += firstName;                                 // name is "Hopper, Grace"
```

Use a template literal

```
const name = `${lastName}, ${firstName}`;          // name is "Hopper, Grace"
```

Constants for the next two examples

```
const greeting = "Hello";      // string data type
const price = 15.99;           // number data type
const isValid = true;          // Boolean data type
```

Use the + operator with an expression that spans multiple lines

```
const message = greeting + "! Is the price really just " + price + "?" +
    "Answer: " + isValid + ".";

// message is "Hello! Is the price really just 15.99? Answer: true."
```

Use a template literal that spans multiple lines

```
const message = `${greeting}! Is the price really just ${price}?
    Answer: ${isValid}.`;

// message is "Hello! Is the price really just 15.99?
                  Answer: true."
```

Description

- To *concatenate*, or *join*, two or more strings, you can use the + or += operators.
- A *template literal* provides a way to join strings by embedding values directly within a string literal that functions as a template.
- A template literal is enclosed in tick marks (` `` `) rather than quotation marks. Within the template literal, the embedded strings are enclosed in braces ({}) that are preceded by a dollar sign ($).
- You can join strings with values of other data types such as numbers and Boolean values. When you do, JavaScript converts the non-string value to a string and then joins it.

Figure 2-13   How to join strings

How to include special characters in strings

The first table in figure 2-14 summarizes four of the many *escape sequences* that you can use when you work with strings. These sequences let you include characters in a string that you can't include just by pressing the appropriate key on the keyboard. For instance, the `\n` escape sequence is equivalent to pressing the Enter key in the middle of a string. And the `\'` sequence is equivalent to pressing the key for a single quotation mark.

Escape sequences are needed so the JavaScript engine can interpret code correctly. For instance, if you use double quotes to identify the start and end of a string, coding a double quote within the string would cause a syntax error. But if the quote is preceded by a backslash, the JavaScript engine can interpret it correctly.

The first example in this figure shows four ways that you can put quotes in a string. The first two statements use escape sequences to insert the quotes into a string. The third statement uses double quotes within a string that's enclosed by single quotes. This works because the single quotes identify the start and end of the string. As a result, you don't need an escape sequence to insert a double quote within the string. The fourth statement works similarly, but it uses double quotes to identify the start and end of the string and single quotes within the string.

The second and third examples show how two other escape sequences work. In the second example, the new line sequence starts a new line. In the third example, the backslash sequence inserts two backslashes into the string.

The second table in this figure summarizes four of the many codes that you can use to include *Unicode characters* in strings. These codes let you include letters from other languages in a string, such as letters that include accents, umlauts, and tildes. They also let you include Korean, Chinese, and Japanese ideographs, as well as symbols like the copyright symbol and the registered trademark symbol.

The example below the table uses the alert() method to display a string that contains Unicode characters in a dialog. If you study the dialog that displays this string, you can see that it contains a heart symbol, a trademark symbol, a smiley face symbol, and a copyright symbol. In addition, it contains a new line character that causes the copyright notice to be displayed on its own line. This shows that dialogs use whitespace characters such as new lines, tabs, and spaces when they display strings.

Some of the escape sequences that can be used in strings

Operator	Description
\'	Single quotation mark in a single quoted string
\"	Double quotation mark in a double quoted string
\n	New line character
\\	Backslash

Four ways to include quotation marks in a string

```
"Type \"x\" to exit"         // Type "x" to exit
'Type \'x\' to exit'         // Type 'x' to exit
'Type "x" to exit'           // Type "x" to exit
"Type 'x' to exit"           // Type 'x' to exit
```

A new line character in a string

```
"Title: Modern JavaScript\nPrice: 59.50"    // Title: Modern JavaScript
                                            // Price: 59.50
```

Two backslashes in a string

```
"C:\\murach\\javascript"                    // C:\murach\javascript
```

Some of the codes for Unicode characters

Code	Character	Description
\u00A9	©	Copyright
\u00AE	®	Registered trademark
\u263A	☺	Smiley face
\u2665	♥	Heart

Unicode characters in a string

```
alert("I \u2665 Murach\u00AE Publishing! \u263A \n(\u00A9 2024)");
```

This page says

I ♥ Murach® Publishing! ☺
(© 2024)

OK

Description

- You can use *escape sequences* to insert special characters within a string, such as a return character that starts a new line or a quotation mark.

- You can use *Unicode characters* to include letters, punctuation, scripts, and ideographs from most languages, as well as some symbols.

Figure 2-14   How to include special characters in strings

How to get input and display output

Some of the examples in this chapter have already used the alert() method to display output to a user in a dialog. Now, this chapter explains the alert() method in more detail and also shows how to use a dialog to get input from a user.

How to use dialogs

Figure 2-15 begins by presenting two methods that you can use to display dialogs for input and output. Both of these methods are available from the window object. Since the *window object* is the *global object* for JavaScript apps being run in a browser, it's the default object. As a result, you don't need to code the object name and the dot operator when calling a method from the window object.

The first example shows two ways to call the alert() method of the window object. The first statement includes the name of the window object, a dot operator, and the alert() method. However, the second statement omits the name of the window object and the dot operator. Both statements display a dialog that says "Hello!".

The second and third examples show how to use the prompt() method of the window object to get a value from the user. The prompt() method accepts two parameters. The first parameter specifies the message that's displayed in the dialog, and the second specifies an optional default value. Since the second parameter is optional, you can omit it as shown by the second example. Then, if the user doesn't enter a value before clicking the OK button, the prompt() method returns an empty string.

The third example shows how the second parameter works. When this prompt() method executes, it displays a dialog like the one in this example. This dialog displays the message parameter above the text box and the default value parameter within the text box. At this point, the user can change the default value or leave it as is. If the user clicks the OK button, the statement assigns the entry to the constant named monthlyInvestment. Or, if the user clicks the Cancel button, the statement assigns null to the constant named monthlyInvestment.

If you don't code the name of the window object when calling alert() or prompt(), it looks like you're calling a function, not a method. However, alert() and prompt() perform actions that are related to the window object. As a result, they are methods.

Two methods of the window object

Method	Description
`alert(`*`str`*`)`	Displays a dialog that contains the string specified by the parameter and an OK button.
`prompt(`*`str, default`*`)`	Displays a dialog that contains the string specified by the first parameter, a text box that contains the default value specified by the optional second parameter, an OK button, and a Cancel button. If the user clicks OK, this method returns a string for the value in the text box or an empty string if the box is empty. If the user clicks Cancel, this method returns null.

Two ways to call a method of the window object

```
window.alert("Hello!");
alert("Hello!");
```

Get input from a user

```
const firstName = prompt("Please enter your first name");
```

The dialog that's displayed

```
This page says
Please enter your first name

|

                                OK      Cancel
```

Get input from a user and supply a default value

```
const monthlyInvestment = prompt("Enter the monthly investment", 100);
```

The dialog that's displayed

```
This page says
Enter the monthly investment

100

                                OK      Cancel
```

Description

- The *window object* is the *global object* for JavaScript in a browser, which means it's the default object.
- Because the window object is the default object, you can omit the object name and dot operator when calling methods from it.

Figure 2-15   How to use dialogs to get input and display output

How to parse numbers

If you want to use the prompt() method to get a number from the user, you need to convert the string that it returns to a number. To do that, you can use the two built-in functions presented in figure 2-16. The parseInt() function converts a string to an integer, and the parseFloat() function converts a string to a decimal. If these functions can't convert a string to a number, they return a value of *NaN*, which means "Not a Number".

The first example presents three statements that show how these functions work. The first statement passes the string "12345.6789" to the parseInt() function. This returns the integer 12345. In other words, it truncates the decimal portion of the number rather than rounding it. The second statement passes the same string to the parseFloat() function. This returns the decimal 12345.6789. The third statement passes the string "Hello" to the parseInt() function. This returns NaN because the parseInt() function can't convert "Hello" to an integer.

The parseInt() and parseFloat() functions can convert values that consist of one or more numeric characters followed by one or more nonnumeric characters. In that case, these functions drop the nonnumeric characters. For example, the parseFloat() function converts the string "72.5%" to the decimal 72.5.

The second example shows how to convert user input to numbers. This is necessary because the value that's returned by the prompt() method is a string, not a number. So, if you want to work with it as a number, you must convert it. Here, the first statement uses the prompt() method to get a string for the number of months from the user. Then, the second statement uses the parseInt() function to convert the user entry to an integer. The third and fourth statements are similar, but they use the parseFloat() function to convert the user entry to a decimal.

The third example shows how to get the same results by coding the prompt() method as the parameter of the parseInt() and parseFloat() functions. This passes the string that's returned by the prompt() method directly to the parseInt() or parseFloat() function.

Note that the second example declares months and monthlySales as variables because their values change. After the first statement, for instance, the months variable stores a string. After the second statement, it stores an integer.

By contrast, the third example declares months and monthlySales as constants because their values don't change. Since working with constants is safer, the statements in the last example are preferable. However, if you find that coding a method as a parameter of a function makes your code harder to read, it's OK to use variables and less concise code.

The parseInt() and parseFloat() functions are similar to the Number() function in that they convert strings to numbers. However, they're different in that the Number() function can't convert a string that has non-numeric characters. So if you pass the string "72.5%" to the Number() function, it returns NaN.

Like alert() and prompt(), you can call parseInt() and parseFloat() from the window object. However, because parseInt() and parseFloat() don't perform actions related to the window object, they're considered functions, not methods.

Two functions for parsing numbers

Function	Description
parseInt(*str*)	Converts the string it receives to an integer and returns that value as a number. If it can't convert the string to an integer, it returns NaN.
parseFloat(*str*)	Converts the string it receives to a decimal and returns that value as a number. If it can't convert the string to a decimal, it returns NaN.

A special value that can be returned by these functions

Value	Description
NaN	Not a Number.

Convert strings to numbers

```
const num1 = parseInt("12345.6789");     // 12345
const num2 = parseFloat("12345.6789");   // 12345.6789
const num3 = parseInt("Hello");          // NaN
```

Convert user input to numbers

```
let months = prompt("Enter number of months", 12);
months = parseInt(months);

let monthlySales = prompt("Enter monthly sales average");
monthlySales = parseFloat(monthlySales);
```

A more concise way to code these examples

```
const months = parseInt(prompt("Enter number of months", 12));
const monthlySales = parseFloat(prompt("Enter monthly sales average"));
```

Description

- The parseInt() and parseFloat() functions are built-in functions that are provided by JavaScript.

Figure 2-16   How to parse numbers

Two simple apps

With just the skills you've learned so far, you can already code some simple but complete apps. Now, the next two figures show two apps that use these skills.

The Miles to Kilometers app

Figure 2-17 presents a simple app that uses a dialog to get a number of miles from the user. Then, the app calculates the kilometers and displays the user's entry and the calculation in another dialog.

The HTML for the app includes an external JavaScript file by adding a <script> element at the end of the <body> element. The src attribute of the <script> element identifies the file to include. You could also code your JavaScript directly between the opening and closing <script> tags. However, it's considered a best practice to use a separate file to store the JavaScript code because it makes your code easier to maintain and reuse. That's especially true when your apps become more complex.

The JavaScript begins by prompting the user to enter the number of miles. Then, the code parses the user's entry into an integer and assigns it to a constant named miles. After that, the code calculates the kilometers by multiplying the miles by a decimal value and assigns the resulting value to a constant named kilometers.

After calculating the kilometers, this code uses the concatenation operator to create a string that includes the miles and kilometers. Here, the string uses a new line escape sequence (\n) to specify the start of a new line. Then, the code passes this string to the alert() method to display it in a dialog.

Another approach to displaying the result would be to use a template literal to create the string like this:

```
const results = `Miles: ${miles}
Kilometers: ${kilometers.toFixed(2)}`;
```

Here, the Enter key is used to start a new line within the template literal. To avoid including spaces at the beginning of the second line, the code doesn't indent "Kilometers", which makes the code a little harder to read. In general, when creating strings like this one, you should choose the approach that you think is the easiest to read and maintain.

Can you guess what happens if the user enters invalid data in the first dialog? In that case, the parseFloat() function returns NaN instead of a number. Then, NaN is used in the calculation, and the result is also NaN. In other words, invalid data doesn't cause the app to crash. Instead, the app displays the second dialog with NaN for both miles and kilometers.

This figure shows the dialogs that are displayed by a Chrome browser. If you use another browser, the dialogs will work the same way. However, they may look slightly different.

The first dialog

```
This page says
Miles:

120|

                              OK      Cancel
```

The second dialog

```
This page says

Miles: 120
Kilometers: 193.12

                                      OK
```

The HTML

```html
<!DOCTYPE html>
<html>
<head>
    <title>Miles to Kilometers</title>
</head>
<body>
    <script src="miles_to_kms.js"></script>
</body>
</html>
```

The JavaScript

```javascript
"use strict";

// get miles from user
const miles = parseFloat(prompt("Miles:"));

// calculate kilometers
const kilometers = miles * 1.60934;

// display results
const results = "Miles: " + miles + "\n" +
                "Kilometers: " + kilometers.toFixed(2);

alert(results);
```

Figure 2-17   The Miles to Kilometers app

The Test Scores app

Figure 2-18 presents a simple app that uses dialogs to let the user enter three test scores. Then, it calculates the average test score. Finally, it displays all three test scores and the average test score in another dialog.

Although this app has an HTML file that includes an external JavaScript file, the HTML isn't shown here. That's because the HTML for this app works like the app in the previous figure. As a result, this figure only shows the JavaScript for the app.

The JavaScript starts by declaring a variable named total and initializing it to 0. This code declares a variable instead of a constant because the total changes as the user enters the test scores.

After declaring the total variable, three statements use the prompt() method to ask the user to enter a test score. Each statement converts the user's entry to an integer and assigns it to a constant. Then, the value of that constant is added to the total variable.

After getting the test scores and updating the total variable, the code calculates the average test score by dividing the total variable by 3. Then, it passes the result of that calculation to the round() method so the average is rounded to an integer, and it assigns the average to a constant.

Finally, the constants that store the user's entries and average score are concatenated with some string literals, and the resulting string is passed as a parameter to the alert() method. This displays the scores and the average in a dialog.

Like the app in the previous figure, the JavaScript for this app begins with the "use strict" directive. As mentioned earlier in this chapter, this is considered a best practice because it prevents certain "bad" coding practices. For example, if you don't enable strict mode and you mistype the name of a constant or variable, JavaScript will create a new constant or variable. This makes it hard to find and fix the error. On the other hand, if you enable strict mode and mistype the name of a constant or variable, JavaScript throws an error. This makes it easy to find and fix the error.

The first dialog

The last dialog

```
This page says

Score 1 = 98
Score 2 = 89
Score 3 = 94
Average score = 94

                                              OK
```

The JavaScript

```javascript
"use strict";

// initialize total variable
let total = 0;

// get 3 scores from user and add them together
const score1 = parseInt(prompt("Enter first test score"));
total += score1;

const score2 = parseInt(prompt("Enter second test score"));
total += score2;

const score3 = parseInt(prompt("Enter third test score"));
total += score3;

// calculate the average
const average = Math.round(total/3);

// display the scores
const result = "Score 1 = " + score1 + "\n" +
               "Score 2 = " + score2 + "\n" +
               "Score 3 = " + score3 + "\n" +
               "Average score = " + average;

alert(result);
```

Figure 2-18   The Test Scores app

Perspective

In this chapter, you learned the basic building blocks for coding apps using JavaScript. You can now work with variables, constants, and built-in functions, as well as methods and properties of built-in objects. Furthermore, you can create simple apps that get input, perform calculations, and display output to either a dialog or a browser console. You are already well on your way to becoming a JavaScript programmer.

Terms

syntax	constant
directive	reserved word
strict mode	keyword
statement	camel case
whitespace	snake case
comment	expression
block comment	operator
single-line comment	arithmetic expression
comment out code	arithmetic operator
uncomment code	operand
primitive data type	order of precedence
number data type	assignment statement
integer	compound assignment operators
decimal	console object
floating-point number	object method
floating-point notation	call a method
string data type	dot operator
string	parameter
empty string	function
Boolean data type	property
literal value	concatenate
literal	join
variable	concatenation operator
declare a variable	string expression
initialize a variable	template literal
assignment operator	escape sequence
numeric literal	Unicode character
string literal	window object
undefined data type	global object
null data type	NaN

Exercise 2-1   Use the console

This exercise guides you through using the console to test some of the expressions and statements presented in this chapter.

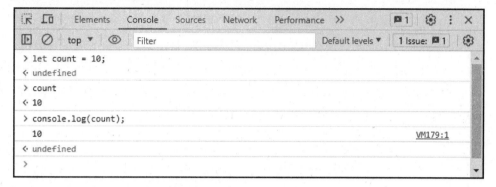

Create a variable in the console

1. Open Chrome and press F12 to open the developer tools.

2. Click the Console tab.

3. Enter a statement that declares a new variable named count and assign it a value of 10. Note that this returns a value of undefined.

4. Enter the name of the variable to view its value.

5. Enter a statement that uses the console.log() method to print the value of the variable. Note that this displays the value followed by a return value of undefined.

6. Enter the expressions and statements shown in figure 2-7 and observe the results.

Work with constant variables

7. Create a constant variable named quantity and assign it a value of 5.

8. Try to assign a new value to the constant and observe the error.

9. Create a new variable named price and initialize it to the constant.

10. Assign a new value to the price variable.

Work with null and undefined variables

11. Create a new variable named tax and assign a null value to it.

12. Add the price and tax variables together and observe the result.

13. Create a new variable named bonus but don't initialize it.

14. Add the price and bonus values together and observe the result.

Use a script to test some variables

15. Start VS Code.

16. Open the index.html file in this folder:

    `exercises/ch02/scripts`

    Note that this file contains a <script> element that sends two lines of data to the console.

17. Run this HTML file in a browser.

18. Press F12 to open the developer tools and click on the Console tab.

19. Check to make sure the data in the console is correct.

20. In the index.html file, add a statement that creates a constant that stores your name. Then, add another statement that sends that constant to the console. Don't forget to save your changes.

21. Run this HTML file in a browser again and view the console to make sure the code you added is working correctly.

Exercise 2-2   Work with strings

This exercise lets you practice working with strings by using dialogs to get three strings and then join them together into a longer string.

Review the starting code

1. Open the index.html file at the path shown below:

   `exercises/ch02/strings`

2. Review the code. Note that it includes a <script> element where you can enter JavaScript code.

Get three strings from the user

3. Write code that prompts the user to enter their first name and assign the result to a constant.

4. Write code that prompts the user to enter their last name and assign the result to a constant.

5. Write code that prompts the user to enter their age and assign the result to a constant.

Format the strings and display them to the user

6. Display a dialog that uses a template literal to display the user's first name, last name, and age on a single line. For example, if the user enters Scott as the first name, McCoy as the last name, and 27 as the age, the dialog should display the following:

   `Scott McCoy is 27 years old`

7. Display a second dialog that uses concatenation and a new line character to display the user's information on two lines like this:

   `Name: Scott McCoy`
   `Age: 27`

Exercise 2-3   Work with numbers

This exercise lets you practice the skills you learned for working with numbers.

Review the starting code

1. Open the index.html file located at the path shown below:

    ```
    exercises/ch02/numbers
    ```

2. Review the code. Note that it includes a <script> element where you can enter JavaScript code.

Calculate the perimeter and area of a rectangle

3. Assume you have a rectangle with two sides (A and B) that are at a right angle to each other.

4. Use a prompt to get the length of side A.

5. Use a prompt to get the length of side B.

6. Calculate the perimeter of the rectangle formed by sides A and B.

7. Send the result to the console to make sure your calculation works correctly.

8. Calculate the area of the rectangle formed by sides A and B.

9. Send the result to the console to make sure your calculation works correctly.

Calculate the hypotenuse of a right triangle

10. Use the Pythagorean theorem (c = squareRoot($a^2 + b^2$)) to calculate the hypotenuse of the triangle formed by sides A and B.

11. Send the result to the console to make sure your calculation works correctly.

12. Display the result of the all of the calculations in a dialog like this:

    ```
    Side A: 10
    Side B: 20
    Perimeter: 60
    Area: 200
    Hypotenuse: 22.3607
    ```

    Make sure the hypotenuse is rounded to 4 decimal places.

3

How to code control statements

This chapter shows how to code the statements that let you control the execution of an app. These statements include if statements as well as looping statements. Before you learn how to use these statements, you'll learn how to code the conditional expressions that they use.

How to code conditional expressions

Conditional expressions are expressions that evaluate to either true or false based on the result of a comparison between two or more values. You use these expressions in control statement*s*.

How to use the relational operators

Figure 3-1 shows how to code conditional expressions that use *relational operators*. To start, the table summarizes these operators. Then, the examples show how these operators work.

The first two expressions use the *equality operator* (==). In the first expression, if the value of lastName is equal to "Hopper", the expression returns true. Otherwise, it returns false. Similarly, in the second expression, if the value of testScore is equal to 10, the expression returns true. Otherwise, it returns false. The next two expressions are similar, but they use the *inequality operator* (!=) to test for inequality.

The next five expressions work similarly, but they use the >, <, >=, and <= operators. These expressions show that conditional expressions can mix and match constants, variables, and literal values. In addition, they show that conditional expressions can use other expressions such as an arithmetic expression.

The last four expressions illustrate the difference between the equality operator and the *strict equality operator*. The first expression uses the equality operator to compare the number 10 to the string "10". Since the equality operator performs *type coercion*, it converts (or coerces) the string "10" to the number 10, compares the two, and returns true. By contrast, the second expression uses the strict equality operator, which doesn't perform type coercion. Instead, it compares the number 10 to the string "10". Since these two values have different data types, this expression returns false.

A similar thing happens when you use the equality operator to compare null and undefined. In this case, the equality operator doesn't actually convert null to undefined or vice versa. However, it still returns true because both null and undefined represent the absence of a value. By contrast, the strict equality operator returns false because null and undefined are different data types.

When comparing values for equality, you should be aware of a couple common problems. First, as you learned in chapter 2, JavaScript doesn't store floating-point numbers as exact values. Because of this, you can get unexpected results when you use the equality, inequality, strict equality, or strict inequality operators to compare decimal values. One way to correct for this is to use the techniques from chapter 2 to round values before you compare them.

Second, when you use the equality operator, you need to remember to use two equal signs (==), not one (=). That's because one equal sign is the assignment operator, not the equality operator. This is a common mistake when you're learning to program, and it causes a syntax error.

The relational operators

Operator	Description	Returns true if...
==	Equal to	Both operands are equal.
!=	Not equal to	The operands are not equal.
===	Identical to	Both operands are identical.
!==	Not identical to	The operands are not identical.
>	Greater than	The left operand is greater than the right operand.
<	Less than	The left operand is less than the right operand.
>=	Greater than or equal to	The left operand is greater than or equal to the right operand.
<=	Less than or equal to	The left operand is less than or equal to the right operand.

Conditional expressions

```
lastName == "Hopper"
testScore == 10

firstName != "Grace"
months != 0

testScore > 100
age < 18

distance >= limit          // compare a variable and a constant
stock <= reorder_point

rate / 100 >= 0.1          // compare an arithmetic expression to a literal

10 == "10"                 // true
10 === "10"                // false

null == undefined          // true
null === undefined         // false
```

Description

- A *conditional expression* uses the *relational operators* to compare the results of two operands and return a Boolean value. An operand can be any type of expression.

- The *equality operator* (==) and the *inequality operator* (!=) perform *type coercion* when comparing values of different data types. That means they convert (coerce) data from one type to another so they can be compared.

- The *strict equality operator* (===), also called the *identity operator*, and the *strict inequality operator* (!==) do not perform type coercion. If the two operands are of different types, the result will always be false.

- Because floating-point numbers aren't exact, you should be careful when using operators to check decimal values for equality (==, !=, ===, !==, >=, <=).

- Confusing the assignment operator (=) with the equality operator (==) is a common programming error.

Figure 3-1   How to use the relational operators

How to use the isNaN() function

When writing JavaScript, you often need to check whether a string can be converted to a number. To do that, you can create a conditional expression by calling the isNaN() function that's presented in figure 3-2. First, you create the conditional expression by passing the string to this method. Then, this method returns true if the string is not a number. Otherwise, it returns false.

How to use the logical operators

To code a *compound conditional expression*, you use the *logical operators* shown in figure 3-2 to combine two or more conditional expressions. If you use the AND operator (&&), the compound expression returns true if both expressions are true. If you use the OR operator (| |), the compound expression returns true if at least one expression is true. If you use the NOT operator (!), the value returned by the expression is reversed. For instance, !isNaN() returns true if the parameter is a number. As a result, isNaN("10") returns false, but !isNaN("10") returns true.

This figure uses three expressions to show how these operators work. The first expression uses the AND operator to combine two conditional expressions. As a result, it evaluates to true if the expression on its left *and* the expression on its right are both true. Similarly, the second expression uses the OR operator to combine two conditional expressions. As a result, it evaluates to true if the expression on its left *or* the expression on its right is true.

When you use the AND and OR operators, JavaScript evaluates the expressions from left to right, and the second expression is evaluated only if necessary. That's why these operators are known as *short-circuit operators*. If, for example, the first expression in an AND operation is false, the second expression isn't evaluated because the entire expression will be false. Similarly, if the first expression in an OR operation is true, the second expression isn't evaluated because the entire expression will be true.

The third expression shows how to use the NOT operator to reverse the value of an expression. As a result, this expression evaluates to true if the age variable *is* a number.

When an expression uses more than one logical operator, JavaScript uses the *order of precedence* shown in this figure to determine the order in which it evaluates the operators. This order of precedence shows that JavaScript evaluates NOT operators, then AND operators, and then OR operators. This order is typically what you want. If it isn't, you can override it by using parentheses.

The isNaN() function

Function	Description
isNaN(*expression*)	Checks whether an expression can be converted to a number. It returns true if the expression is not a number. Otherwise, it returns false.

Two expressions that use the isNaN() function

```
isNaN("Hopper") // Returns true since "Hopper" is not a number
isNaN("123.45") // Returns false since "123.45" can be converted to a number
```

The logical operators

Operator	Name	Description
&&	AND	Returns true if both expressions are true. This operator only evaluates the second expression if necessary.
||	OR	Returns true if at least one expression is true. This operator only evaluates the second expression if necessary.
!	NOT	Reverses the value of the Boolean expression.

Three expressions that use logical operators

The AND operator
```
age > 17 && score < 70
```

The OR operator
```
isNaN(rate) || rate < 0
```

The NOT operator
```
!isNaN(age)
```

Order of precedence

1. NOT operator
2. AND operator
3. OR operator

Description

- A *compound conditional expression* joins two or more conditional expressions using the *logical operators*.
- If logical operators are used to join more than two conditional expressions, the sequence in which the operations are performed is determined by the *order of precedence* of the operators. To clarify or change the order of precedence, you can use parentheses.
- The AND and OR operators only evaluate the second expression if necessary. As a result, they are known as *short-circuit operators*.

Figure 3-2   How to use the logical operators

How to get started with the selection structure

Like all programming languages, JavaScript provides *control statements* that let you control the execution of an app. One type of control statement known as a *selection structure* determines which code to execute based on a condition. There are several types of selection structures, but the if statement is the most common.

How to code an if statement

An *if statement* lets you control the execution of statements based on the results of conditional expressions. Figure 3-3 begins by showing the syntax of the if statement. In this syntax, the brackets ([]) identify a part of the syntax that is optional, and the ellipsis (...) indicates that an element can be repeated multiple times. As a result, this syntax shows that each if statement must start with an *if clause*. Then, it can have one or more *else if clauses*, but they are optional. Last, it can have an *else clause*, but that clause is also optional.

After the syntax, the first example shows an if statement with an else clause. Here, if age is greater than or equal to 18, the first message is displayed. Otherwise, the second message is displayed.

The second example shows an if statement with two else if clauses and an else clause. Here, if rate is not a number, the first message is displayed and the rest of the if statement is skipped. If rate is less than zero, the second message is displayed and the rest of the if statement is skipped. If rate is greater than 12, the third message is displayed and the rest of the if statement is skipped. Otherwise, the message in the else clause is displayed.

The third example shows an if statement with a compound conditional expression that tests whether userEntry is not a number or, if it is a number, whether it's less than or equal to zero. If either expression is true, a message is displayed. If both expressions are false, nothing is done because this if statement doesn't have an else if or else clause.

The fourth example shows two ways to test whether a Boolean variable or constant is true. Here, the first if statement uses the equality operator to test whether the variable is equal to true. You can also just code the name of the variable or constant as shown by the second if statement. Since the second way of testing a Boolean variable or constant is shorter and easier to read, that's the recommended approach.

The fifth example works like the fourth example, but it shows two ways to test whether a Boolean variable or constant is false. In this example, the second if statement uses the not operator (!) to reverse the value of the variable or constant. Here again, since the second if statement is shorter, that's the recommended approach.

The syntax of the if statement

```
if (condition-1) { statements }
[ else if (condition-2) { statements }
...
else if (condition-n) { statements } ]
[ else { statements } ]
```

An if statement with an else clause

```
if (age >= 18) {
    alert("You may vote.");
} else {
    alert("You are not old enough to vote.");
}
```

An if statement with else if and else clauses

```
if (isNaN(rate)) {
    alert ("You did not provide a number for the rate.");
} else if (rate < 0) {
    alert ("The rate may not be less than zero.");
} else if (rate > 12) {
    alert ("The rate may not be greater than 12.");
} else {
    alert ("The rate is: " + rate + ".");
}
```

An if statement with a compound conditional expression

```
if (isNaN(userEntry) || userEntry <= 0) {
    alert ("Please enter a valid number greater than zero.");
}
```

Two ways to test whether a Boolean variable is true

```
if (isValid == true) { }
if (isValid) { }                  // same as isValid == true
```

Two ways to test whether a Boolean variable is false

```
if (isValid == false) { }
if (!isValid) { }                 // same as isValid == false
```

Description

- An *if statement* always has one *if clause*. It can also have one or more *else if clauses* and one *else clause* at the end. Because of that, it can also be referred to as an *if-else statement*.

- The statements in a clause execute when its condition is true. Otherwise, control passes to the next clause. If none of the conditions in the preceding clauses are true, the statements in the else clause execute. If there is no else clause, no code executes.

Figure 3-3   How to code an if statement

How to code a nested if statement

When coding if statements, you may sometimes need to code one if statement within a clause of another if statement. This is known as a *nested if statement*, and it is illustrated by the first example in figure 3-4.

In this example, the outer if statement checks for two customer type codes. The if clause tests for the "r" code (retail), and the else if clause tests for the "w" code (wholesale). If neither test evaluates to true, no code executes and the discountPercent variable remains 0.

Within the outer if clause, a nested if statement sets the discount percent for a retail customer based on the value of the invoice total. Similarly, the outer else if clause uses a nested if statement to set the discount percent for a wholesale customer.

The second example gets the same results without nesting if statements. Instead, this statement uses a series of compound conditions. The problem with this example is that it duplicates the Boolean expression that checks the customer type in each clause. As a result, it makes your code more difficult to maintain. If, for example, the code for retail customers changes from "r" to "retail", you'd need to make that change in three places. That's both tedious and error prone. By contrast, you'd only need to change the code in one place in the first example.

In the first example, the second nested if statement could use an else clause instead of the last else if clause like this:

```
if (invoiceTotal < 500) {
    discountPercent = .4;
} else {
    discountPercent = .5;
}
```

The advantage of this approach is that it uses less code. As a result, it's easier to maintain. However, the code in the figure has the advantage of clearly stating the condition for each discount.

An if statement that contains two nested if statements

```
let discountPercent = 0;

if (customerType === "r") {                                    // retail
    if (invoiceTotal >= 100 && invoiceTotal < 250) {
        discountPercent = .1;
    } else if (invoiceTotal >= 250) {
        discountPercent = .2;
    }
} else if (customerType === "w") {                             // wholesale
    if (invoiceTotal < 500) {
        discountPercent = .4;
    } else if (invoiceTotal >= 500) {
        discountPercent = .5;
    }
}
```

An if statement that gets the same results

```
let discountPercent = 0;

if (customerType === "r" &&                                    // retail
    invoiceTotal >= 100 && invoiceTotal < 250) {
    discountPercent = .1;
} else if (customerType === "r" && invoiceTotal >= 250) {
    discountPercent = .2;
} else if (customerType === "w" && invoiceTotal < 500) {   // wholesale
    discountPercent = .4;
} else if (customerType === "w" && invoiceTotal >= 500) {
    discountPercent = .5;
}
```

Description

- It's possible to code one if statement within a clause of another if statement. The result is known as a *nested if statement*.

- In most cases, you can use the logical operators to get the same results that you get with nested if statements. However, this can be more difficult to read and lead to some duplication of code.

Figure 3-4   How to code nested if statements

The Guess the Number app

Figure 3-5 presents a simple Guess the Number app where the user competes with the computer to guess a number between 1 and 20. Whichever guess is closer to the number generated by the app is the winner.

The HTML for the Guess the Number app works like the HTML for the apps shown in the previous chapter. As a result, the HTML for the Guess the Number app isn't shown in this figure.

The JavaScript for this app starts by generating a random number between 1 and 20. Then, it generates a random number for the computer's guess. Next, it prompts the user to enter a guess.

After getting the number and the guesses, the code uses a nested if statement to process the guesses. The outer if clause uses the isNaN() method to check whether the user entered a string that can't be converted to a number. In that case, the code notifies the user and the else if and else clauses are skipped, which ends the app.

The outer else if clause uses the OR operator to combine two conditional expressions that check whether the user entered a number between 1 and 20. Since this clause is only evaluated when the outer if clause is false, you can be sure that the userGuess constant contains a valid number. If the user didn't enter a number within the range, the else if clause notifies the user and the else clause is skipped, which ends the app.

The outer else clause contains most of the code for the app. It is evaluated only if none of the preceding clauses are true. So you can be sure that the userGuess constant contains a valid number between 1 and 20.

The code in the outer else clause starts by building a message string to notify the user of the number, the user's guess, and the computer's guess. Then, it calculates which guess is closest to the number. To do that, it subtracts each guess from the number to get the difference. Then, it uses the Math.abs() method to get the absolute value of the result. This converts a negative number to a positive number.

Finally, an inner if statement determines the winner. If the values for the differences are equal, there's no winner. If the user's difference is less than the computer's difference, the user is the winner. Otherwise, the computer is the winner. Each clause of the inner if statement updates the message variable with the result of the comparison. Then, the code uses the alert() method to display a dialog that contains the message.

To save space, this figure doesn't include the "use strict" directive at the top of the JavaScript. However, most of the apps in this book include the "use strict" directive to enable strict mode because that's a best practice for modern JavaScript.

The dialog that asks the user for a number

This page says

Enter a number between 1 and 20

12

OK   Cancel

The dialog that displays the guess results

This page says

The number is 17.
You guessed 12 and the computer guessed 4.
You WIN!

OK

The JavaScript

```javascript
// get a random number between 1 and 20
const num = Math.ceil(Math.random() * 20);

// get the computer's guess
const computerGuess = Math.ceil(Math.random() * 20);

// get the user's guess
const userGuess = parseInt(prompt("Enter a number between 1 and 20"));

if (isNaN(userGuess)) {
    alert("Not a valid number. Computer wins.")
} else if (userGuess < 1 || userGuess > 20) {
    alert("Not a number between 1 and 20. Computer wins.");
} else {
    let message = "The number is " + num + ".\n" +
        "You guessed " + userGuess +
        " and the computer guessed " + computerGuess + ".\n";

    // compute the difference between the guesses and the number
    const computerDiff = Math.abs(num - computerGuess);
    const userDiff = Math.abs(num - userGuess);

    // determine the winner and notify the user
    if (userDiff === computerDiff) {
        message += "It's a tie!";
    } else if (userDiff < computerDiff) {  // user's guess is closer
        message += "You WIN!";
    } else {
        message += "Computer wins.";
    }
    alert(message);
}
```

Figure 3-5   The Guess the Number app

More skills for working with the selection structure

Now that you know the basics of using the if statement, you're ready to learn more skills for working with the selection structure.

How to use a non-Boolean value in a conditional expression

So far, this chapter has shown how to code conditional expressions that use relational and logical operators to return a Boolean value of true or false. However, JavaScript also evaluates non-Boolean values such as numbers or strings to either true or false. Because of that, they can be used in conditional expressions. When used in a conditional expression, these values are often called *truthy* or *falsy* to indicate that they aren't actually Boolean values, even though they evaluate to true or false.

Figure 3-6 shows how you can use non-Boolean values in conditional expressions. To start, it presents the non-Boolean values that JavaScript evaluates as false (falsy values) and true (truthy values). The values that it evaluates as false are the number 0, null, undefined, NaN (not a number), an empty string, and an empty array. The values that it evaluates as true are any number that isn't zero, any string or array that isn't empty, and any object.

The examples in this figure show how to use a non-Boolean value as the condition for an if statement. The first example declares a variable named val but doesn't initialize it. Because of that, the value is undefined. Then, an if statement tests whether the val variable is false. In this case, because the value of val is undefined, it evaluates to false and the code in the if block executes. If you initialized the val variable to null, zero, or an empty string, you'd get the same result.

The second example uses a dialog to get a string from the user, and it assigns that string to the constant named name. Then, an if statement tests the name constant to determine if the user entered any text in the dialog. If so, name evaluates to true, and the if block executes. Otherwise, name evaluates to false and the else block executes. For example, if the user clicks OK in the dialog without entering any text, name contains an empty string, which evaluates to false. Or, if the user clicks Cancel in the dialog, name contains null, which also evaluates to false.

Values that JavaScript evaluates as false

- 0
- null
- undefined
- NaN
- an empty string
- an empty array

Values that JavaScript evaluates as true

- any number other than zero
- any string that isn't empty
- any array that isn't empty
- any object

Check if a variable has a value

```
let val;
if (!val) {
    alert("Variable 'val' does not have a value");
}
```

Check if a variable contains a string

```
const name = prompt("Please enter a name");
if (name) {
    alert("You entered " + name);
} else {
    alert("You did not enter a name");
}
```

Description

- JavaScript allows you to use non-Boolean as well as Boolean values in conditional expressions.
- Non-Boolean values that are used in this way are called *truthy* or *falsy* to indicate that they aren't actual Boolean values but can still be used in conditional expressions.
- You can use non-Boolean values to test for conditions like uninitialized variables or strings that are empty.

Figure 3-6   How to use a non-Boolean value in a conditional expression

How to use the conditional operator

Figure 3-7 shows how to use JavaScript's *conditional operator*. This is JavaScript's only *ternary operator*, which means that this operator has three operands. By contrast, a *unary operator*, such as **++**, has one operand (the value being incremented), and a *binary operator*, such as *****, has two operands (the two values being multiplied).

Since the conditional operator has three operands, it needs two symbols to separate them. The syntax in this figure shows that the conditional operator uses the question mark (**?**) and colon (**:**) to separate its three operands.

When executed, the conditional operator begins by evaluating the first operand, which is a conditional expression. Then, if the conditional expression is true, JavaScript returns the second operand. If the conditional expression is false, JavaScript returns the third operand.

After the syntax, the examples show how to use the conditional operator. The first example sets a constant named message to one of two values based on a condition. If the age is 18 or more, it assigns "Can vote" to the constant. Otherwise, it assigns "Cannot vote" to the constant.

The second example shows how to use an expression in one of the operands. If hours are over 40, the second operand calculates overtime by multiplying the hours over 40 by 1.5. Otherwise, the third operand sets overtime to 0.

The third example shows how to select a singular or plural ending for use in a message. If errorCount is 1, the ending is an empty string. Otherwise, the ending is a string of "s".

Code that uses a conditional operator can always be rewritten as an if statement. To illustrate, each example shows the conditional operator rewritten as an if statement. In general, if statements typically result in code that's easier to read. As a result, if your top priority is readability, it's a good practice to use if statements.

However, the conditional operator can sometimes reduce code duplication. For example, to write the first example in this figure as an if statement, you need to code the name of the message variable three times. However, the equivalent conditional operator only uses the name of the message variable once. This makes the code shorter and easier to maintain. As a result, you may want to use the conditional operator when it makes your code easier to maintain.

The syntax of the conditional operator

```
(conditional-expression) ? value-if-true : value-if-false
```

Set a message based on a comparison

```
const message = (age >= 18) ? "Can vote" : "Cannot vote";
```

Written with an if statement

```
let message = null;
if (age >= 18) {
    message = "Can vote";
} else {
    message = "Cannot vote";
}
```

Calculate overtime pay

```
const overtime = (hours > 40) ? (hours - 40) * rate * 1.5 : 0;
```

Written with an if statement

```
let overtime = null;
if (hours > 40) {
    overtime = (hours - 40) * rate * 1.5;
} else {
    overtime = 0;
}
```

Select a singular or plural ending based on a value

```
const ending = (errorCount == 1) ? "" : "s";
const message = "Found " + errorCount + " error" + ending + ".";
```

Written with an if statement

```
let ending = null;
if (errorCount == 1) {
    ending = "";
} else {
    ending = "s";
}
const message = "Found " + errorCount + " error" + ending + ".";
```

Description

- The *conditional operator* begins by evaluating its first operand, which is a conditional expression. Then, if the condition is true, it returns the value of the second operand. Otherwise, it returns the value of the third operand.

- The conditional operator provides a concise way to write certain types of if statements.

Figure 3-7   How to use the conditional operator

How to code a switch statement

A *switch statement* provides a convenient way to code some types of selection structures and can be used instead of an if statement. Specifically, it can be used instead of an if statement with multiple else if clauses that test the same expression for equality with different values. This is illustrated in figure 3-8.

The switch statement starts with the *switch* keyword followed by a *switch expression* inside of parentheses. A switch expression is not a conditional expression that evaluates to true or false. Instead, a switch expression returns a value that determines the code that should be executed. A switch expression is often as simple as a single constant or variable.

A switch statement begins by checking each of the values in its *case labels*. If it finds one that's equal to the result of the switch expression, it executes the code that follows that case label. It continues executing until it reaches a *break statement* or the end of the switch statement.

If no case labels match the value in the switch expression, the switch statement executes the code that follows the default label. However, the default label is optional. If it's omitted and no case labels match the expression, the switch statement doesn't execute any code. A switch statement can only have one default case, and it's usually coded as the last case in the statement. However, it can be coded anywhere in the switch statement.

In the first example, the switch expression is a constant named letterGrade that should contain a letter. Then, each case label checks the value of this constant. For example, if letterGrade is "B", the switch statement executes the code after the label for that case and sets the message variable to "above average". Then, it encounters a break statement and exits the switch statement. However, if letterGrade is "Z", the switch statement executes the code after the default label and sets the message to "invalid grade".

In the second example, code execution *falls through* some case labels. This occurs when code executes at one case label and doesn't encounter a break or return statement. In that case, execution falls through to the next case label. Although this is often the result of accidentally forgetting to code a break statement at the end of a case label, it can be a useful technique if done intentionally as shown in this example.

Here, the switch statement executes the same code for a letterGrade of "A" or "B". Instead of repeating the code, this example places two case labels before the code. Then, for a letterGrade of "A", execution falls through to the code after the case for "B". Similarly, for a letterGrade of "D", execution falls through to the code after the case for "F".

The syntax of the switch statement

```
switch (switch-expression) {
    case value-1: [ statements ]
    [ case value-2: [ statements ]
        ...
        case value-n: [ statements ] ]
    [ default: [ statements ] ]
}
```

A switch statement with a default case

```
let message = null;
switch (letterGrade) {
    case "A":
        message = "well above average";
        break;
    case "B":
        message = "above average";
        break;
    case "C":
        message = "average";
        break;
    case "D":
        message = "below average";
        break;
    case "F":
        message = "failing";
        break;
    default:
        message = "invalid grade";
        break;
}
```

A switch statement with fall through

```
switch (letterGrade) {
    case "A":
    case "B":
        message = "Scholarship approved.";
        break;
    case "C":
        message = "Application requires review.";
        break;
    case "D":
    case "F":
        message = "Scholarship not approved.";
        break;
}
```

Description

- The *switch statement* evaluates the *switch expression* in the parentheses and then executes the code for the *case label* with the value that matches that expression.
- Execution jumps to the end of a switch statement when it reaches a *break statement*.
- If a case doesn't contain a break statement, execution *falls through* to the next label.
- If the value of the switch expression doesn't match any of the case labels, the code for the default label executes if that label is present.

Figure 3-8   How to code a switch statement

The Magic Eight Ball app

Figure 3-9 presents an app that prompts the user to enter a yes or no question. Then, the app generates and displays one of nine responses in the style of the classic Magic Eight Ball toy.

The JavaScript for this app starts by displaying a dialog that asks the user to enter a yes or no question. Then, it assigns the string that's returned to a constant named question. Next, it uses this constant as the conditional expression of an if statement.

As a result, if the user clicks the OK button without entering any text, the question is an empty string. Similarly, if the user clicks the Cancel button, the question is null. Since both an empty string and null evaluate to false, this causes the else clause to execute. In that case, the code displays a dialog that indicates that the user didn't enter a question, and the app ends.

However, if the user enters some text and clicks the OK button, the question constant evaluates to true. As a result, the code in the if clause processes the question. To do that, the code initializes a variable named answer to an empty string. Then, it generates a random number between 1 and 9 and assigns that number to the num constant.

The switch statement uses the num constant as its switch expression to set the value of the answer variable. To save space, this figure only shows the first three cases. However, you can view all nine possible answers in the code that's included in the download for this book. After the switch statement finishes executing, this code displays the question and answer in a dialog.

The dialog that asks for a question

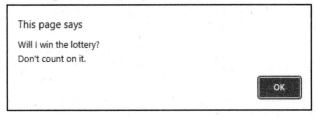

The dialog that displays the question and answer

```
This page says

Will I win the lottery?
Don't count on it.

                                        OK
```

The JavaScript

```javascript
// get user's question
const question = prompt("Please enter a yes or no question.")

if (question) {
    let answer = "";

    // get a random number from 1 to 9
    const num = Math.ceil(Math.random() * 9);

    switch (num) {
        case 1:
            answer = "It is certain.";
            break;
        case 2:
            answer = "Reply hazy, try again.";
            break;
        case 3:
            answer = "Don't count on it.";
            break;

        // cases 4 through 9 go here - see download

        default:
            answer = "Something went wrong.";
            break;
    }
    alert(question + "\n" + answer);
} else {
    alert("You didn't enter a question.");
}
```

Figure 3-9   The Magic Eight Ball app

How to code the iteration structure

Besides the selection structure, most languages provide for an *iteration structure*. Since this structure provides a way to repeatedly execute a block of statements, it's also known as a *repetition structure*. In JavaScript, the iteration structure is implemented by while, do-while, and for statements

How to code while and do-while loops

Figure 3-10 starts by presenting the syntax of the *while statement* that you can use to create *while loops*. This statement executes the block of code that's in the loop while its conditional expression is true.

The first example uses a while loop to get the sum of the numbers 1 through 5. Before the while statement starts, a variable named sum is set to zero and a *counter variable* named i is set to 1. A counter variable counts the number of times a loop is run, and it is traditionally named i for integer (or index). Then, the condition for the while statement says that the loop should repeat as long as i is less than or equal to 5.

Within the while loop, the first statement adds the value of i to the sum variable. Then, the value of i is increased by 1. As a result, JavaScript executes this loop five times, one time each for the i values 1, 2, 3, 4, and 5. The loop ends when i is no longer less than or equal to 5.

The second example uses a while loop to make sure that a user enters a positive number. Here, the first statement initializes a variable named years with a value entered by the user. Then, the while loop checks to see if the value is not a number or if it's less than or equal to zero. If so, the user is prompted again. As a result, this loop continues to run until the user enters a positive number.

After the second example, this figure presents the syntax for the *do-while statement* that you can use to create *do-while loops*. A do-while statement works much like a while statement. However, a do-while statement tests its condition at the end of the loop instead of at the start. As a result, the statements in a do-while loop are always executed at least once.

To illustrate, the third example uses a do-while loop to get the same results as the while loop in the second example. In other words, it continues to loop until a user enters a positive number. However, since the code within the do-while loop always runs at least once, this example only needs to code one prompt statement. The while version, on the other hand, prompts the user before the loop starts, and then again within the loop if the user enters invalid data.

If the condition for a while or do-while statement doesn't ever become false, the loop continues indefinitely. This is known as an *infinite loop*. When you first start programming, it's common to code an infinite loop by mistake. If you do that, you can end the loop by closing the browser tab or window for the app.

In general, you use a while or do-while loop when you don't know in advance how many times the loop needs to run. That's the case with the loops in this figure that run until the user enters a positive number.

The syntax of a while loop

```
while (condition) { statements }
```

A while loop that gets the sum of the numbers 1 through 5

```
let sum = 0;
let i = 1;
while (i <= 5) {
    sum += i;                    // adds i to sum
    i++;
}
alert(sum);                      // displays 15
```

A while loop that makes sure a user enters a positive number

```
let years = parseInt(prompt("Enter number of years."));
while (isNaN(years) || years <= 0) {
    years = parseInt(prompt("Years must be a valid positive number."));
}
```

The syntax of a do-while loop

```
do { statements } while (condition);
```

A do-while loop that makes sure a user enters a positive number

```
let years = null;
do {
    years = parseInt(prompt("Enter number of years.\n" +
        "(Must be valid positive number)"));
}
while (isNaN(years) || years <= 0);
```

Description

- The *while statement* creates a *while loop* that contains a block of code that's executed while its condition is true. This condition is tested at the beginning of the loop, and the loop ends without executing any code if the condition is false.

- The *do-while statement* creates a *do-while loop* that contains a block of code that is executed while its condition is true. However, its condition is tested at the end of the loop instead of the beginning. As a result, the code in the loop is always executed at least once.

- If the condition for a while or do-while loop never evaluates to false, the loop never ends. This is known as an *infinite loop*. You can end an infinite loop by closing the tab or browser window.

- You typically use a while or do-while loop when you don't know in advance how many times the loop needs to run.

- A *counter variable* is used to keep track of how many times a loop has run. It's a common coding practice to name a counter variable i for integer (or index).

Figure 3-10   How to code while and do-while loops

How to code for loops

Figure 3-11 shows how to use the *for statement* to create *for loops*. Within the parentheses of a for statement, you initialize a counter variable that's used within the loop. Then, you code a condition that determines when the loop ends. Last, you code an expression that specifies how the counter variable should be incremented.

The first example in this figure shows how this works. Here, the first statement in the parentheses declares a counter variable named i and initializes it to 1. Then, the condition in the parentheses determines that the loop should continue as long as the counter variable is less than or equal to 5. Next, the expression in the parentheses increments i by 1 each time through the loop. Within the loop, the statement adds the value of i to the variable named sum.

If you compare this example with the first while loop in the previous figure, you can see that both get the same results. However, the for statement is designed for working with a counter variable. As a result, it's a better way to code this loop.

The second example calculates the future value of an investment amount of 10,000 at an interest rate of 7.0% for 10 years. This time, the counter variable named i is initialized to zero and the loop continues as long as the value of the counter variable is less than the number of years. As a result, the loop executes once for each of the 10 years.

Within the code block, the statement calculates the interest for the year by using this expression:

```
futureValue * annualRate / 100
```

Then, the **+=** operator adds the interest to the futureValue variable. In this statement, the annualRate needs to be divided by 100 to convert the annual rate to a percentage.

In the first two examples in this figure, the counter is incremented by 1 each time through the loop, which is usually the way this statement is coded. However, if you need to, you can increment the counter variable by other amounts, and you can decrement the counter variable. For instance, the third example increments the counter variable by 2 instead of by one. To do that, this code uses the compound assignment operator (**+=**). Similarly, the fourth example decrements the counter variable rather than incrementing it. To do that, this code uses the decrement operator (**--**).

Unlike while and do-while loops, you typically use for loops when you know in advance how many times the loop needs to run. For example, you know you need to run the loop that calculates the future value once for each year.

The syntax of a for statement

```
for (counter-initialization; condition; increment-expression) {
    statements
}
```

A for loop that gets the sum of the numbers 1 through 5

```
let sum = 0;
for (let i = 1; i <= 5; i++) {
    sum += i;                        // adds i to sum
}
alert(sum);                          // displays 15
```

A for loop that calculates the future value of an investment

```
const investment = 10000;
const annualRate = 7.0;
const years = 10;

let futureValue = investment;
for (let i = 0; i < years; i++) {
    futureValue += futureValue * annualRate / 100;
}
alert(futureValue.toFixed(0));       // displays 19672
```

A for loop that increments the counter by two

```
let message = "";
for (let i = 0; i <= 10; i += 2) {
    message += i + " ";
}
alert(message);                      // displays 0 2 4 6 8 10
```

A for loop that decrements the counter

```
let message = "";
for (let i = 3; i > 0; i--) {
    message += i + "...";
}
message += "Blast off!";
alert(message);                      // displays 3...2...1...Blast off!
```

Description

- The *for statement* is used when you need to increment or decrement a counter that determines how many times the *for loop* is executed.

- Within the parentheses of a for statement, you code an expression that initializes a counter variable, a conditional expression that determines when the loop ends, and an increment expression that indicates how the counter should be incremented or decremented each time through the loop.

- You typically use a for loop when you know how many times the loop needs to execute.

Figure 3-11   How to code for loops

How to use the break and continue statements

The break and continue statements give you additional control over loops. The *break statement* breaks out of a loop by causing execution to jump to the statement that follows the loop. This causes the loop to end. The *continue statement* continues a loop by causing execution to jump to the top of the loop. This causes the loop to execute again by reevaluating its condition.

The first example in figure 3-12 shows how to use the break statement. Here, the condition for a while statement is set to true. This creates an infinite loop. However, you can use the break statement to end the loop when a certain condition is met. In this case, the loop ends when the user enters a valid number in the dialog. At that point, the break statement ends the loop, and the statement after the loop displays the number entered by the user.

The second example shows how to use the continue statement. Here, a for loop runs while a number ranges from 1 to 40. Then, within the loop, the number is divided by 5 and the remainder is tested to see whether it is zero. If it isn't, the continue statement skips to the start of the loop. If it is, the number is added to the sum variable. As a result, this code adds numbers that are divisible by 5 to the sum but doesn't add any other numbers to the sum.

The break statement in a while loop

```
let number = 0;
while (true) {
    number = parseInt( prompt("Enter a number from 1 to 10.") );
    if (isNaN(number) || number < 1 || number > 10) {
        alert("Invalid entry. Try again.");
    } else {
        break;
    }
}
alert(number);
```

The continue statement in a for loop

```
let sum = 0;
for (let number = 1; number <= 40; number++) {
    if (number % 5 !== 0) {
        continue;                       // if number isn't divisible by 5
    }
    sum += number;
}
alert(sum);          // displays 180, the sum of 5, 10, 15, 20, 25, 30, 35, 40
```

Description

- The *break statement* ends a loop. In other words, it jumps out of the loop without executing any additional code.

- The *continue statement* ends the current iteration of a loop, but allows the next iteration to proceed. In other words, it jumps to the start of the loop and executes it again.

Figure 3-12   How to use the break and continue statements

The Future Value app

Figure 3-13 presents a Future Value app that uses a for loop to calculate the future value of an investment amount. This app starts by getting the investment amount, interest rate, and number of years from the user. Here, the code uses while loops to continue displaying a dialog until the user enters a valid number.

After getting the values from the user, a for loop uses them to calculate the future value of the investment. To do that, it initializes a counter variable named i to 0 and increments that variable by 1 each time through the loop. It does that as long as the counter is less than the number of years entered by the user. As a result, the loop runs once for each year. For example, if the user enters 10 for the number of years, the loop runs 10 times.

Within the for loop, a single statement calculates the future value. To do that, it uses an expression to calculate the interest for the year. Then, it adds the result of that expression to the current value of the futureValue variable.

After the for loop finishes, this app uses the alert() method to display the values the user entered, as well as the calculated future value. Here, the toFixed() method is called on the futureValue variable to round it to two decimal places.

As you can see, this app uses both while loops and for loops. It uses while loops to get data from the user because it doesn't know in advance how many times it will take for a user to enter valid data. Once it gets a valid number of years from the user, however, the app knows how many times the loop that calculates the future value needs to execute. Because of that, it uses a for loop to do the calculation.

The first of three input dialogs with a default value

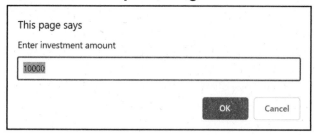

This page says

Enter investment amount

`10000`

OK   Cancel

The dialog that displays the future value

This page says

Investment amount: $10000
Interest rate: 4.5%
Years: 10
Future Value: $15529.69

OK

The JavaScript

```javascript
// get investment amount - loop until user enters a number
let investment = NaN;
while (isNaN(investment)) {
    investment = parseFloat(
        prompt("Enter investment amount", 10000));
}

// get interest rate - loop until user enters a number
let rate = NaN;
while (isNaN(rate)) {
    rate = parseFloat(prompt("Enter interest rate", 4.5));
}

// get number of years - loop until user enters a number
let years = NaN;
while (isNaN(years)) {
    years = parseInt(prompt("Enter years", 10));
}

// calulate future value
let futureValue = investment;
for (let i = 0; i < years; i++) {
    futureValue += futureValue * rate / 100;
}

// display results
alert("Investment amount: $" + investment + "\n" +
    "Interest rate: " + rate + "%\n" +
    "Years: " + years + "\n" +
    "Future Value: $" + futureValue.toFixed(2));
```

Figure 3-13   The Future Value app

Perspective

Now that you understand the selection and iteration structures, you can control the flow of execution in your apps. In fact, using only what you've learned so far, you can write programs of considerable complexity. By mastering the skills in this chapter, you have achieved one of the most important skills for programming in not just JavaScript, but in any programming language.

Terms

conditional expression
relational operator
equality operator
inequality operator
type coercion
strict equality operator
identity operator
strict inequality operator
compound conditional expression
logical operator
order of precedence
short-circuit operator
control statement
selection structure
if statement
if clause
else if clause
else clause
if-else statement
nested if statement
truthy value

falsy value
conditional operator
ternary operator
unary operator
binary operator
switch statement
switch expression
case label
fall through
iteration structure
repetition structure
while statement
while loop
do-while statement
do-while loop
infinite loop
counter variable
for statement
for loop
break statement
continue statement

Exercise 3-1   Work with selection structures

This exercise guides you through the process of creating an app that simulates a coin flip. After the user enters a guess, it should display the result formatted like this:

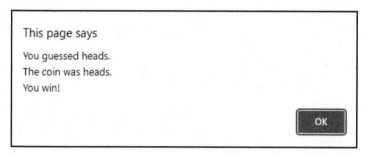

> This page says
>
> You guessed heads.
> The coin was heads.
> You win!
>
> OK

Review the starting code

1. In VS Code's Explorer window, expand this folder:

    `exercises\ch03\coin_flip`

2. View the code for the index.html file. Note that it contains code that prompts the user to enter "heads" or "tails" as well as code that displays the result of the user's guess.

3. Run the app in a browser to verify that it works correctly.

Add if statements to validate and check the user's guess

4. Use an if statement to check whether the user's guess is valid. The only valid entries should be "heads" or "tails".

5. If the user's guess is *not* valid, use a dialog to display an appropriate message.

6. If the user's guess is valid, use the Math.random() method to simulate a coin flip by returning a value of 1 or 2.

7. Within the clause that checks for a valid guess, add a nested switch statement that converts the value of 1 or 2 to "heads" or "tails".

8. In the same clause, add a nested if statement that checks whether the user's guess of "heads" or "tails" matches the coin flip and sets an appropriate message, such as "You win!".

9. Use a dialog to display the user's guess, the result of the flip, and the message.

Exercise 3-2   Work with iteration structures

This exercise guides you through the process of using iteration structures to control the flow of an app.

Set up the files

1.   Open the index.html file at the following path:

     `exercises/ch03/stairs`

Write the code for printing some stairs

2.   Write a for loop that prints one, two, and three # characters to the console. To do that, you'll need to use a counter variable that's incremented by 1 each time through the loop and a stairs variable that stores the # characters. The output should print three stairs going up like this:

     ```
     #
     ##
     ###
     ```

3.   Test the code to ensure that it works correctly. For the browser to display the result correctly, you may need to uncheck the "Group similar messages in console" box in the settings for the Console tab.

4.   Write a while loop that prints two stairs going down. You can reuse the stairs variable as a starting point, and you can use the substring() method to shorten the stairs string for every iteration like this:

     `stairs = stairs.slice(0, -1)`

     The final output of the app should look like the following:

     ```
     #
     ##
     ###
     ##
     #
     ```

Print the stairs according to the user's specification

5.   Write a statement that gets a height from the user.

6.   Modify the code to print the stairs according to the height specified.

Exercise 3-3   Use the break and continue statements

This exercise gives you additional practice with loops and lets you use break and continue statements.

1. Open the guess_number.js file at the following path:

    exercises/ch03/guess_number

2. Review the code and run the app to see how it works.

3. Surround the JavaScript code with a while loop that causes the app to run forever (or until the browser is closed).

4. Add a prompt to the end of the while loop that asks if the user would like to play again.

5. Add an if statement that checks what the user entered. If they entered "y" or "yes", use a continue statement to run the loop again. If they entered anything else, use a break statement to end the loop.

4

How to work with arrays and strings

So far, this book has shown you how to work with constants and variables that store a single item of data such as a number, a string, or a Boolean value. In programming, however, you often need to store a collection of data items. For example, you might need to store a collection of related strings or a collection of related numbers.

This chapter begins by showing you how to use an array to store a collection of data items. Then, it presents some more skills for working with strings. As you'll see, some of these skills are similar to the skills for working with arrays. That's because a string is essentially a collection of characters.

How to get started with arrays

An *array* is an object that contains zero or more items called *elements*. Each of these elements can be a primitive data type or an object. Although the elements of an array typically contain the same type of data or object, they can contain different types if necessary. The *length* of an array indicates the number of elements that it contains.

How to create and use an array

Figure 4-1 shows how to create an array. To do that, you can assign an array literal to a constant. An *array literal* consists of a list of zero or more values enclosed in brackets. If the list contains no values, the assignment creates an Array object with no elements, also known as an empty array. If the list contains one or more values, the assignment creates an Array object that contains one element for each value, and it assigns the values to the elements.

To refer to the elements in an array, you use an *index* that ranges from zero to one less than the number of elements in an array. For example, an array with 12 elements has index values that range from 0 to 11.

To use an index, you code it within brackets after the name of the array as shown by the first example. Here, the first statement creates an empty array named amounts by assigning an array literal that consists of an empty set of brackets. Then, the next three statements add values for the first three elements of the array.

The second example creates an array and assigns values to the first three elements in a single statement. To do that, it includes the values in a list within the brackets of an array literal. This creates an Array object with three elements.

Once you create an array and assign values to its elements, you can use an index to refer to those elements as shown in the third example. Here, the literal values of 0, 1, and 2 refer to the first, second, and third elements in the array. However, you can also use a constant or variable as the index for an array element. In either case, if you try to access an element that hasn't been assigned a value, JavaScript returns a value of undefined.

The fourth example shows how to work with the array's length property. The length property returns the number of elements in an array. Since the indexes of an array start at zero, this property will always be 1 more than the highest index used in the array. For example, the indexes for the amounts array range from 0 to 2, but its length is 3.

In this figure, the first two examples assign the amounts array to a constant. Although you might think that you'd have to assign an array to a variable to be able to add elements to it, that's not the case. That's because an array isn't a primitive type that stores a single value. Instead, an array is an object that stores elements. As a result, you can assign an array to a constant and still change the elements that it stores. However, you can't assign a new value to the constant such as a null value or another array. If you need to do that, you need to assign the array to a variable, not a constant.

The syntax for creating an array using an array literal

```
const arrayName = [values];
```

The syntax for referring to an element of an array

```
arrayName[index]
```

A property of an array

Property	Description
length	The number of elements in the array.

Create an array and add three elements

```
const amounts = [];
amounts[0] = 141.95;
amounts[1] = 212.25;
amounts[2] = 411;
```

Create an array and add three elements with a single statement

```
const amounts = [141.95, 212.25, 411];
```

Refer to the elements in an array

```
amounts[0]        // refers to the first element   - returns 141.95
amounts[1]        // refers to the second element  - returns 212.25
amounts[2]        // refers to the third element   - returns 411
amounts[3]        // element doesn't exist         - returns undefined
```

Determine how many elements are in an array

```
const count = amounts.length;        // 3
```

Code that fails when you assign a new array to a constant

```
amounts = [550.95, 620.50, 722];   // TypeError: Assignment to constant
                                   // variable.
```

Description

- An *array* can store zero or more *elements*. The *length* of an array is the number of elements in the array.

- One way to create an array is to code a set of brackets, called an *array literal*.

- When you use an array literal, you can add elements to the array by coding a list of values within the brackets, separated by commas.

- To refer to the elements in an array, you use an *index* where 0 is the first element, 1 is the second element, and so on.

- When you assign an array to a constant, you can change the values of the array's individual elements, but you can't assign a new value to the constant itself.

Figure 4-1   How to create and use an array

How to add, replace, and delete array elements

Figure 4-2 shows how to add and delete elements in an array. To add an element to the end of an array, you can use the length property of the array as the index of the new element as shown by the first example in this figure. Since the length property is always one more than the highest index used in the array, this adds the new element to the end of the array.

To add an element at a specific index, you use its index to refer to the element and assign a value to it as shown by the second example. If you use an index that's greater than the length of the array, JavaScript assigns an *empty slot* to the indexes that you skipped over. Although an empty slot doesn't store an element, the length property of an array counts empty slots when calculating the array's length. This is shown by the last statement in this example.

The third example shows that you can replace an element at a specific index. To do that, you refer to the element by its index and assign a new value to it.

To delete an element from an array, you can use the delete operator as shown by the fourth example. When you use the delete operator, JavaScript replaces the deleted element with an empty slot. In other words, JavaScript doesn't shift the elements in the array to fill in the gap where the deleted element was. If you try to access an empty slot, JavaScript returns a value of undefined. That's because an empty slot doesn't contain an element.

To remove all elements in an array, you can set the length property of the array to zero as shown by the fifth example. This works differently than using the delete operator because JavaScript doesn't leave the elements in the array as empty slots. Instead, it removes the elements completely, leaving an array with no elements.

You can also truncate an array by setting its length property to a value that's less than its length. Then, JavaScript completely removes all elements that no longer fit in the array. In addition, you can set the length property to a value that's greater than the length of the array. Then, JavaScript adds empty slots to the array for the new elements.

The delete operator

Operator	Description
delete	Deletes the contents of an element and sets the element to an empty slot, but doesn't remove the element from the array.

Add an element to the end of an array

```
const numbers = [1, 2, 3];          // array is 1,2,3
numbers[numbers.length] = 4;        // array is 1,2,3,4
```

Add an element at a specific index

```
const numbers = [1, 2, 3];          // array is 1,2,3
numbers[5] = 6;                      // array is 1,2,3,,,6
const len = numbers.length;         // len is 6
```

Replace an element at a specific index

```
const numbers = [1, 2, 3];          // array is 1,2,3
numbers[1] = 20;                     // array is 1,20,3
```

Delete an element at a specific index

```
const numbers = [1, 2, 3];          // array is 1,2,3
delete numbers[1];                   // array is 1,,3
const num = numbers[1];             // num is undefined
```

Remove all elements

```
const numbers = [1, 2, 3];          // array contains three elements
numbers.length = 0;                  // removes all elements from array
```

Description

- You can add an element to the end of an array by using the length property as the index of the new element.

- An *empty slot* doesn't store an element, but the length property of an array counts empty slots as part of the array's length.

- If you add an element at a specific index that isn't the next one in sequence, JavaScript adds empty slots to the array between the end of the original array and the new element.

- When you use the delete operator to delete an element, JavaScript deletes the element's value but keeps an empty slot for the element.

- To remove all the elements from an array, you can set the array's length property to zero. Unlike the delete operator, this removes all the elements, not just the elements' values.

Figure 4-2   How to add, replace, and delete array elements

How to use a for loop with an array

Since arrays usually contain collections of related elements, it's common to use loops to work with them. Figure 4-3 shows how you can use a for loop to process all of the elements in an array. When you do that, you can use the counter variable for the loop as the index for the array.

The first example shows how to create an array and fill it with the numbers 1 through 10. To start, this code creates an empty array named numbers. Then, it uses a for loop to add the numbers 1 through 10 to the array. The statement in the body of this loop stores the result of the counter variable plus 1 in the array using the counter variable as the index for the element. As a result, the element at index 0 stores 1, the element at index 1 stores 2, and so on.

The second example displays the values in the numbers array. First, this code creates an empty string named displayString. Then, it uses a for loop to access the elements in the array. In the declaration of the for loop, the length property of the array controls how many times the loop executes. This allows the code to work with arrays of different lengths. Inside the for loop, the value in the element and a space are concatenated to the end of displayString. After the for loop, the code calls the alert() method and passes the displayString to it. This displays the ten numbers stored in the array, separated by spaces.

The third example creates an array named amounts that's used by the next two examples. This array contains four elements where each element stores a number.

The fourth example uses a for loop to add the numbers in the amounts array. To do that, it begins by defining a variable named total and initializing it to 0. Then, it uses a for loop to loop through the four amounts in the array and add them to the total variable.

The fifth example displays the amounts and the total. To do that, it begins by defining a variable named amountsString and initializing it to an empty string. Then, it uses a for loop to concatenate each amount in the array with the amountsString variable. Finally, after the loop, the code calls the alert() method to display a message that includes the amountsString variable and the total variable from the previous example.

Put the numbers 1 through 10 into an array

```
const numbers = [];
for (let i = 0; i < 10; i++) {
    numbers[i] = i + 1;
}
```

Display the numbers in the array

```
let displayString = "";
for (let i = 0; i < numbers.length; i++) {
    displayString += numbers[i] + " ";
}
alert(displayString);    // displays 1 2 3 4 5 6 7 8 9 10
```

Put four amounts into an array

```
const amounts = [];
amounts[0] = 141.95;
amounts[1] = 212.25;
amounts[2] = 411;
amounts[3] = 135.75;
```

Total the amounts in the array

```
let total = 0;
for (let i = 0; i < amounts.length; i++) {
    total += amounts[i];
}
```

Display the amounts and the total

```
let amountsString = "";
for (let i = 0; i < amounts.length; i++) {
    amountsString += amounts[i] + "\n";
}
alert("The amounts are:\n" +
      amountsString + "\n" +
      "Total: " + total);
```

The message that's displayed

This page says

The amounts are:
141.95
212.25
411
135.75

Total: 900.95

OK

Description

- When you use a for loop to work with an array, you can use the counter for the loop as the index for the array.

Figure 4-3   How to use a for loop with an array

How to use for-in and for-of loops with an array

Since it's so common to need to loop through all of the elements in an array, JavaScript provides some specialized for loops that make it easier to do that. Figure 4-4 shows how these types of loops work.

The first example in this figure creates an empty array, assigns it to a constant named amounts, and then adds four elements with numeric values. The other examples in this figure work with this array.

The second example shows how to use a *for-in loop* to work with the array. The syntax shows that a for-in loop doesn't require separate expressions to initialize, test, and increment an index counter. Instead, you just declare a variable that refers to the index of each element. Then, within the loop, you can use this index to access each element in the array.

The code that uses a for-in loop shows how to total the values in the amounts array. Here, the variable named i refers to the index of each element in the array. Then, within the loop, the statement uses that index to get the value of the current element and add it to the total variable.

With a for-in loop, the index value is a string, not a number. As a result, if you need to do any arithmetic calculations with the index value, you can use the parseInt() method to convert it to a number first. This works differently than a regular for loop where the index value is a number, not a string.

The third example shows how to use a *for-of loop* to work with the amounts array. The syntax shows that a for-of loop uses a variable to refer to the value of an element. If you need to get the value for every element in an array, this is the most concise way to do it.

The code that uses a for-of loop shows how to total the values in the amounts array. Here, the variable named amount refers to the value of each element in the amounts array. Then, within the loop, the statement adds the amount to the total.

The examples in this figure use the *let* keyword to declare variables that refer to the index or value of the current element in the array. However, you can also use the *const* keyword to declare constants. With for-in and for-of loops, either approach works equally well. On the other hand, with a regular for loop, you must use the *let* keyword to declare the index as a variable.

Now that you know how to use for loops, for-in loops, and for-of loops, you might be wondering when to use each one. In general, for-of loops are the easiest to code and read. As a result, if you need to get the value of every element in an array, it's a good practice to use a for-of loop. However, if you also need access to the element's index, you can use a for-in loop, which is also easy to code and read. In addition, a for-in loop allows you to assign a value to an array element while a for-of loop does not.

For all other situations, you can use a for loop. For example, you might use a for loop if you don't need to access every element, if you need to increment the counter by a value other than 1, or if you need to decrement the counter.

If you're working with an array that contains empty slots, you need to know that for-in loops skip the empty slots, but for-of loops and for loops don't. As a result, if you're using a for-of or for loop, you may need to add an if statement

Put four amounts into an array

```
const amounts = [];
amounts[0] = 141.95;
amounts[1] = 212.25;
amounts[2] = 411;
amounts[3] = 135.75;
```

How to use the for-in loop

The syntax

```
for (let index in array) {
    statements
}
```

Total the numbers in the array

```
let total = 0;
for (let i in amounts) {       // variable i holds the current index
  total += amounts[i];         // use the index to get current value
}
alert(total);                  // displays 900.95
```

How to use the for-of loop

The syntax

```
for (let element of array) {
    statements
}
```

Total the numbers in the array

```
let total = 0;
for (let amount of amounts) {  // variable amount holds the current value
  total += amount;
}
alert(total);                  // displays 900.95
```

Description

- In a *for-in loop*, you declare a variable that stores the *index* of the current element in the array.

- In a *for-of loop*, you declare a variable that stores the *value* of the current element in the array.

- In a for-in loop, the index variable has a data type of string, not number. If you want to use that variable in a calculation, you can to convert it to a number using the parseInt() method.

- With for-in and for-of loops, you can use the *let* keyword or the *const* keyword to declare a variable or constant that refers to the index or value of each element. Either approach works equally well.

- If an array contains empty slots, for-in loops skip the empty slots, but for-of loops don't. As a result, with a for-of loop, you may need to add an if statement to handle any undefined values returned by empty slots.

Figure 4-4   How to use for-in and for-of loops with an array

that checks for an empty slot before processing each element. To do that, the if statement can check whether the value of the element is undefined.

The Test Scores app

Figure 4-5 presents another version of the Test Scores app that was first presented in chapter 2. This version of the app stores the scores entered by the user in an array. Because of that, it allows the user to enter as many scores as they want, rather than allowing the user to enter just three scores.

The first dialog in this figure prompts the user to enter a score. The app displays this dialog repeatedly until the user enters "x" or presses the Cancel button. Then, the second dialog displays the scores the user entered followed by the average score.

The JavaScript for this app starts by declaring an empty array named scores. Then, it uses a while loop to get the user entries. Since the conditional expression of this loop is the *true* keyword, the loop runs until it encounters a break statement.

Within the loop, the code prompts the user to enter a score and then checks that value. If it's "x", that means the user is done entering scores. If it's null, that means the user clicked the Cancel button. In either case, the code uses the break statement to end the loop.

If the user didn't enter "x" or click the Cancel button, the code uses the parseInt() method to convert the value to an integer. Remember, this method returns the value NaN if the value it receives can't be converted.

Then, the code uses an if-else statement to check the value entered by the user. If it's greater than or equal to 0 and less than or equal to 100, the value is added to the scores array. Otherwise, the user is notified that they need to enter a valid value. Since the value NaN isn't within the valid range of values, the app also displays this message if the user enters a value that can't be converted to an integer.

When the while loop ends, an if statement checks that the array contains at least one element. If it doesn't, that means the user entered "x" or pressed Cancel for the first entry. In that case, the user is notified and processing ends.

If the array contains one or more elements, a for-in loop processes the scores in the array. Then, the code uses the loop's index variable to retrieve the elements from the scores array.

Each time through the loop, the code adds the value of the array element to the total variable and also to a string that will display the elements. In this string, the code includes the score number so the user can see which score it is. To do that, the score number is set to the index value plus 1 so the scores are displayed starting with 1 rather than with 0 ("Score 1", "Score 2", etc.). However, because the variable for a for-in loop is a string, this code has to use the parseInt() method to convert the string to an integer before it can add 1 to it.

When the for-in loop ends, the code calculates the average test score and assigns it to the constant named average. This calculation divides the total variable by the length of the scores array, which is the number of scores in the array. Finally, the app uses a dialog to display the scores and the average score.

The dialog that prompts the user for scores

This page says

Enter a test score. Or, enter 'x' to exit.

OK   Cancel

The dialog that displays the scores and their average

This page says

Score 1: 90
Score 2: 100
Score 3: 85
Average score is 91.67

OK

The JavaScript

```
const scores = [];

// get scores from the user
while (true) {
    const entry = prompt("Enter a test score. Or, enter 'x' to exit.");
    if (entry === 'x' || entry === null) {
        break;
    }

    const score = parseInt(entry);
    if (score >= 0 && score <= 100) {
        scores[scores.length] = score;
    } else {
        alert("Score must by a valid number from 0 through 100.");
    }
}

// calculate total and average and display, or notify user if no scores
if (scores.length === 0) {
    alert("You didn't enter any scores.");
} else {
    let total = 0;
    let scoresString = "";
    for (let i in scores) {
        total += scores[i];
        scoresString += `Score ${parseInt(i) + 1}: ${scores[i]}\n`;
    }
    const average = total/scores.length;

    // display the scores and their average
    alert(`${scoresString}Average score: ${average.toFixed(2)}`);
}
```

Figure 4-5   The Test Scores app

More skills for working with arrays

The Array object includes several methods that you can use to work with the elements in an array. The topics that follow show how to use some of these methods.

How to modify or copy an array

Figure 4-6 summarizes some of the methods of the Array object that you can use to modify or copy the elements in an array. Except for the slice() method, these methods change the original array. The slice() method, on the other hand, copies some or all of an array's elements into a new array and doesn't change the original array.

The first example in this figure declares and initializes an array named names. This array contains three strings.

The second example shows how to use the push() and pop() methods to add elements to and remove elements from the end of an array. These functions let you use an array as a data structure known as a stack. In a *stack*, the last element added to the collection is the first element removed (last-in, first-out). You can think of this as adding a plate to a stack of plates where the last plate you add is the first plate you remove.

The third example shows how to use the unshift() and shift() methods. These methods work just like the push() and pop() methods, except they add elements to and remove elements from the beginning of an array instead of the end of an array.

The splice() method lets you remove, replace, or add elements in an array. To remove elements, you call the splice() method with the index of the first element to remove and the number of elements to remove. To replace elements, you call the splice() method with the index of the first element to replace, the number of elements to be replaced, and a list of the replacement values. To add elements, you call the splice() method with the index where you want the first element added, zero for the number of elements to remove, and a list of the values to add.

The fourth example shows how to use the splice() method to remove, add, and replace elements from a specific index. Here, the first statement removes two elements starting at index 1. Then, the second statement adds two elements starting at index 1. Note that to add elements, you code 0 for the second parameter. Next, the third statement replaces two elements starting at index 1.

The slice() method lets you create a new array from part or all of an array without modifying the original array. The first parameter indicates the index of the element where the copy starts, and the second parameter indicates the index up to which the elements are copied. In other words, the element at the index specified by the second parameter isn't copied.

The fifth example shows how the slice() method works. Here, the first statement copies the elements with indexes 1 and 2 into a new array, and the second statement copies all but the last element. To do this, the second statement passes a negative number as the second parameter, which counts back from the

Methods that modify or copy an array

Method	Description
push(*elements*)	Adds one or more elements to the end of the array and returns the new length.
pop()	Removes the last element in the array, decrements the length, and returns the value of the removed element.
unshift(*elements*)	Adds one or more elements to the beginning of the array, shifts other elements to the right by incrementing their indexes, and returns the new length of the array.
shift()	Removes the first element, shifts all elements one index to the left by decrementing their indexes, decrements the length of the array, and returns the value of the removed element.
splice(*start, number, elements...*)	Removes the number of elements specified by the second parameter starting with the index specified by the first parameter. Replaces the removed elements with the ones in the optional third parameter, or adds the elements at the start index if the second parameter is 0. If used to remove elements, returns an array containing those elements.
slice(*start, end*)	Returns a new array from the start index to the element before the end index. If no parameters are provided, it returns a new array with all elements. If end index is negative, it counts back from the end. This method doesn't change the original array.

An array that's used by the following examples

```
const names = ["Grace","Charles","Ada"];
```

Add and remove elements from the end of the array

```
names.push("Alan", "Linus"); // ["Grace","Charles","Ada","Alan","Linus"]
let removed = names.pop();    // removed is Linus
                             // ["Grace","Charles","Ada","Alan"]
```

Add and remove from the beginning of the array

```
names.unshift("Linus");      // ["Linus","Grace","Charles","Ada","Alan"]
removed = names.shift();     // removed is Linus
                             // ["Grace","Charles","Ada","Alan"]
```

Remove, add, and replace elements from a specific index

```
removed = names.splice(1, 2);          // removed is ["Charles","Ada"]
                                       // ["Grace","Alan"]
names.splice(1, 0, "Charles", "Ada");  // ["Grace","Charles","Ada","Alan"]
names.splice(1, 2, "Mary", "Linus");   // ["Grace","Mary","Linus","Alan"]
```

Copy some elements to a new array

```
const partialCopy = names.slice(1, 3); // partialCopy is ["Mary","Linus"]
const allButLast = names.slice(0, -1); // allButLast is
                                       // ["Grace","Mary","Linus"]
```

Copy all the elements to a new array

```
const fullCopy = names.slice();        // fullCopy is
                                       // ["Grace","Mary","Linus","Alan"]
```

Figure 4-6   How to modify or copy an array

end. Here, the second parameter is -1, so the elements up to the last element are copied.

You can also use the slice() method to copy all of the elements of an array to a new array. To do that, you omit the parameters of this method as shown in the last example in figure 4-6.

Finally, note that each of these methods returns a value or an array. For example, the push() and shift() methods return the new length of the array. The pop() and shift() methods return the value of the removed element. The slice() method returns a new array with elements from an existing array. And, when used to remove elements, the splice() method returns an array of the removed elements. However, you don't need to assign the returned value or array to a variable or constant if you won't use it in your code. In that case, the value or array is discarded. This is illustrated by the second and third statements in the fourth example that use the splice() method.

How to inspect or transform an array

Figure 4-7 summarizes some of the methods of the Array object that inspect and transform the elements of an array. For example, the indexOf() and lastIndexOf() methods let you search for a specific value in the array from either the beginning or end of the array. Each of these methods has a second optional parameter that allows you to indicate the index where the search starts. Both methods return the index of the value being searched for, or -1 if the value isn't found in the array.

The includes() method also searches for a value in the array and has an optional second parameter that allows you to indicate the index where the search starts. Unlike the indexOf() and lastIndexOf() methods, however, the includes() method doesn't return an index value or -1. Instead, it returns true if the value is found and false if it isn't. This method can make your code easier to read if you just need to know whether the value is in the array. To illustrate, the second example shows that an if statement that uses the includes() method is easier to read than an if statement that uses the indexOf() method.

The at() method provides another way to get the element in an array that's at the specified index. However, in addition to using positive values like you do when you use brackets, the at() method allows you to use negative index values to retrieve elements by counting from the end of the array. For instance, an index of -1 gets the last element in the array, -2 gets the second to last element, and so on. This is a more concise way to get elements at the end of an array as shown by the third example.

The join() and toString() methods create a string that lists the array's elements. However, the join() method lets you specify a separator for the elements, while the toString() method always uses a comma as the separator. The fourth example shows how this works. Note that if an array contains empty slots or elements that are undefined or null, the join() and toString() methods will use an empty string to represent that slot.

The reverse() method reverses the order of the elements in the array. The fifth example shows how this works.

Methods that inspect or transform an array

Method	Description
indexOf(*value*, *start*)	Returns the first index at which the value is found, or -1 if the value isn't found. The optional second parameter specifies the index to start searching from.
lastIndexOf(*value*, *start*)	Returns the last index at which the value is found, or -1 if the value isn't found. The optional second parameter specifies the index to start searching from.
includes(*value*, *start*)	Returns a Boolean value that indicates whether the value is in the array. The optional second parameter specifies the index to start searching from.
at(*index*)	Returns the element at the specified index, or undefined if the index is out of range. Negative indexes count back from the last item in the array.
join(*separator*)	Returns all elements after they have been converted to a string. The optional parameter provides a string to separate the elements. Otherwise, the elements are separated with commas.
toString()	Same as the join() method when used without the separator parameter.
reverse()	Reverses the order of the elements.

An array that's used by the following examples

```
const numbers = [1,2,3,4,5,6,7,8,9,10];
```

Two ways to check if a specific value is in the array

```
if (numbers.includes(5)) { ... }
if (numbers.indexOf(5) != -1) { ... }
```

Two ways to get the last element in the array

```
let last = numbers[numbers.length - 1];    // last is 10
last = numbers.at(-1);                      // last is 10
```

Three ways to convert an array to a string

```
let str = numbers.join();        // str is "1,2,3,4,5,6,7,8,9,10"
str = numbers.join(", ");        // str is "1, 2, 3, 4, 5, 6, 7, 8, 9, 10"
str = numbers.toString();        // str is "1,2,3,4,5,6,7,8,9,10"
```

Reverse the elements in an array

```
numbers.reverse();               // numbers is [10,9,8,7,6,5,4,3,2,1]
```

Description

- When you search an array of strings, the search is case-sensitive.

Figure 4-7   How to inspect or transform an array

The Test Scores 2.0 app

Figure 4-8 presents an enhanced version of the Test Scores app that displays all of the entered scores, the total, and the average score. In addition, it displays a list of the last three scores in the reverse sequence from which they were entered.

To start, the JavaScript creates an empty array named scores. Then, it uses an infinite while loop to get scores from the user.

Within the while loop, the first statement prompts the user to enter a test score or 'x' to exit. Then, it checks whether the user entered 'x' or clicked on the Cancel button, which returns null. If so, the break statement causes the infinite loop to end.

Otherwise, the code converts the user's entry to an integer. Then, it checks whether the score is within a valid range. If so, the code uses the push() method to add the score to the end of the scores array. Otherwise, it displays a message that indicates that the score wasn't valid.

When the loop ends, the code assigns the length property of the array to a constant named len. This simplifies the following code that refers to the length of the array. Then, the code checks the len constant to see if the user entered any scores. If not, the code displays an appropriate message to the user.

If the user did enter one or more scores, the code calculates the total of the scores and the average score. To calculate the total of the scores, the code uses a for-of loop. This works because the code that adds elements to the array ensures that the array doesn't contain any empty slots.

Next, this code gets the last three scores that were entered by the user, in the reverse order in which they were entered. To do that, it uses the conditional operator to check if the length of the array is less than or equal to three. If it is, the code uses the slice() method with no parameters to copy all scores in the array to a new array named lastScores. Otherwise, the code uses the slice() method with parameters to copy the last three elements of the array to the lastScores array. To do that, it uses the length of the array minus three as the starting index and the length as the ending index. The length works as the ending index because the slice() method doesn't return the element at that index.

After getting an array that stores the last three scores, this code uses the reverse() method to reverse the order of the elements in that array. Then, it displays the score data to the user. To display the scores entered by the user and the last three scores, the code uses the join() method with a separator of a comma and a space.

The dialog that displays the results

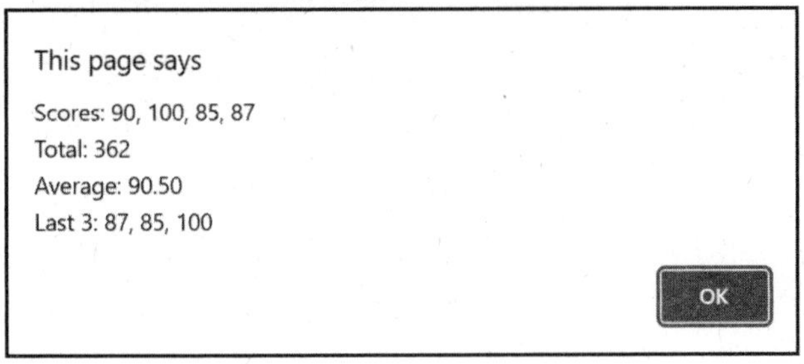

```
This page says

Scores: 90, 100, 85, 87
Total: 362
Average: 90.50
Last 3: 87, 85, 100

                                          OK
```

The JavaScript

```javascript
const scores = [];

while (true) {
    const entry = prompt("Enter a test score. Or, enter 'x' to exit.");
    if (entry === 'x' || entry === null) {
        break;
    }

    const score = parseInt(entry);
    if (score >= 0 && score <= 100) {
        scores.push(score);
    } else {
        alert("Score must by a valid number from 0 through 100.");
    }
}

const len = scores.length;
if (len === 0) {
    alert("You didn't enter any scores.");
} else {
    // calculate total and average
    let total = 0;
    for (let score of scores) {
        total += score;
    }
    const average = total/len;

    // get the last 3 scores in reverse order
    const lastScores =
        (len <= 3) ? scores.slice() : scores.slice(len - 3, len);
    lastScores.reverse();

    // display score data
    alert("Scores: " + scores.join(", ") + "\n" +
        "Total: " + total + "\n" +
        "Average: " + average.toFixed(2) + "\n" +
        "Last 3: " + lastScores.join(", "));
}
```

Figure 4-8   The Test Scores 2.0 app

More skills for working with strings

In chapter 2, you learned some basic skills for working with strings. Now, this chapter shows some more skills for working with strings, including how to use the properties and methods of a String object.

How to inspect a string

Figure 4-9 describes one property and several methods that you can call from a String object to learn more about the string. Remember that you can also call properties and methods from a variable, constant, or literal that contains a string. In that case, JavaScript automatically converts the string to a String object before it calls the property or method.

The length property returns the number of characters in the string. To show how this works, the first example in this figure declares a constant named str and initializes it with a string value of "JavaScript". This constant is used by the examples that follow. Then, the second example uses the length property to get the number of characters in the string.

The third example shows how to use the at() method. Here, the first expression gets the character at the position 4, which is the S in JavaScript. Then, the second expression gets the last character in the string. To do that, it passes an index value of -1 to the at() method. To get the second to last character in a string, this example could pass an index value of -2.

The fourth example shows the use of the indexOf() method. Here, the first expression shows that the search starts at the beginning of the string if you don't pass a start parameter. However, if you pass a start parameter, the search starts at the specified index as shown by the second expression. If the search string is found, the method returns the index that corresponds to the search string. However, if the search string isn't found, the method returns -1.

The fifth example shows how to use the startsWith(), endsWith(), and includes() methods. Here, the first two expressions show that the search is case-sensitive for all of these methods. Then, the last two expressions show that you can pass a start parameter to the includes() method to begin the search at the specified index. This shows that "JavaScript" includes a string of "ava" if you start the search at the beginning of the string but doesn't include "ava" if you start the search at the index of 2.

Properties and methods for inspecting a string

Property	Description
`length`	The number of characters in the string.
Method	**Description**
`at(position)`	Returns the character at the specified position, or undefined if the position is out of range. Negative position indexes count back from the last character in the string.
`indexOf(search, start)`	Returns the index of the first occurrence of the search string, or -1 if the search string isn't found. If the optional second parameter is provided, the search starts at that index.
`startsWith(search)`	Returns a Boolean value that indicates whether the string starts with the specified string.
`endsWith(search)`	Returns a Boolean value that indicates whether the string ends with the specified string.
`includes(search, start)`	Returns a Boolean value that indicates whether the string contains the specified string. If the optional second parameter is provided, the search starts at that index.

The constant that's used by the following examples
```
const str = "JavaScript";
```

Get the length of a string
```
str.length            // 10
```

Get one character
```
str.at(4)             // "S"
str.at(-1)            // "t"
```

Get index values
```
str.indexOf("a")      // 1
str.indexOf("a", 2)   // 3
str.indexOf("s")      // -1
```

Check whether a string contains the specified text
```
str.startsWith("Java")    // true
str.startsWith("java")    // false
str.endsWith("Script")    // true
str.includes("ava")       // true
str.includes("ava", 2)    // false
```

Description
- The methods that search a string are case-sensitive.

Figure 4-9   How to inspect a string

How to modify a string

Figure 4-10 presents methods of the String object that you can use to modify a string. All of these methods return a new string.

The first example declares and initializes a constant with a string value that's used by most of the examples in this figure. Then, the second example shows how to use the substring() method to return part of a string. Note that the character at the index specified by the end parameter for this method is *not* included in the result. Also, if you happened to specify an end index that's greater than the length of the string, JavaScript replaces it with the length of the string.

The third example shows how to use the toLowerCase() and toUpperCase() methods. A common use of these methods is to perform a case-insensitive test for equality between two strings, like this:

```
str1.toLowerCase() === str2.toLowerCase()
```

Otherwise, the == and === operators are case-sensitive.

The fourth example shows how to use the padStart() and padEnd() methods to add spaces to the beginning or end of a string. Here, both expressions pass a parameter that specifies the length of the new string after the padding is done. As a result, the first expression adds three spaces to the beginning of the string, and the second expression adds three spaces to the end of the string.

The fifth example shows how to use the trimStart(), trimEnd(), and trim() methods to remove whitespace (spaces, tabs, and line breaks) from a string. But first, this example declares another constant and initializes it with a string that has three blank spaces at its start and end.

The sixth example shows how to use the replace() and replaceAll() methods to replace part of the string with a new string. Here, you can see that the replace() method only replaces the first instance of the string "a" with the new string "@". By contrast, the replaceAll() method replaces all instances of the string.

The seventh example shows how to use the repeat() method. This method accepts an integer that specifies the number of times to repeat the string. In this example, the expression calls the repeat() method from a string literal of "*". Then, it passes a parameter of 20 to the repeat() method. This repeats the string 20 times. It also shows that you can call the methods of the String object from a string literal as well as from a variable or constant that stores a string.

Methods for modifying a string

Method	Description
substring(*start, end*)	Returns the substring from the start index to the end of the string. Or, if the optional end index parameter is provided, the substring ends just before that index.
toLowerCase()	Returns the string with all letters converted to lowercase.
toUpperCase()	Returns the string with all letters converted to uppercase.
trimStart()	Returns the string with whitespace removed from the beginning.
trimEnd()	Returns the string with whitespace removed from the end.
trim()	Returns the string with whitespace removed from the beginning and the end.
padStart(*length*)	Returns the string with spaces added to its beginning until it's the specified length.
padEnd(*length*)	Returns the string with spaces added to its end until it's the specified length.
replace(*old, new*)	Returns the string with the first instance of the old string replaced with the new string.
replaceAll(*old, new*)	Returns the string with all instances of the old string replaced with the new string.
repeat(*times*)	Returns the string repeated the specified number of times.

A constant used by the following examples
```
const str = "JavaScript";
```

Get substrings
```
str.substring(4)          // "Script"
str.substring(0, 4)       // "Java"
```

Convert case
```
str.toLowerCase()         // "javascript"
str.toUpperCase()         // "JAVASCRIPT"
```

Pad the start or end of a string
```
str.padStart(str.length + 3) // "   JavaScript"
str.padEnd(str.length + 3)   // "JavaScript   "
```

Trim whitespace from the start or end of a string
```
const str2 = "   JavaScript   ";
str2.trimStart()          // "JavaScript   "
str2.trimEnd()            // "   JavaScript"
str2.trim()               // "JavaScript"
```

Replace a substring with a new string
```
str.replace("a", "@");    // "J@vaScript"
str.replaceAll("a", "@"); // "J@v@Script"
```

Repeat a string
```
"*".repeat(20);           // "********************"
```

Figure 4-10   How to modify a string

How to create an array from a string

Figure 4-11 presents the split() method of the String object. You can use this method to split a string into an array of substrings based on a separator that can consist of one or more characters. This creates an array with each of the substrings as an element, and it eliminates the separator.

The first example in this figure declares and initializes two constants that are used by the following examples. The first constant stores a string that consists of a first name, a middle initial, and a last name separated by spaces. The second stores a string for a date whose date parts are separated by hyphens.

The second example shows how to split the full name string into an array using a space as the separator. This results in an array that contains the elements "Grace", "M", and "Hopper". Then, it gets the length of the new array and assigns it to a constant named len. Next, it assigns the element at the last index in the array (len - 1) to a constant named lastName. Similarly, the third example shows how to split the date string into an array using a hyphen as the separator.

The fourth example shows a split() method that uses two characters as the separator. Here, the first statement defines a constant that stores a list of names separated by a comma and a space. Then, the second statement uses a split() statement with a separator that consists of a comma and a space to split the string into an array of names.

The fifth example shows how to split the fullName string into individual characters. To do that, you call the split() method and specify an empty string as the separator.

The sixth example shows what happens if the separator character isn't in the string. Here, the date constant contains a string that has hyphens, but the split() method is called with a slash as the separator. In this case, the resulting array only has one element with the same value as the original string.

The last example shows what happens if the separator character is the first or last character in the string. Here, a constant named path stores a string with a slash character as its first and last characters. Then, the split() method is called with a slash as the separator. In this case, the resulting array has an empty string element at the beginning and at the end of the array.

A method for creating an array from a string

Method	Description
`split(separator)`	Splits the string into an array based on the specified separator and returns the array.

Two constants that are used by the following examples

```
const fullName = "Grace M Hopper";
const date = "7-4-2023";
```

Split a string that's separated by spaces into an array

```
const names = fullName.split(" ");      // names is ["Grace","M","Hopper"]
const len = names.length;               // len is 3
const lastName = names[len - 1];        // lastName is "Hopper"
```

Split a string that's separated by hyphens into an array

```
const dateParts = date.split("-");      // dateParts is ["7","4","2023"]
const month = dateParts[0];             // month is "7"
const year = dateParts[2];              // year is "2023"
```

Split a string that's separated by commas and spaces into an array

```
const names = "Bob, Anne, Mike";
const namesParts = names.split(", "); // namesParts is ["Bob","Anne","Mike"]
```

Split a string into an array of characters

```
const characters = fullName.split("");
// ["G","r","a","c","e"," ","M"," ","H","o","p","p","e","r"]
```

What happens if the string doesn't contain the separator

```
const dateParts = date.split("/");      // dateParts is ["7-4-2023"]
len = dateParts.length;                 // len is 1
```

What happens if the string contains the separator at the beginning or end

```
const path = "/directory/";
const pathParts = path.split("/"); // pathParts is ["","directory",""]
```

Description

- A separator can consist of one or more characters.

- If the separator is an empty string, each character in the string becomes an element in the array that's returned by the method.

- If the string includes the separator at the beginning or end of the string, an empty string is included as an element at the beginning or end of the array.

Figure 4-11   How to create an array from a string

How to chain method calls

When a method returns a primitive data type such as a string or an object such as an array, you can chain a call to another method directly from the first method using a technique known as *method chaining*. When you use method chaining, you don't have to assign the return value of the first method to a constant or variable. As a result, code that uses method chaining is shorter, and it's usually easier to read. Figure 4-12 shows how method chaining works.

The first example starts by showing how to capitalize the first letter of a name that's assigned to a variable without using method chaining. To do that, it uses three statements. The first statement calls the substring() method to get the first letter of the name and assign it to a variable. Then, the second statement uses the toUpperCase() method to capitalize the letter. Finally, the third statement uses the substring() method to get the rest of the name, concatenates it with the first letter, and assigns it back to the name variable.

Next, this example shows how to use method chaining to do the same thing. To do that, just one statement is used. This statement calls the substring() method to get the first letter of the name. Then, since the substring() method returns a string, the statement uses method chaining to call the toUpperCase() method directly from the substring() method to capitalize the letter. Finally, the statement concatenates the rest of the string with the first letter and assigns it back to the name variable. In addition to making the code shorter, this can make the code easier to read, especially if you need to chain multiple method calls as shown in the second example.

This example starts by showing how to remove punctuation and leading and trailing spaces from a string and then convert it to lowercase without using method chaining. The code begins by declaring a constant named words and initializes it with a string that contains leading and trailing whitespace, some new line characters, some commas, and a period. This string is defined as a template literal that spans three lines. Then, the code uses the replaceAll() method three times to remove the new line characters, the commas, and the period from the string. Next, it uses the trim() method to remove the leading and trailing whitespace from the string. Finally, it uses the toLowerCase() method to convert all of the letters in the string to lowercase. Since this code doesn't use method chaining, it must assign the result of each method call to a variable.

Next, this example shows how to use method chaining to do the same thing. In this case, the code only requires a single statement. That's because it doesn't need to assign the result of each method to a variable. Instead, it can call each method from the previous method and assign the result to a constant. As a result, the code is simpler and easier to read. To make this code even easier to read, each method call is coded on its own line, starting with the dot operator that begins the method call.

While the first two examples show how to use method chaining with strings, the third example shows that you can also use it with objects such as an Array object. This example uses the split() method to convert a string named words into an array of words. Then, it chains a call to the at() method of the Array object to get the third word in the array.

Capitalize the first letter of a name

```
let name = "grace";
```

Without method chaining

```
let firstLetter = name.substring(0, 1);
firstLetter = firstLetter.toUpperCase();
name = firstLetter + name.substring(1);
```

With method chaining

```
name = name.substring(0, 1).toUpperCase() + name.substring(1);
```

Convert a string to lowercase without punctuation or extra spaces

```
const text = `    JavaScript, often abbreviated as JS,
is a programming language that is one of the core technologies
of the World Wide Web, alongside HTML and CSS.       `;
```

Without method chaining

```
let words = text.replaceAll("\n", "");
words = words.replaceAll(",", "");
words = words.replaceAll(".", "");
words = words.trim();
words = words.toLowerCase();    // `javascript often abbreviated as js...`
```

With method chaining

```
const words = text
    .replaceAll("\n", " ")
    .replaceAll(",", "")
    .replaceAll(".", "")
    .trim()
    .toLowerCase();             // `javascript often abbreviated as js...`
```

Use method chaining to get the third word in a string of words

```
const thirdWord = words.split(" ").at(2);
```

Description

- When a method returns a primitive value or an object, you can chain a call to another method directly from the first method without assigning the return value to a constant or variable. This is known as *method chaining*.

- Method chaining often yields code that's more concise and readable than code that doesn't use method chaining.

- If you use a string function with a template literal, it's applied to any embedded strings as well as any literal characters in the template.

Figure 4-12   How to chain method calls

The Email Check app

Figure 4-13 presents an app that uses a dialog to prompt the user to enter an email address. Then, if the email address doesn't follow one of the specified rules, it displays a dialog that explains why the email address isn't valid. However, if the email address follows all the rules, the app displays a dialog that indicates that the email is valid.

The JavaScript for this app starts by setting a variable named isValid to false. Then, a while loop executes until the isValid variable is set to true.

Within the loop, the first statement prompts the user to enter an email address. Then, an if statement checks whether the email is valid. To do this, the if clause uses the startsWith() method to check if the email address starts with one of the forbidden characters, and the three else if clauses use the includes() and indexOf() methods to check that the email address contains the required characters in the correct order.

If any of the conditional expressions for these clauses are true, the statement that's executed displays a dialog that indicates why the email is invalid. In addition, the isValid variable remains at its initial value of false. As a result, the loop runs again and prompts the user for another email address.

However, if the user enters an email address that follows all the rules, the statements in the else clause execute. These statements display a dialog that indicates that the email address is valid and set the isValid variable to true. This causes the loop to end.

One of the dialogs that displays when the email address is invalid

This page says

Email address must contain an @ symbol.

OK

The dialog that displays when the email address is valid

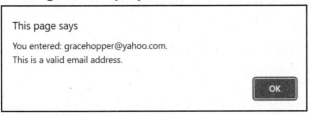

This page says

You entered: gracehopper@yahoo.com.
This is a valid email address.

OK

The email address rules that the app uses

- The email address may not start with a period or an underscore.
- The email address must contain an @ symbol and a period.
- The period must come after the @ symbol.

The JavaScript

```
let isValid = false;

while (!isValid) {
    const email = prompt("Enter your email address:");

    if (email.startsWith("_") || email.startsWith(".")) {
        alert("Email address may not start with a period or underscore.");
    } else if (!email.includes("@")) {
        alert("Email address must contain an @ symbol.");
    } else if (!email.includes(".")) {
        alert("Email address must contain a period.");
    } else if (!email.includes(".", email.indexOf("@"))) {
        alert("The period must come after the @ symbol.");
    } else {
        alert(`You entered: ${email}.\nThis is a valid email address.`);
        isValid = true;
    }
}
```

Figure 4-13   The Email Check app

The Bio app

Figure 4-14 presents an app that prompts the user for their name, date of birth, and favorite colors. To keep things simple, this app assumes that the user will enter data in the correct format and will enter at least two colors. Then, the app reformats the bio data and displays it back to the user.

Note that all three prompt statements chain a method call to the split() method to convert the string value the user enters into an array. But each statement uses a different separator to split the string. Specifically, the name is split on the spaces, the date is split on the hyphens, and the list of colors is split on the commas.

After getting the user entries, the code loops through the names array, capitalizes the first letter of each name and each initial, and converts all the other letters to lowercase. To do that, it uses the substring() method to get the first letter and then chains a method call to the toUpperCase() method to convert the letter to uppercase. Then, it uses the substring() method to get the remaining letters and then chains a method call to the toLowerCase() method to convert the letters to lowercase. Finally, it concatenates the first letter and the rest of the name and updates the element in the array.

For this to work, the code that capitalizes the name uses a for-in loop, not a for-of loop. That's because if you want to change an element while you're looping through an array, you must use an index to access that element. So you need to use a for loop or a for-in loop.

The code doesn't do any processing of the array that holds the date of birth values. However, it adjusts the elements in the array that holds the favorite colors so they don't contain any leading or trailing spaces. That's necessary because the user might enter the colors separated by a comma and a space, like the example shown here. Since the split() method that splits the colors uses a comma as the separator, this could lead to extra spaces in the color elements. To correct for that, the code uses a for-in loop to call the trim() method on each color and then updates the element in the array.

To create a display string for the colors, the code adds "and" between the last and the second-to-last element. To do that, it uses the slice() method to get a new array that contains all but the last element, and it uses the at() method to get the last element. In both cases, it uses negative indexes to work from the end of the array. Finally, it calls the join() method on the new array using a comma and a space as the separator, and it concatenates the resulting string and the last element.

Once all the processing is done, the code displays the bio data in a dialog. It uses the join() method to convert the name array back to a string, with the names and initials separated by spaces. It uses an index of 2 to get the year from the array that holds the date of birth values. And it uses the length property of the colors array and the color string to display the number and list of favorite colors.

The dialogs that prompt the user for their bio information

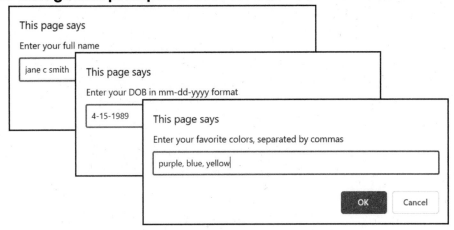

The dialog that displays the user's bio

This page says

Hello, my name is Jane C Smith.
I was born in 1989.
I have 3 favorite colors: purple, blue and yellow.

OK

The JavaScript

```javascript
// get name, dob, and colors and split into arrays
const names = prompt("Enter your full name").split(" ");
const dob = prompt("Enter your DOB in mm-dd-yyyy format").split("-");
const colors = prompt("Enter your favorite colors, separated by commas")
    .split(",");

// capitalize each name in array
for (let i in names) {
    const firstLetter = names[i].substring(0, 1).toUpperCase();
    const restOfName = names[i].substring(1).toLowerCase();
    names[i] = firstLetter + restOfName;
}

// trim any spaces from colors
for (let i in colors) {
    colors[i] = colors[i].trim();
}

// create a display string for the colors
const firstColors = colors.slice(0, -1);
const lastColor = colors.at(-1);
const colorString = `${firstColors.join(", ")} and ${lastColor}`;

// display bio
alert(`Hello, my name is ${names.join(" ")}.
I was born in ${dob[2]}.
I have ${colors.length} favorite colors: ${colorString}.`);
```

Figure 4-14   The Bio app

Perspective

Arrays are the optimal data structure to use if you want to keep a collection of elements in an indexed sequence and use those indexes to quickly access and modify the elements. In this chapter, you learned most of the skills you need for working with arrays, including many useful methods that are available from an array. However, chapter 11 presents more skills for working with arrays, including how to sort an array.

Terms

array	empty slot
array element	for-in loop
array length	for-of loop
array literal	stack
index	method chaining

Exercise 4-1   Work with arrays

This exercise asks you to get an array of prices, process those prices, calculate a total, and display the results like this:

```
This page says

Old total: 49.96
4 items earns a 10% discount!
New total: 44.96

                                                    OK
```

Review the starting code

1. Open the index.html file in this folder:

    `exercises\ch04\prices`

2. Review the code. Note that it uses a dialog to get an array of prices and that it displays the array in the console.

3. Run the code in a browser. At the prompt, accept the default entry.

4. Open the browser's development tools and use the console to view the array that's displayed in the console. Expand the node for the array. Note that the five elements in the array are strings.

Convert and validate the data

5. Use a for-in loop to convert the elements in the array from strings to numbers.

6. Use a for-in loop to delete any element that isn't greater than 0. When you do this, display a dialog that indicates that an invalid element is being deleted and include the value of that element.

Calculate the total of valid prices

7. Use a for-of loop to create a new array that only contains valid prices, not any undefined elements such as the negative price that was deleted earlier. To do that, you can use an if statement to make sure an element is defined before adding it to the new array.

8. Use a for-of loop to calculate the total of the valid prices.

Check the count of valid prices and display the result

9. Use an if statement to check the count of valid prices.

10. If there are more than three valid prices, display a dialog like the one shown above that displays the old total, the number of items, and a new total with a 10% discount.

11. If there are three or fewer valid prices, display a dialog that only displays the total without a discount.

Exercise 4-2   More skills for working with arrays

This exercise gives you more practice working with arrays. The code for this exercise maintains an array of three countries. It doesn't allow duplicate countries, and it doesn't allow more than three countries to be in the array at once. When you're done, your code should display each country on its own like this:

Review the starting code

1. Open the index.html file in this folder:

    `exercises/ch04/countries`

2. Note that this code defines an array named countries and a while loop that prompts the user to enter the name of a country.

Write code that adds countries to the array

3. Write code that gets the name of a country from the user.

4. Use an if-else statement to check if the country is already in the array. If it is, display a dialog to notify the user. If not, use the push() method to add the country to the array.

5. Use an if statement to check if more than three countries are in the array. If there are, use the shift() array method to remove the first country in the array. Then, display a dialog to notify the user that the country has been removed.

6. After the if statements, add code that displays a dialog with each country on its own line.

Exercise 4-3   Work with strings

This exercise asks you to work with a long string and display some data about it in the console. When you're done, the console should look like this:

```
It was the best of times it was the worst of times
    it was the age of wisdom it was the age of foolishness
    it was the epoch of belief it was the epoch of incredulity
    it was the season of Light it was the season of Darkness
    it was the spring of hope it was the winter of despair
    we had everything before us we had nothing before us
    we were all going direct to Heaven
    we were all going direct the other way in short the period
    was so far like the present period that some of its noisiest
    authorities insisted on its being received for good or for evil
    in the superlative degree of comparison only
Line count: 11
Word count: 119
```

Review the starting code

1. Open the index.html file in this folder:

    `exercises/ch04/words`

2. Note that this code defines a constant for the first sentence from a famous book and that it displays this constant in the console.

3. Run the index.html file and open the browser's developer tools to view what this sentence looks like when displayed in the console.

Write code that modifies a string

4. Remove all punctuation (commas, dashes, and periods) from the string. To do that, use the replaceAll() method to replace the punctuation characters with an empty string or a space. Remember that you can chain multiple calls to the replaceAll() method.

5. Use the trim() method to remove leading and trailing spaces.

6. Use the console.log() function to display the modified string in the console. Note that the leading spaces have only been removed from the first line.

Display a count of the lines

7. Use the split() method to split the string into an array based on the new line character.

8. Based on the length of this array, display a message in the console that indicates the number of lines.

Display a count of the words

9. Write a for-in loop to remove any leading or trailing spaces from each line.

10. Join the lines in the array into a new string using a space as the separator.

11. Split this new string into an array based on the space character.

12. Based on the length of this array, display a message in the console that indicates the number of words.

5

How to code functions and handle events

In this chapter, you'll learn how to use functions to organize your code into blocks of statements. You'll also learn how to run a function in response to an event such as a user clicking a button on a web page. When you finish this chapter, you'll be able to start developing useful apps that use functions to handle events that occur on web pages.

Three ways to work with functions

A *function* is a block of statements that performs an action. Once you've defined a function, you can run it by *calling* it. When you do that, you can pass *parameters* to it, and it can return a value.

So far in this book, you've been using built-in functions that are provided by JavaScript. Now, you'll learn how to define and call your own. In JavaScript, there are three ways to define a function. You can use a function declaration, a function expression, or an arrow function.

How to work with a function declaration

Figure 5-1 shows how to use a *function declaration* to define a function. To do that, you start by coding the *function* keyword followed by a name for the function. When naming a function, it's a good practice to start the name with a verb that indicates what the function does.

After the function name, you code a set of parentheses. Within the parentheses, you can code a list of parameters separated by commas. After the parentheses, you code a set of braces. Within the braces, you code the statements for the function. Everything within the braces is known as the *function body*.

To *call* a function, you code the name of the function, followed by a set of parentheses. Within the parentheses, you pass values to the parameters for the function. Then, the function uses these values as it executes its block of code.

The first example in this figure defines a function named showInvalidMessage(). This function doesn't require any parameters and doesn't return a value. When called, it displays a message in a dialog.

The second example defines a function named toKilometers() that converts miles to kilometers. This function defines one parameter named miles and returns a value for the calculated kilometers. In the function body, the code calculates the number of kilometers by multiplying the number of miles by 1.60934. Then, it uses the *return* keyword to return the result of that calculation. In this example, the calling code passes a parameter of 100 to the function, so the function returns a value of 160.934 kilometers.

The third example defines a function named calculateTax() that requires two parameters and returns a value. It calculates a sales tax amount, rounds it to two decimal places, and returns that rounded value as a string.

The examples in this figure pass literal values as parameters to the functions being called. However, you can also pass constants, variables, objects, and even other functions as parameters. When you do, you must pass the parameters in the same sequence as the parameters in the function.

In a file, you can code a statement that calls a function declaration before the function declaration as shown by the fourth example. This works because JavaScript *hoists* function declarations to the top of the script that contains them.

Incidentally, some programmers treat parameter and argument as synonyms and use them interchangeably. Others use parameter only to refer to a variable defined by the function and argument only to refer to a value passed to the function. In this book, we use parameter to refer to both.

The syntax for a function declaration

```
function functionName(parameters) {
    // statements that run when the function is executed
}
```

A function declaration with no parameters that doesn't return a value

```
function showInvalidMessage() {
    alert("That value is invalid. Please try again.");
}
```

Call the function

```
showInvalidMessage();
```

A function declaration with one parameter that returns a value

```
function toKilometers(miles) {
    return miles * 1.60934;
}
```

Call the function

```
const kms = toKilometers(100);                    // kms is 160.934
```

A function declaration with two parameters that returns a value

```
function calculateTax(subtotal, taxRate) {
    const tax = subtotal * taxRate;
    return tax.toFixed(2);
}
```

Call the function

```
const salesTax = calculateTax(85, 0.05);   // salesTax = "4.25"
```

What happens if you call a function declaration before you code it

```
sayHello();                        // prints "Hello" to the console
function sayHello() {
    console.log("Hello");
}
```

Description

- A *function* contains a block of code that can be *called* (or *invoked*) by a statement.
- A function can define one or more *parameters* that must be passed to it when it's called. In the calling statement, these parameters can also be referred to as *arguments*.
- A function can return a value to the statement that called it. To do that, it uses a *return statement* to return the specified value and end the function.
- To *call* a function, code its name followed by a set of parentheses. Within the parentheses, code any parameters required by the function. You must code these parameters in the same sequence they're defined in the function.
- A *function declaration* defines a function that has a name, or a *named function*.
- A function declaration is *hoisted* to the top of the file that contains it. Because of that, it doesn't have to be coded before any statements that call it.

Figure 5-1   How to work with a function declaration

How to work with a function expression

A *function expression* defines a function within an expression. For example, figure 5-2 shows how to define a statement that assigns a function expression to a constant. This syntax is similar to a function declaration, except that you can omit the name after the function keyword to create a function that doesn't have a name, also known as an *anonymous function*.

When you assign a function expression to a constant, you should code a semicolon after the closing brace. This indicates the end of the assignment statement. Then, you can call the function expression by using the name of the constant to refer to the function.

After you assign a function expression to a constant, you call it using techniques similar to the techniques you use to call a function declaration. The only difference is that you refer to the function expression by the name of the constant it's assigned to as shown by the three examples in this figure.

These three function expressions perform the same actions as the function declarations shown in the previous figure. The showInvalidMessage() function doesn't have any parameters and doesn't return a value. The toKilometers() function requires the number of miles and returns the result of the calculation that converts miles to kilometers. And the calculateTax() function requires the subtotal and tax rate and returns the sales tax amount as a string rounded to two decimal places.

The fourth example in this figure shows that, unlike a function declaration, a function expression isn't hoisted to the top of the script. As a result, if you code the statement that calls a function expression before you define the function expression, you'll get an error.

Although you can assign a function expression to a variable instead of a constant, you typically don't need to do that. In general, it's considered a best practice to assign function expressions to constants as shown in this figure.

The syntax for a function expression

```
const name = function(parameters) {
    // statements that run when the function is executed
};
```

A function expression with no parameters that doesn't return a value

```
const showInvalidMessage = function() {
    alert("That value is invalid. Please try again.");
};
```

Call the function

```
showInvalidMessage();
```

A function expression with one parameter that returns a value

```
const toKilometers = function(miles) {
    return miles * 1.60934;
};
```

Call the function

```
const kms = toKilometers(100);
```

A function expression with two parameters that returns a value

```
const calculateTax = function(subtotal, taxRate) {
    const tax = subtotal * taxRate;
    return tax.toFixed(2);
};
```

Call the function

```
const salesTax = calculateTax(85, 0.05);    // salesTax = "4.25"
```

What happens if you call a function expression before you code it

```
sayHello();                                  // ReferenceError
const sayHello = function() {
    console.log("Hello");
};
```

Description

- A *function expression* can define a function that doesn't have a name, also known as an *anonymous function*.
- To call a function expression, you can assign it to a constant. Then, you can use the name of the constant to call the function expression.
- In contrast to a function declaration, a function expression isn't hoisted. As a result, a function expression must be coded before any statements in the file that call it.

Figure 5-2   How to work with a function expression

How to work with an arrow function

An *arrow function* is similar to a function expression, but with a more concise syntax and some other improvements. Figure 5-3 shows how to code an arrow function. This works like coding a function expression, except that you don't code the *function* keyword followed by a list of parameters. Instead, you code a list of parameters followed by the *arrow operator* (=>).

The first example shows an arrow function assigned to a constant named calculateTax. Here, you can think of the arrow operator as pointing to the code that the function executes. You can call this arrow function the same way you call a function expression. That is, you code the name of the constant that the arrow function is assigned to followed by a set of parentheses. Within the parentheses, you code any parameters separated by commas.

The second example shows that an arrow function that has just one parameter can be coded more concisely by omitting the parentheses that are coded around the parameter. If you want, you can still include the parentheses around the parameter, but many programmers omit them.

The third example shows that an arrow function that has just one statement in its body can be coded even more concisely by omitting the braces. In addition, if this statement is a return statement, the arrow function can omit the *return* keyword.

The fourth example shows that an arrow function that has no parameters must include the parentheses. These parentheses indicate that the arrow function doesn't have any parameters.

In addition to making code shorter, you should know that arrow functions differ from function expressions in how they handle the *this* keyword, which can be used to refer to an object that's available to the function. However, for modern JavaScript development, it's considered a best practice to avoid using the *this* keyword within functions. As a result, you are unlikely to encounter this scenario when working with modern JavaScript.

At this point, you may be wondering when it makes sense to use function declarations, and when it makes sense to use function expressions or arrow functions. In general, it's a matter of personal preference. Some programmers prefer to use function declarations because they're the easiest to read. Some programmers prefer to use function expressions because they're not hoisted, so you can't call a function before it's coded. And others prefer to use arrow functions because they're more concise than function expressions.

In this book, we sometimes use function declarations because they're the easiest to read for named functions. However, we often use arrow functions too, especially to handle events, as shown later in this chapter. We don't use function expressions at all because they're not as readable as function declarations and arrow functions are preferred for handling events.

The syntax for an arrow function

```
const name = (parameters) => {
    // statements that run when the function is executed
};
```

An arrow function

```
const calculateTax = (subtotal, taxRate) => {
    const tax = subtotal * taxRate;
    return tax.toFixed(2);
};
```

Call the function

```
const salesTax = calculateTax(85, 0.05);        // salesTax = "4.25"
```

An arrow function with one parameter

```
const toKilometers = miles => {                 // no parens around param
    return miles * 1.60934;
};
```

An arrow function with one parameter that executes one statement

```
const toKilometers = miles => miles * 1.60934;  // no braces or return
```

An arrow function with no parameters that executes one statement

```
const sayHello = () => console.log("Hello");    // empty parens
```

Description

- An *arrow function* provides a more concise way of coding a function expression.
- To code an arrow function, you omit the *function* keyword and code an *arrow operator* (=>) after the parameter list.
- If a function has only one parameter, you can omit the parentheses around the parameter list.
- If a function has no parameters, you must include parentheses around the empty parameter list.
- If a function body consists of a single statement, you can omit the braces around that statement. In addition, you can omit the *return* keyword if there is one.
- You call an arrow function the same way you call a function expression.

Figure 5-3   How work with an arrow function

The Future Value app

Figure 5-4 presents an updated version of the Future Value app from chapter 3. This version uses three functions to organize its code.

The getNumber() function defines two parameters, a message for a prompt and a default value. Then, the body of the function uses these parameters to get a number from the user. To start, it initializes the num variable to NaN. Then, it uses a while loop to prompt the user for a value and converts the string entered by the user to a number. If the user enters a string that's not a number, the while loop continues and prompts the user again. Once the while loop ends, the function returns the valid number from the user.

The getNumber() function provides two main benefits. First, it reduces code duplication because the app doesn't need to use three while loops to get the three numbers it needs. Instead, the app just calls the getNumber() function three times. Second, it makes this code easier to reuse. That's because getting a number from a user is a common task. As a result, you might be able to reuse this function in other apps.

The calcFutureValue() function defines parameters for the investment amount, interest rate, and number of years. Then, it uses a for loop to calculate the future value based on these parameters. When the loop ends, the function returns the future value.

The displayResults() function accepts parameters for the investment amount, interest rate, and years as well as the future value. However, instead of returning a value, this function uses a statement to display the results in a dialog.

The main benefit of the calcFutureValue() and displayResults() functions is that they organize this app's code in smaller chunks. In other words, these functions don't reduce code duplication, and they're not likely to be reused in other apps. However, breaking lengthy code into smaller chunks often makes your code more readable and easier to maintain.

In addition, if you name your functions well, the names of the functions indicate what the code is doing and reduce the need for comments. For example, there's less need to include a comment that explains that the getNumber() function gets a number from the user. Similarly, there's less need to include a comment to explain that the calcFutureValue() function calculates the future value of an investment. In other words, well-named functions help to make self-documenting code.

The first dialog that gets input

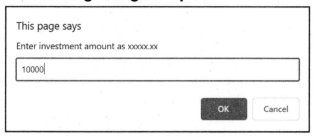

This page says

Enter investment amount as xxxxx.xx

10000|

OK   Cancel

The dialog that displays the results

This page says

Investment amount: $10000
Interest rate: 7.5%
Years: 10
Future Value: $20610.32

OK

The JavaScript

```
function getNumber(promptMsg, defaultValue) {
    let num = NaN;
    while (isNaN(num)) {
        num = parseFloat(prompt(promptMsg, defaultValue));
    }
    return num;
}

function calcFutureValue(investment, rate, years) {
    let futureValue = investment;
    for (let i = 0; i < years; i++) {
        futureValue += futureValue * rate / 100;
    }
    return futureValue;
}

function displayResults(investment, rate, years, futureValue) {
    alert("Investment amount: $" + investment + "\n" +
          "Interest rate: " + rate + "%\n" +
          "Years: " + years + "\n" +
          "Future Value: $" + futureValue.toFixed(2));
}

const investment = getNumber("Enter investment amount as xxxxx.xx", 10000);
const rate = getNumber("Enter interest rate as xx.x", 7.5);
const years = getNumber("Enter number of years", 10);
const futureValue = calcFutureValue(investment, rate, years);
displayResults(investment, rate, years, futureValue);
```

Figure 5-4   The Future Value app

More skills for working with functions

Now that you know the basics of defining and calling functions, you're ready to learn some more skills for working with functions, including how to work with scope, how to include default parameters, and how to work with the rest and spread operators.

How to work with scope

Scope refers to the visibility of your code. In other words, it tells you where you can use the variables and constants that you've defined.

In JavaScript, variables and constants that are defined outside of functions have *global scope*. This means they can be used by any function in the app without passing them to the function as parameters.

The first example in figure 5-5 illustrates the use of global scope. It begins by declaring a constant and a variable outside of any functions. As a result, they have global scope. Then, this example defines a function named calculateTax() that uses the global taxRate variable to calculate a tax amount. Next, it assigns the tax amount to the global tax variable. As a result, the function doesn't need to return the tax variable. Instead, a statement outside of the function can refer to the tax variable because it has global scope.

By contrast, variables and constants that are defined within functions, either in the parameter list or the function body, have *local scope*. This means that they can only be used within the function that defined them.

The second example illustrates the use of local scope. Here, the calculateTax() function defines subtotal and taxRate parameters, uses these parameters to calculate the tax, assigns the tax to a local variable, and returns the tax. In this example, a statement outside of the function can't refer to the tax variable because it has local scope.

Although it may seem easier to use global scope than to pass data to a function and return data from it, global scope often creates problems. That's because any function can modify a global variable, and it's all too easy to misspell a variable name or modify the wrong variable, especially in large apps. That in turn can create debugging problems. This problem is even worse if you don't use strict mode.

By contrast, local scope reduces the likelihood of naming conflicts. For instance, two different functions can use the same names for local variables or constants without causing conflicts. This leads to fewer errors and debugging problems. As a result, it's considered a best practice to define functions so all of the variables and constants are local.

When you work with local variables and constants, it's a best practice to use the *let* and *const* keywords to define them. When you use these keywords, the variable or constant has *block scope* and is only available within the block of code where it's defined as shown by the third example. By contrast, if you use the *var* keyword, the variable has *function scope* and is available throughout the

Global scope (not recommended)

```
const taxRate = 0.074;                  // declare global constant
let tax = 0;                            // declare global variable

function calculateTax(subtotal) {
    tax = subtotal * taxRate;           // use global constant and variable
    tax = tax.toFixed(2);
}

calculateTax(100);
alert(tax);                             // tax is "7.40"
```

Local scope (recommended)

```
function calculateTax(subtotal, taxRate) {
    let tax = subtotal * taxRate;       // declare local variable
    tax = tax.toFixed(2);
    return tax;
}

const tax = calculateTax(100, 0.074);
alert(tax);                             // tax is "7.40"
```

Block scope

```
function displayCount() {
    for (let i = 0; i < 5; i++) {       // start block
        console.log(i);                 // i in scope
    }                                   // end block
    console.log(i);                     // i not in scope - ReferenceError
}
```

Description

- The *scope* of a variable or constant determines what code has access to it.

- Variables and constants declared outside of functions have *global scope*, and the code in all functions has access to all global variables and constants.

- Variables and constants that are declared inside a function have *local scope*. Local variables and constants can only be referred to by the code within the function.

- Variables and constants declared inside a block of code, such as a block for an if or for statement, have *block scope*. That means they can only be referred to by the code in that block.

- In general, it's a best practice to use local variables and constants instead of global ones.

- It's a best practice to use the *let* and *const* keywords, not the *var* keyword, to declare variables and constants. That's because scope works differently with the *var* keyword in ways that can lead to bugs that are hard to find and fix.

Figure 5-5   How to work with scope

entire function. This is generally considered a bad practice because it can lead to bugs that are difficult to find and fix.

How to work with default parameters

If you omit a parameter when you call a function, the value of the parameter is undefined. Usually, this isn't what you want.

To make sure a parameter value isn't undefined, you can code your functions to check for undefined parameters before they're used. Then, you can assign a default value to the parameter. To do that, you can use the *undefined* keyword, like this:

```
if (paramName == undefined) {
    paramName = defaultValue;
}
```

However, a simpler way to handle this is to assign a default value when you code the parameter as shown in figure 5-6.

The first example presents a function named calculateTax() that provides a default value of 0.074 for its taxRate parameter. As a result, if the calling code doesn't pass a value to the taxRate parameter, the function uses the default tax rate of 0.074. On the other hand, if the calling code passes a value to this parameter, the function uses that value instead of the default. This is shown by the first two statements that call this function.

The third and fourth statements show what happens if you pass null or undefined as a parameter. Because JavaScript considers null to be a valid value, the calculateTax() function doesn't use the default value. Instead, it uses null in the calculation and returns a value of 0.00. On the other hand, JavaScript considers undefined an invalid value. Because of that, the fourth statement uses the default value.

A default value can be a literal value, a constant, a variable, or an expression. In addition, you can use an earlier parameter as a default value for a later parameter. In an arrow function, if you provide a default value for a single parameter, you must enclose that parameter in parentheses as shown by the second example.

The third example shows that a function can have more than one default parameter in a parameter list. However, to pass a value for a parameter that's later in the parameter list, you must provide values for all of the parameters that come before it. For instance, the fourth call to the toPlaces() function returns a value of NaN because it assigns a value of "floor" to the places parameter, which expects a number. To pass "floor" so it's assigned to the type parameter while still using the default value for places, the code needs to pass a value of undefined to the places parameter as shown in the fifth call to this function. This causes the function to use the default value of 2 for the places parameter.

Unlike many other programming languages, JavaScript doesn't require you to code parameters with default values at the end of the parameter list. However, it's generally considered a good practice to do so. That way, you don't need to pass a value of undefined to optional parameters before you pass values to the required parameters.

A function with a default parameter

```
function calculateTax(subtotal, taxRate = 0.074) {
    const tax = subtotal * taxRate;
    return tax.toFixed(2);
}
```

Call the function

```
const tax1 = calculateTax(100);              // tax1 is "7.40"
const tax2 = calculateTax(100, 0.087);       // tax2 is "8.70"
const tax3 = calculateTax(100, null);        // tax3 is "0.00"
const tax4 = calculateTax(100, undefined);   // tax4 is "7.40"
```

An arrow function with a single parameter and a default value

```
const getPI = (places = 15) => Number(Math.PI.toFixed(places));
```

Call the function

```
const pi = getPI();          // pi is 3.141592653589793
const pi2 = getPI(4);        // pi2 is 3.1416
```

A function with two parameters that have default values

```
function toPlaces(num, places = 2, type = "round") {
    num = num * (10 ** places);     // move decimal point right
    if (type == "floor") {
        num = Math.floor(num);
    } else if (type == "ceil") {
        num = Math.ceil(num);
    } else {
        num = Math.round(num);
    }
    return num / (10 ** places);    // move decimal point left
}
```

Call the function

```
const num1 = toPlaces(5.22873);                    // num1 is 5.23
const num2 = toPlaces(5.22873, 4);                 // num2 is 5.2287
const num3 = toPlaces(5.22873, 4, "ceil");         // num3 is 5.2288
const num4 = toPlaces(5.22873, "floor");           // num4 is NaN
const num5 = toPlaces(5.22873, undefined, "floor"); // num5 is 5.22
```

Description

- You can assign a default value to a function parameter. If the code that calls the function doesn't provide a value for that parameter, the function uses the default value.

- The default value can be a literal value or an expression. Parameters that come later in the parameter list can use the value of earlier parameters as their default value.

- In an arrow function, a single parameter with a default value must be coded within parentheses.

- A function can define multiple parameters with default values. These parameters aren't required to be coded at the end of the parameter list, though they usually are.

- To pass a value to a parameter, you must also pass values to all parameters that come before that parameter.

- To use the default value of a parameter, you can pass undefined.

Figure 5-6   How to work with default parameters

How to work with the rest and spread operators

Figure 5-7 shows how to use the *rest operator* (...) to define a *rest parameter* that collects one or more values into an array. This provides a convenient syntax for defining a *variadic function*, which is a function that accepts a varying number of parameters.

The first example in this figure defines a calculateTaxAll() function. This function has a taxRate parameter and a subtotals parameter that's prepended with the rest operator. Because of the rest operator, any parameters coded after the taxRate parameter are collected in the subtotals parameter as elements in an array. In the body of the function, the code loops through this array to calculate the tax for each subtotal amount and adds it to the overall tax amount.

When you code a rest parameter, you can only code one per function, and it must be the last parameter in the list. In other words, a rest parameter collects the *rest* of the values that are passed to the function.

The second example shows how to call the calculateTaxAll() function. Here, the first three statements call the function with varying numbers of parameters. Then, the fourth and fifth statements show how to use the *spread operator* (...) when calling a function. The spread operator looks identical to the rest operator. The difference depends on when and where the operator is used.

The fourth statement creates a new array named taxRateAndAmounts and initializes it with five values. Then, the fifth statement passes this array to the calculateTaxAll() function. However, since this array is prepended with the spread operator, JavaScript passes the array elements as individual parameters. In other words, the elements in the array are *spread* out into individual parameters.

The next three statements show how to use multiple spread operators when you call a function. These spread operators don't need to come at the end of the parameter list. In addition, they can be mixed with literal values. Here, the code that calls the calculateTaxAll() function prepends the two arrays with the spread operator and passes a final parameter that's a numeric literal. This produces the same result as passing the values individually.

Although these examples use the spread operator with variadic functions, the spread operator can also be used with non-variadic functions. For example, this code calls the toPlaces() function that's in the previous figure:

```
const paramArray = [5.22873, 4, "ceil"];
const num6 = toPlaces(...paramArray);        // num6 is 5.2288
```

When you use the spread operator this way, any additional elements in the array beyond those needed for the parameters are ignored by the function.

A function with a rest parameter

```
function calculateTaxAll(taxRate, ...subtotals) {
    let tax = 0;
    for (let subtotal of subtotals) {     // rest parameter provides an array
        tax += subtotal * taxRate;
    }
    return tax.toFixed(2);
}
```

Three ways to call this function

With a list of parameters

```
const tax1 = calculateTaxAll(0.074, 100);                    // tax1 is "7.40"
const tax2 = calculateTaxAll(0.074, 100, 200);               // tax2 is "22.20"
const tax3 = calculateTaxAll(0.074, 100, 200, 400, 500);     // tax3 is "88.80"
```

With a single spread operator

```
const taxRateAndAmounts = [0.074, 100, 200, 400, 500];
const tax4 = calculateTaxAll(...taxRateAndAmounts);          // tax4 is "88.80"
```

With multiple spread operators

```
const rateAndAmounts = [0.074, 100];
const moreAmounts = [200, 400];
const tax5 = calculateTaxAll(...rateAndAmounts,
                             ...moreAmounts, 500);           // tax5 is "88.80"
```

Description

- You can use the *rest operator* (...) to accept a variable number of parameters and put them in an array. The parameter with the rest operator is called a *rest parameter.*

- A function can only define one rest parameter, and it must be the last parameter in the parameter list.

- A function which accepts a varying number of parameters is called a *variadic function.* All functions with a rest parameter are variadic functions.

- You can use the *spread operator* (...) to pass the elements in an array to a function as individual parameters.

- A function call can use more than one spread operator, and the spread operator doesn't need to be the last argument.

Figure 5-7   How to work with the rest and spread operators

The Bio app

Figure 5-8 presents an updated version of the Bio app from chapter 4. This version uses five functions to organize its code. In addition, one of these functions has a parameter with a default value, and three have a rest parameter.

The getAsArray() function accepts a message string and a separator value and uses these parameters to get information from the user. It passes the separator value to the split() method of the string returned by the prompt() method to convert the information from the user to an array. If this function is called without a value for the separator parameter, the default value is used and the string is split on the spaces.

The next three functions each have a single rest parameter. Because of that, they can be called with a comma-separated list of parameters or with an array and a spread operator.

The capitalize() function starts by creating a new array to hold capitalized words. Then, it loops through the array named words that's collected by the rest operator, capitalizes the first letter of each word, converts the rest of the letters to lower case, and adds the capitalized word to the new array. When the loop completes, the function returns the new array with the capitalized words. Note that this code creates a new array and doesn't change the initial array.

The trim() function starts by creating a new array to hold the trimmed items. Then, it loops through the array named items collected by the rest operator, trims any spaces, and adds each trimmed value to the new array. When the loop completes, the function returns the new array with the trimmed items. This function also doesn't change the initial array.

The getColorsString() function creates a display string that adds the conjunction "and" between the last and the second-to-last elements of the array collected by the rest operator. To do that, it uses the slice() method to get a new array that contains all elements but the last, and it uses the at() method to get the last element. Then, the function returns a string that concatenates the string returned by the join() method with the last element. Once again, this code doesn't change the original array.

The displayBio() function displays the bio data in a dialog. It uses the join() method to convert the name array back to a string, with the names and initials separated by spaces. It uses the at() method and a negative index to get the last element from the dob array, which is the year. And it uses the length property of the colors array and the string returned by getColorsString() to display the favorite colors.

The last five statements in this figure use these functions to get input from the user, capitalize names, trim spaces, format strings, and display the result to the user. The first call to getAsArray() doesn't pass a separator, so it splits the name on the spaces. By contrast, the second call to this function splits the date on the dashes, and the third call splits the colors on the commas.

The statements that call the capitalize() and trim() functions use the values returned by the getAsArray() function as parameters. For that to work, the code prepends the spread operator to the call to getAsArray(). This spreads out the elements in the array returned by that function into individual parameters.

The dialog that displays the user's bio

```
This page says

Hello, my name is Jane C Smith.
I was born in 1989.
I have 3 favorite colors: purple, blue and yellow.

                                              OK
```

The JavaScript

```javascript
function getAsArray(promptMsg, separator = " ") {
    return prompt(promptMsg).split(separator);
}

function capitalize(...words) {
    const capitalizedWords = [];
    for(let word of words) {
        const firstLetter = word.substring(0,1).toUpperCase();
        const restOfWord = word.substring(1).toLowerCase();
        capitalizedWords.push(firstLetter + restOfWord);
    }
    return capitalizedWords;
}

function trim(...items) {
    const trimmedItems = [];
    for(let item of items) {
        trimmedItems.push(item.trim());
    }
    return trimmedItems;
}

function getColorsString(...items) {
    const firstItems = items.slice(0, -1);
    const lastItem = items.at(-1);
    return `${firstItems.join(", ")} and ${lastItem}`;
}

function displayBio(names, dob, colors) {
    alert("Hello, my name is " + names.join(" ") + ".\n" +
        "I was born in " + dob.at(-1) + ".\n" +
        "I have " + colors.length + " favorite colors: " +
        getColorsString(...colors) + ".");
}

const names = capitalize(...getAsArray("Enter your full name"));
const dob = getAsArray("Enter your DOB in mm-dd-yyyy format", "-");

const msg = "Enter your favorite colors, separated by commas";
const colors = trim(...getAsArray(msg, ","));

displayBio(names, dob, colors);
```

Figure 5-8   The Bio app

How to handle events

JavaScript apps commonly respond to actions like a browser loading a web page or a user clicking a button. These actions are called *events*, and the functions that handle these events are called *event handlers*. To make this work, you *attach* the functions to the events.

Event handlers can seem complicated at first. However, they're easier to understand when you see them in action. For example, the Guess the Number app that's presented in figure 5-11 shows two simple event handlers in action.

How to work with events

Figure 5-9 begins by summarizing some of the events that are commonly handled by JavaScript apps. For instance, the load event of the window object occurs when the browser has loaded the entire page, including external images and style sheets. The DOMContentLoaded event of the document object is similar but occurs earlier, when the HTML document is loaded and ready to be used. And the click event of an element object such as a button occurs when the user clicks the element.

An event handler is a function that's executed when an event occurs. In other words, the function "handles" the event. You code an event handler just like any other function. They are commonly coded as arrow functions.

To attach an event handler to an event, you use the addEventListener() method. The first parameter for this method is the event to *listen* for, and the second parameter is the function that handles the event when it occurs. For most apps, you won't need to detach an event hander. However, if you should ever need to do that, you can use the removeEventListener() method.

The first example in this figure shows how to attach an event handler. To start, the first statement defines an arrow function that displays a message in a dialog, and it assigns this function to a constant. Then, the second statement attaches the showMessage() function to the DOMContentLoaded event of the document object. To do that, the code calls the addEventListener() method of the document object and passes it a string of "DOMContentLoaded" to identify the event, and it passes the name of the constant to identify the function that will handle this event.

Note that this code doesn't include the parentheses after the name of the constant that refers to the function. That's because this code is *attaching* the function, not *calling* it. If you code parentheses after showMessage, the code calls the function right away and doesn't attach it to the event.

If you only need an event handler for one event, you can code an arrow function directly as the second parameter of the addEventListener() method. This technique is shown by the second example.

Incidentally, there's another way to attach an event handler that you may see in legacy code. With that technique, the event handler function is assigned to a property, such as onclick or onblur. However, using the addEventListener() method is more flexible and is generally considered a best practice for attaching event handlers.

Common events

Object	Event	Occurs when...
window	load	The whole page has been loaded into the browser, including external style sheets and images.
document	DOMContentLoaded	The HTML document has been loaded into the browser and is ready.
	keydown	The user presses a key on the keyboard.
	keyup	The user releases a key on the keyboard.
element	click	The user clicks on the element.
	dblclick	The user double-clicks on the element.
	mouseover	The user moves the mouse over the element.
	mousein	The user moves the mouse into the element.
	mouseout	The user moves the mouse out of the element.

Two methods available to window, document, and element objects

Method	Description
addEventListener(*event, function*)	Attaches the function as the handler for the event.
removeEventListener(*event, function*)	Detaches the function as the handler for the event.

Define and attach an event handler for the DOMContentLoaded event

```
// define an arrow function and assign it to a constant
const showMessage = () => alert("I'm ready!");

// attach the function to an event
document.addEventListener("DOMContentLoaded", showMessage);
```

A more concise way to code the previous example

```
document.addEventListener("DOMContentLoaded", () => alert("I'm ready!") );
```

Description

- An *event handler* is a function that executes when an *event* occurs. It's a common practice to use arrow functions for event handlers.

- To *attach* the same event handler to multiple events, assign the arrow function to a constant. Then, pass that constant as the second parameter of the addEventListener() method.

- When you pass a constant that refers to an event handler to the addEventListener() method, you don't code the parentheses after the constant name. If you do, the event handler will be called rather than attached.

- If you only want to attach an event handler to a single event, you don't need to assign the arrow function to a constant. Instead, you can code an arrow function as the second parameter of the addEventListener() method.

Figure 5-9   How to work with events

How to attach events to HTML elements

In addition to attaching event handlers to an event of the document object, you often need to attach an event handler to an event of an HTML element. For instance, you may need to attach a function to the event that fires when a button is clicked. To do that, you need to work with the *Document Object Model,* or *DOM*. The DOM represents all the HTML elements on the page. To access the DOM, you can use the document object.

The first table in figure 5-10 presents the querySelector() method of the document object. This method accepts a parameter that's a CSS selector, and it returns an object that represents the first HTML element that matches that selector. For example, you can use the **#** prefix to select an element by its id.

The second table presents the textContent property that's available to most element objects. This property allows you to get or set the text between the opening and closing tags of an element. As a result, it's available from elements that store text between their opening and closing tags, such as the <p>, <span>, and <label> elements.

The third table presents the value property that's available from text boxes. You can use the value property to get or set the text that's stored in a text box.

The first example shows the HTML for a text box, a button, and a label. Here, the text box has an id of "text_box", the button has an id of "show_button", and the label has an id of "label".

The second example shows a function named setLabel() that can be used to handle an event. This event handler starts by using the querySelector() method to get the HTML elements with ids of "label" and "text_box". Then, it uses the value property of the text box to set the textContent property of the label.

The third example shows how to attach the event handler named setLabel() to the click event of the button. To start, it adds an event handler for the DOMContentLoaded event of the document object. Within this event handler, the first statement gets the button element with the id of "show_button". Then, the second statement calls the addEventListener() method of the button element to attach the setLabel() function to the click event of the button.

In most cases, it makes sense to attach event handlers for HTML elements within the event handler for the DOMContentLoaded event. That way, you can be sure the browser has loaded the DOM and all the HTML elements exist. Occasionally, though, you may need to make sure the window is fully loaded, including images and scripts. In those cases, you can use the load event of the window object to attach the event handlers.

If you code a <script> element at the end of the <body> element, the browser executes that code after the DOM has been loaded. In that case, you don't need to put the code that attaches event handlers within the event handler for the DOMContentLoaded event. However, it's still considered a best practice to attach event handlers within the event handler for the DOMContentLoaded event. That way, your code will work correctly even if the <script> element later gets moved to the beginning of the HTML document.

A method of the document object

Method	Description
`querySelector(selector)`	Returns an Element object that represents the first HTML element that matches the selector. The selector must be a valid CSS selector.

A property available to most elements

Property	Description
`textContent`	Gets or sets the text between the opening and closing tag of an element.

A property available to text boxes

Property	Description
`value`	Gets or sets the text that's stored in a text box.

The HTML for a text box, button, and label

```
<input id="text_box" type="text"><br>
<button id="show_button">Show</button><br>
<label id="label"></label>
```

An event handler

```
const setLabel = () => {
    const label = document.querySelector("#label");
    const textBox = document.querySelector("#text_box");
    label.textContent = "You entered: " + textBox.value;
};
```

Code that attaches the event handler to the click event of the button

```
document.addEventListener("DOMContentLoaded", () => {
    const showButton = document.querySelector("#show_button");
    showButton.addEventListener("click", setLabel);
});
```

Description

- The *Document Object Model (DOM)* represents all the HTML elements on the page.
- The document object allows you to use the DOM to select and work with individual HTML elements.
- To select a specific HTML element with the querySelector() method, pass its id as the parameter prefixed with **#** and enclosed in quotes.
- It's a common practice to use the event handler for the DOMContentLoaded event of the document object to attach event handlers for other elements. This makes sure they are attached only after the DOM has been built.

Figure 5-10   How to attach events to HTML elements

The Guess the Number app

Figure 5-11 presents an updated version of the Guess the Number app from chapter 3. This version uses HTML elements rather than prompt statements to get the guess from the user. In addition, rather than competing against the computer, this version provides feedback to the user so they can keep trying until they guess correctly. When the user guesses the number, this version lets them know how many tries it took. If the user wants to play again, they can start a new game by clicking the Play Again button.

The HTML for the app includes an external CSS file in the <head> element for styling. In the <body> element, it displays a level-1 heading, a paragraph with some information about the game, a text box, two buttons, and a label. At the bottom of the <body> element, the <script> element includes an external JavaScript file.

The text box, button, and labels all have id attributes. This is what the code uses to select these elements. Note that the id attribute for the Play Again button uses snake case rather than camel case. That's because snake case is commonly used in HTML documents.

The CSS in the external file begins by defining the styles for the <body> element. This includes setting the fonts, the background color, the width of the body, the padding, the margins, and a thin black border with rounded corners. For the <h1> element, the CSS sets the color of the text. For the text box and button, the CSS sets the margins to provide some spacing to the left and below these elements.

The app after a user has made a guess

Guess the Number

It's between 1 and 10.

```
5                         [ Guess ]  [ Play again ]
```
Too small. Try again.

The HTML

```html
<!DOCTYPE html>
<html>
    <head>
        <meta charset="UTF-8">
        <meta name="viewport" content="width=device-width, initial-scale=1">
        <title>Guess the Number</title>
        <link rel="stylesheet" href="main.css">
    </head>
    <body>
        <h1>Guess the Number</h1>
        <p>It's between 1 and 10.</p>

        <input type="text" id="number">
        <button id="guess">Guess</button>
        <button id="play_again">Play again</button><br>
        <label id="message"></label>

        <script src="guess.js"></script>
    </body>
</html>
```

The CSS

```css
body {
    font-family: Arial, Helvetica, sans-serif;
    background-color: white;
    margin: 1em auto;
    width: 600px;
    padding: 0 2em 1em;
    border: 1px solid black;
    border-radius: 1em;
}
h1 {
    color: cornflowerblue;
}
input, button {
    margin: 0 0.5em 1em 0;
}
```

Figure 5-11   The Guess the Number app (part 1)

Part 2 of figure 5-11 presents the JavaScript for the Guess the Number app. It starts by declaring two global variables. The randomNum variable stores the number that the user is trying to guess, while the tries variable keeps track of how many tries it takes the user to guess the number. Although it's generally considered a best practice to avoid global variables, this app uses these global variables to keep the code simple while you're getting started with event handlers. As you progress through this book, you'll learn several techniques you can use to avoid using global variables like these.

The getRandomInt() function is a helper function that generates and returns a random number. A *helper function* is a function that helps another function by performing a task for it. The getRandomInt() function has a parameter named max with a default value of 100. As a result, if no max value is passed in, this function returns a random number between 1 and 100.

The guessClick() and playAgainClick() functions handle the events that occur when the user clicks a button. The guessClick() function is attached to the click event of the Guess button, and the playAgainClick() function is attached to the click event of the Play Again button.

The guessClick() function starts by getting the value the user entered in the text box and passing it to the parseInt() method. Then, it declares a message variable and uses an if statement to process the guess. If the user entered an invalid number or a number outside the range of 1 to 10, the code sets an appropriate message. Otherwise, it compares the guess to the random number, sets an appropriate message, and increments the tries variable. When the if statement completes, the function displays the message in the message label.

The playAgainClick() function starts by calling the getRandomInt() function to generate a new number to guess. Then, it passes a parameter of 10, so the number generated is between 1 and 10. If this code didn't pass a parameter of 10, the getRandomInt() function would use its default value of 100 and generate a number between 1 and 100, which wouldn't be right for this app. After that, this code resets the tries variable to zero, clears the number text box by setting its value property to an empty string, and clears the message label by setting its textContent property to an empty string.

The button event handlers are attached within the event handler for the DOMContentLoaded event. In addition, this event handler calls the playAgainClick() function to initialize a new game. It's common to use the event handler of the DOMContentLoaded event to set the initial state of the app, such as setting initial values or setting the focus on an HTML element.

It's generally considered a best practice to use arrow functions for event handlers. That's because function declarations and function expressions handle the *this* keyword in a way that can cause problems in some scenarios. So, this app uses arrow functions to handle the DOMContentLoaded event of the document and the click events of the buttons. For consistency, the helper function is also coded as an arrow function. However, it would work equally well if it was coded as a function declaration.

The JavaScript

```
"use strict";

// global variables
let randomNum = 0;
let tries = 0;

// helper function
const getRandomInt = (max = 100) => {
    let num = Math.random() * max;   // get a random number from 1 to max
    num = Math.ceil(num);            // round up to nearest integer
    return num;
};

// event handler functions
const guessClick = () => {
    const guess = parseInt(document.querySelector("#number").value);

    let message = "";
    if (isNaN(guess)) {
        message = "Not a valid number. Please enter a valid number."
    } else if (guess < 1 || guess > 10) {
        message = "Invalid number. Enter a number between 1 and 10.";
    } else if (guess < randomNum) {
        message = "Too small. Try again.";
        tries++;
    } else if (guess > randomNum) {
        message = "Too big. Try again.";
        tries++;
    } else if (guess === randomNum) {
        tries++;
        const lastWord = (tries === 1) ? "try" : "tries";
        message = `You guessed it in ${tries} ${lastWord}!`;
    }
    document.querySelector("#message").textContent = message;
};

const playAgainClick = () => {
    randomNum = getRandomInt(10);
    tries = 0;
    document.querySelector("#number").value = "";
    document.querySelector("#message").textContent = "";
};

document.addEventListener("DOMContentLoaded", () => {
    playAgainClick(); // initialize a new game

    document.querySelector("#guess").addEventListener(
        "click", guessClick);
    document.querySelector("#play_again").addEventListener(
        "click", playAgainClick);
});
```

Figure 5-11   The Guess the Number app (part 2)

How to work with the Event object

When an event occurs, modern browsers automatically pass an Event object to the function that's handling the event. This object provides properties and methods that you can use to work with that event. Figure 5-12 begins by presenting one of those properties and one of those methods.

The currentTarget property contains an object that represents the HTML element that the event handler is attached to, such as the button that was clicked. You can use this property to work with that element.

The preventDefault() method stops the *default action* for the event from occurring. Not every event has a default action. For example, the default action of the click event for a submit button submits the form to the server. However, a button without a type attribute of submit or reset doesn't have a default action for its click event. The second table lists some common default actions.

The HTML in this figure defines two <a> elements. The default action of the click event for these elements loads the page at the URL specified by the href attribute.

The JavaScript below the HTML presents an event handler function that handles the click event of both <a> elements. This function has a single parameter named event that provides a way to access the Event object that the browser automatically passes to the event handler. Although this example uses a name of event, you can give this parameter any name you want. Many programmers use a shorter name such as e or evt.

Within the event handler function, the code uses the currentTarget property of the Event object to get the <a> element that was clicked. Then, it uses the textContent property to get the text between the opening and closing tags of the <a> element. Next, it displays this text to the user and asks if they want to navigate to an external website. To do that, the code uses the confirm() method of the window object. This is similar to the prompt() method, but it returns true if the user clicks OK and false if they click Cancel.

If the user doesn't want to leave, the code uses the preventDefault() method of the Event object to stop the default action of the click event. As a result, this prevents the browser from loading the page at the URL specified by the <a> element.

The Event object has many other properties and methods besides those presented here. Furthermore, JavaScript provides specialized Event objects for mouse actions (MouseEvent objects), keyboard actions (KeyboardEvent objects), and so on. These objects provide properties such as the name of the key that triggered an event or the x and y coordinates of the mouse during an event.

One property and one method of the Event object

Property	Description
`currentTarget`	Get the HTML element that triggered the event.

Method	Description
`preventDefault()`	Stops the default action for the event from occurring.

Common HTML elements that have default actions for the click event

Element	Default action for the click event
`<a>`	Load the page or image in the href attribute.
`<input>`	Submit the form if the type attribute is set to submit. Reset the form if the type attribute is set to reset.
`<button>`	Submit the form if the type attribute is set to submit. Reset the form if the type attribute is set to reset.

Two HTML <a> elements

```
<a id="g" href="https://google.com">Google</a>
<a id="fb" href="https://facebook.com">Facebook</a>
```

An event handler for the click event of both <a> elements

```
const confirmLeave = event => {
    const destination = event.currentTarget.textContent;
    const leave = confirm("This is an external website. " +
                          "Continue to " + destination + "?");
    if (!leave) {
        event.preventDefault();
    }
};

document.addEventListener("DOMContentLoaded", () => {
    document.querySelector("#g").addEventListener("click", confirmLeave);
    document.querySelector("#fb").addEventListener("click", confirmLeave);
});
```

A property of the KeyboardEvent object

Property	Description
`key`	Get a string representing the key that triggered the event.

Description

- Modern browsers send an Event object to the event handler for the event.
- You can use the currentTarget property to get the element that the event handler is attached to.
- If the event being listened for has a *default action*, you can use the preventDefault() method to stop that action from occurring.
- Specialized event objects like the KeyboardEvent object and MouseEvent object have additional properties and methods available.

Figure 5-12   How to work with the Event object

The Typewriter app

Figure 5-13 presents the Typewriter app. This app displays the text that a user types on the web page. It allows the user to press Backspace to delete the last typed character or Enter to start a new line. However, the Delete key and the arrow keys don't do anything.

The HTML for this app defines an <h1> element and a <pre> element. The <pre> element displays the text between its tags in a fixed width font. In addition, unlike other HTML elements, it preserves spaces and line breaks. As a result, it works well as a typewriter.

The CSS for this app is similar to the CSS for the Guess the Number app. However, it doesn't have a border, and there are no text boxes or buttons to style.

The event handler functions for the Typewriter app are coded directly within the addEventListener() methods as arrow functions. This is a common way to code event handlers.

The event handler for the DOMContentLoaded event starts by attaching the event handler for the keydown event of the document object. This event handler receives a KeyboardEvent object that has a key property that indicates the key that the user pressed.

The event handler for the keydown event begins by getting the <pre> element from the DOM. Then, it defines a string that includes all valid characters for the app. These characters include all letters (lowercase and uppercase), all numbers, and some special characters such as punctuation marks.

After defining the valid characters, this event handler uses an if statement to check the key property of the KeyboardEvent object. If the user pressed a valid character, the code adds the character to the text for the <pre> element. If the user pressed Enter, the code adds a new line character to the end of the text of the <pre> element. And if the user pressed Backspace, the code removes the last character from the text of the <pre> element. To do that, it uses the slice() method of the string object, which works just like the slice() method of an array object. However, if the user pressed any other character such as an arrow key or Delete, the code doesn't do anything, which is what you want for this app.

The app after a user has typed some content

My Typewriter App

```
Hello! Welcome to my typewriter app!
I can backspace to delete the last character,
and I can hit 'Enter' to start a new line.
But I can't arrow to insert or delete - sorry :(
```

Some of the HTML

```
<body>
    <h1>My Typewriter App</h1>
    <pre id="text"></pre>
    <script src="typewriter.js"></script>
</body>
```

The CSS

```
body {
    font-family: Arial, Helvetica, sans-serif;
    background-color: white;
    margin: 1em;
    padding: 0 2em 1em;
}
h1 {
    color: cornflowerblue;
}
```

The JavaScript

```
document.addEventListener("DOMContentLoaded", () => {

    document.addEventListener("keydown", event => {
        const pre = document.querySelector("#text");

        const validChars = `abcdefghijklmnopqrstuvwxyz
            ABCDEFGHIJKLMNOPQRSTUVWXYZ
            1234567890~!@#$%^&*()_+-=\;:'",.`;

        if (validChars.includes(event.key)) {
            pre.textContent += event.key;
        }
        else if (event.key.toLowerCase() === "enter") {
            pre.textContent += "\n";
        }
        else if (event.key.toLowerCase() === "backspace") {
            pre.textContent = pre.textContent.slice(0, -1);
        }
    });
});
```

Description

- The <pre> element displays text in a fixed-width font and preserves spaces and line breaks.
- The key property of the KeyboardEvent object gets the key that was pressed.

Figure 5-13   The Typewriter app

Perspective

In this chapter, you learned how to code functions and handle events. Along the way, you were introduced to some basic techniques for modifying the DOM based on input from a user, which is one of the most important uses of JavaScript. If you understand the code presented in this chapter, you're ready to learn more about modifying the DOM as shown in the next chapter.

Terms

function	global scope
call a function	local scope
invoke a function	block scope
parameter	function scope
argument	rest operator
return statement	rest parameter
function declaration	variadic function
named function	spread operator
hoist	event handler
function body	event
function expression	attach a function
anonymous function	Document Object Model (DOM)
arrow function	helper function
arrow operator	default action
scope	

Exercise 5-1   Work with functions

This exercise asks you to use functions to organize some existing code.

Review the starting code

1. Open the index.html file in this folder:

    `exercises\ch05\dice_roller`

2. Review the code. Note that it gets input from the user and uses a loop to simulate the rolling of multiple dice.

3. Run the code in a browser. At the prompts, accept the default entries. Note that this rolls four six-sided dice. However, you can change the default entries to roll different numbers of dice or to change the number of sides.

Break the code up into two functions

4. Declare a function named rollDie() and move the code that rolls the die into it. This function should accept a parameter that specifies the numbers of sides, and it should return the value of the die after it has been rolled.

5. Test the code to make sure it still works.

6. Declare a function named rollDice() and move the code that rolls the dice into it. This function should accept parameters for the number of dice to roll and the number of sides per die. In addition, it should return an array of values after the dice have been rolled.

7. Add a statement that calls the rollDice() function and assign the array that's returned to a constant.

8. Modify the call to the alert() method so it displays the values in the array that's returned by the rollDice() function.

9. Test the code to make sure it still works.

Add a default value to a function

10. In the rollDice() function, add a default value of 6 to the sides parameter.

11. Modify the statement that calls the rollDice() function so it doesn't pass a sides parameter.

12. Comment out the statement that gets the sides from the user.

13. Test the code to make sure it still works. It should display the number of dice specified by the user, but they should be the default six-sided dice.

Convert the function declarations to arrow functions

14. Convert the function declarations to arrow functions.

15. Test the code to make sure it still works. Remember that any code that calls an arrow function must be coded after the arrow function.

Exercise 5-2 Handle DOM events

This exercise shows you how to add functions and event handlers for a Dice Roller app that looks like this:

Dice Roller

Enter the number of sides per dice

6

Enter the number of dice to roll

2		Roll

Dice: 3 2

Review the starting code

1. View the files in this folder:

    exercises\ch05\dice_roller_dom

2. Open the index.html file and review its code. Note that it defines an HTML document and provides id attributes that you can use to get elements from the DOM.

3. Open the dice_roller.js file and review its code. Note that it doesn't do much except set a message that says the DOM is loaded and ready.

4. Run the app and test it. It should display a message when it's loaded, but clicking on the Roll button shouldn't do anything since it doesn't have an event handler yet.

Attach the event listener

5. Add code that adds the rollButtonClick() function as the event handler for the click event of the Roll button.

6. Run the app and make sure the event handler has been attached correctly. When you click the Roll button, it should change the message that's displayed at the bottom of the page.

Add the rollDie() and rollDice() functions

7. Add a function named rollDie(). This function should accept a parameter that specifies the number of sides for the die, and it should return the value of the die after it has been rolled.

8. Add a function named rollDice(). This function should accept parameters for the number of dice to roll and the number of sides per die, and it should return an array of values after the dice have been rolled.

9. Modify the rollButtonClick() function so it uses the rollDice() function to get and display the values of the dice.

10. Run the app and test it. It should work correctly if you enter valid values.

Debug the app

11. Run the app again but don't enter a value for the number of sides. Note that the app returns NaN for the dice values.

12. To fix this issue, use the isNaN() function to check if the sides variable is NaN. If so, set the sides variable equal to 6. In addition, set the value of the first text box to 6.

13. Run the app again without entering a value for the number of sides. This time, the app should use 6 as the number of sides.

Exercise 5-3   The Movie List app

This exercise shows you how to add functions and event handlers for a Movie List app that looks like this:

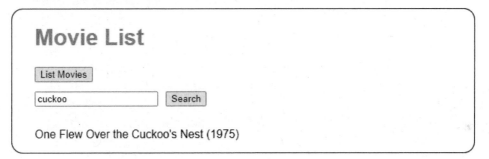

Review the starting code

1. View the files in this folder:

   `exercises\ch05\movie_list`

2. Open the index.html file and review its code. Note that it provides id attributes that you can use to get some of the HTML elements.

3. Open the movie.js file and review its code. Note that it defines an array of strings and assigns those strings to a constant named movies.

Code the event handler for the List Movies button

4. Add a function named listMovies() that has no parameters. This function should display all of the strings in the movies array in the HTML element that has an id of "message". To do that, it should separate each movie with a pipe character (|).

5. Add the DOMContentLoaded event handler to the end of the JavaScript file. This event listener should attach the listMovies() function as the event handler for the click event of the List Movies button.

6. Run the app and click the List Movies button to make sure it displays all of the movies in the movies array.

Code the event handler for the Search button

7. Add a function named searchMovies() that has no parameters. This function should:

    - Get the search term from the text box.

    - Create an empty array to store the selected movies.

    - Loop though each movie in the movies array and check if the movie name includes the search term. If so, this code should add the movie name to the array of selected movies.

    - Display the selected movies in the HTML element that has an id of "message".

8. Modify the DOMContentLoaded event handler so it attaches the searchMovies() function as the event handler for the click event of the Search button.

9. Run the app and click the Search button to make sure it displays all of the movies on the HTML page.

6

How to script the DOM

At this point, you have all of the JavaScript skills that you need to get started with DOM (Document Object Model) scripting. Now, you just need to learn how to use some of the properties and methods that are provided by the DOM specifications, as well as some skills for scripting forms, controls, and images.

How to get started with DOM scripting

To script the DOM, you use properties and methods of the objects that make up the document model. These properties and methods are implemented by all modern browsers.

DOM scripting concepts

Before you learn how to write code that scripts the DOM, you should understand the DOM scripting concepts presented in figure 6-1. First, when a browser loads a web page, it builds the *Document Object Model*, or *DOM*, for that page. The DOM is a hierarchical collection of nodes in the browser's memory that represents the web page as it is currently displayed by the browser.

To visualize the DOM, the diagram in this figure shows the *nodes* that represent the elements and text of the HTML at the top of this figure. *Element nodes* correspond to individual HTML elements, such as a <body> element or <a> element, and are represented by ovals. *Text nodes* hold text for elements and are represented by rectangles. For instance, the left-most text node contains the text for the <title> element: "Join Email List". The one to the right of that contains the text for the <h1> element in the body: "Please join our email list". And so on.

For simplicity, this diagram only includes the element and text nodes, but the DOM also contains *attribute nodes*. Each attribute node can also have a text node that holds the attribute's value.

When working with the DOM nodes, you will come across terms like parent, child, sibling, and descendant. A *parent* node has one or more *child* nodes. In this figure, the form node is a parent node that has three child nodes. A *sibling* node has the same parent as another node. In this figure, the label, input, and span nodes are sibling nodes because they have the same parent node. And a *descendant* node descends from the same node as another node. In this figure, the h1, form, label, input, and span nodes are all descendants of the body node.

The indentation for the HTML also shows these relationships. In this figure, for example, the indentation shows the <label>, <input>, and <span> elements are child nodes of the <form> element.

This chapter shows how to write JavaScript code that changes the DOM. Whenever that happens, the browser displays the results of the change. As a result, by changing, or *scripting*, the DOM you can change anything on a web page in real time according to user input, a response from the server, a timer, or another event.

The HTML for a web page

```html
<!DOCTYPE html>
<html>
    <head>
        <title>Join Email List</title>
    </head>
    <body>
        <h1>Please join our email list</h1>
        <form id="join_form" action="join.html" method="post">
            <label for="email_address">Email Address:</label>
            <input type="text" id="email_address" name="email_address">
            <span id="email_error">*</span><br>
        </form>
    </body>
</html>
```

The DOM for the web page

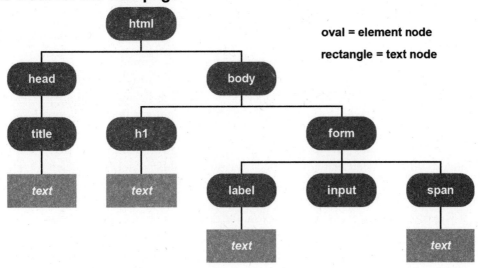

oval = element node

rectangle = text node

Description

- The *DOM* (*Document Object Model*) is a hierarchical collection of nodes in the browser's memory that represents the current web page.
- The browser builds the DOM for a web page as it loads the page.
- A *node* can represent an HTML element, an HTML attribute, or the text for an element or attribute.
- A *parent* node has one or more *child* nodes. In this figure, the form node is a parent node that has three child nodes.
- A *sibling* node has the same parent as another node. In this figure, the label, input, and span nodes are sibling nodes because they have the same parent node.
- A *descendant* node descends from the same node as another node. In this figure, the h1, form, label, input, and span nodes are all descendants of the body node.
- JavaScript can modify the web page in the browser by modifying the DOM. Whenever the DOM changes, the browser displays the results of the change.

Figure 6-1   DOM scripting concepts

How to get elements

Figure 6-2 begins by summarizing two methods that you can use to get element objects from the DOM. Typically, you call these methods from the document object. However, you can also call these methods from an element object.

The querySelector() method returns an element object that represents the first HTML element that matches the specified CSS selector. For instance, the first example in this figure passes a selector of "#email_address" to the querySelector() method. This returns an object for the HTML element that has an id attribute of "email_address".

You can also pass a CSS selector that's an element name or a class name. In that case, the method returns the first element that matches that selector. For instance, the second example passes a selector of "a". This returns an object for the first <a> element in the document. However, if you passed a selector of ".small", this would return the first element that's assigned to the CSS class named "small".

The querySelectorAll() method returns an array of all elements that match the selector. For instance, the third example passes a selector of "a". This returns an array of all the <a> elements in the document. However, if you passed a selector of ".small", it would return an array of all the elements that are assigned to the CSS class named "small".

Technically, the querySelectorAll() method returns a NodeList object that contains all elements that match the selector. However, this NodeList object works so much like an Array object that this chapter refers to the object that's returned by this method as an array, even though it's technically a node list.

If you call either of these methods from the document object, they get the first element or all of the elements in the document. However, if you call these methods from an element, they get the first element or all of the elements that are descendants of that element as shown by the fourth and fifth examples.

The fourth example defines a <ul> (unordered list) element with an id of "image_list" that has two child <li> (list item) elements. Then, the first statement in the fifth example uses the querySelector() method of the document object to get the <ul> element by its id, and it assigns that element to a constant named list. Next, the second statement uses the querySelectorAll() method of the element to get an array of all of the <li> elements that are children of the <ul> element.

The sixth example shows another way to get the same array. To do that, this example calls the querySelectorAll() method from the document object. However, it passes a descendant selector that selects all <li> elements within the element with an id of "image_list".

To work with the DOM, you can use the *DOM API* (*application programming interface*). This API provides *interfaces* that define the properties and methods for the objects available from the DOM. For example, the Document interface defines the querySelector() and querySelectorAll() methods that are available from the document object. Similarly, the Element interface defines these methods for element objects.

Two methods of the document object and element objects

Method	Description
`querySelector(selector)`	Returns the first HTML element that matches the CSS selector that's passed to it.
`querySelectorAll(selector)`	Returns all the HTML elements that match the CSS selector that's passed to it.

Get an element by its ID

```
const textBox = document.querySelector("#email_address");
```

Get the first <a> element in a document

```
const firstLink = document.querySelector("a");
```

Get an array of all <a> elements in a document

```
const links = document.querySelectorAll("a");
```

A <ul> element that contains two <li> elements

```
<ul id="image_list">
    <li><img src="images/lion.png"></li>
    <li><img src="images/tiger.png"></li>
</ul>
```

Get an array of all <li> elements within the <ul> element

```
const list = document.querySelector("#image_list");
const items = list.querySelectorAll("li");
```

Another way to get the same array

```
const items = document.querySelectorAll("#image_list li");
```

Description

- To work with the DOM, you can use the *DOM API* (*application programming interface*).
- The DOM API provides *interfaces* that define properties and methods that are available from the objects of the DOM.
- The Document interface defines the properties and methods of the document object that provide access to the DOM.
- The Element interface defines the properties and methods of the element objects of the DOM.

Figure 6-2   How to get elements

How to script elements

Figure 6-3 begins by summarizing six of the most useful properties for working with elements. These properties are defined by the Node interface of the DOM API. You can use the first five properties to get objects from the DOM, and you can use the sixth property to get or set the text in an element.

The first example in this figure shows an HTML <span> element with three child elements. The <b> element displays text in bold, the <u> element underlines text, and the <i> element displays text in italics. These three elements are siblings of each other and are children of the <span> element. Additionally, these three elements each have a child text node.

The second example uses the querySelector() method of the document object to get an element object that represents the <span> element from the first example. This code assigns the element object to a constant named span.

The third example shows how to get objects for the child elements of the <span> element. The first statement uses the firstChild property of the <span> element to get the <b> element. The second statement is similar. However, after it gets the <b> element, it chains the nextElementSibling property to get the <u> element. And the third statement uses the lastChild property of the <span> element to get the <i> element.

The fourth example shows how to use the textContent property to get the text for the second child node, which is the <u> element. Since the second child node contains text of "Back", this displays "Back" in the console.

The fifth example shows how to use the textContent property to get the text for the <span> element and all of its descendant nodes. As a result, this code displays the text for all descendant nodes. However, it doesn't include the HTML tags for the descendant nodes.

The sixth example shows how to use the textContent property to set the text for the first child element of the <span> element, which is the <b> element. To do that, this example gets the first child node. Then, it assigns new text content of "Hurry " to that node.

The seventh example shows that you can also use the textContent property to set the text for the entire <span> element. However, this replaces all of the child nodes for the element with a single text node.

Some properties for working with nodes

Property	Description
parentNode	Gets the parent node. If no parent node exists, returns null.
childNodes	Gets an array of child nodes. If no child nodes exist, returns an empty array.
firstChild	Gets the first child node. If no child nodes exist, returns null.
lastChild	Gets the last child node. If no child nodes exist, returns null.
nextElementSibling	Gets the next sibling element. If no next sibling exists, returns null.
textContent	Gets or sets the text that's stored in an element and all of its descendant nodes. If the element doesn't contain any text, returns an empty string.

A <span> element with three child elements

```
<span><b>Welcome </b><u>Back</u><i>!</i></span>
```

Get the <span> element

```
const span = document.querySelector("span");
```

Get the child elements of the <span> element

```
const bElem = span.firstChild;                      // first child
const uElem = span.firstChild.nextElementSibling;   // second child
const iElem = span.lastChild;                        // third child
```

Get the text from a child element

```
console.log(uElem.textContent);          // displays "Back"
```

Get the all the text in the <span> element

```
console.log(span.textContent);           // displays "Welcome Back!"
```

Set the text of the first child element

```
span.firstChild.textContent = "Hurry ";
console.log(span.textContent);           // displays "Hurry Back!"
```

Set the text of the <span> element

```
span.textContent = "Hi";                 // replaces all child elements
console.log(span.textContent);           // displays "Hi"
```

Description

- The Node interface of the DOM API defines some basic properties and methods that you can use to work with elements and their text nodes.

- When you use the textContent property to set the text for an element, it replaces any existing child nodes for the element with a single, new text node.

Figure 6-3   How to script elements

How to script element attributes

Figure 6-4 begins by summarizing four methods for scripting the attributes of an element. The first example shows some HTML that defines a <ul> element that has two attributes, an id attribute and a class attribute. Then, the second example gets an object for the <ul> element and assigns it to a constant named list.

The third example uses the hasAttribute() method to check if the list element has a class attribute. If so, the code displays a message in the console.

The fourth example uses the getAttribute() method to get the value of the class attribute of the <list> element. Since the first example assigned a class named "close" to the <ul> element, this example gets a value of "close" and assigns it to a constant.

The fifth example shows how to use the setAttribute() method to set the class attribute of the <list> element to "open". If the element didn't already have a class attribute, this statement would add the class attribute to the element before setting its value.

Finally, the sixth example uses the removeAttribute() method to remove the class attribute from the <list> element. This removes the attribute and its value from the element.

Four methods available from an element

Method	Description
hasAttribute(*name*)	Returns true if an attribute with the specified name exists.
getAttribute(*name*)	Returns the value of the attribute with the specified name, or an empty string if an attribute with that name isn't set.
setAttribute(*name*, *value*)	Sets the attribute with the specified name to the specified value. If the attribute doesn't already exist, it's created.
removeAttribute(*name*)	Removes the attribute with the specified name.

A list element that has two attributes

```
<ul id="image_list" class="close">
    <li><img src="images/lion.png"></li>
    <li><img src="images/tiger.png"></li>
</ul>
```

Get the element

```
const list = document.querySelector("#image_list");
```

Check if the element has an attribute

```
if (list.hasAttribute("class")) {
    console.log("list has class attribute");
}
```

Get an attribute

```
const listClass = list.getAttribute("class");
```

Set an attribute

```
list.setAttribute("class", "open");
```

Remove an attribute

```
list.removeAttribute("class");
```

Figure 6-4   How to script element attributes

More skills for scripting attributes

So far, this chapter has shown some of the objects, properties, and methods available from the DOM API. However, there's another API called the *HTML DOM API* that provides properties that make it easier to work with some HTML elements. Figure 6-5 summarizes some of these properties and shows you how to use them.

When you work with the HTML DOM API, you should know that its properties don't provide new functionality. Instead, they provide shortcuts that make it easier to work with the DOM nodes of an HTML document. In addition, these two APIs work together, so you can use both to script the same document.

The first example in this figure shows the HTML for an <a> element. This element has two attributes, an href attribute and a title attribute.

The second example shows how the HTML DOM API can make it easier to work with attributes. To start, this example gets the <a> element defined in the first example and assigns it to a constant named link. Then, it shows how to use the DOM API or the HTML DOM API to get and set the title attribute of this element. This shows that you can use the getAttribute() and setAttribute() methods of the DOM API, or you can use the title property of the HTML DOM API. Since using the HTML DOM API leads to code that's shorter and easier to read, it typically makes sense to use the properties of the HTML DOM API.

In most cases, the HTML DOM API names its properties so they correspond to the names of HMTL attributes. For instance, the second example shows that you can use the title property of an element object to work with the title attribute of an HTML element.

However, sometimes the HTML DOM API names a property in a way that's different than the name of the attribute name that's used in the HTML. For instance, the third example shows that the HTML DOM API provides a className property that you can use to get and set the class attribute of an HTML element.

The fourth example shows how to get and set the href attribute of the <a> element from the first example. This changes the href attribute so it refers to the Amazon website instead of the Murach Books website.

The fifth example shows how to get and set the src attribute of an <img> element. To set the src attribute, the third statement gets the string for the src attribute and replaces "lion.png" with "tiger.png". Then, the fourth statement sets the resulting string as the src attribute for the image. As a result, the src attribute for this element now uses the same path but points to a different image.

The sixth example shows how to enable or disable an <input> element. To do that, the code gets the element and sets its disabled attribute to true or false.

The HTML DOM API provides specialized interfaces that define the properties and methods available from the objects of the DOM. For example, it provides the HTMLElement interface that defines the first three properties shown in this figure. Similarly, it provides the HTMLAnchorElement interface that defines the href property that's available from an object for an <a> element.

Most of the time, you don't need to know which interface defines the property or method that you're using. Usually, you'll be able to use the element's

Some properties that make it easier to script attributes

Element	Property	Attribute
(all)	id	The id attribute
	title	The title attribute
	className	The class attribute. To set multiple class names, separate the names with spaces.
\<a>	href	The href attribute
\<img>	src	The src attribute
	alt	The alt attribute
\<input>	disabled	The disabled attribute

The HTML for an \<a> element

```
<a href="https://www.murach.com" title="Murach">Visit our website</a>
```

Two ways to get and set the title attribute of an element

```
const link = document.querySelector("a");
```

With the DOM API
```
console.log(link.getAttribute("title"));    // displays "Murach"
link.setAttribute("title", "Amazon");       // sets title to "Amazon"
```

With the HTML DOM API
```
console.log(link.title);                    // displays "Amazon"
link.title = "Murach";                      // sets title to "Murach"
```

Set and get a class attribute that has two class names

```
const div = document.querySelector("div");
div.className = "open plus";                 // class attribute is "open plus"
console.log(div.className);                  // displays "open plus"
```

Get and set the href attribute of an \<a> element

```
const link = document.querySelector("a");
console.log(link.href);                     // displays "https://murach.com"
link.href = "https://amazon.com";           // sets href to "https://amazon.com"
```

Get and set the src attribute of an \<img> element

```
const image = document.querySelector("#image");
console.log(image.src);                      // displays the src attribute
const source = image.src.replace("lion.png", "tiger.png");
image.src = source;                          // sets the new src attribute
```

Disable and enable an \<input> element

```
document.querySelector("#play_button").disabled = true;
document.querySelector("#play_button").disabled = false;
```

Description

- The HTML DOM API provides interfaces that define specialized properties and methods for the objects in the DOM. These properties and methods are often shorter and easier to use than the properties and methods defined by the DOM API.

Figure 6-5   More skills for scripting attributes

attribute name as the property name in your code. For example, you can use the href property to work with the href attribute of an <a> element. However, if that doesn't work, you can search the internet to find the property name that you need.

How to script the class attribute

So far, this chapter has only shown how to replace or remove the entire value of the class attribute of an element. However, that's often not what you want. For instance, suppose an element already has one or more class names and you want to add another. In that case, you need to get the existing attribute value, add the new class name to the string, and assign the updated string as the new value of the class attribute.

It's even more complicated if there are multiple class names in the class attribute and you want to remove some but not all of them. Then, you need to get the string that contains the class names and use the techniques you learned in chapter 4 to manually edit the string to remove some of the class names. This can be tedious and error-prone.

Fortunately, an element has a classList property that makes it easier to work with the class attribute. This property gets an object that contains the class names that are in that attribute, and that object has properties and methods for working with those names. The tables in figure 6-6 present some of these properties and methods.

The examples in this figure show how to use the classList property. The first example defines an <h2> element with a class attribute that has a single CSS class named "first". Then, the second example selects that <h2> element and assigns the object that represents it to a constant named h2.

The third example uses the add() method of the classList property to add a CSS class named "blue" to the class attribute. Then, the fourth example uses the replace() method of the classList property to replace the CSS class named "blue" with a CSS class named "red". And the fifth example uses the remove() method of the classList property to remove the CSS class named "red" from the class attribute.

The statements in the sixth example use the toggle() method of the classList property to alternate between adding and removing the CSS class named "blue". Before the first statement executes, the value of the class attribute is "first". So, when the first statement calls the toggle() method, it adds the "blue" class to the attribute. Then, when the second statement executes the toggle() method again, it removes the "blue" class from the attribute value, and the third statement adds it again.

The seventh example uses the contains() method of the classList property to check if the CSS class named "blue" already exists in the class attribute. If it does, the add() method adds the CSS class named "bold".

Another property of an element

Property	Description
`classList`	Gets an object that contains the class names in the class attribute and provides properties and methods for working with them.

Common properties and methods of the classList object

Property	Description
`length`	Gets the number of class names in the class attribute.
`value`	Gets the class names in the class attribute in a single, space-delimited string.

Method	Description
`contains(className)`	Returns true if the specified class name is in the attribute.
`add(className)`	Adds the specified class name to the attribute.
`remove(className)`	Removes the specified class name from the attribute.
`replace(oldName,newName)`	Replaces the specified old class name with the specified new class name.
`toggle(className)`	Removes the specified class name if it's in the attribute or adds it if it isn't.

A heading element

```
<h2 class="first">Welcome to our website!</h2>
```

Get the heading element

```
const h2 = document.querySelector("h2");
```

Add a CSS class

```
h2.classList.add("blue");            // class attribute is "first blue"
```

Replace a CSS class

```
h2.classList.replace("blue", "red");    // attribute is "first red"
```

Remove a CSS class

```
h2.classList.remove("red");          // attribute is "first"
```

Toggle a CSS class

```
h2.classList.toggle("blue");         // attribute is "first blue"
h2.classList.toggle("blue");         // attribute is "first"
h2.classList.toggle("blue");         // attribute is "first blue"
```

Check for a CSS class before taking an action

```
if (h2.classList.contains("blue")) {
    h2.classList.add("bold");        // attribute is "first blue bold"
}
```

Figure 6-6   How to script the class attribute

The FAQs app

Figure 6-7 presents a FAQs (Frequently Asked Questions) app that uses the properties and methods of the document and element objects to script the DOM. In this app, if the user clicks on a heading with a plus sign before it, some text is displayed below it and the plus sign is changed to a minus sign. Similarly, if the user clicks on a heading with a minus sign before it, the text below it is hidden and the minus sign is changed to a plus sign. The user can display the text below all three headings at the same time, and the user can hide the text below all three headings at the same time.

The HTML for this app stores each of the questions within an <a> element within an <h2> element. In addition, it stores the answer to each question in a <div> element that's coded immediately after its corresponding <h2> element. Note that the href attributes in the <a> elements are coded as # signs so these links don't go anywhere.

Because <a> elements are coded within the <h2> elements, a user can use the Tab key to move the browser's focus from one heading to the next. Then, when a user "tabs" to a heading and presses the Enter key, the effect is the same as clicking on the heading. This makes this app easier to use for motor-impaired users who can't use a mouse. In addition, it makes the app work better for everyone by providing additional functionality.

The HTML in this figure includes an external CSS style sheet in its head section, and an external JavaScript file at the end of its body. The code that's stored in these files is shown in part 2 of this figure.

The FAQs app

The HTML for the <body> element

```html
<body id="faqs">
    <h1>JavaScript FAQs</h1>

    <h2><a href="#">What is JavaScript?</a></h2>
    <div>
        <p>JavaScript is a scripting language that you can use to make
            websites interactive.</p>
    </div>

    <h2><a href="#">Why use JavaScript?</a></h2>
    <div>
        <ul>
            <li>It has simple syntax that's easy to learn.</li>
            <li>It's versatile.</li>
            <li>It's one of the most popular programming languages.</li>
        </ul>
    </div>

    <h2><a href="#">Which browsers support JavaScript?</a></h2>
    <div>
        <p>All the major modern browsers support JavaScript.</p>
    </div>

    <script src="faqs.js"></script>
</body>
```

Figure 6-7   The FAQs app (part 1)

Part 2 of figure 6-7 begins by showing the CSS for the FAQs app. This CSS uses the focus and hover pseudo-classes for <a> elements to set the color of this element to blue. That way, the <a> elements look the same whether the user hovers the mouse over a link or tabs to the link.

The first style rule for the <h2> elements applies to all of the <h2> elements. This rule sets the cursor to a pointer when the user hovers the mouse over an <h2> element. It also applies a background property that includes an image named plus.png. This image is displayed just once (no-repeat) to the left of the element and it is vertically centered.

The second style rule for the <h2> elements applies to elements that have a class property set to "minus". This style rule applies a background property that uses an image named minus.png. That's the image that's used when the text below a heading is displayed.

The first style rule for the <div> elements sets the display property to "none", which hides the contents of the <div> element. By contrast, the second style rule applies to <div> elements that have a class attribute set to "open". It sets the display property to block, which displays the contents.

Part 2 of this figure also shows the JavaScript for this app. It consists of an event handler for the click event of each <h2> element and an event handler for the DOMContentLoaded event.

The toggleVisibility() function defines the click event handler for each <h2> element. This function begins by defining a parameter named evt for the Event object. Here, the first statement assigns the currentTarget property of the Event object to a constant named h2. This is the <h2> element that was clicked to trigger the event. Then, the second statement gets the <div> element that follows the clicked <h2> element.

The third statement uses the toggle() method of the classList property to modify the class attribute of the <h2> element. If that attribute contains the "minus" CSS class, it's removed. If it doesn't, it's added. This changes the background image from a plus sign to a minus sign or vice versa. The fourth statement does the same with the <div> element and the "open" CSS class. This changes the <div> from hidden to visible or vice versa.

The DOMContentLoaded event handler attaches the toggleVisibility() event handler to the click event of each <h2> element. To do that, it uses a descendant selector to get all the <h2> elements in the element with an id of "faqs". Then, it assigns the <h2> elements to a constant named h2s. Finally, it uses a for-of loop to loop through the <h2> elements and attach the toggleVisibility() event handler to the click event of each one.

The DOMContentLoaded event handler ends by setting the focus to the <a> element that's the child of the first <h2> element. It does that by using an index of 0 to refer to the first element in the h2Elements constant, and then uses the firstChild property to refer to the first child of that element, which is its <a> element.

Some of the CSS

```
a {
    color: black;
    text-decoration: none;
}
a:focus, a:hover {
    color: blue;
}
h2 {
    cursor: pointer;
    background: url(images/plus.png) no-repeat left center;
}
h2.minus {
    background: url(images/minus.png) no-repeat left center;
}
div {
    display: none;
}
div.open {
    display: block;
}
```

The JavaScript

```
// the event handler for the click event of each <h2> element
const toggleVisibility = evt => {
    const h2 = evt.currentTarget;          // get the <h2> element
    const div = h2.nextElementSibling;     // get the <div> element

    h2.classList.toggle("minus");
    div.classList.toggle("open");

    evt.preventDefault();  // cancel default action of child <a> element
};

document.addEventListener("DOMContentLoaded", () => {
    // get the <h2> elements
    const h2s = document.querySelectorAll("#faqs h2");

    // attach event handler for each <h2> element
    for (let h2 of h2s) {
        h2.addEventListener("click", toggleVisibility);
    }
    // set focus on first <a> element
    h2s[0].firstChild.focus();
});
```

Description

- The first statement in the handler for the DOMContentLoaded event creates an array of the <h2> elements in the element that has "faqs" as its id.

- The for-of loop in that event handler is executed once for each of the <h2> elements. It attaches the toggle event handler to the click event of each <h2> element.

Figure 6-7   The FAQs app (part 2)

How to script forms and controls

It's common to use DOM scripting to work with forms and controls as shown in the figures that follow. A *form* contains one or more *controls* such as text boxes and buttons. The controls that accept user entries are also known as *fields*.

How forms work

Figure 6-8 shows how to create a form that contains three controls: two text boxes and a button. To start, you code the <form> element. Within the opening tag, you code the action and method attributes. The action attribute specifies the URL of the file on the web server that processes the data that's sent when the form is submitted. The method attribute specifies the HTTP method that's used to send the data to the web server.

In this example, the form specifies a method value of "post" to use the HTTP POST method when the user clicks the Join List button to submit the data to the server. Then, the server uses the code in the file named join.php to process the data in the form.

When you use the GET method, the form data is sent as part of the URL for the HTTP request. As a result, the data is visible in the address bar of the browser. By contrast, when you use the POST method, the form data is packaged as part of an HTTP request and isn't visible in the browser. It's generally considered a best practice to use the POST method to send data to the server and to use the GET method only when you are getting data from the server.

In addition to the action and method attributes, you can code an id attribute in the opening <form> tag. This is helpful if you need to select the form by id in your JavaScript. However, this attribute is optional.

Within the <form> element, you code the controls for the form. In this example, the first two <input> elements define text boxes for an email address and first name. The third <input> element has a type attribute of "submit", which means that it defines a *submit button*. When it's clicked, the browser submits the data in the form to the server.

If an <input> element has a type attribute of "reset", it defines a *reset button*. When that type of button is clicked, the browser resets all of the controls in the form to their starting HTML values.

When a browser submits a form to the server, the server-side code should validate all of the data before it processes that data. Then, if any of the data isn't valid, the server should send the form back to the browser with appropriate error messages so the entries can be corrected. This is referred to as *data validation*.

Typically, the client-side code that's running in the browser also validates the form data before submitting it to the server. However, the client-side validation doesn't have to be as thorough as the server-side validation. If the browser validation catches 80 to 90% of the entry errors, it will significantly increase the performance of an app by preventing many unnecessary round trips to the server.

A form in a browser

Email Address:	grace@yahoo.com
First Name:	Grace
	Join our List

Attributes of the <form> element

Attribute	Description
`action`	The URL of the file that will process the data in the form.
`method`	The HTTP method for submitting the form data. It can be set to either "get" or "post". The default value is "get".

The HTML for the form

```
<form action="join.php" method="post">
    <label for="email_address">Email Address:</label>
    <input type="text" id="email_address" name="email_address">
    <br>
    <label for="first_name">First Name:</label>
    <input type="text" id="first_name" name="first_name">
    <br>
    <label> </label>
    <input type="submit" value="Join our List">
</form>
```

Description

- A *form* contains one or more *controls* (or *fields*) like text boxes, radio buttons, lists, or check boxes that can receive data.

- When you click on a *submit button* for a form (type attribute of "submit"), the form data is sent to the server as part of an HTTP request.

- When you click on a *reset button* for a form (type attribute of "reset"), the form data is reset to its default values.

- When a form is submitted to the server for processing, the data in the controls is sent along with the HTTP request.

- When you use the "get" method to submit a form, the URL that requests the file is followed by a question mark and name/value pairs containing the submitted data, separated by ampersands.

- When you use the "post" method to submit a form, the name/value pairs for the data are stored in the body of the HTTP request, not the URL.

- *Data validation* refers to checking the data collected by a form to make sure it's valid, and complete data validation should always be done on the server. Then, if any invalid data is detected, the form is returned to the client so the user can correct the entries.

- To save round trips to the server when the data is invalid, some validation is usually done on the client before the data is sent to the server. However, this validation doesn't have to be as thorough as the validation that's done on the server.

Figure 6-8   How forms work

How to script text boxes, text areas, and select lists

Text boxes, text areas, and select lists are common controls that often need to be scripted. A *text box* provides a single line for an entry, a *text area* provides multiple lines for an entry, and a *select list* provides a list of options that the user can select from, usually in a drop-down list.

The table in figure 6-9 shows two properties that are common to most controls: value and name. With a text box or text area, the value property gets or sets the text that's displayed in the control. With a select list, by contrast, the value property gets or sets the selected option.

The name property is used by server-side code to get data that's submitted to the server. As a result, it typically makes sense to set the name attribute for all controls within a form. The HTML in this figure sets the name and id attribute for each control to the same value because that's generally considered a best practice. Note that the name property is available to all <input> elements, not just text boxes.

The HTML in this figure uses these controls to get a user's name, comments, and country. Note that the <select> element's initial option has a display string of "Select a country…" and a value attribute of an empty string. This encourages the user to select an option when the browser first loads the page.

The first JavaScript example shows how to use the value property of these controls to get the values the user entered or selected. The first three statements use the querySelector() method to store the text box, text area, and select list values in constants named name, comment, and country.

After storing the value of the selected option in the constant named country, this example checks the value of that constant and performs different processing depending on the selected country. If the user selected a country, the code displays the name of the country in a dialog. Otherwise, it displays a dialog asking the user to select a country.

In addition to using the value property to retrieve the content of these controls, you can use it to set the content of the controls. The second JavaScript example in this figure shows how this works. In this case, each of the controls on the form has its value property set to an empty string. This is a common way to clear a form, but you can set the value property to any string.

When you set the value property for a text box or area, the value is displayed in the text box or area. However, when you set the value of a select list, it selects the option in the list with that value. In this figure, for example, setting the value property of the select list to "can" selects the Canada option. However, if you set the value property to a value that doesn't correspond to an option, the browser doesn't select any option, not even the default option. (The default option is the first option in the list, or the option that has a selected attribute.)

When working with a text area, you may need to think about how to handle line returns. For instance, if the user presses the Enter key, a *hard return* is entered and becomes a character in the value property, even if the user didn't type any other text. If that's not what you want, you can use the trim() or

Two properties available from most controls

Property	Description
`name`	A name that's typically used by server-side code.
`value`	Gets or sets the value attribute. For a text box or text area, gets or sets the text stored in the control. For a select list, gets or sets the value attribute of the selected option.

HTML for a text box, text area, and select list

```html
<label for="name">First Name:</label>
<input type="text" name="name" id="name"><br>

<label for="comment">Comment:</label>
<textarea name="comment" id="comment" rows="5" cols="40"></textarea><br>

<label for="country">Country:</label>
<select name="country" id="country">
    <option value="">Select a country...</option>
    <option value="usa">USA</option>
    <option value="can">Canada</option>
    <option value="mex">Mexico</option>
</select><br>
```

JavaScript to get the text box, text area, and select list values

```javascript
const name = document.querySelector("#name").value;
const comment = document.querySelector("#comment").value;
const country = document.querySelector("#country").value;

if (country == "usa") {
    alert("You selected USA.");
} else if (country == "can") {
    alert("You selected Canada.");
} else if (country == "mex") {
    alert("You selected Mexico.");
} else {
    alert("Please select a country.");
}
```

JavaScript to set the text box, text area, and select list values

```javascript
document.querySelector("#country").value = "";
document.querySelector("#name").value = "";
document.querySelector("#comment").value = "";
```

Description

- It's considered a best practice to set the name and id attributes of these controls to the same value. Although JavaScript doesn't typically use the name attribute, the server-side code uses this attribute to get the data that's sent to the server.

- When the user presses the Enter key while typing in a text area, a *hard return* is entered into the text. Hard returns appear as characters in the value property.

- When the user types past the end of a line in a text area and a new line is automatically started, a *soft return* occurs. Soft returns do not appear as characters in the value property.

Figure 6-9   How to script text boxes, text areas, and select lists

replace() methods to remove hard returns from the string that's returned by the value property.

In contrast to hard returns, *soft returns* occur automatically when the user enters text that overflows onto the next line. These returns don't become characters in the value property, so you don't need to check for them.

How to script radio buttons and check boxes

Radio button and check boxes are two other types of controls that often need to be scripted. Both of these controls let a user select an option. *Radio buttons* let a user select one of several options in a group. When the user clicks one button in a group of radio buttons, the other buttons in the group are deselected. By contrast, *check boxes* let a user select an option independent of other options. That's because selecting one check box has no effect on any other check box.

The table in figure 6-10 summarizes the checked property that's available from radio buttons and check boxes. This property returns a Boolean value that indicates whether the radio button or check box is checked.

The HTML in this figure defines two radio buttons and a check box. When you create a group of radio buttons, they must have the same name so the browser knows they're in the same group. However, they must have different id values. In this example, both radio buttons have the name "contact", but one has an id of "text" while the other has an id of "email". Note that the id and value attributes don't have to be the same, but they often are.

When you create a check box, it must have a unique name and the name and id attributes must be set to the same value. In the example, the check box has a name and id of "accept".

The first JavaScript example begins by getting the user's choices from the radio buttons. First, it checks if the radio button with an id of "text" is checked. If so, the code does the processing for a selection of "text". Otherwise, the code checks if the radio button with an id of "email" is checked. If so, the code does the processing for a selection of "email". Since only one member of a radio button group can be checked, only one of these radio buttons is going to have its checked property set to true.

After checking the radio buttons, this example checks whether the user selected the check box. To do that, it checks whether the value of the checked property is true. If so, the code processes the choice. Otherwise, this code displays a dialog that asks the user to accept the terms of service.

The second JavaScript example shows how to use code to select or deselect a radio button or check box. In this example, the code deselects the radio buttons and selects the check box. To do that, it sets the checked property of these controls to true or false.

A property of radio buttons and check boxes

Property	Description
checked	If true, the control is selected. If false, the control is not selected.

HTML for two radio buttons and a check box

```
<label>Contact me by:</label>
<input type="radio" name="contact" id="text" value="text" checked>Text
<input type="radio" name="contact" id="email" value="email">Email<br>

<label>Terms of Service:</label>
<input type="checkbox" name="accept" id="accept">I accept<br>
```

JavaScript to get the radio button and check box values

```
if (document.querySelector("#text").checked) {
    /*text processing*/
} else if (document.querySelector("#email").checked) {
    /*email processing*/
}

if (document.querySelector("accept").checked) {
    /*accept processing*/
} else {
    alert("You must accept our terms of service.");
}
```

JavaScript to set the radio button and check box values

```
document.querySelector("#text").checked = false;
document.querySelector("#email").checked = false;
document.querySelector("#accept").checked = true;
```

Description

- All *radio buttons* in a group must have the same name, but different ids. Only one button in a group may be checked at a time, but none of the buttons has to be checked.

- Each *check box* is independent of the other check boxes on the page. The name and id attributes of a check box should be set to the same value.

- To select a radio button, set its checked property to true. When you select a radio button, any other checked button in the same group will be cleared.

- To clear a radio button, set its checked property to false. When you clear a radio button, no other button will become checked.

- To select a check box, set its checked property to true. To clear a check box, set its checked property to false.

Figure 6-10 How to script radio buttons and check boxes

How to use methods and events with forms and controls

Figure 6-11 presents some methods and events that you are likely to use with forms and controls. The first table summarizes two methods that are commonly used with forms. The submit() method submits the form to the web server for processing, and the reset() method resets the data in the controls.

HTML <input> and <button> elements with a type attribute of "submit" or "reset" call the submit() and reset() methods automatically when they are clicked. However, if you want to validate the data in a form before you submit it to the server, that's not what you want. In that case, you can use an <input> element with its type attribute set to "button" or a <button> element with no type attribute. Then, you can use JavaScript to call the form's submit() or reset() method when you're ready to submit or reset the form.

The second table in this figure summarizes three methods that you are likely to use with controls. To start, you can use the focus() method to move the focus to a control, and you can use the blur() method to remove the focus from a control. In addition, you can use the select() method to highlight text in controls that display text such as text boxes or text areas.

The third table summarizes six events that you are likely to use with controls. So far, this book has shown how to attach an event handler to the click event of an element. However, you can also attach event handlers to other events and work with controls like text boxes, select lists, text areas, and links. For instance, you can write an event handler for the change event of a text box or the blur event of a link.

The examples in this figure show how you can use these methods and events. The second example shows that you call the reset() and submit() methods from a form, not a control. Then, the third example shows how to write one event handler for the change event of a text box and another for the dblclick event of a text box. Both of these event handlers are coded within the event handler for the DOMContentLoaded event of the document object. These event handlers use the focus() and blur() methods to move the focus to one text box and to remove it from another.

Two methods that are commonly used with forms

Method	Description
`submit()`	Submits the form and its data to the server.
`reset()`	Resets the controls in the form to their starting values.

Three methods that are commonly used with controls

Method	Description
`focus()`	Moves the focus to the control.
`blur()`	Removes the focus from the control.
`select()`	Selects all the text in a text box or text area.

Common control events

Event	Description
`click`	The user clicks the control.
`dblclick`	The user double-clicks the control.
`focus`	The control receives the focus.
`blur`	The control loses the focus.
`change`	The value of the control changes.
`select`	The user selects text in a text box or text area.

A custom function that's used by the following examples

```
const getElement = selector => document.querySelector(selector);
```

Submit a form

```
getElement("#registration_form").submit();
```

An event handler that attaches two other event handlers

```
document.addEventListener("DOMContentLoaded", () => {

    getElement("#investment").addEventListener("change", () => {
        calculateClick();                      // perform calculation
        getElement("#investment").blur();   // remove focus
    };

    getElement("#years").addEventListener("dblclick", => {
        getElement("#years").value = "";    // clear text box
    };

    getElement("#years").focus();
};
```

Description

- An <input> or <button> element with its type attribute set to "submit" or "reset" automatically submits or resets a form.

Figure 6-11   How to use methods and events with forms and controls

The Register app

Figure 6-12 presents a Register app that consists of several controls on a form. If an entry is required, a red asterisk is displayed to the right of the control. Then, when the user clicks the Register button, the app checks the entries to make sure they're valid. If any of them aren't valid, the app displays an error message to the right of the corresponding field. If all are valid, the app submits the form.

If the user clicks the Reset button, the app resets the controls to their starting values. To do that, the app calls the reset() method for the form. In addition, the app also clears any error messages and restores the starting asterisks, which isn't done by the reset() method.

Part 1 of figure 6-12 shows the HTML for the form and its controls. Here, the form uses the HTTP POST method to submit the values of the controls to a URL that's a file named confirm.html. As a result, it just displays a web page. In real life, though, the form would send the data to a server for processing.

Within the form, there are two text boxes named "email_address" and "phone", a select list named "country", a radio button group named "contact", and a check box named "terms". Within the radio button group are three radio buttons with ids of "text", "email", and "none". The first radio button has a checked attribute, which means that radio button is checked by default when the page loads.

Below these controls, the HTML defines two buttons named "register" and "reset_form". These buttons have a type attribute of "button". As a result, they don't automatically submit or reset the form. Instead, the app uses JavaScript methods to submit or reset the form.

After some controls, the HTML defines <span> elements. The starting values of these <span> elements are asterisks (*). These asterisks indicate that these entries are required. These <span> elements are also where the app displays error messages if the user enters invalid data. In this app, the CSS for <span> elements looks like this:

```
span { color: red; }
```

As a result, the app displays both starting asterisks and any error messages in red.

The Register app

Register for an Account

E-Mail: [   ] This field is required.

Mobile Phone: [   ] This field is required.

Country: [Select a country ▾] Please select a country.

Contact me by: ⦿ Text ○ Email ○ Don't contact me

Terms of Service: ☐ I accept This box must be checked.

[Register] [Reset]

The HTML for the form and controls

```
<h1>Register for an Account</h1>
<form action="confirm.html" method="post">
    <div>
        <label for="email_address">E-Mail:</label>
        <input type="text" name="email_address" id="email_address">
        <span>*</span></div>
    <div>
        <label for="phone">Mobile Phone:</label>
        <input type="text" name="phone" id="phone">
        <span>*</span></div>
    <div>
        <label for="country">Country:</label>
        <select name="country" id="country">
            <option value="">Select a country</option>
            <option value="usa">USA</option>
            <option value="can">Canada</option>
            <option value="mex">Mexico</option></select>
        <span>*</span></div>
    <div>
        <label>Contact me by:</label>
        <input type="radio" name="contact" id="text"
            value="text" checked>Text
        <input type="radio" name="contact" id="email"
            value="email">Email
        <input type="radio" name="contact" id="none"
            value="none">Don't contact me</div>
    <div>
        <label>Terms of Service:</label>
        <input type="checkbox" name="terms" id="terms" value="yes">I accept
        <span>*</span></div>
    <div>
        <label> </label>
        <input type="button" id="register" value="Register">
        <input type="button" id="reset_form" value="Reset"></div>
</form>
```

Figure 6-12   The Register app (part 1)

Part 2 of figure 6-12 presents the JavaScript for this app, which consists of four functions starting with the getElement() function. Although it isn't shown here, the JavaScript for this app includes the "use strict" directive just like the rest of the apps presented in this book.

The processEntries() function is an event handler that's executed when the user clicks the Register button. It starts by assigning the objects that represent the email address and phone text boxes, the country select list, and the terms checkbox to constants named email, phone, country, and terms. That's because this app needs to refer to the objects for these controls to work with the <span> elements that follow them.

After getting the control objects it needs, this code declares a Boolean variable named isValid and initializes it to true. Then, it uses a series of if statements to check the values entered by the user. The first two if statements use the value property to check that the user entered values in the email address and phone number text boxes. The third if statement uses the value property to check that the user selected a value in the country select list. And the fourth if statement uses the checked property to be sure that the user checked the terms checkbox.

If any entry is invalid, the code sets an error message in the <span> element that follows the control. It does that by using code like this:

```
email.nextElementSibling.textContent = "This field is required.";
```

This sets the message in the text node of the next sibling element, which is the related <span> element. In addition, the code sets the isValid variable to false. However, if the entry is valid, the code sets an empty string in the <span> element, which removes the asterisk or any previous error message.

After this code checks if the data is valid, a final if statement checks whether the isValid variable is true. If so, it submits the form to the server. To do that, it uses the getElement() function to get the form. Then, it calls the form's submit() method. Otherwise, if the isValid variable is false, the form isn't submitted so the user can correct the entries.

The resetForm() function is an event handler that's executed when the user clicks the Reset button. It starts by calling the form's reset() method, which resets all of the values in the controls to their starting values. Then, the next four statements reset the values in the <span> elements to asterisks. Finally, the last statement moves the focus to the first text box.

The last function is the event handler for the DOMContentLoaded event of the document object. It just attaches the two event handlers to the click events of the Register and Reset buttons. Then, it moves the focus to the first text box.

The JavaScript

```javascript
const getElement = selector => document.querySelector(selector);

const processEntries = () => {
    const email = getElement("#email_address");
    const phone = getElement("#phone");
    const country = getElement("#country");
    const terms = getElement("#terms");

    let isValid = true;
    if (email.value == "") {
        email.nextElementSibling.textContent = "This field is required.";
        isValid = false;
    } else {
        email.nextElementSibling.textContent = "";
    }
    if (phone.value == "") {
        phone.nextElementSibling.textContent = "This field is required.";
        isValid = false;
    } else {
        phone.nextElementSibling.textContent = "";
    }
    if (country.value == "") {
        country.nextElementSibling.textContent = "Please select a country.";
        isValid = false;
    } else {
        country.nextElementSibling.textContent = "";
    }
    if (!terms.checked) {
        terms.nextElementSibling.textContent = "This box must be checked.";
        isValid = false;
    } else {
        terms.nextElementSibling.textContent = "";
    }

    if (isValid) {
        getElement("form").submit();
    }
};

const resetForm = () => {
    getElement("form").reset();
    getElement("#email_address").nextElementSibling.textContent = "*";
    getElement("#phone").nextElementSibling.textContent = "*";
    getElement("#country").nextElementSibling.textContent = "*";
    getElement("#terms").nextElementSibling.textContent = "*";
    getElement("#email_address").focus();
};

document.addEventListener("DOMContentLoaded", () => {
    getElement("#register").addEventListener("click", processEntries);
    getElement("#reset_form").addEventListener("click", resetForm);
    getElement("#email_address").focus();
});
```

Figure 6-12   The Register app (part 2)

How to modify the DOM

So far, you've learned some of the most useful skills for working with existing nodes of the DOM. However, you can also modify the DOM by adding, replacing, and deleting nodes.

How to add, replace, and delete nodes

Before you can add a new node to the DOM, you need to create it. To do that, you can use the two methods of the document object summarized in the first table in figure 6-13. You can use the createElement() method to create a new HTML element. For instance, you can create a new <a> element by passing a string of "a" to this method. Similarly, you can use the createTextNode() method to create a new text node. This method assigns the string it receives to that node.

The second table in this figure presents five more methods of the Node interface. The appendChild() method adds a child node to the end of any other child nodes. For instance, to add a new <li> element as a child of a <ul> element, you can call appendChild() on the <ul> element and pass the <li> element to the method. When you use this method, it adds the new node as the last child of the parent node. By contrast, when you use the insertBefore() method, it adds the new node before the specified child node.

Like the insertBefore() method, the replaceChild() method accepts a new node and an existing child node as parameters. However, the replaceChild() method replaces the specified child node with the new node.

The last two methods let you remove a node. The removeChild() method removes the specified child node, and the remove() method removes the node that called the method.

The rest of this figure shows some of these methods in action. The HTML defines two <p> elements with text nodes and an <input> element for a button. Then, when a user clicks the button, the JavaScript in this figure adds a new <p> element between the two existing <p> elements. The two screens in this figure show what the page looks like before and after the button is clicked.

The event handler for the button's click event starts by creating a new <p> element. Then, it creates a new text node that stores a string of "Middle paragraph" and adds that text node as a child of the new <p> element.

Next, the code gets the first <p> element from the document, as well as that element's parent. In this figure, the parent element isn't shown in the HTML. That's OK, though, because you don't need to know what the parent element is to work with it.

Finally, the code inserts the new <p> element before the second <p> element. To do that, it passes the first <p> element's next sibling as the second parameter. Since the next sibling is the second <p> element, the new <p> element is inserted before that element.

Two more methods of the document object

Method	Description
`createElement(element)`	Creates a node for the specified element.
`createTextNode(value)`	Creates a text node with the specified value.

Five methods for adding, replacing, and removing nodes

Method	Description
`appendChild(node)`	Adds the specified node after any existing child nodes.
`insertBefore(new, child)`	Adds the new node before the specified child node.
`replaceChild(new, child)`	Replaces the specified child node with the new node.
`removeChild(node)`	Removes the specified child node.
`remove()`	Removes the node that called the method.

A button that that adds a new <p> element to the DOM

Before button is clicked   **After button is clicked**

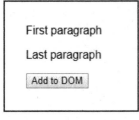

The HTML

```
<p>First paragraph</p>
<p>Last paragraph</p>
<input type="button" id="add" value="Add to DOM">
```

The click event handler for the button

```
document.querySelector("#add").addEventListener("click", () => {
    // create a new <p> element
    const newParagraph = document.createElement("p");

    // create a new text node and add it to the new <p> element
    const text = document.createTextNode("Middle paragraph");
    newParagraph.appendChild(text);

    // get the first <p> element in the document and its parent
    const firstParagraph = document.querySelector("p");
    const parent = firstParagraph.parentNode;

    // insert the new <p> element after the first <p> element (that is,
    // before the element that comes after the first <p> element)
    parent.insertBefore(newParagraph, firstParagraph.nextElementSibling);
});
```

Figure 6-13   How to add, replace, and delete nodes

The updated Register app

Figure 6-14 presents an updated Register app that displays a summary of error messages above the form instead of displaying those messages to the right of each control. This is a common way of displaying error messages. It has the advantage of saving horizontal space, allowing for longer error messages, and allowing for more than one error message per control.

This figure also presents the CSS for the "messages" class, which is used by the <ul> element that displays the error messages. This CSS class adds a red border with rounded corners around the element, sets the font color to red, adds some padding on all sides, and adds a bottom margin. Although this figure doesn't present the HTML for the updated Register app, it's identical to the HTML for the original Register app presented in figure 6-12.

The updated JavaScript for this version of the app doesn't show the custom getElement() function, but it's also the same as the original Register app. By contrast, the displayErrorMsgs() function is new to the updated Register app. This function receives a single parameter named msgs that contains an array of the error messages. This function starts by creating a new <ul> element. Then, it adds the CSS class named "messages" to that element's class attribute.

Next, a for-of loop processes each error message in the msgs array that's passed to this function as a parameter. For each message, this loop creates a new <li> element and a new text node for the current message. Then, it adds the text node as a child of the <li> element, and it adds the <li> element as a child of the <ul> element.

After that, this function checks if the DOM already has a <ul> element. That's necessary because when this app starts, the DOM doesn't contain a <ul> element. However, if the user clicked the Register button and errors were detected, the app has already added a <ul> element to the DOM.

To check for a <ul> element, this code uses the getElement() function to select the first <ul> element and assign it to the constant named node. If that constant is null, there's no <ul> element in the DOM. Otherwise, there is.

If there's no <ul> element in the DOM, this code uses the getElement() function to get an object for the <form> element. Then, it adds the new <ul> element to the parent of the <form> element. In other words, it adds the new <ul> element right before the <form> element. That way, the <ul> element with the error messages displays above the controls on the form.

On the other hand, if there's already a <ul> element, the code doesn't add the new <ul> element it created. If it did, the page would display both the old error messages and the new ones. Instead, it replaces the old <ul> element with the new one.

The updated Register app

Register for an Account

- Please enter an email address.
- Please enter a mobile phone number.
- Please select a country.
- You must agree to the terms of service.

E-Mail: [   ] *

Mobile Phone: [   ] *

Country: [Select a country ▾] *

Contact me by: ◉ Text ○ Email ○ Don't contact me

Terms of Service: ☐ I accept *

[Register] [Reset]

The CSS for the error messages

```css
.messages {
    color: red;
    padding: 1em 2em;
    margin-bottom: 2em;
    border: 2px solid red;
    border-radius: 1em;
}
```

The updated JavaScript

```javascript
const displayErrorMsgs = msgs => {
    const ul = document.createElement("ul");        // create a new ul
    ul.classList.add("messages");

    for (let msg of msgs) {                          // for each message...
        const li = document.createElement("li");     // create li
        const text = document.createTextNode(msg);   // create text node
        li.appendChild(text);                        // add text to li
        ul.appendChild(li);                          // add li to new ul
    }
    const node = getElement("ul");                   // get ul from form
    if (node == null) {                              // if it doesn't exist...
        const form = getElement("form");
        form.parentNode.insertBefore(ul, form);      // add new ul before form
    } else {
        node.parentNode.replaceChild(ul, node);      // otherwise, replace it
    }
};
```

Figure 6-14   The updated Register app (part 1)

Part 2 of figure 6-14 presents the processEntries() and resetForm() event handlers for the updated version of the Register app. Both of these event handlers have significant changes from the original version of the Register app.

Like before, the processEntries() function starts by assigning the objects that represent the email address and phone text boxes, the country select list, and the terms checkbox to constants named email, phone, country, and terms. After that, though, it creates an array named msgs. This array holds any error messages for invalid entries.

Next, the code checks each user entry just as it did before. This time, though, the code adds an error message to the msgs array if an entry is invalid.

Finally, this function checks the length property of the array. If the length is zero, there aren't any error messages in the array and the user's entries are valid. In that case, the code calls the submit() method of the form to submit the data to the server.

On the other hand, if there are error messages in the array, the code calls the displayErrorMsgs() function and passes the array as the parameter. This function either inserts a summary of error messages above the controls of the form if one doesn't already exist, or it replaces the summary if it does exist.

Like before, the resetForm() function starts by calling the reset() method of the form. This resets all the form controls to their starting values. It also removes the <ul> element if it's been added to display error messages. However, this function no longer needs to reset the text in the related <span> elements.

Finally, this figure shows the event handler for the DOMContentLoaded event of the document object. This event handler is unchanged from the original version of the Register app.

The updated JavaScript (continued)

```javascript
const processEntries = () => {
    // get form controls to check for validity
    const email = getElement("#email_address");
    const phone = getElement("#phone");
    const country = getElement("#country");
    const terms = getElement("#terms");

    // create array for error messages
    const msgs = [];

    // check user entries for validity
    if (email.value === "") {
        msgs.push("Please enter an email address.");
    }
    if (phone.value === "") {
        msgs.push("Please enter a mobile phone number.");
    }
    if (country.value === "") {
        msgs.push("Please select a country.");
    }
    if (!terms.checked) {
        msgs.push("You must agree to the terms of service.");
    }

    // submit the form or notify user of errors
    if (msgs.length === 0) {        // no error messages
        getElement("form").submit();
    } else {
        displayErrorMsgs(msgs);
    }
};

const resetForm = () => {
    // no longer need to clear span elements
    getElement("form").reset();

    // remove error messages if any
    const ul = getElement("ul");
    if (ul !== null) ul.remove();

    getElement("#email_address").focus();
};

document.addEventListener("DOMContentLoaded", () => {
    getElement("#register").addEventListener("click", processEntries);
    getElement("#reset_form").addEventListener("click", resetForm);
    getElement("#email_address").focus();
});
```

Figure 6-14   The updated Register app (part 2)

How to work with images

Many web apps use DOM scripting to manipulate images. To do that, they script the <img> element that displays an image in a browser.

How to create an image object

Figure 6-15 lists some of the attributes of the <img> element. The src attribute tells the browser where to find the image to display, and it's required. The alt attribute should also be coded for <img> elements. You can use this attribute to provide information about the image if it can't be displayed or if the page is being accessed using a screen reader.

To create an object that represents an <img> element, you can use the createElement() method just as you would for any other HTML element. When you do, the code looks like this:

```
const image = document.createElement("img");
```

However, you can also create an object that represents an <img> element by using the Image() constructor. A *constructor* is a special method for creating new objects. To call a constructor, you code the *new* keyword followed by the name of the constructor, which is usually the same as the name of the object. For instance, the first example in this figure shows how to call the Image() constructor to create an image object. This results in code that is more concise and easier to read.

How to preload images

In apps that load an image in response to a user event, the image isn't loaded into the browser until the JavaScript changes the src attribute of the <img> element. For large images or slow connections, this can cause a delay of a few seconds before the browser is able to display the image.

To solve this problem, an app can load the images before the user event occurs. This is known as *preloading images*. Then, the browser can display the images without delays. Although this may result in a page taking longer to load initially, the user won't encounter any delays after the app has loaded.

The second example in figure 6-15 shows how to preload an image. First, it uses the Image() constructor to create an image object. Then, it sets the src property to the URL of the image to be preloaded. This causes the web browser to preload the image.

The third example shows how to preload the images for all the links on a page. This assumes that the href attribute in each link contains the URL of each image. First, the querySelectorAll() method gets an array of all the links and assigns it to a constant named links. Then, this code uses a for-of loop to process each link in the array.

Within the loop, the first statement creates a new image object. Then, the second statement sets the src property of the image object to the href property of

Four attributes of the <img> element

Attribute	Description
`src`	The URL of the image to display.
`alt`	Alternate text to display in place of the image.
`width`	The width of the image in pixels.
`height`	The height of the image in pixels.

Create an object that represents an <img> element

```
const image = new Image();
```

Preload an image

```
const image = new Image();
image.src = "image_name.jpg";
```

Preload all images referenced by the <a> elements in a document

```
const links = document.querySelectorAll("a");

for (let link of links) {
    const image = new Image();
    image.src = link.href;
}
```

Description

- The HTML <img> element displays an image that's identified by the src attribute.

- If an image can't be displayed, the text for the alt attribute is displayed instead. This text is also read aloud by screen readers.

- The height and width attributes can be used to indicate the size of an image so the browser can allocate the correct amount of space on the page, or to resize an image.

- The HTMLImageElement interface defines properties for an image object that correspond with the attributes of the <img> element.

- To create an image object, you can use the *new* keyword to call the Image() *constructor*, which is a special method that's used to create a new object.

- When an app *preloads images*, it loads all of the images that it's going to need in the browser's cache when the page loads. Then, the browser can display them whenever they're needed without any noticeable delay.

- To preload an image, you create a new image object. Then, you set its src attribute to the URL for the image you want to preload.

Figure 6-15   How to work with images

the link. This preloads the image. As a result, this code preloads all of the images referenced by the links on the page.

The Image Swap app

Figure 6-16 shows an image swap app, which is a common type of JavaScript app. Here, the main image is swapped whenever the user clicks on one of the small (thumbnail) images. In this example, the user has clicked on the third thumbnail, so the app displays the larger version of that image. This app also changes the caption above the large image as part of the image swap.

The HTML for this app uses <img> elements to display the four thumbnail images. However, this HTML places these elements within <a> elements to make the images clickable and able to receive the focus. In the <a> elements, the href attributes identify the images to be swapped when the links are clicked, and the title attributes provide the text for the related captions. In this case, the HTML places both the <a> and <img> elements within <li> elements of a <ul> element.

After the <ul> element, the HTML defines an <h2> element for the caption and an <img> element for the main image on the page. The contents of the <h2> element provide the caption for the first image, and the src attribute of the <img> element provides the location for the first image. That way, when the app first starts, it displays the first caption and image.

This figure highlights the three ids that the JavaScript uses. First, the id of the <ul> element is set to "image_list" so the JavaScript can get its child <a> elements. Second, the id of the <h2> element is set to "caption" so the JavaScript can change the caption. And third, the id of the main <img> element is set to "main_image" so the JavaScript can change the image.

For the motor-impaired, this HTML provides accessibility by coding the <img> elements for the thumbnails within <a> elements. Then, when this app starts, its JavaScript sets the focus on the first <a> element. That way, the user can access the thumbnail links by pressing the Tab key, and the user can swap the main image by pressing the Enter key when a thumbnail has the focus, which starts the click event handler.

The CSS for this page sets the display property for each <li> element to inline. As a result, this app displays the thumbnail images stored in these elements from left to right instead of from top to bottom.

The Image Swap app

The HTML for the \<body\> element

```
<body>
    <h1>Fishing Images</h1>
    <p>Click on an image to enlarge.</p>
    <ul id="image_list">
        <li><a href="images/release.jpg" title="Catch and Release">
            <img src="thumbnails/release.jpg" alt="release fish"></a></li>
        <li><a href="images/deer.jpg" title="Deer at Play">
            <img src="thumbnails/deer.jpg" alt="deer"></a></li>
        <li><a href="images/hero.jpg" title="The Big One!">
            <img src="thumbnails/hero.jpg" alt="big fish"></a></li>
        <li><a href="images/bison.jpg" title="Roaming Bison">
            <img src="thumbnails/bison.jpg" alt="bison"></a></li>
    </ul>
    <h2 id="caption">Catch and Release</h2>
    <p><img id="main_image" src="images/release.jpg"
        alt="Catch and Release"></p>
</body>
```

The CSS for the \<li\> elements

```
li {
    display: inline;
}
```

Figure 6-16   The Image Swap app (part 1)

Part 2 of figure 6-16 presents the JavaScript for this app. In the event handler for the DOMContentLoaded event, the first two statements get the objects for the <img> element that displays the main image and the <h2> element for the caption. Then, the third statement creates an array of the <a> elements within the <ul> element and assigns it to a constant named imageLinks. Next, the code uses a for-of loop to process each of the links in the array.

The for-of loop starts by preloading the image that will be swapped. Then, it attaches an event handler to the click event of each link. Note that the function for each event handler has a parameter named evt that allows the event handler to access the Event object.

Within the event handler, the first statement changes the src attribute of the image to the href attribute of the clicked link. The second statement changes the alt attribute of the image to the title attribute of the clicked link. And the third statement changes the textContent property of the caption to the title attribute of the clicked link. When the user clicks on a thumbnail, these statements change the DOM. As a result, the browser immediately changes the image and caption on the web page. Note that this code works because the <a> elements were coded in a way that corresponds with the images to display.

This event handler ends by canceling the default action of the link. Since the default action for a link displays the file identified by the href attribute, canceling this action is necessary for the app to work correctly. Otherwise, clicking on the link would open a new browser window or tab and display the image that's specified by the href attribute.

When the for-of loop ends, the code moves the focus to the first link. This allows the user to tab through the thumbnail images and press the Enter key to swap the main image.

The JavaScript

```
const getElement = selector => document.querySelector(selector);

document.addEventListener("DOMContentLoaded", () => {
    // get the main image and caption elements
    const mainImage = getElement("#main_image");
    const caption = getElement("#caption");

    // get all the <a> elements in the <ul> element
    const imageLinks = document.querySelectorAll("#image_list a");

    // process image links
    for (let link of imageLinks) {

        // preload image
        const image = new Image();
        image.src = link.href;

        // attach event handler for click event of <a> element
        link.addEventListener("click", evt => {
            mainImage.src = link.href;
            mainImage.alt = link.title;
            caption.textContent = link.title;

            evt.preventDefault(); // cancel the default action of the link
        });
    }

    // set focus on first image link
    imageLinks[0].focus();
});
```

Figure 6-16   The Image Swap app (part 2)

Perspective

This chapter has presented some of the most useful skills for scripting the DOM. To do that, it presented four different apps. The FAQs app showed how to script the elements and attributes of the DOM. The Register app showed how to use DOM scripting to validate the data in forms. The updated Register app showed how you can add and remove elements from the DOM. And the Image Swap app showed how to work with images, including how to preload images.

Terms

DOM (Document Object Model)	control
node	field
parent node	submit button
child node	reset button
sibling node	data validation
descendant node	hard return
element node	soft return
text node	text box
attribute node	text area
scripting the DOM	select list
API (application programming interface)	radio button
interface	check box
DOM API	constructor
HTML DOM API	preload an image
form	

Exercise 6-1   The Register 3.0 app

The Register 3.0 app enhances the Register 2.0 app that you worked with in this chapter. When you're done, it should look like this:

Add new elements to the HTML file

1. Open the index.html file in this folder:

   `exercises\ch06\register_3.0`

   Note that it doesn't include elements that get the state or the zip code.

2. Add a \<div\> element for the state. To code this element, you can use the existing \<div\> element for the email address as a model.

3. Add a \<div\> element for the zip code.

Add validation for the new text boxes

4. Open the register.js file.

5. In the processEntries() function, add code that makes sure the user has entered a value for the state and the zip code.

6. Run the app and test it. It should display an appropriate message if you don't enter a value for the state or the zip code.

Enhance the validation for the email text box

7. Add code that checks if the email address contains an @ symbol and a period. If not, display an appropriate message that indicates that the email is invalid.

8. Run the app and test it. It should display a message if the email doesn't have an @ symbol or a period.

Exercise 6-2 The Movie Ranker app

The Movie Ranker app uses the buttons to the right of each movie to rank the movies.

Movie Ranker

#1	The Matrix	Up Down
#2	The Godfather	Up Down
#3	The Social Network	Up Down

Review the starting code

1. View the files in this folder:

    `exercises\ch06\movie_ranker`

2. Open the index.html file. Note that it includes id attributes for many of its elements.

3. Run the app and click the buttons. Note that they don't do anything yet.

Add the functions that get elements

4. Open the mover.js file.

5. Add a getElement() function like the one shown in this chapter that gets the first element for the specified CSS selector.

6. Add a getElements() function that uses the querySelectorAll() method to get all elements for the specified CSS selector.

Add code that swaps the first two movie titles

7. Add a function named swapFirstTwo(). This function should use the getElements() function to get an array for all of the elements for movie titles.

8. Get the text for the first two movie titles in the array and assign the text to two constants.

9. Use the two constants to swap the text for first two elements.

10. Attach the swapFirstTwo() function as the event handler for the click event of the Down button in the first row and the Up button in the second row.

11. Run the app and test it. Clicking either of the two buttons should swap the first two titles.

Add code that swaps the last two movie titles

12. Add a function named swapLastTwo(). This function should use the getElements() function to get an array for all of the elements for movie titles.

13. Get the text for the last two movie titles in the array and assign the text to two constants.

14. Use the two constants to swap the text for last two elements.

15. Attach the swapLastTwo() function as the event handler for the click event of the Up button in the third row and the Down button in the second row.

16. Run the app and test it. Clicking either of the two buttons should swap the last two titles.

Exercise 6-3   The Image Carousel app

The Image Carousel app uses the Left and Right buttons to rotate through a list of images. Only three images are displayed at a time, but there are four images total so one image will always be hidden. For example, when the Left button is clicked, the image on the left is hidden and the other images shift to the left.

Review the starting code

1. View the files in this folder:

   `exercises\ch06\image_carousel`

2. Open the index.html file. Note that it uses three <img> elements to display the three images.

3. Open the carousel.js file. Note that it contains some starting code that includes the click event handlers for the Left and Right buttons as well as an array that contains the paths to the four images.

Write the code for the Left event handler

4. Add code to the DOMContentLoaded event handler that gets the three <img> elements from the HTML page.

5. Add code to the click event handler for the Left button. This code should remove the first item in the imagePaths array, shift all other items to the left, and add the first item to the end of the array.

6. Add code that assigns the first three paths in the imagePaths array to the src attribute of the three <img> elements on the page.

7. Run the app and make sure that the Left button works correctly.

Write the code for the Right event handler

8. Add code to the click event handler for the Right button. This code should remove the last item from the imagePaths array, shift all other items in the array to the right, and add the last item to the beginning of the array.

9. Add code that assigns the first three paths in the imagePaths array to the src attribute of the three <img> elements on the page.

10. Run the app and make sure that the Right button works correctly.

7

How to test
and debug an app

As you develop a JavaScript app, you need to test it to make sure that it performs as expected. Then, if there are any problems, you need to debug your app to correct those problems. This chapter shows you how to do both.

An introduction to testing and debugging

When you *test* an app, you run it to make sure that it works correctly. As you test the app, you try different combinations of input data and user actions to be certain that the app works in every case. In other words, the goal of testing is to make an app fail.

When you *debug* an app, you fix the errors (*bugs*) that you discover during testing. Each time you fix a bug, you test again to make sure that the changes you made didn't affect any other aspects of the app.

The Future Value app

Figure 7-1 presents the Future Value app that's used throughout this chapter. This app calculates the future value of an investment at a specified annual interest rate after a specified number of years.

This app has already been tested and debugged to work as intended. So, you can use the code in this figure as a reference as you read the rest of this chapter and try the examples for yourself.

The HTML for this app uses three text boxes to get input from the user. These text boxes have ids of investment, rate, and years. Then, to display the future value, this HTML uses a fourth text box with an id of future_value. The element for this text box includes a disabled attribute. That way, the JavaScript can use this text box to display data to the user, but the user can't enter data into it. Next, this HTML defines a Calculate button that the user can click to calculate the future value. It has an id of calculate.

The CSS for this app displays the labels as an inline block. As a result, each <input> element that's coded after a <label> element is displayed to the right of the label, not below the label. In addition, the CSS sets the width of each label to 11 ems and right aligns its text. On the other hand, the CSS for the <input> elements sets the width of each <input> element to 15 ems with a left margin of 1 em. This provides for a small space between the labels and the <input> elements.

The Future Value app

The HTML for the <body> element

```html
<body>
    <h1>The Future Value Calculator</h1>
    <div>
        <label for="investment">Total investment:</label>
        <input type="text" id="investment">
    </div>
    <div>
        <label for="rate">Annual interest rate:</label>
        <input type="text" id="rate">
    </div>
    <div>
        <label for="years">Number of years</label>
        <input type="text" id="years">
    </div>
    <div>
        <label>Future value:</label>
        <input type="text" id="future_value" disabled>
    </div>
    <div>
        <label> </label>
        <input type="button" id="calculate" value="Calculate">
    </div>
    <script src="future_value.js"></script>
</body>
```

The CSS for the <label> and <input> elements

```css
label {
    display: inline-block;
    width: 11em;
    text-align: right;
}
input {
    width: 15em;
    margin-left: 1em;
}
```

Figure 7-1   The Future Value app (part 1)

The JavaScript for this app begins by defining a getElement() function that gets an element for the specified CSS selector. Then, it defines a function named isNotValid() that returns true if the specified value is not a number or if the number is less than or equal to zero. In other words, the function returns true if the value is not valid. Otherwise, it returns false.

The calcFutureValue() function contains the code that calculates the future value based on the investment, annual interest rate, and number of years. To do that, it begins by initializing a variable named futureValue to the amount of the original investment. Then, it uses a loop to calculate the interest for each year and to add that interest to the futureValue variable. As part of the calculation, the code divides the interest rate by 100 to convert it to a percent. If it didn't do that, this calculation wouldn't yield the correct result.

The calcButtonClick() function handles the click event of the Calculate button. This event handler begins by clearing any previous text from the text box for the future value. Then, it gets the strings stored in the first three text boxes and converts them to numbers that correspond to the investment, annual interest rate, and number of years.

After getting the values for the first three text boxes, this code checks whether each user entry is valid. If not, the code adds an error message and moves the focus to the text box for that entry. Then, the code checks whether any error messages have been set. If no error messages have been set, all three entries are valid. In that case, the app calls the calcFutureValue() function to calculate the future value and displays it in the future value text box. Otherwise, it uses the alert() method to display the error messages in a dialog.

After the calcButtonClick() function, the code defines an arrow function that handles the DOMContentLoaded event. Within this function, the first statement attaches the calcButtonClick() function to the click event of the Calculate button. Then, the second statement sets the focus on the first text box. As a result, when the app first loads, the app is ready for the user to enter data into the first text box.

The JavaScript

```javascript
function getElement(selector) {
    return document.querySelector(selector);
}

function isNotValid(val) {
    return isNan(val) || val <= 0;
}

function calcFutureValue(investment, rate, years) {
    let futureValue = investment;
    for (let i = 1; i <= years; i++) {
        futureValue += futureValue * rate / 100;
    }
    return futureValue;
}

function calcButtonClick() {
    // clear any previous calculation
    getElement("#future_value").value = "";

    // get values user entered in textboxes
    const investment = parseFloat(getElement("#investment").value);
    const rate = parseFloat(getElement("#rate").value);
    const years = parseInt(getElement("#years").value);

    // check user entries and set error message
    let errorMsg = "";
    if (isNotValid(investment)) {
        errorMsg += "Investment amount must be a positive number.\n";
        getElement("#investment").focus();
    }
    if (isNotValid(rate)) {
        errorMsg += "Interest rate must be a positive number.\n";
        getElement("#rate").focus();
    }
    if (isNotValid(years)) {
        errorMsg += "Number of years must be a positive number.";
        getElement("#years").focus();
    }

    // if user entries are valid, calculate and display future value
    if (errorMsg == "") {
        const futureValue = calcFutureValue(investment, rate, years);
        getElement("#future_value").value = futureValue.toFixed(2);
    } else {
        alert(errorMsg);
    }
}

document.addEventListener("DOMContentLoaded", () => {
    // attach the click event handler for the button
    getElement("#calculate").addEventListener("click", calcButtonClick);

    // set focus on first text box on initial load
    getElement("#investment").focus();
});
```

Figure 7-1   The Future Value app (part 2)

Three types of errors

As you test an app, three types of errors can occur. These errors are described in figure 7-2.

Syntax errors violate the rules for coding JavaScript statements. These errors are detected by the JavaScript engine when the browser loads the JavaScript for a page. However, as you learned in chapter 1, some syntax errors are detected by IDEs like VS Code before the browser loads the JavaScript for a page.

Runtime errors occur after a page has been loaded into a browser and the app is running. Then, when the JavaScript engine encounters a statement that it can't execute, it throws an error that stops the execution of the app.

Logic errors are errors in the logic of the coding: an arithmetic expression that delivers the wrong result, a comparison that uses the wrong relational operator, and so on. Since this type of error doesn't stop the execution of the app, it's often the most difficult to find and fix.

For example, the code for the Future Value app in this figure has a logic error that results in an incorrect result. In this case, it's hard to tell what the correct future value should be or what statement caused the error. However, this chapter presents some techniques that can help you find and fix these types of errors.

The Future Value app with a logic error

The Future Value Calculator

Total investment: `1000`

Annual interest rate: `3.5`

Number of years: `10`

Future value: `3405062891.60`

Calculate

The goal of testing
- To find all errors before the app is put into production.

The goal of debugging
- To fix all errors before the app is put into production.

The three types of errors that can occur
- *Syntax errors* violate the rules for how JavaScript statements must be written. These errors are caught by the JavaScript engine when the browser loads the JavaScript for a page.
- *Runtime errors* occur after a page is loaded and the app is running. When the JavaScript engine encounters a statement that it can't execute, it throws an error that stops the execution of the app.
- *Logic errors* are errors in the logic of your code. They don't stop the execution of the app, but they produce the wrong results.

Description
- To *test* a JavaScript app, you run it to make sure that it works correctly even if you enter invalid data or perform other unexpected actions.
- When you *debug* an app, you fix all of the errors (*bugs*) that you find when you test the app.

Figure 7-2   Three types of errors

Common JavaScript errors

Figure 7-3 presents some common coding errors for JavaScript. If you've been doing the exercises, you have most likely encountered several of these errors already. It may seem counterintuitive, but making errors is a natural and inevitable part of programming, and finding and fixing those errors helps you grow as a programmer.

If you're using a text editor or IDE that provides good support for JavaScript, you can avoid most of these errors by noting the error markers and warnings that are displayed as you enter the code. For instance, VS Code helps you avoid most of the syntax errors described in this figure. However, it doesn't help you avoid errors with HTML references and data types.

The fourth heading illustrates a problem that can occur if you're not using strict mode. In this example, the code defines a function. Within this function, the first statement declares and initializes a variable named salesTax. As a result, this variable has local scope. However, the second statement misspells salesTax as salestax when it tries to assign a new value to the variable. Since a variable named saletax hasn't been declared, JavaScript creates it and gives it global scope, causing a bug.

Since it's easy to misspell the name of a variable, this was a common and tricky bug to find in early versions of JavaScript. Fortunately, with modern JavaScript, you can prevent this type of bug by using strict mode. Then, the JavaScript engine throws an error if you use a variable before it's declared. This forces you to fix the error before you can run your code, which is what you want.

Common syntax errors

- Misspelled names.
- Incorrect case for names.
- Omission of required parentheses, quotation marks, or braces.
- Use of the assignment operator (=) instead of the equality (==) or strict equality (===) operator to test for equality.

A problem with HTML references

- Incorrect reference to an HTML component.

Problems with data types

- Not making sure that a user entry is the right data type before processing it.
- Not converting a user entry to a numeric value before using it in arithmetic operations.

A problem you can avoid by using strict mode

- If you don't use strict mode and you assign a value to a variable that hasn't been declared, the JavaScript engine treats it as a global variable, as in this example:

```
function calculateTax(subtotal, taxRate) {
    let salesTax = subtotal * taxRate;          // salesTax is local
    salestax = Number(salesTax.toFixed(2));     // salestax is global
    return salesTax;         // salesTax isn't rounded but salestax is
}
```

Figure 7-3   Common JavaScript errors

How to plan the test runs

When you test an app, you typically do so in at least two phases. In the first phase, you test the app with valid data. In the second phase, you test the app with invalid data. This is illustrated in figure 7-4.

As your apps become more complex, it helps to create a plan for testing an app. A *test plan* is a table or spreadsheet that shows what test data you're going to enter and what the results should be. Many programmers also use unit testing frameworks to allow them to automate testing, although that's beyond the scope of this book.

In the valid testing phase, you should start with test data that produces results that can be easily verified. This is illustrated by the Future Value app in this figure. Here, the first test data entries are an investment of 1000, an annual interest rate of 10 percent, and 1 year. This makes it easy to see that the result should be 1100, and it is.

Next, you should use test data that is more likely to produce an inaccurate result. That involves using a range of valid entries and verifying that the results are accurate. To do that, of course, you need to know what the results should be. For apps that perform simple calculations, like the Miles To Kilometers app, that's not a problem. For apps like the Future Value app that perform more complex calculations, it can be difficult to determine what the results should be. That's why this chapter presents some of the debugging techniques that you can use to help determine if the result of a calculation is correct.

For the invalid testing phase, your test data should include all kinds of invalid entries. This is illustrated by the second screenshot in this figure. This shows a test run of the Future Value app where the investment is blank, the interest rate is a negative number, and the number of years value is a positive number. As you can see, this displays an error message showing that the investment and interest rate values are invalid.

When you create a test plan for invalid data, you try to make the program fail by testing various combinations of valid data, invalid data, and user actions. This should include random user actions like pressing the Enter key or clicking the mouse at the wrong time or place.

The Future Value app with valid data

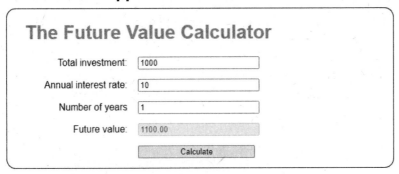

The Future Value app with invalid data

The two test phases
1. Test the app with valid input to make sure the results are correct.
2. Test the app with invalid input and unexpected user actions.

How to make a test plan
1. List the valid entries that you're going to make and the correct results for each set of entries. Then, make sure that the results are correct when you test with these entries.
2. List the invalid entries that you're going to make. These should include entries that test the limits of the allowable values. Then, make sure your app handles these entries appropriately.

Two common testing problems
*   Not testing a wide enough range of entries.
*   Not knowing what the results of each set of entries should be and assuming that the results are correct.

Description
*   It's easy to find syntax and runtime errors because the JavaScript engine won't run the code until you fix them.
*   It's harder to find logic errors because they can slip through your test runs if you don't check that the results are correct.

Figure 7-4   How to plan the test runs

How to debug with Chrome's developer tools

Chapter 1 showed how to use the Console panel of Chrome's *developer tools* to find and fix some simple errors. Now, this chapter reviews those skills. In addition, it presents some other debugging features available from Chrome that you can use to debug more complicated errors.

This chapter doesn't present all of the debugging features available from Chrome. Instead, it presents a subset of those features that should help you get started with debugging. Then, if you later decide that you want to use some of the other features, you have a solid foundation for learning about them.

How to find errors

Although there are several ways to open and close the developer tools, you typically use the F12 key as described in figure 7-5. That's why the developer tools for Chrome and other browsers are often referred to as the *F12 tools*.

One of the primary uses of Chrome's developer tools is to get error messages when a JavaScript app throws an error and stops running. To get the error message, you open the developer tools and click the Console tab. This displays the Console panel, which shows the error message. Then, you can click on the link to the right of the message to switch to the Sources panel with the statement that caused the error highlighted. In the Sources panel, you can hover your mouse over the error icon (an X in a red circle) to view the error message.

In this figure, the problem is that the isNaN() function in the statement uses incorrect case. This shows how easy it can be to find an error.

Sometimes, the statement that's highlighted isn't the one that caused the error. However, this still gives you a clue that can help you find the statement that actually caused the error.

When you're testing and debugging your code, the error message that's displayed is for the first error that's detected, even if there are multiple errors in the code. To fix all errors, you have to fix the first error and test the app again. Then, if there are other errors, you repeat the process until you have fixed them all and the app runs correctly.

Chrome with an open Console panel that shows an error

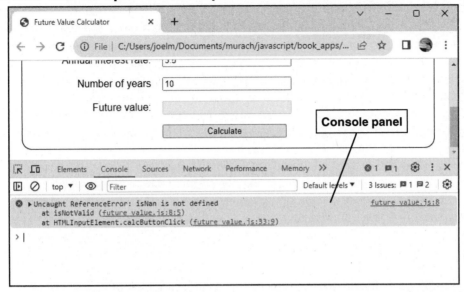

The Sources panel after the link in the Console panel has been clicked

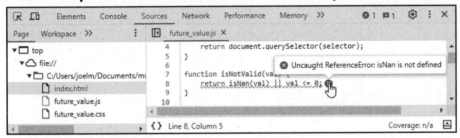

How to use the developer tools

- To open or close the developer tools, press F12 or look up the specific shortcut key for your browser.
- To change where the developer tools are displayed, click the More Actions (three vertical dots) menu and select a Dock Side item.
- To display a panel, click its tab.

How to get more information about an error

1. In the Console panel, click the link to the right of the error message that indicates the line number that caused the error. This opens the Sources panel and displays the statement that caused the error.
2. Hover your cursor over the red X to view the error message.

Description

- Chrome's *developer tools* provide some excellent debugging features.
- Because you typically start the developer tools by pressing the F12 key, these tools are often referred to as the *F12 tools*.

Figure 7-5   How to use Chrome to find errors

How to set breakpoints

A *breakpoint* is a point you can set where the execution of your app deliberately stops. Then, you can examine the values of variables and constants to see if your code is executing as expected. You can also step through the execution of the code from that point on. These techniques can help you solve difficult errors.

Figure 7-6 shows you how to set breakpoints, step through the code, and view the values of variables and constants using the Sources panel of Chrome. In this example, a breakpoint has been set on line 40 of the JavaScript file for the Future Value app.

When you run your app, it stops at the first breakpoint that it encounters and highlights the line of code next to the breakpoint. While your code is stopped, you can hover your mouse over an object's name in the Code Editor pane of the Sources panel to display the current value of that object. In addition, the current values of variables and constants are displayed to the right of the statements that declare them.

At a breakpoint, you can also view the current variables and constants in the Debugging pane. In the Scope section, you can see the variables and constants that are used by the function that is being executed.

You can also see the values of other variables, constants, and expressions by clicking the Watch tab in the Debugging pane to display the Watch section. Then, you can click the plus sign and type a variable or constant name that you want to watch. Or, you can enter an expression that you want to watch.

How to step through code

To step through the execution of an app after it stops at a breakpoint, you can use the Step Into, Step Over, and Step Out buttons. These buttons are displayed above the Debugging pane. Or, you can press the key associated with these operations, as shown in the table in this figure.

If you repeatedly click the Step Into button, you will execute the code one statement at a time and the next statement to be executed will be highlighted. After each statement is executed, you can use the Local or Watch section of the Debugging pane to observe any changes in the variables.

As you step through an app, you can use Step Over if you want to execute a called function without taking the time to step through it. Or, you can use Step Out to step out of a function that you don't want to step all the way through. When you want to return to normal execution, you can use Resume. Then, the app will run until it reaches the next breakpoint.

These are powerful debugging features that can help you find the causes of most problems. Stepping through an app is also a good way to understand how its code works. For example, stepping through the for loop in the Future Value app while watching the value of the futureValue variable might help you to better understand how it works.

A breakpoint in the Sources panel

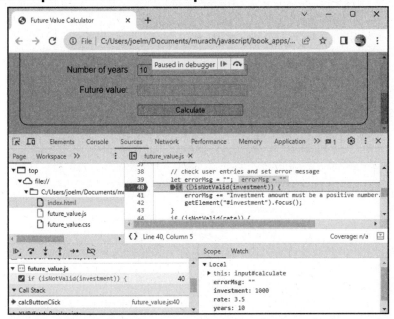

How to set or remove a breakpoint in the Sources panel

- In the Sources panel, click on the JavaScript file in the Page section to display the JavaScript code. Then, find the line of code you want to add or remove a breakpoint to and click on its corresponding line number in the Code Editor pane.

The buttons and keys for stepping through the JavaScript code

Button	Key	Description
Step Into	F11	Step through the code by executing one statement at a time.
Step Over	F10	Run any called functions without stepping through them.
Step Out	Shift+F11	Execute the rest of a function without stepping through it.
Resume	F8	Resume normal execution.

How to view the current data values at each step

- Hover the mouse pointer over a variable or constant name in the Code Editor pane.
- View the current values in the Scope section of the Debugging pane.
- In the Debugging pane, click the Watch tab. Then, in the Watch section, click the plus sign and type the variable name, constant name, or expression that you want to watch.
- The values are also displayed to the right of the declarations in the Code Editor pane.

Description

- When the JavaScript engine encounters a *breakpoint*, it stops before executing the statement with the breakpoint. You can set a breakpoint on any line except a blank line.
- A blue arrow around the line number marks a breakpoint, and a light blue highlight marks the next statement to be executed as you step through your code.

Figure 7-6   How to use breakpoints and step through code using Chrome

Other debugging techniques

With just the techniques you've learned so far, you can already find and fix most bugs in JavaScript. However, in some cases, the techniques presented in the next few figures may be helpful.

How to trace code execution

When you *trace* the execution of an app, you monitor the sequence in which the JavaScript engine executes the statements in the app. One way to do that is to add statements to your code that display messages or variable values at key points in the code.

For instance, the example in figure 7-7 uses the log() method of the console object to display messages in the Console panel. Here, two statements that use the log() method have been added to the calcFutureValue() function of the Future Value app. The first statement is coded at the beginning of the function. It displays a message that lets you know the function has started. The second statement is coded in the body of the for loop. It displays a message that includes the value of the counter variable and the future value at each iteration of the loop.

The output from the log() methods shows that the calculation is incorrect because the loop only executes nine times, but it should execute ten times, once for each year. That indicates that the conditional expression that determines when the loop should end is probably incorrect. In this case, you can fix the error by changing the less than operator (<) to less than or equal to (<=).

When you use this technique, you usually start by adding just a few statements that call the log() method to the code. Then, if that doesn't help you solve the problem, you can add more. Often, this is all you need for solving simple debugging problems, and it's sometimes quicker than setting breakpoints and stepping through the code.

For example, tracing often works better than stepping through code when you're working with loops. To illustrate, let's say you've got an error that occurs inside a loop that performs a calculation on each element of an array with 1000 elements. In that case, it would be daunting to step through the entire array to find the error. However, adding a statement that calls the log() method makes it easy to send the loop's index and the element's value to the console on each iteration. Then, you can review the data displayed in the console to find the cause of the error.

You can also use the alert() method to trace the execution of your code. This has the benefit of displaying the trace data in a dialog without having to open the Console panel. However, using the alert() method doesn't allow you to see all of the generated messages at once, which makes it harder to use for tracing. In addition, you have to click OK after each dialog, which can be intrusive, especially if the alert() method is coded within a loop.

Code with two log() methods that trace its execution

```
function calcFutureValue(investment, rate, years) {

    console.log("calcFutureValue() has started");

    let futureValue = investment;
    for (let i = 1; i < years; i++ ) {
        futureValue += futureValue * rate / 100;

        console.log(`year ${i} future value is ${futureValue}`);
    }
    return futureValue;
}
```

The messages in the Console panel

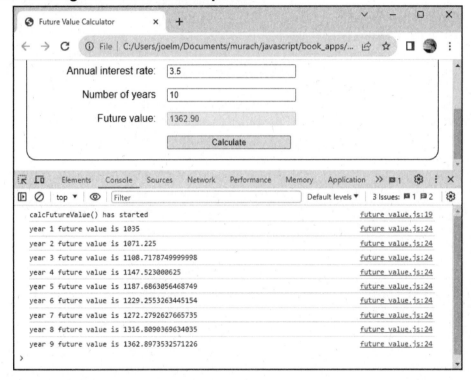

Description

- To *trace* the execution of your code, you can call the console.log() method at key points in your code to display messages in the Console panel. These messages can display the values of variables or constants.

- You can also use the alert() method to trace code execution by displaying messages in dialogs. However, responding to these dialogs becomes intrusive.

Figure 7-7   How to trace code execution

More methods for tracing execution

Figure 7-8 presents three more methods of the console object. Like the log() method, you can use these methods to display messages about your code in the Console panel.

Unlike the log() method, these methods provide a stack trace. A *stack trace* is a list of all the functions that have been called in your code. This can be useful in more complex debugging scenarios where you need more information about the code.

The messages displayed by the error() and warn() methods differ from the messages displayed by the log() method in three ways. First, the Console panel displays error and warning messages in different colors so they're more visible. In this figure, the Console panel displays the error messages in red and the warning messages in yellow.

Second, the Console panel displays icons with the error and warning messages to make them more visible. In this figure, the Console panel displays an X in a red circle for an error message and an exclamation point in a yellow triangle for a warning message.

Third, the Console panel displays an expander arrow (▶) between the icon and the message. When you click the expander arrow, the Console panel displays a stack trace that lists all of the functions that have been called in your code up to the point of the warning or error.

The first example in this figure shows a function named isNotValid() that displays an error message if the value it receives isn't a number. Or, if the value it receives is less than or equal to zero, it displays a warning message. Below the code example, this figure shows how these messages look in the Console panel. Here, the expander arrows for the messages have been clicked so the stack trace is displayed for both.

Like the error() and warn() methods, the trace() method displays a stack trace. However, it differs from those methods in three ways. First, the stack trace displays automatically. That is, you don't need to click the expander arrow to display it. Second, the trace message doesn't display any icons. And third, if you call the trace() method as shown in the second example, it displays "console. trace" as the message.

The second example shows the calcFutureValue() function with a call to the trace() method at the start of its code. Then, the stack trace that's displayed in the Control panel shows that the calcFutureValue() function was called by the calcButtonClick() function, that both functions are stored in the same JavaScript file, and the line number for each function.

Three more methods of the console object

Method	Description
error(*string*)	Outputs an error message in red to the Console panel with an icon of an X in a red circle and an arrow to display a stack trace.
warn(*string*)	Outputs a warning message in yellow to the Console panel with an icon of an exclamation point in a yellow triangle and an arrow to display a stack trace.
trace()	Outputs a stack trace to the Console panel.

Code that sends an error or warning message to the Console panel

```
function isNotValid(val) {
    if (isNaN(val)) {
        console.error("Value is not a number");
    } else if (val <= 0) {
        console.warn(`Value ${val} is not greater than zero.`);
    }
    return isNaN(val) || val <= 0;
}
```

Messages after running the code twice with invalid data

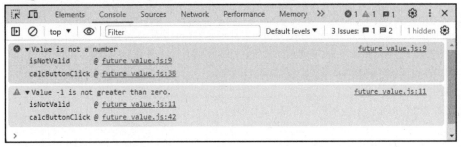

Code that sends a stack trace to the Console panel

```
function calcFutureValue(investment, rate, years) {
    console.trace();
...
```

The stack trace in the Console panel

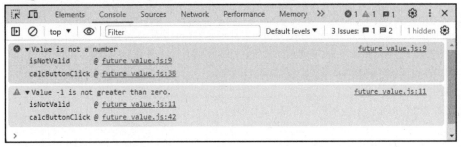

Description

- A *stack trace* lists all the functions that the code has called up to that point.
- You can click on the link for a function in a stack trace to go to its code.

Figure 7-8   More methods for tracing execution

How to view the HTML and CSS for a web page

If you need to review the HTML and CSS for your app, you can use the Elements panel of Chrome's developer tools as shown in figure 7-9. This panel lets you drill down into the document's HTML. For example, the screenshot in this example shows that the <body> element and the first <div> element have been expanded so you can view their content.

In addition, the Styles pane shows the CSS that has been applied to the selected element. In this figure, the Styles pane is displayed below the Elements panel. However, by default, it's displayed on the right side of the Elements panel.

The Styles pane shows all of the styles that have been applied from all of the style sheets that are attached to the web page. If a style in this pane has a line through it, that means it has been overridden by another style. This pane can be invaluable when you're trying to solve complicated formatting problems with cascading style sheets.

Another benefit of the Elements panel is that it reflects any changes to the HTML that your JavaScript has made. For instance, if your JavaScript added any nodes to the DOM, like new <p> elements, this panel would show those new nodes.

You can also view the HTML code for your app by right-clicking the browser window and selecting View Page Source. However, this only displays the code that's initially loaded into the browser. In other words, it doesn't include any changes made to the DOM by JavaScript.

The HTML and CSS for a web page in the Elements panel

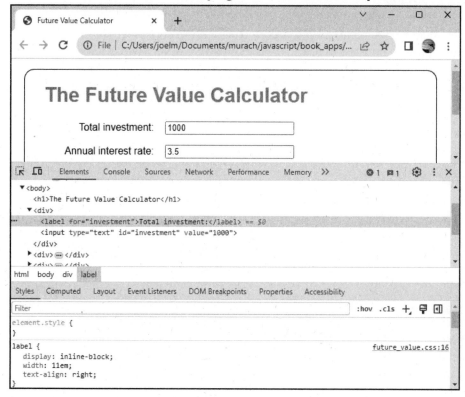

Description

- To display the Elements panel, open the developer tools and click on the Elements tab.
- The Elements panel displays the HTML nodes for a document. You can expand these nodes to view an HTML element.
- If your JavaScript code changes the DOM, such as by adding or removing nodes, the HTML changes in the Elements panel as well.
- To select a node, click on it. Then, you can see the CSS that's applied to the element in the Styles pane.
- You can view the initial HTML for a web page by right-clicking the page and selecting View Page Source. However, when you view the HTML this way, it doesn't show any changes to the DOM made by your JavaScript code.

Figure 7-9   How to view the HTML and CSS for a web page

Perspective

Before you put an app into production, you should test and debug it thoroughly. If you do a good job of it, your app won't encounter unexpected errors and crash, and it will deliver correct results. Now that you've completed this chapter, you should have all the skills you need for testing and debugging apps like the ones in this book.

Terms

test an app	test plan
debug an app	developer tools
bug	F12 tools
syntax error	breakpoint
runtime error	trace
logic error	stack trace

Exercise 7-1   Debug the Future Value app

In this exercise, you'll use Chrome's developer tools to find a syntax error and a logic error, set a breakpoint, and step through the Future Value app.

Review the starting code

1. View the files in this folder:

    `exercises\ch07\future_value`

2. Run the app in Chrome, enter valid values in all three text boxes, and click on the Calculate button. Note that this button doesn't work correctly.

Fix a runtime error

3. Open the developer tools and use the Console panel to view the error. Read the error message carefully. This should give you an idea of what caused the error.

4. Click the link for the error to view the statement that caused the error in the Sources panel.

5. Switch to VS Code. Then, use it to fix the error and save the file.

6. Run the app, enter valid values, and click the Calculate button. This time, the app should display the future value.

Create a test plan and fix a logic error

7. Create a test plan for valid data. This can be a handwritten table or a spreadsheet that includes the test data for three or four test runs as well as the expected results.

8. Run the app, enter valid values from your test plan, and click the Calculate button. This should show that the future value that's calculated doesn't match the expected result.

9. View the console again. Note that it doesn't display any messages. That's because the error is a logic error, not a runtime error.

10. Switch to VS Code and find the for loop in the calcFutureValue() function. Within this loop, add a statement that displays the value of the futureValue variable in the console.

11. Run the app, perform the calculation again, and view the console. This should display the future value for each year. Note that the future value is growing too quickly each year.

12. Switch to VS Code, review the code, and fix the problem.

13. Run the app and perform the calculation again. This time, the calculation should match the expected result on your test plan.

Set a breakpoint and step through code

14. Switch to the Sources panel. If necessary, click on the future_value.js file to display the code for this file.

15. Set a breakpoint on the first statement in the calcButtonClick() function that handles the click event of the Calculate button.

16. Run the app, enter valid data in the three text boxes, and click the Calculate button. The app should stop at the breakpoint.

17. Use the Step Into button or press F11 to step through the app. At each step, note the values that are displayed in the Local section of the Debugging pane and the values that are displayed in the Sources panel next to the code.

    Note: To step out of a long function, use the Step Out button or press Shift+F11.

18. When you finish stepping through the app, note that it displays the result in the browser.

19. Run the app, enter valid data, and click the Calculate button.. It should stop at the breakpoint.

20. Use the Step Over button or press F10 to step through the app. Note that this steps over most (but not all) of the called functions.

21. When you finish stepping through the app, remove the breakpoint.

Exercise 7-2   Debug the Movie Ranker app

This app gives you some practice for using Chrome's developer tools to debug an app.

Review the starting code

1. View the files in this folder:

   `exercises\ch07\movie_ranker`

2. Run the app and click the buttons. Note that none of them are working.

3.   Display Chrome's developer tools and navigate to the Console panel. This should display several error messages depending on how many times you clicked the buttons.

Fix a syntax error that occurs when the DOM is loaded

4.   Refresh the page in your browser. This should remove all error messages from the console except one.

5.   Click the link for the error to view the statement that caused the error in the Sources panel.

6.   Switch to VS Code. Then, open the mover.js file, navigate to the statement that caused the error, and examine the code, paying special attention to the function name.

7.   Fix the error, save your changes, and refresh the page in your browser. This should remove the syntax error from the console. If it doesn't, repeat the previous two steps until it does.

Fix a runtime error that occurs when you click two of the buttons

8.   Click the Down button in the first row and note that it still doesn't work.

9.   In the console, read the error message and note the line number of the error.

10. Switch to VS Code and examine the code at the line number, paying special attention to the code that accesses the movieElements array.

11. Fix the error, save your changes, refresh the page in the browser, and test the Down button in the first row again. It should work now. If it doesn't, repeat the previous two steps until it does.

12. Test the Up button in the second row. It should also work now.

Fix a logic error that occurs when you click the other two buttons

13. Click the Down button in the second row and note that it still doesn't work.

14. Set a breakpoint on the first statement in the moveUp() function.

15. Test the app again and click on the Down button in the second row. The app should stop at the breakpoint.

16. Click the Step Into button or press F11 to step through the application. At each step, note the values that are displayed in the Local section of the Debugging pane. That should help you determine the cause of the error.

17. Fix the error, save your changes, refresh the page in the browser, and test the Down button in the second row again. It should work now. If it doesn't, repeat the previous two steps until it does.

18. Test the Up button in the third row. It should also work now.

Section 2

Master the essential skills

In section 1, you learned the essential JavaScript skills you need to create apps that script the DOM. Now, section 2 presents some more essential skills that every JavaScript developer should have. When you're done, you'll have all the skills you need to be able to create complex apps and work with popular libraries and frameworks.

8

How to work with dates, times, and timers

So far, this book has focused on using three of JavaScript's primitive data types to work with strings, numbers, and Boolean values. Now, this chapter shows how to use a Date object to work with dates and times. In addition, this chapter shows how to use a timer to run code after a specified interval of time. These are important skills because dates, times, and timers are used in a wide range of apps, from business apps to games.

How to work with dates and times

JavaScript doesn't provide a primitive data type for dates and times. Instead, it provides a Date object that can store both dates and times with methods for working with both.

In JavaScript, dates are represented by the number of milliseconds since midnight, January 1, 1970. Positive values come after this date while negative values come before. Internally, the dates are stored in *Coordinated Universal Time* (*UTC*), the primary time standard for the world and successor to *Greenwich Mean Time* (*GMT*). However, JavaScript has access to the time zone on the client's computer and can adjust dates to the local time.

How to create Date objects

Figure 8-1 begins by summarizing some of the parameters you can use with the Date() *constructor*, which is a special method that you can use to create a Date object. To call a constructor, you code the *new* keyword followed by the constructor name as shown by the examples in this figure.

To start, these examples show six ways to create a Date object. First, you can call the Date() constructor with no parameters. This creates a Date object that's set to the local time on the user's computer.

Second, you can call the Date() constructor with a string parameter that specifies a date and time in a local date format. Here, the hours must be specified in 24-hour (or military) time. For example, 3:15pm is 15:15 on a 24-hour clock. If you omit the time, the Date object uses a default value of midnight. Also, to avoid problems, it's a good practice to use 4 digits to specify the year.

Third, you can call the Date() constructor with a string parameter that's in the universal date/time format. This format specifies a date in YYYY-MM-DD format. To include a time, you add the letter T and a time in HH:mm:ss:sss format. When you use the universal format and you only specify a date, JavaScript uses UTC time, not local time. However, if you specify a date and a time, JavaScript offsets the date/time value to the local time. As a result, if you want to get a date in local time, you can specify a time of 00:00. For instance, you can specify a string of "2024-11-05T00:00" to specify the date in local time.

Fourth, you can call the Date() constructor with numeric parameters for the parts of the date. Here, year and month are required. Then, if day is omitted, the Date object uses a default of 1. And if any of the remaining values are omitted, the Date object uses a default of 0 for them. When you use this technique, it's important to know that the months are numbered from 0 through 11 where 0 is January and 11 is December.

Fifth, you can call the Date() constructor and pass it another Date object. This lets you modify the copy of the Date object without modifying the original.

Sixth, you can call the Date() constructor and pass it a *timestamp*, which is the number of milliseconds since midnight, January 1, 1970 UTC, offset to the local time on the user's computer.

How the Date() constructor works with different parameters

Parameters	Description
None	Creates a new Date object set to the current date and time.
String value	Creates a new Date object set to the date and time of the string.
Numeric values	Creates a new Date object set to the year, month, day, hours, minutes, seconds, and milliseconds of the numbers. Year and month are required.
Date object	Creates a new Date object that's a copy of the Date object it received.
Timestamp	Creates a new Date object set to the milliseconds since midnight, Jan 1, 1970.

Six ways to create a Date object

Get the current date and time

```
const now = new Date();
```

Specify a string using a local format

```
const electionDay = new Date("11/5/2024");
const grandOpening = new Date("2/16/2024 8:00");
const departureTime = new Date("4/6/2024 18:30:00");
```

Specify a string using the universal format

```
const electionDay = new Date("2024-11-05");          // UTC, not local
const grandOpening = new Date("2024-02-16T08:00");    // local time zone
const departureTime = new Date("2024-04-06T18:30:00"); // local time zone
```

Specify numeric values

```
const electionDay = new Date(2024, 10, 5);          // 10 is November
const grandOpening = new Date(2024, 1, 16, 8);      // 1 is February
const departureTime = new Date(2024, 3, 6, 18, 30); // 3 is April
```

Copy another Date object

```
const today = new Date(now);        // copy Date object from first example
```

Specify a timestamp

```
const timestampDate = new Date(1704096000000);      // 1/1/2024
```

What happens when an invalid date is passed to the Date constructor

```
const badDate = new Date("6/32/2024");              // Invalid date
```

Description

- A *constructor* is a special method that creates an object. To call a constructor, code the *new* keyword followed by the name of the constructor and any parameters within parentheses.

- In JavaScript, dates are represented by the number of milliseconds since midnight, January 1, 1970.

- The universal date/time format (YYYY-MM-DDTHH:mm:ss.sss) uses a T to separate the time from the date. Components other than the year and month are optional.

- When you create a Date object, JavaScript usually offsets the date and time to use the local time that's specified on the user's computer. However, if you use the universal date/time format to specify a date only (no time component), it uses the UTC time.

- Month numbers start with 0 where January is 0, February is 1, and so on.

Figure 8-1   How to create Date objects

The seventh example in figure 8-1 shows what happens if you pass an invalid value to the Date() constructor. In that case, JavaScript creates a Date object that stores a NaN value to indicate that the date is invalid.

How to use the methods of a Date object

Figure 8-2 describes several methods provided by a Date object. The first four methods convert a Date object to a string. However, as the examples show, these methods don't allow you to control the format of the string that they return. In addition, although it isn't shown in the examples, the strings returned by the toString() and toTimeString() methods include a time zone, formatted like this:

```
"Sun Jan 07 2001 08:25:00 GMT-0800 (Pacific Standard Time)"
```

When JavaScript converts a Date object to a string that includes a time, it shows the offset from GMT, which is the same as the offset from UTC. For instance, the examples in this figure use GMT-0800 to show that the time is offset by 08 hours and 00 minutes from GMT. That's because these examples were run from a computer that's in Pacific Standard Time, which is offset 8 hours from UTC.

The methods in the second table get the parts of a Date object. Here, all of the methods except the getTime() method return the date/time parts using the local time. By contrast, the getTime() method uses universal time, which is the number of milliseconds since midnight, January 1, 1970 UTC.

So, what happens if you use the getTime() and toString() methods with an invalid date? In that case, the getTime() method returns a value of NaN, and the toString() method returns a string of "Invalid Date".

In addition to the get methods shown in this figure, JavaScript also provides a getYear() method that returns a two-digit year. However, it's generally considered a best practice to use the getFullYear() method to avoid ambiguity and possible errors.

The methods in the third table set new values for the parts in a Date object. These methods let you use values that are outside the allowed range. Then, any value over or under the allowed range causes the next most significant date part to roll over.

For example, if you set the hours of a Date object to 25, it adds one hour and one day to the Date object. Or, if you set the day of the month to 0, the Date object rolls the month back to the previous month and sets the day to the last day of that month. By letting you use values that are out of the allowed range, JavaScript provides a mechanism for performing calculations on Date objects using any of the parts of the date or time as shown in the next figure.

As you've learned, the methods that get and set parts of the Date object, with the exception of getTime(), work with the local time on the user's computer. However, there are complementary methods for each set and get method that work with universal time. The names of these methods start with getUTC and setUTC, such as getUTCFullYear() and setUTCMinutes().

Four methods for converting a Date object to a string

Method	Description
`toString()`	Returns a string representing the date and time in local time using the client's time zone.
`toDateString()`	Returns a string representing just the date in local time.
`toTimeString()`	Returns a string representing just the time in local time.
`toISOString()`	Returns a string representing the date and time in universal time.

Get a string representation of a date or time

```
const birthday = new Date(2001, 0, 7, 8, 25);
alert(birthday.toString());       // "Sun Jan 07 2001 08:25:00 GMT-0800"
alert(birthday.toDateString());   // "Sun Jan 07 2001"
alert(birthday.toTimeString());   // "08:25:00 GMT-0800"
alert(birthday.toISOString());    // "2001-01-07T16:25:00.000Z"
```

Some get methods of a Date object

Method	Description
`getTime()`	Returns the number of milliseconds since midnight, January 1, 1970 UTC.
`getFullYear()`	Returns the four-digit year in local time.
`getMonth()`	Returns the month in local time, starting with 0 for January.
`getDate()`	Returns the day of the month in local time.
`getDay()`	Returns the day of the week (1=Sunday, 2=Monday, and so on).
`getHours()`	Returns the hour in 24-hour format in local time.
`getMinutes()`	Returns the minutes in local time.
`getSeconds()`	Returns the seconds in local time.
`getMilliseconds()`	Returns the milliseconds in local time.

Some set methods of a Date object

Method	Description
`setFullYear(year)`	Sets the four-digit year in local time.
`setMonth(month)`	Sets the month in local time.
`setDate(day)`	Sets the day of the month in local time.
`setHours(hour)`	Sets the hour in 24-hour format in local time.
`setMinutes(minutes)`	Sets the minutes in local time.
`setSeconds(seconds)`	Sets the seconds in local time.
`setMilliseconds(ms)`	Sets the milliseconds in local time.

Description

- Except for the getTime() method, the get and set methods use the time zone specified on the user's computer to work with local time.

- There are complementary get and set methods that start with getUTC and setUTC that work with universal time.

Figure 8-2   How to use the methods of a Date object

How to format dates

The first example in figure 8-3 shows how to format a date by using the get methods presented in the previous figure. To start, the first statement creates a new Date object that contains a date and time. Then, the second statement uses the getDate() method to get the day of the month and pads it with a leading 0 if it's only one digit. To do that, this code uses the optional second parameter of the padStart() method to specify "0" as the character to add to the start of the string.

Next, the third statement uses the getMonth() method to get the month, adds 1 to the month, converts the result to a string, and pads it with a leading 0 if it's one digit. Then, the fourth statement uses the getFullYear() method to get the four-digit year. Finally, the fifth statement creates a string in YYYY-MM-DD format by joining the day and month strings with the four-digit year.

How to perform calculations on dates

The second example shows how to calculate the number of days from the current date until the New Year. To start, this code gets a Date object for the current date and time. Then, it uses the values of the first Date object to create a second date object set to January 1st of the following year.

After creating the two Date objects, this code calculates the number of milliseconds between the two Date objects by subtracting the values returned by the getTime() method. Then, it calculates the number of milliseconds in a day by multiplying the number of hours in a day (24) by the number of minutes in an hour (60) by the number of seconds in a minute (60) by the number of milliseconds in a second (1000). Next, it calculates the number of days by dividing the number of milliseconds between the two dates by the number of milliseconds in one day and rounding that value up using the Math.ceil() method.

The third example shows how to calculate a due date. Here, the code begins by creating an invoiceDate constant that's initialized to a Date object for the current date. Then, it creates a dueDate constant and initializes it to a copy of the first Date object. Next, the code uses the setDate() function to add 21 days to the dueDate object. As a result, the due date is 21 days after the invoice date.

At this point, you may be wondering how it's possible for this code to change the dueDate constant. The answer is that this code doesn't assign a new value or object to the dueDate constant. Instead, it changes the values stored inside the Date object that's already assigned to the dueDate constant. If you want to assign a new value to the dueDate constant, such as null or another Date object, you need to assign the Date object to a variable, not a constant.

The fourth example shows how to find the last day of the current month. To start, the first statement creates an endOfMonth constant that's initialized to today's date. Then, the second statement adds 1 to the month. Next, the third statement sets the day to 0, which is one day before the first day of the month. This rolls the month back to the previous month and sets the day to the last day of that month. For example, if the current date is December 2, adding 1 to the

Format a date

```
const departTime = new Date(2024, 3, 16, 18, 30); // April 16, 2024 6:30pm

// get day - pad if only 1 digit
const day = departTime.getDate().toString().padStart(2, "0");

// get month (add 1 since month is zero based) - pad if only 1 digit
const month = (departTime.getMonth() + 1).toString().padStart(2, "0");

const year = departTime.getFullYear();

const dateText = `${year}-${month}-${day}`;

// dateText is "2024-04-16"
```

Calculate the days until the New Year

```
// get current date and time
const now = new Date();

// create new date for Jan 1 of following year - 0 is January
const newYear = new Date(now.getFullYear() + 1, 0, 1);

// get time difference in milliseconds
const timeLeft = newYear.getTime() - now.getTime();

// calculate milliseconds in a day: hrs * mins * secs * milliseconds
const msInOneDay = 24 * 60 * 60 * 1000;

// convert milliseconds to days
const daysLeft = Math.ceil(timeLeft / msInOneDay);

// if today is November 5, 2024, daysLeft is 57
```

Calculate a due date

```
const invoiceDate = new Date();

// make a copy of invoice date
const dueDate = new Date(invoiceDate);

// set the due date to 3 weeks (21 days) in the future
dueDate.setDate(invoiceDate.getDate() + 21);

// if invoice date is 9/3/2024, due date is 9/24/2024
```

Find the end of the month

```
const endOfMonth = new Date();

// set the month to next month
endOfMonth.setMonth(endOfMonth.getMonth() + 1);

// set the day to one day before the start of the month
endOfMonth.setDate(0);

// if today is 12/2/2024, endOfMonth is 12/31/2024
```

Figure 8-3   How to format dates and perform calculations on them

month changes the date to January 2. Then, when the day is set to 0, the Date object rolls the month back to December, and sets the day to the last day of December, which is December 31.

The Countdown app

Figure 8-4 presents the Countdown app. This app accepts the name and date of an event from the user and calculates the number of days between the current date and that event. It displays a different message if the date is today, is in the future, or is in the past. In addition, it performs data validation to make sure the user enters both a name and a date, and that the date is valid.

Part 1 of this figure shows the HTML and some of the CSS for the Countdown app. The HTML includes two text boxes and a button. When the user enters data into the text boxes and clicks the button, that app displays a message in the label that's below the button. To make it easy for JavaScript to work with these elements, the HTML sets the id attributes for these elements.

The CSS in this figure shows the style rule for the element that has an id of "message". This sets the font color to red and the font weight to bold.

The user interface for the Countdown app

The HTML

```html
<!DOCTYPE html>
<html lang="en">
<head>
    <meta charset="UTF-8">
    <meta name="viewport" content="width=device-width, initial-scale=1">
    <title>Countdown</title>
    <link rel="stylesheet" href="countdown.css">
</head>
<body>
    <h1>Countdown To...</h1>
    <div>
        <label for="event">Event Name:</label>
        <input type="text" id="event">
    </div>
    <div>
        <label for="date">Event Date:</label>
        <input type="text" id="date"><br>
    </div>
    <div>
        <label> </label>
        <button id="countdown">Countdown!</button>
    </div>
    <div>
        <label id="message"></label>
    </div>
    <script src="countdown.js"></script>
</body>
</html>
```

The CSS for the message element

```css
#message {
    color: red;
    font-weight: bold;
    width: auto;

}
```

Figure 8-4   The Countdown app (part 1)

Part 2 of figure 8-4 shows the JavaScript for this app. To start, it defines a getElement() function that gets an element for the specified CSS selector. Then, it codes an event handler for the DOMContentLoaded event.

The DOMContentLoaded event handler starts by attaching the click event handler for the Countdown button. Then, it sets the focus on the first text box, which is the text box for the event name.

The click event handler for the Countdown button starts by getting the values the user entered for the event name and date. Then, it gets the label element with an id of "message" and assigns it to a constant named messageLbl. Next, it validates the data entered by the user.

First, it checks if the user entered some text for the name and date of the event. If not, the code sets the textContent property of the message label to an appropriate error message and executes a return statement. As a result, if the user doesn't enter something in both text boxes, this code displays a message and exits the event handler.

Second, the code checks if the user entered a valid date string. To do that, it checks if the toString() method of the Date object returns a string of "Invalid Date". If so, the user didn't enter a valid date. In that case, the code displays an error message and exits the event handler.

However, if the event date is valid, the code calculates the number of days between the current date and the event date. To do that, it creates a new Date object for the current date and assigns it to the today constant. Then, it subtracts the milliseconds for today from the milliseconds for the event date, and assigns the resulting value to the msFromToday constant. Next, it calculates the number of milliseconds in a day and assigns that value to the msForOneDay constant. After that, it divides the msFromToday value by the msForOneDay value and uses the Math.ceil() method to round the resulting value up and assign it to the daysToDate constant.

After calculating the number of days, this event handler builds a message to display to the user. To do that, it assigns the result of the toDateString() method to a constant named displayDate. Then, it declares a variable named msg that holds the message to be displayed. Next, it checks the daysToDate variable. If it's zero, the date entered by the user is today. If it's greater than zero, the date is in the future. And if it's less than zero, the date is in the past. For each condition, the code constructs an appropriate message using a template literal. Finally, it displays the message by assigning it to the textContent property of the message label.

The JavaScript

```javascript
const getElement = selector => document.querySelector(selector);

document.addEventListener("DOMContentLoaded", () => {

    getElement("#countdown").addEventListener("click", () => {
        // get the values entered by the user
        const eventName = getElement("#event").value;
        const eventDateString = getElement("#date").value;

        // get the message label element
        const messageLbl = getElement("#message");

        // make sure user entered an event name and date
        if (eventName == "" || eventDateString == "") {
            messageLbl.textContent = "Please enter both a name and a date.";
            return;
        }

        // convert event date string to Date object and check for validity
        const eventDate = new Date(eventDateString);
        if (eventDate.toString() == "Invalid Date") {
            messageLbl.textContent = "Please enter a valid date.";
            return;
        }

        // calculate days
        const today = new Date();
        const msFromToday = eventDate.getTime() - today.getTime();
        const msForOneDay = 24 * 60 * 60 * 1000;
        const daysToDate = Math.ceil(msFromToday / msForOneDay);

        // create and display message
        const displayDate = eventDate.toDateString();
        let msg = "";
        if (daysToDate == 0) {
            msg = `Hooray! Today is ${eventName}! (${displayDate})`;
        } else if (daysToDate > 0) {
            msg = `${daysToDate} day(s) until ${eventName}! (${displayDate})`;
        } else if (daysToDate < 0) {
            msg = `${eventName} happened ${Math.abs(daysToDate)}
                day(s) ago. (${displayDate})`;
        }
        messageLbl.textContent = msg;
    });

    // set focus on first text box
    getElement("#event").focus();
});
```

Figure 8-4   The Countdown app (part 2)

How to work with timers

A *timer* lets you call a function after a specified period of time has elapsed. Timers are useful in a wide range of apps, especially apps that script the DOM. The next two figures describe two types of timers.

How to use a one-time timer

The first type of timer calls its function only once. To create this type of timer, you use the global setTimeout() method that's shown in figure 8-5. Its first parameter specifies the function that the timer calls. Its second parameter specifies the number of milliseconds to wait before calling that function.

When you use the setTimeout() method to create a timer, it returns a reference to the timer that's created. Then, if necessary, you can use this reference to cancel the timer. To do that, you pass this reference to the clearTimeout() method.

The example in this figure presents an app that asks a trivia question and gives the user 10 seconds to answer. This app uses a one-time timer to replace the trivia question with another message after a delay of 10 seconds.

The HTML for this app defines a <div> element with an id of "question". Within the <div> element, the HTML defines a <p> element that tells the user how much time they have to answer, a <label> element that displays the question, and radio buttons that present three answers to choose from.

The JavaScript starts by declaring a global variable for the timer and a global constant for the <div> element with the id of "question". As a result, they are available to the following functions. Then, it defines two functions, timesUp() and processAnswer().

The timesUp() function displays a message that indicates that the time has expired. To do that, it updates the textContent property of the <div> element to remove the question and display a message instead.

The processAnswer() function begins by using the clearTimeout() method to stop the timer that's started by the setTimeout() method. If this function is called before the timer calls the timesUp() function, it prevents the timesUp() function from running. Then, this function checks the user's answer and displays a message to the user that indicates whether the user's answer is correct or not.

The DOMContentLoaded event handler begins by using the setTimeout() method to set the global timer variable to a timer that calls the timesUp() function after a delay of 10 seconds (10,000 milliseconds). Then, it attaches the processAnswer() function to the click event for all the radio buttons in the <div> element. That way, if the user answers the question before the 10 seconds elapse, the processAnswer() function cancels the timer. In that case, the app doesn't call the timesUp() function.

Two methods for working with a timer that calls a function once

Method	Description
setTimeout(*function*, *delay*)	Creates a timer that calls the specified function once after the specified delay in milliseconds has elapsed.
clearTimeout(*timer*)	Cancels a timer created by the setTimeout() method.

A page that times out after 10 seconds

My Trivia

You have 10 seconds to answer.

What is the capitol of Vermont? ○ Burlington ○ Montpelier ○ Concord

My Trivia

Time's up!!

Some of the HTML

```
<h1>My Trivia</h1>
<div id="question">
    <p>You have 10 seconds to answer.</p>
    <label>What is the capitol of Vermont? </label>
    <input type="radio" name="city" value="Burlington">Burlington
    <input type="radio" name="city" value="Montpelier"> Montpelier
    <input type="radio" name="city" value="Concord">Concord
</div>
```

The JavaScript

```
let timer = null;
const div = document.querySelector("#question");

const timesUp = () => div.textContent = "Time's up!!";

const processAnswer = evt => {
    clearTimeout(timer);
    if (evt.currentTarget.value === "Montpelier") {
        div.textContent = "Correct!! The capitol of Vermont is Montpelier.";
    } else {
        div.textContent = "Sorry - the capitol of Vermont is Montpelier.";
    }
};

document.addEventListener("DOMContentLoaded", () => {
    timer = setTimeout(timesUp, 10000);          // 10,000 ms = 10 secs
    const options = div.querySelectorAll("input");
    for (let opt of options) {
        opt.addEventListener("click", processAnswer);
    }
});
```

Figure 8-5   How to use a one-time timer

How to use an interval timer

The second type of timer calls its function repeatedly at the specified interval. To create this type of timer, you use the global setInterval() method shown in figure 8-6. Its first parameter specifies the function to be called. Its second parameter specifies the time interval between function calls. To cancel this type of timer, you pass a reference to the timer to the clearInterval() method.

The example in this figure shows how to use an interval timer to improve the app presented in the previous figure. This version counts down the 10 seconds the user has to answer the question one second at a time. That way, the user can see how much time they have left.

The HTML for this version of the app includes a <span> element with an id of "seconds". The text of this span element is set to 10 when the page initially loads. Then, the code decrements it once per second. This figure shows how the app looks when the user has four seconds left to answer the question.

The JavaScript starts by declaring a global timer variable for the timer and a global div constant for the <div> element whose id is "question". Then, it defines two functions, updateTime() and processAnswer().

The updateTime() function is called each time the interval time elapses. To start, it gets the number of seconds from the <span> element with the id of "seconds" and decrements that number by 1. Then, it checks if the number of seconds is equal to 0. If so, the code stops the interval timer and displays a message that notifies the user that the time has expired. Otherwise, it updates the textContent property of the <span> element to display the number of seconds left in the countdown.

The processAnswer() function is essentially the same as it was in the previous figure. The only difference is that it passes the timer object to the clearInterval() method, not the clearTimeout() method.

The DOMContentLoaded event handler is also much the same as it was in the previous figure. This time, though, it uses the setInterval() method to start the timer so its function executes at intervals of one second (1,000 milliseconds).

When you use the setInterval() method to create a timer, you should know that the timer waits for the specified interval to elapse before executing the function the first time. So, if you want the function to execute immediately, you need to explicitly call it first, before you create the timer.

Two methods for working with a timer that calls a function repeatedly

Method	Description
`setInterval(function, interval)`	Creates a timer that calls a function each time the specified interval in milliseconds has elapsed.
`clearInterval(timer)`	Cancels a timer created by the setInterval() method.

The page updated to count down

> # My Trivia
>
> You have 4 seconds to answer.
>
> What is the capitol of Vermont? ◯ Burlington ◯ Montpelier ◯ Concord

The updated HTML for the <p> element

```
<p>You have <span id="seconds">10</span> seconds to answer.</p>
```

The JavaScript

```
let timer = null;
const div = document.querySelector("#question");

const updateTime = () => {
    const span = document.querySelector("#seconds");
    const seconds = parseInt(span.textContent) - 1;

    if (seconds == 0) {
        clearInterval(timer);
        div.textContent = "Time's up!!";
    } else {
        span.textContent = seconds;
    }
};

const processAnswer = evt => {
    clearInterval(timer);
    if (evt.currentTarget.value === "Montpelier") {
        div.textContent = "Correct!! The capitol of Vermont is Montpelier.";
    } else {
        div.textContent = "Sorry - the capitol of Vermont is Montpelier.";
    }
};

document.addEventListener("DOMContentLoaded", () => {
    timer = setInterval(updateTime, 1000);                  // 1,000 ms = 1 sec

    const options = div.querySelectorAll("input");
    for (let opt of options) {
        opt.addEventListener("click", processAnswer);
    }
});
```

Figure 8-6   How to use an interval timer

The Clock app

Figure 8-7 presents a Clock app that requires the use of an interval timer. When this app starts, it displays the current time and date. Then, it updates the time and date every second.

The HTML has two <p> elements. The element with an id of "time" displays the current time in hours, minutes, and seconds. To do that, it uses a 12-hour clock, not a 24-hour clock. The element with an id of "date" displays the current date, including the day of the week.

The code starts by defining two helper functions. The getElement() function gets the first element specified by the CSS selector, and the padValue() function returns the value it receives padded with "0" to two digits. In other words, the padValue() function adds a leading zero to single-digit numbers.

The displayClock() function displays the current time and date on the web page. To start, this function creates a Date object that's set to the current date and time. The subsequent statements get the various time parts.

To get the AM/PM value, the code checks the 24-hour time returned by the getHours() method. If this value is greater than or equal to 12, the time is 12 noon or later. In that case, the string "PM" is assigned to the ampm constant. Otherwise, the string "AM" is assigned.

To get the hours, the code again checks the value returned by the getHours() method. If this value is greater than 12, the code subtracts 12 from the 24-hour time and assigns the result to the hours constant. Otherwise, the value returned by getHours() is assigned.

To get the minutes and seconds, the code calls the getMinutes() and getSeconds() methods, respectively. Then, it passes the values returned by those methods to the padValue() function. This pads single-digit values with a leading zero before assigning them to the minutes and seconds constants.

Once the time parts are ready, the code uses the getElement() method to get the element with the id of "time" and set its textContent property to display the current hour, minutes, seconds, and AM/PM value. Then, the code uses the getElement() method to get the element with the id of "date" and set its textContent property to the value returned by the toDateString() method.

The DOMContentLoaded event handler starts by calling the displayClock() method. This displays the time and date when the page is first loaded. Then, the code starts the clock by calling the setInterval() method. This statement passes the displayClock() function as the first parameter and 1,000 milliseconds as the second parameter. As a result, this app displays the current time and date every second. Also, since this app doesn't need to stop the timer, this statement doesn't assign the value returned by setInterval() to a variable.

The Clock app

My Clock

1:08:20 PM

Fri Jul 21 2023

Some of the HTML

```
<h1>My Clock</h1>
<p id="time"></p>
<p id="date"></p>
```

The JavaScript

```javascript
const getElement = selector => document.querySelector(selector);

const padValue = value => value.toString().padStart(2, "0");

const displayClock = () => {
    // calculate and format current time and date
    const now = new Date();
    const ampm = (now.getHours() >= 12) ?
        "PM" : "AM";
    const hours = (now.getHours() > 12) ?
        now.getHours() - 12 : now.getHours();
    const minutes = padValue(now.getMinutes());
    const seconds = padValue(now.getSeconds());

    // display time and date
    getElement("#time").textContent =
        `${hours}:${minutes}:${seconds} ${ampm}`;
    getElement("#date").textContent = now.toDateString();
};

document.addEventListener("DOMContentLoaded", () => {
    // set initial clock time and then start interval for clock
    displayClock();
    setInterval(displayClock, 1000);
});
```

Figure 8-7   The Clock app

The Timer app

Figure 8-8 presents a Timer app that requires the use of an interval timer. When the user clicks the Start Timer button, a prompt asks for a number of minutes between 1 and 10. Then, the timer is displayed above the button, and it counts down one second at a time. When the timer gets to zero, the app displays a message and clears the display.

The HTML defines a <p> element with an id of "display_timer" where the timer countdown is displayed. In addition, it defines a <button> element with an id of "start_timer" that starts the timer.

The code starts by defining two global variables: the timer variable for the timer object returned by setInterval() and the endTime variable for the Date object that contains the end time of the timer. Then, it defines four functions. The first two work the same as in the Clock app presented in the previous figure.

The displayTimer() function displays the countdown timer. To start, it creates a Date object that's set to the current date and time. Then it uses the getTime() method of the Date object to get the difference in milliseconds between the current time and the end time of the timer. Next, the code checks this difference. If the difference is less than or equal to zero, the timer has expired. In that case, the code calls the clearInterval() method, clears the timer display, and displays a dialog that notifies the user.

Otherwise, the code displays the number of minutes and seconds left on the timer. To do that, it creates a new Date object by passing the value of the diff constant to the Date() constructor. This creates a date that's the specified number of milliseconds past midnight, January 1, 1970 GMT, adjusted to the local time of the user's computer. For instance, if a user in the Pacific time zone sets a five minute timer, the Date() constructor produces the date Wed Dec 31 1969 16:05:00 GMT-0800. However, the app is only interested in the minutes and seconds (05:00) of this object, so it can ignore the rest of the date parts.

After creating the Date object, the code passes the return values of the getMinutes() and getSeconds() methods of the new date to the padValue() function. This pads single-digit values with a leading zero before assigning them to the minutes and seconds constants. Then, the code uses these values to update the timer display.

The startTimer() function uses a while loop to prompt the user until they enter a number of minutes from 1 to 10. Then, it sets the endTime global variable to the current time and adds the specified number of minutes. Next, the code calls the displayTimer() method to display the initial minutes and seconds of the timer. After that, the code starts the timer by calling the setInterval() method, passing it the displayTimer() function and 1,000 milliseconds. The timer object returned by setInterval() is assigned to the timer variable so the display-Timer() function can use it to stop the timer when the time is up.

The DOMContentLoaded event handler only contains a single statement. This statement attaches the startTimer() function to the click event of the Start Timer button.

The Timer app

Some of the HTML

```html
<h1>My Timer</h1>
<p id="display_timer"></p>
<button id="start_timer">Start Timer</button>
```

The JavaScript

```javascript
let timer = null;
let endTime = null;

const getElement = selector => document.querySelector(selector);
const padValue = value => value.toString().padStart(2, "0");

const displayTimer = () => {
    const now = new Date();
    const diff = endTime.getTime() - now.getTime();
    if (diff <= 0) {
        clearInterval(timer);
        getElement("#display_timer").textContent = "";
        alert("Time's up!!");
    } else {
        const timerDate = new Date(diff);
        const minutes = padValue(timerDate.getMinutes());
        const seconds = padValue(timerDate.getSeconds());
        getElement("#display_timer").textContent = `${minutes}:${seconds}`;
    }
};

const startTimer = () => {
    let minutes = NaN;
    while (!(minutes > 0 && minutes < 10)) {
        minutes = parseInt(prompt("Please enter 1 to 10 minutes."));
    }
    endTime = new Date();
    endTime.setMinutes(endTime.getMinutes() + minutes);
    displayTimer();
    timer = setInterval(displayTimer, 1000);
};

document.addEventListener("DOMContentLoaded", () => {
    getElement("#start_timer").addEventListener("click", startTimer);
});
```

Figure 8-8   The Timer app

The Slide Show app

Figure 8-9 presents a Slide Show app that requires the use of an interval timer. This app displays a new image and caption every two seconds.

The HTML defines four <a> elements within a <ul> element. Each of these <a> elements uses its href attribute to specify the location of an image in the slide show. In addition, each <a> element uses its title attribute to specify a caption for its image.

After the unordered list, the HTML defines the <img> element that displays the image for each slide. This element is followed by the <h2> element that displays the caption for each slide.

To keep this app simple, it doesn't provide any controls for stopping the slide show or moving through the slides manually. As a result, you should be aware that this app doesn't meet the best standards for usability or accessibility.

The CSS defines a style rule for the <ul> element that contains the list. Since the purpose of this list is to provide the captions and images for the slide show, the list shouldn't be displayed. That's why this CSS sets its display property to none.

The Slide Show app

Some of the HTML

```
<h1>Fishing Slide Show</h1>
<ul id="image_list">
    <li><a href="images/release.jpg" title="Catch and Release"></a></li>
    <li><a href="images/deer.jpg" title="Deer at Play"></a></li>
    <li><a href="images/hero.jpg" title="The Big One!"></a></li>
    <li><a href="images/bison.jpg" title="Roaming Bison"></a></li>
</ul>
<p><img id="main_image"></p>
<h2 id="caption"></h2>
```

The CSS for the <ul> element

```
ul {
    display: none;
}
```

Figure 8-9   The Slide Show app (part 1)

The second part of figure 8-9 presents the JavaScript for the Slide Show app. It starts by defining the getElement() helper function. Then, it defines the DOMContentLoaded event handler. To start, this event handler gets the nodes for the <img> element for the slide show and the <h2> element for the caption and assigns them to two constants. Next, it uses the querySelectorAll() method to get an array that contains one object for each <a> element in the <ul> element. In other words, it gets an array of links.

After getting the array of links, this code creates a constant named imageCache that's initialized to a new array. In addition, it creates a variable named image that's initialized to null. Then, this code loops through each of the <a> elements in the links array. Within this loop, the first three statements preload each image and set the alt property of each image to the title property of the current link. Next, the fourth statement adds the Image object to the imageCache array so it can be used later.

After preloading the images and adding them to the imageCache array, this code sets the initial image and caption to the first image in the array. To do that, it uses the properties of the first Image object.

At this point, the event handler starts the slide show by calling the setInterval() method. To do that, this code passes an anonymous function as the first parameter. Then, it passes 2,000 (two seconds) as the second parameter.

The anonymous function displays the next slide at the specified time interval. To start, it sets a variable named imageCounter to a value that determines which slide in the imageCache array to display next. To do that, it adds one to imageCounter, which was initialized to a value of zero. Then, it uses the modulus operator (%) to get the remainder when the imageCounter property is divided by the length of the imageCache array.

This causes the imageCounter property to range from 0 through one less than the length of the array. For example, if the imageCache array contains 4 images, the counter values will range from 0 through 3 (1%4=1; 2%4=2; 3%4=3; 4%4=0; 5%4=1, and so on). Since this code uses the counter as the index of the imageCache array, this anonymous function loops through the elements in the array and the index never becomes greater than 3.

The second statement in this anonymous function uses imageCounter as the index for the imageCache array and assigns that Image object to the image variable. The third statement sets the src attribute of the <img> element to the src attribute of the Image object. The fourth statement sets the alt attribute of the <img> element to the alt attribute of the Image object. And the last statement sets the text for the caption node to the alt attribute of the Image object. As soon as the code makes these changes to the DOM, the app displays the next image and caption in the browser.

The JavaScript

```javascript
const getElement = selector => document.querySelector(selector);

document.addEventListener("DOMContentLoaded", () => {
    // get elements for the image and caption
    const mainImage = getElement("#main_image");    // the <img> element
    const caption = getElement("#caption");         // the <h2> element

    // get all the <a> elements in the <ul> element
    const links = document.querySelectorAll("#image_list a");

    // process images
    const imageCache = [];
    let image = null;

    for (let link of links) {
        // Preload image
        image = new Image();
        image.src = link.href;
        image.alt = link.title;

        // add image to array
        imageCache.push(image);
    }

    // set initial image and caption
    mainImage.src = imageCache[0].src;
    mainImage.alt = imageCache[0].alt;
    caption.textContent = imageCache[0].alt;

    // start slide show
    let imageCounter = 0;
    setInterval(() => {  // first parameter - anonymous function
        // calculate the index for the current image
        imageCounter = (imageCounter + 1) % imageCache.length;

        // get image object from array
        image = imageCache[imageCounter];

        // set image and caption with values from image object
        mainImage.src = image.src;
        mainImage.alt = image.alt;
        caption.textContent = image.alt;
    },
    2000);                // second parameter - 2 second interval
});
```

Description

- The Slideshow app codes an anonymous arrow function directly as the first parameter of the setInterval() method. This is a common way to pass a function as a parameter.

- The Slideshow app doesn't need to stop the timer, so it doesn't assign the object returned by the setInterval() method to a variable.

Figure 8-9   The Slide Show app (part 2)

Perspective

Now that you've completed this chapter, you should be able to use Date objects to work with dates and times. In addition, you should be able to use timers to run a function after a specified interval of time. These skills are useful for a wide range of JavaScript apps.

Terms

constructor
Coordinated Universal Time (UTC)
Greenwich Mean Time (GMT)
timestamp
timer

Exercise 8-1   The Display Invoice app

This exercise has you write code that displays information about an invoice and calculates the number of days until it's due.

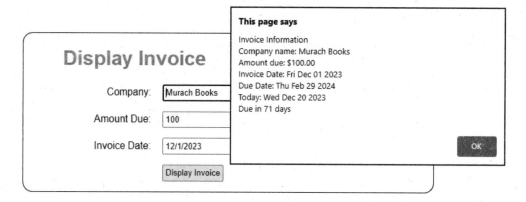

When you finish this exercise, you will have a dialog formatted as follows:

Invoice Information
Company name: Murach Books
Amount due: $100.00
Invoice Date: Fri Dec 01 2023
Due Date: Thu Feb 29 2024
Today: Wed Dec 20 2023
Due in 71 days

Review the starting code

1. View the files in this folder:

    `exercises\ch08\invoices`

2. Run the app. Then, click on the Display Invoice button and note that it displays a dialog that shows the data in the three text boxes.

Display the invoice date in the correct format

3. Open the display_invoice.js file and locate the displayInvoice() function.

4. Edit the statement that gets the invoice date so that it converts the string for the invoice date to a Date object.

5. Edit the statement that adds the invoice date to the invoice information so that it uses the toDateString() method of the Date object to display the string in the dialog.

6. Run the app. It should display the invoice date in the format shown above.

Calculate and display the due date

7. Within the displayInvoice() function, create a new Date object for a due date by making a copy of the invoice date.

8. Use the setDate() method of the due date to set it 90 days later than the invoice date. To do that, you can use the getDate() method of the invoice date and add 90 to it.

9. Add the due date to the displayed invoice information, formatted as shown above.

10. Run the app. It should display the due date in the format shown above.

Calculate and display the number of days until due

11. Within the displayInvoice() function, create a Date object for the current date and add code that displays that date in the dialog, formatted as shown above.

12. Calculate the number of milliseconds until the invoice is due by subtracting the number of milliseconds for the due date from the number of milliseconds for the current date and assign the result to a constant named msUntilDue.

13. Calculate the number of milliseconds in a day and assign it to a constant named msPerDay.

14. Calculate the number of days until the invoice is due. To do that, you can divide the msUntilDue constant by the msPerDay constant and use the Math. ceil() method to round the result up.

15. Check the number of days until the invoice is due and add an appropriate message to the dialog. If the number of days is 0, the message should say the invoice is due today. Otherwise, the message should indicate the number of days until the invoice is due or the number of days that the invoice is overdue.

16. Run the app and test it with invoice dates that cause the invoice to display all three messages.

Exercie 8-2   The Stopwatch App

This exercise has you create a Stopwatch app that uses three buttons. The Start button starts the stopwatch, the Stop button pauses it, and the Reset button resets it. If the stopwatch is stopped, you can resume timing by clicking Start again.

Review the starting code

1. View the files in this folder:

    `exercises\ch08\stopwatch`

2. Run the app. Click on the buttons and note that they don't work correctly.

3. Open the stopwatch.js file. Note that it contains the starting code for two functions and three event handlers. This includes a padNum() function that you can use to add leading zeros to a number.

Write the code for the Start button

4. Declare a global variable named startMS and initialize it to 0. This variable will store the number of milliseconds for the moment the timer was started.

5. Modify the code in the updateDisplay() function so it displays the minutes, seconds, and milliseconds for the amount of time that has elapsed since the timer was started. This function should use the padNum() function so the app displays the time with the mm:ss:mmm format.

6. In the startClick() event handler, use the getTime() function to set the startMS global variable to the number of milliseconds for the current time. Then, call the setInterval() function so it executes the updateDisplay() function every 10 milliseconds.

7. Run the app and test it to make sure the Start button works correctly.

Write the code for the Stop button

8. Declare a timer as a global variable, and modify the startClick() event handler so it assigns the timer returned by setInterval() to that global variable.

9. In the stopClick() event handler, use the clearInterval() function to stop the timer.

10. Run the app and test it to make sure the Stop button works. It should pause the timer. However, if you click Start to restart the stopwatch, the timer should start over instead of resuming from the elapsed time.

11. Declare a global variable named elapsedMS and initialize it to 0.

12. Modify the stopClick() event handler so it calculates the milliseconds for the elapsed time and assigns that value to the elapsedMS global variable. To do that, you can subtract the starting time from the current time.

13. Modify the startClick() event handler so it uses the global elapsedMS variable to set the global startMS variable to the correct value. To do that, you can subtract the elapsed time from the current time.

14. Run the app and test it to make sure the Stop and Start buttons now work correctly.

Write the code for the Rest button

15. In the resetClick() event handler, call the stopClick() event handler to stop the timer. Then, set the global elapsedMS variable to 0, and set the text of the time element to display a time of 00:00:000.

16. Run the app and test it to make sure that all three buttons work correctly.

9

How to work with data validation and exceptions

In chapter 6, you learned how to use DOM scripting to validate data by checking user entries and displaying error messages when the data is invalid. In this chapter, you'll learn two more ways to do that.

First, you'll learn how to use some of the features that are built into HTML and how to use JavaScript to customize those features. Then, you'll learn how to work with exceptions. When you finish this chapter, you'll have the skills you need to work with data validation and exceptions.

How to use HTML data validation

Data validation refers to checking data to make sure it's valid. For example, when a user enters data in a form and submits it to the server, the server-side code should perform complete data validation. Then, if any data is invalid, the server should return the form to the client so the user can correct the data.

To save round trips to the server, the client-side code typically performs some data validation as well. However, this validation doesn't have to be as thorough as the validation that's done on the server.

As you've already seen, you can use JavaScript to perform data validation on the client. However, HTML also provides features for data validation that don't require you to write any JavaScript code.

How to use input controls for data validation

Figure 9-1 begins by summarizing some types of input controls that can provide basic data validation for common input such as email addresses, numbers, and dates. Here, the type attribute of the <input> element indicates the type of data that the user should enter. Then, in some cases, the browser can validate the data that's entered. In other cases, the browser can assist the user in entering a valid value.

For example, if you set the type attribute to "email", all major browsers provide basic data validation for the email address that's entered into the text box, such as checking for the @ symbol and a domain name. If you set the type attribute to "number", all major browsers implement the control as a text box with up and down arrows that let the user increase or decrease the current value. And if you set the type attribute to "date", most major browsers provide a popup calendar that allows the user to select a date.

This figure also summarizes two HTML attributes for working with controls. First, the autofocus attribute moves the focus to the control when the form is loaded. As a result, you don't need to use JavaScript to do that. Second, the placeholder attribute puts some text in a control, which you can use to help the user enter the correct data in a valid format. When the user starts to enter data in the control, the browser removes the placeholder text. Note that this works differently than a default value because the browser doesn't submit placeholder text to the server.

The code example in this figure illustrates some of these controls and attributes. To start, the <input> element that accepts an email address has its type attribute set to "email". In addition, this element includes the autofocus attribute. As a result, the browser moves the focus to this control when the page is first displayed. The form in this figure shows the error message that's displayed in Chrome when an invalid entry is made in this control.

The input control that accepts a telephone number has its type attribute set to "tel". Although none of the current browsers provide data validation for this type, it's still considered a good practice to use this attribute for telephone numbers because it clearly identifies the content of your web page. This control

Common types of input controls

Type	Description
email	Gets an email address with validation done by the browser.
url	Gets a URL with validation done by the browser.
tel	Gets a telephone number with no validation done by the browser.
number	Gets a numeric entry with min, max, and step attributes, browser validation, and up and down arrows.
range	Gets a numeric entry with min, max, and step attributes, browser validation, and a slider control.
date	Gets a date entry with min and max attributes and may include a popup calendar or up and down arrows.
time	Gets a time entry with min and max attributes and may include up and down arrows.

Two attributes for working with controls

Attribute	Description
autofocus	Tells the browser to set the focus on the control when the page is loaded.
placeholder	A message in the control that is removed when an entry is made by the user.

A form that uses some of these controls and attributes

```
<form action="join.php" method="post">
    <label for="email_address">Email Address:</label>
    <input type="email" id="email_address" name="email_address" autofocus><br>

    <label for="name">Name:</label>
    <input type="text" id="name" name="name"><br>

    <label for="phone">Phone Number:</label>
    <input type="tel" id="phone" name="phone" placeholder="999-999-9999"><br>

    <label> </label>
    <input type="submit" id="join_list" value="Join our List"><br>
</form>
```

The form in Chrome with an error message for the email address

Description

- The <input> element provides basic data validation for some common types of input.

Figure 9-1   How to use input controls for data validation

also uses the placeholder attribute to indicate the format of the phone number should be 999-999-9999. Note that Chrome displays this placeholder in a lighter color than the value for the email control.

How to use attributes for data validation

In addition to the input controls presented in the last figure, HTML provides some attributes specifically for data validation. Figure 9-2 begins by summarizing these attributes. To start, the required attribute causes the browser to check whether a control is empty before it submits the form for processing. If the control is empty, the browser displays a message and doesn't submit the form.

If you code a title attribute for a control, the browser displays the value of that attribute when the mouse hovers over the control. It may also display that value at the end of the browser's standard error message for a control.

The pattern attribute provides for data validation through the use of regular expressions. Regular expressions are patterns that can be used to validate user entries like credit card numbers, zip codes, dates, or phone numbers. Regular expressions are supported by many programming languages, including JavaScript and HTML.

If you want to stop a control or form from being validated, you can code the novalidate attribute. And if you want to turn the auto-completion feature off for a control, you can set its autocomplete attribute to "off". By default, all modern browsers set autocomplete to "on". As a result, a browser displays a list of entry options when the user starts the entry for a control. These options are based on the entries the user has previously made for controls with similar names.

The code example in this figure shows how you can use some of these attributes. This form has the same controls as the form presented in the previous figure. However, it includes the required attribute for each input control. As a result, the user must make an entry for each control. In addition, it turns off the auto-completion feature for the email control, and it specifies a pattern and title for the phone control. You'll learn how this pattern works in the next figure.

The form below the code example shows the error message that's displayed if the user enters a phone number with an invalid format. This error message includes the browser's standard error message as well as the text that's specified by the title attribute for this control.

HTML attributes for data validation

Attribute	Description
required	Indicates that a value is required for a control.
title	Text that is displayed in a tooltip when the mouse hovers over a control. This text may also display as part of the browser's default error message.
pattern	A regular expression that is used to validate the entry in a control.
novalidate	Tells the browser that it shouldn't validate a form or a control.
autocomplete	Set this attribute to "off" to tell the browser to disable auto-completion for a form or a control.

A form that uses attributes for data validation

```
<form action="join.php" method="post">
    <label for="email_address">Email Address:</label>
    <input type="email" id="email_address" name="email_address"
        required autofocus autocomplete="off"><br>

    <label for="name">Name:</label>
    <input type="text" id="name" name="name" required><br>

    <label for="phone">Phone Number:</label>
    <input type="tel" id="phone" name="phone" required
        pattern="\d{3}[\-]\d[3][\-]\d{4}"
        title="Must be 999-999-9999"><br>

    <label> </label>
    <input type="submit" id="join_list" value="Join our List"><br>
</form>
```

The form in Chrome with an error message for the phone control

How HTML data validation is limited

* The HTML controls and attributes for data validation may not be implemented the same way by all browsers.
* HTML is limited in the types of validation it can do. For example, HTML can't check whether one control is equal to another.

Figure 9-2   How to use attributes for data validation

An introduction to regular expressions

Figure 9-3 presents some of the basics for working with regular expressions. A *regular expression* (or *regex* for short) defines a *pattern* that can be searched for in a string. The trick to using regular expressions is coding the patterns. The first thing to know is that letters and numbers usually represent themselves in a pattern.

The first table in this figure shows how to include special characters in a pattern. To do that, you start with the *escape character*, which is the backslash. For instance, `\\` is equivalent to one backslash; `\/` is equivalent to one forward slash; and `\xA9` is equivalent to `\u00A9`, which is equivalent to the copyright symbol.

However, this table doesn't include all of the special characters that you need to precede with backslashes. For instance, the second table points out that you need to use `\.` to represent a period and `\[` to represent a bracket.

The second table shows how to match types of characters instead of specific characters. For example, the pattern `MB\d` matches the letters MB followed by any digit. And the pattern `MB...` matches MB followed by any three characters.

The third table shows how to group and match a *subpattern* that's coded in parentheses. If you code more than one subpattern in a pattern, the patterns are numbered from left to right.

The fourth table presents *quantifiers* that match repeating characters, types, or subpatterns. For instance, `\d{3}` matches any three digits in succession, and `\${1,3}` matches from one to three occurrences of a dollar sign.

The example presents two input controls where each control has a pattern attribute that contains a regular expression. The first regular expression validates a phone number. The first part of the regular expression, `\d{3}`, matches three digits. Then the next part, `[\-]`, matches a dash. The rest of the regular expression is similar, matching three digits, a dash, and then four digits. This regular expression matches phone numbers like 555-123-4567 but not 555.123.4567.

The second regular expression validates a zip code that's five or nine digits. The first part of the regular expression, `\d{5}`, matches five digits. The rest of the regular expression is within parentheses that are followed by the question mark quantifier. The parentheses indicate a subpattern, and the quantifier matches zero or one occurrences of this subpattern. The first part of the subpattern, `[\-]`, matches a dash. The rest of the subpattern, `\d{4}`, matches four digits. This regular expression matches zip codes like 97234 and 01234-5432.

The information in this figure should get you started coding regular expressions of your own. Before you try to code a complex pattern, though, you might want search the internet to see if you can find the regular expression you're looking for. You'll probably find that someone else has already written the pattern you need. Just be sure to test the regular expression thoroughly to make sure it works correctly.

How to match special characters

Pattern	Matches
\\	Backslash
\/	Forward slash
\t	Tab
\n	New line
\udddd	The Unicode character whose value is the four hexadecimal digits.
\xdd	The Latin-1 character whose value is the two hexadecimal digits. Equivalent to \u00dd.

How to match types of characters

Pattern	Matches
.	Any character except a new line (use \. to match a period)
[ ]	Any character in the brackets (use \[or \] to match a bracket)
[^]	Any character not in the brackets
[a-z]	Any character in the range of characters when used inside brackets
\w	Any letter, number, or the underscore
\W	Any character that's not a letter, number, or the underscore
\d	Any digit
\D	Any character that's not a digit
\s	Any whitespace character (space, tab, new line, carriage return, form feed, or vertical tab)
\S	Any character that's not whitespace

How to group and match subpatterns

Pattern	Matches
(subpattern)	Creates a subpattern (use \(and \) to match a parenthesis)
|	Matches either the left or right subpattern (use \\| to match a vertical bar)

How to match a repeating pattern

Pattern	Matches
{n}	Pattern must repeat exactly *n* times (use \{ and \} to match a brace)
{n,}	Pattern must repeat *n* or more times
{n,m}	Subpattern must repeat from *n* to *m* times
?	Zero or one of the previous subpattern (same as {0,1})
+	One or more of the previous subpattern (same as {1,})
*	Zero or more of the previous subpattern (same as {0,})

Input controls that validate a phone number and a zip code

```
<input type="tel" id="phone" name="phone" pattern="\d{3}[\-]\d{3}[\-]\d{4}">
<input type="text" name="zip" id="zip" pattern="\d{5}([\-]\d{4})?">
```

Figure 9-3   An introduction to regular expressions

The Register app

To show you how you can use HTML for basic data validation, figure 9-4 presents the Register app. This app validates the same data as the app presented in chapter 6. However, unlike that version of the app, this one doesn't use any JavaScript. Instead, it uses the features of HTML to validate the user's entries.

To start, this figure shows the user interface for this app. After the user enters data and clicks the Register button, the browser checks the data for validity. Then, if the data isn't valid, the browser displays a message like the one shown here.

The HTML for the form includes three text boxes, a drop-down list, three radio buttons, and a check box. The text boxes, drop-down list, and check box all have a required attribute, so the user must enter some data in these controls. Otherwise, the app shows a message like the one shown in this figure. This is true even for the drop-down list, since the first option has a value of an empty string. As a result, the user must select another option.

The email text box has a placeholder attribute that provides the user guidance on the format that the email entry should follow. In addition, both the email and phone text boxes have the autocomplete attribute set to off.

The email text box has an autofocus attribute. As a result, the browser sets the focus on this text box when the page loads. The phone text box has a pattern attribute with a regular expression for a phone number, as well as a title attribute that explains the format that the regular expression matches.

The DOB text box has a type value of "date". As a result, Chrome provides the placeholder shown in this figure. In addition, it provides a calendar icon that, when clicked, provides a small pop-up calendar that you can use to select a date.

These input controls are followed by a submit button and a reset button. The submit button starts the data validation, and the reset button resets all the controls to their original state.

The Register app with an error message

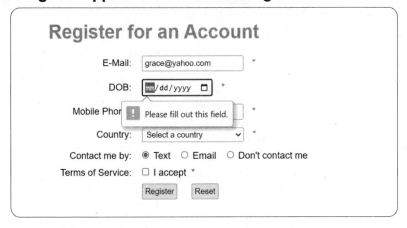

The HTML for the <form> element

```html
<form action="confirm.html" method="post">
    <label for="email_address">E-Mail:</label>
    <input type="email" name="email_address" id="email_address"
        placeholder="name@domain.com" autocomplete="off" autofocus required>
    <span>*</span><br>

    <label for="dob">DOB:</label>
    <input type="date" name="dob" id="dob" required>
    <span>*</span><br>

    <label for="phone">Mobile Phone:</label>
    <input type="tel" name="phone" id="phone" autocomplete="off" required
        pattern="\d{3}[\-]\d{3}[\-]\d{4}" title="Must be nnn-nnn-nnnn">
    <span>*</span><br>

    <label for="country">Country:</label>
    <select name="country" id="country" required>
        <option value="">Select a country</option>
        <option>USA</option>
        <option>Canada</option>
        <option>Mexico</option>
    </select>
    <span>*</span><br>

    <label>Contact me by:</label>
    <input type="radio" name="contact" id="text" value="text" checked>Text
    <input type="radio" name="contact" id="email" value="email">Email
    <input type="radio" name="contact" id="none" value="none">
    Don't contact me<br>

    <label>Terms of Service:</label>
    <input type="checkbox" name="terms" id="terms" required>I accept
    <span>*</span><br>

    <label> </label>
    <input type="submit" id="register" value="Register">
    <input type="reset" id="reset_form" value="Reset">
</form>
```

Figure 9-4   The Register app

How to customize HTML validation

For simple forms, you may be able to get by using input controls and data validation attributes as shown so far in this chapter. However, the data validation that's provided by HTML won't always suit your needs. For example, Chrome displays one validation message at a time, but you might want to display all of the validation messages at once. Similarly, you might want to validate a control based on the value of another control, such as confirming a password.

In that case, you can use the methods and properties provided by the *Constraint Validation API*. This API is implemented by all modern browsers, and it lets you use JavaScript to customize the data validation features available from HTML.

How to validate an element or a form

Figure 9-5 presents a method and a property of an HTML element. If you call the checkValidity() method on an individual element, it checks the data in that element. If you call this method on a form, it checks the data of all the elements on the form. In either case, if the data is valid, the method returns true. Otherwise, it returns false and raises an invalid event. The validationMessage property returns the standard validation message that's provided by the browser.

The first example in this figure presents an HTML form with data validation attributes, including the novalidate attribute. This attribute tells the browser not to display the default validation messages. Instead, the code in the second and third examples provides those validation messages.

The second example shows how to validate the email text box when the blur event fires, which happens when the user moves the focus away from the text box. This can be useful if you want to give the user immediate validation feedback rather than waiting until the form submits.

To start, the code gets the email text box element and attaches an event handler for the blur event. This event handler clears any previous error message in the <span> element that follows the text box. Then, it calls the checkValidity() method of the text box. Next, the code attaches an event handler for the invalid event that's raised by the checkValidity() method if data is invalid. This event handler uses the validationMessage property to display the standard validation message in the <span> element. Finally, it sets the focus on the text box.

The third example shows how to validate all the elements on the form when the form is submitted. This displays all of the validation messages at once.

To start, the code gets the form and loops through all the elements in the form. Within the loop, the code attaches an event handler for the invalid event of each element. This event handler displays the standard validation message in the associated <span> element. Then, this code attaches an event handler for the submit event of the form. This event handler clears any previous error messages in the associated <span> elements for each element. Next, it calls the checkValidity() method of the form. If any of the elements of the form contain invalid data, this method returns false. In that case, the form isn't submitted.

A method and property of an element for data validation

Method/Property	Description
`checkValidity()`	A method that returns true if all the data in a form or element is valid. Otherwise, returns false and raises an invalid event.
`validationMessage`	A property that gets a string for the browser's standard validation message.

The HTML for a form with <span> elements for error messages

```
<form action="join.php" method="post" novalidate>
    <label for="email_address">Email Address:</label>
    <input type="email" id="email_address" name="email_address" required>
    <span>*</span><br>

    <label for="name">Name:</label>
    <input type="text" id="name" name="name" required>
    <span>*</span><br>

    <label> </label>
    <input type="submit" id="join_list" value="Join our List"><br>
</form>
```

Validate the email text box on blur

```
const email = getElement("#email_address");
email.addEventListener("blur", () => {
    email.nextElementSibling.textContent = "*";    // clear previous message
    email.checkValidity();                         // raises invalid event if invalid
});
email.addEventListener("invalid", () => {
    email.nextElementSibling.textContent = email.validationMessage;
    email.focus();
});
```

Validate the form on submit

```
const form = getElement("form");

// attach a handler for the invalid event for each control on the form
for (let element of form.elements) {
    element.addEventListener("invalid", evt => {
        const span = evt.currentTarget.nextElementSibling;
        if (span) span.textContent = evt.currentTarget.validationMessage;
    });
}

form.addEventListener("submit", evt => {
    // clear previous error messages
    for (let element of form.elements) {
        const span = element.nextElementSibling;
        if (span) span.textContent = "*";
    }

    if (!form.checkValidity()) {
        evt.preventDefault();
    }
});
```

Figure 9-5   How to validate an element or a form

In addition, the invalid event for each element with invalid data is raised and handled. This displays all of the validation messages at once.

How to create custom validation

Figure 9-6 presents the setCustomValidity() method of an HTML element. This method accepts a string value and sets this value as a custom validation message for the element. To remove any previous custom validation messages for the element, you pass an empty string to this method.

The first example in this figure presents the form from the previous figure with two more text boxes for the user to enter a password and confirm that password. To save space, the email and name input elements aren't shown here, but they're the same as in figure 9-5.

The second example shows how to add custom validation to the code that validates the form when the submit event fires. Like the code in the previous figure, this code starts by getting the form, attaching an event handler for the invalid event of each element, and attaching an event handler for the submit event of the form.

The submit event handler begins by clearing any previous messages in the <span> elements. Then, it checks whether the values in the password and confirm password text boxes match. If not, the code passes an appropriate error message to the setCustomValidity() method of the confirm password text box. Otherwise, it passes an empty string to the setCustomValidity() method to remove any previous validation message.

After setting or removing the custom message, this code calls the checkValidity() method of the form. If any of the elements of the form contain invalid data, including the custom validation for the confirm password text box, this method returns false. And, as before, the invalid event for each element with invalid data is raised and handled and the validation messages for the invalid elements are displayed. Then, the code prevents the form from being submitted.

A method of an element that customizes a validation message

Method	Description
`setCustomValidity(msg)`	Sets a custom validation message for the element. To remove a previous validation message, set an empty string.

The HTML for a form

```
<form action="join.php" method="post" novalidate>
    <!-- email and name input elements -->

    <label for="password">Password: </label>
    <input type="password" name="password" id="password" required>
    <span>*</span><br>

    <label for="confirm">Confirm Password: </label>
    <input type="password" name="confirm" id="confirm" required>
    <span>*</span><br>

    <label></label>
    <input type="submit" id="join_list" value="Join our List"><br>
</form>
```

Validate the form on submit

```
const form = getElement("form");

// attach a handler for the invalid event for each control on the form
for (let element of form.elements) {
    element.addEventListener("invalid", evt => {
        const span = evt.currentTarget.nextElementSibling;
        if (span) span.textContent = evt.currentTarget.validationMessage;
    });
}

form.addEventListener("submit", evt => {
    // clear previous error messages
    for (let element of form.elements) {
        const span = element.nextElementSibling;
        if (span) span.textContent = "*";
    }

    // check if password and confirm password match
    const password = getElement("#password");
    const confirm = getElement("#confirm");

    if (password.value !== confirm.value) {
        confirm.setCustomValidity("Passwords must match.");
    } else {
        confirm.setCustomValidity(""); // remove any previous message
    }

    if (!form.checkValidity()) {
        evt.preventDefault();
    }
});
```

Figure 9-6   How to create custom validation

The Register app 2.0

Figure 9-7 presents an updated version of the Register app from figure 9-4. This version uses methods and properties from the Constraint Validation API to enhance the data validation. Specifically, it displays all the validation messages at once instead of one at a time, replaces some of the standard messages with more user-friendly messages, and checks to make sure the user is at least 13 years old.

The HTML for this version of the app uses the title attribute to store user-friendly messages for most of the controls on the form. The browser displays these messages when the user hovers over the control. In addition, if the form contains invalid data and the user clicks the Register button, the app displays these messages in the <span> element associated with the control.

In this figure, the <form> element doesn't have a novalidate attribute. That's because the JavaScript for the app adds this attribute.

The Register app with error messages

The HTML for the <form> element

```
<form action="confirm.html" method="post">
    <label for="email_address">E-Mail:</label>
    <!-- same as figure 9-4 -->

    <label for="dob">DOB:</label>
    <input type="date" name="dob" id="dob" required
        title="You must be at least 13 years old." >
    <span>*</span><br>

    <label for="phone">Mobile Phone:</label>
    <input type="tel" name="phone" id="phone" autocomplete="off" required
        placeholder="nnn-nnn-nnnn" pattern="\d{3}[\-]\d{3}[\-]\d{4}"
        title="Must be nnn-nnn-nnnn format." >
    <span>*</span><br>

    <label for="country">Country:</label>
    <select name="country" id="country" required
        title="Please select a country." >
        <option value="">Select a country</option>
        <option>USA</option>
        <option>Canada</option>
        <option>Mexico</option></select>
    <span>*</span><br>

    <label>Contact me by:</label>
    <!-- same as figure 9-4 -->

    <label>Terms of Service:</label>
    <input type="checkbox" name="terms" id="terms" required
        title="Please accept the terms of service.">I accept
    <span>*</span><br>

    <label> </label>
    <!-- same as figure 9-4 -->
</form>
```

Figure 9-7   The Register app 2.0 (part 1)

Part 2 of figure 9-7 presents the JavaScript for the updated Register app. To start, this code defines a getElement() helper function that gets the specified HTML element. Then, it defines a helper function named clearMessages() that accepts an object that represents a form, loops the elements of that form, and resets the text of the associated <span> element with an asterisk.

The DOMContentLoaded event handler starts by getting the form and setting its noValidate property to true. This turns off the default HTML data validation just as if you had coded the novalidate attribute in the <form> element.

After turning off the default HMTL validation, the code loops through the elements of the form and attaches an invalid event handler for each element. This event handler assigns the element that raised the event to a constant named elem.

Then, it sets a constant named msg based on whether that element has a title property. If it does, this code assigns the value of the title property to the msg constant. Otherwise, it assigns the value of the validationMessage property to the msg constant.

Finally, it gets the <span> element that's associated with the element that raised the event. If that element exists, the code assigns the value of the msg constant to its textContent property.

After attaching the invalid event handler to each element on the form, this code attaches an event handler for the submit event of the form. In addition, it attaches an event handler for the click event of the Reset button.

The submit event handler of the form begins by clearing any previous validation messages. Then, it uses custom validation to check if the user is at least 13 years old. To do this, the code gets the string that's stored in the date-of-birth text box and creates a Date object from it. Next, it creates a Date object for the current date and subtracts 13 from the year. This creates a Date object that's exactly 13 years in the past from the current date.

After creating the two Date objects, the code sets a msg constant based on the comparison of the date of birth entered by the user with the date that's 13 years in the past. If the dob value is greater than that date, the user isn't 13 years old. In that case, the code assigns the value of the element's title property to the msg constant. Otherwise, the code assigns an empty string. Then, the code passes the value of the msg constant to the setCustomValidity() method of the date-of-birth text box. If the value is an empty string, this removes any previous validation message. Otherwise, it sets the validation message.

The submit event handler ends by calling the checkValidity() method of the form to check if the controls on the form are valid. If not, this code prevents the form from being submitted and displays the validation messages on the form.

The click event handler for the Reset button begins by clearing any previous validation messages. Then it sets the focus on the first control on the form, which is the email address text box.

The JavaScript

```javascript
const getElement = selector => document.querySelector(selector);

const clearMessages = form => {
    for (let element of form.elements) {
        const span = element.nextElementSibling;
        if (span) span.textContent = "*";
    }
};

document.addEventListener("DOMContentLoaded", () => {
    const form = getElement("form");

    // turn off default HTML validation messages
    form.noValidate = true;

    // attach invalid event handler for form controls
    for (let element of form.elements) {
        element.addEventListener("invalid", evt => {
            const elem = evt.currentTarget;
            const msg = elem.title ? elem.title : elem.validationMessage;

            const span = elem.nextElementSibling;
            if (span) span.textContent = msg;
        });
    }

    form.addEventListener("submit", evt => {
        clearMessages(form);

        // do custom age validation
        const dobElement = getElement("#dob");
        const dob = new Date(dobElement.value);

        const limit = new Date();
        limit.setFullYear(limit.getFullYear() - 13);

        const msg = (dob > limit) ? dobElement.title : "";
        dobElement.setCustomValidity(msg);

        // validate form
        if (!form.checkValidity()) {
            evt.preventDefault();
        }
    });

    getElement("#reset_form").addEventListener("click", () => {
        clearMessages(form);
        getElement("#email_address").focus();
    });
});
```

Figure 9-7   The Register app 2.0 (part 2)

How to work with exceptions

Runtime errors can also be referred to as *exceptions*. Most programming languages provide a way to handle the exceptions that are thrown by an app so the app doesn't crash. This process is referred to as *exception handling*.

How to use try-catch statements

To handle exceptions in JavaScript, you use a *try-catch statement* as shown in figure 9-8. First, you code a *try block* around the statement or statements that may throw an exception. Then, you code a *catch block* that contains the statements to execute if an exception is thrown in the try block.

If necessary, you can also code a *finally block* that's executed whether or not an exception is thrown, but that block is optional. Typically, cleanup code such as releasing resources goes in this block. That way, you can be sure your cleanup code executes even if the code in the catch block has a return statement or unexpectedly throws an exception.

The first example in this figure shows how you can use a try-catch statement to catch any exceptions that are thrown in the try block. Then, if an exception is thrown by one of the statements in that block, the execution of the program jumps to the first statement in the catch block. In this example, the catch block contains a single statement that displays an error message.

When an exception is thrown, JavaScript creates an Error object that contains information about the exception. To access the Error object, you code a parameter name in the parentheses after the catch keyword. Then, you can use the name and message properties of the Error object to process the error. This is illustrated by the catch block in the first example. Here, the code uses a parameter named e to access the Error object. Using e as the parameter name is a common practice, but you can use a longer name such as err or error if you prefer.

Just because you code a parameter within the parentheses of a catch block doesn't mean you have to use that parameter. This is illustrated by the catch block in the second example. Here, the catch block displays a custom message without accessing the Error object. In cases like this, you can omit the parentheses and error parameter from the catch block as shown in the last example.

If JavaScript throws an exception and that exception isn't caught by a try-catch statement, JavaScript passes the exception to the calling function. This passing of the exception continues until the exception is caught or the app ends with a runtime error. When this happens, you can open the Console panel of the developer tools to view information about the error.

An interesting feature of JavaScript is that it throws fewer exceptions than most other languages. For example, JavaScript doesn't throw an exception when it can't convert a string to a number. Instead, it returns a value of NaN. As a result, you need to do less exception handling when you use JavaScript than you do with most other languages.

The syntax for a try-catch statement

```
try { statements }
catch(error) { statements }
[ finally { statements } ]          // the finally block is optional
```

Two properties of the Error object

Property	Description
name	The type of error.
message	A message that describes the error.

A function with a try-catch statement

```
const calcFutureValue = (investment, rate, years) => {
    try {
        let futureValue = investment;
        for (let i = 1; i <= years; i++) {
            futureValue += futureValue * rate / 100;
        }
        return futureValue.toFixed(2);
    }
    catch(e) {
        console.log(e.name + ": " + e.message)
    }
};
```

A catch block that displays a custom message

```
catch(e) {
    console.log("The calcFutureValue function has thrown an error.");
}
```

A catch block with no error parameter

```
catch {
    console.log("The calcFutureValue function has thrown an error.");
}
```

Description

- You can use a *try-catch statement* to process any errors that are thrown by an app. These errors are referred to as *exceptions*, and this process is known as *exception handling*.

- In a try-catch statement, you code a *try block* around any statements that may throw exceptions. Then, you code a *catch block* that contains the statements that are executed when an exception is thrown in the try block.

- The optional *finally block* is executed whether or not the statements in the catch block are executed.

- The parameter in the catch block gives you access to the Error object that's created when an error is thrown. This object has two properties that you can use to display the error type and message.

- If you don't need to use the Error object, you can omit the parameter.

Figure 9-8   How to use try-catch statements

How to create and throw exceptions

In some cases, you want to throw your own, custom exceptions. If, for example, you create functions that other programmers use, you can throw exceptions to let them know when an error has occurred.

To throw an exception, you use the *throw keyword* to create a *throw statement*. The throw statement can throw an Error object that already exists, or it can throw a new Error object as shown in figure 9-9.

To create a new Error object, you can use the *new* keyword to call the Error() constructor and pass it a parameter that provides the message for the error. This sets the message in the message property of the Error object. In general, it's considered a best practice to make your message as specific as possible about what caused the error and where in the code it occurred.

After you create an Error object, you can use a throw statement to throw it. This is illustrated by the first example in this figure. Here, a function that calculates a future value throws an exception if the investment value it receives is invalid. The error message includes information about which function and which parameter caused the problem.

If the code in the first example throws an exception at runtime, execution of the function ends and code execution jumps to the code that called the function. Then, the code that called the function can catch the exception and display its message property. In this figure, the second example uses a try-catch statement to catch the exception.

In general, it's considered a best practice to prevent exceptions from occurring whenever possible instead of allowing them to be thrown and then catching them. For example, it would be a better practice for the second example to make sure that it only passed valid values to the calcFutureValue() function. Then, the call to the function wouldn't cause an exception to be thrown, and the try-catch statement wouldn't be needed. However, for truly exceptional situations, such as when a server is down, it's a best practice to use a try-catch statement to catch the exception that's thrown.

Another use for the throw statement is to test that errors are being caught and handled appropriately. To do that, you can code a throw statement in a try block to be sure the catch block works the way you want.

In some cases, you may want to perform some processing in the catch block when an error occurs and then re-throw the error. To do that, you catch the error, perform the necessary processing, and throw the error again. Then, code execution jumps to the calling code.

The table in this figure shows that JavaScript provides different types of built-in Error objects that you can use. For instance, when a numeric value isn't within an allowable range, you can throw a RangeError object, not a generic Error object. Then, the name property of that object is set to "RangeError", not "Error".

The syntax to create an Error object

```
new Error(message)
```

The syntax to throw an exception

```
throw errorObject;
```

A function that throws an exception

```
const calcFutureValue = (investment, rate, years) => {
    if (isNaN(investment) || investment <= 0) {
        const msg = "calcFutureValue requires investment greater than 0.";
        throw new Error(msg);
    }

    let futureValue = investment;
    for (let i = 1; i <= years; i++ ) {
        futureValue += futureValue * rate / 100;
    }
    return futureValue.toFixed(2);
};
```

A try-catch statement that catches an exception

```
try {
    const fv = calcFutureValue(investment, rate, years);
    getElement("#future_value").value = fv;
} catch(e) {
    console.log(e.name + ": " + e.message);
}
```

Some types of Error objects

Type	Thrown when
Error	A generic error has occurred
RangeError	A numeric value exceeds the allowable range
TypeError	The type of a value is different from what was expected

A statement that throws a range error

```
throw new RangeError("Annual rate must be greater than zero.");
```

Three reasons for using throw statements

- To alert code that calls a function that something is wrong
- To test the operation of a try-catch statement
- To perform some processing after catching an error and then throw the error again

Description

- To create a new Error object, you use the Error() constructor with a string parameter.
- To throw an exception, you use a *throw statement* to throw an Error object.

Figure 9-9   How to create and throw exceptions

The Future Value app

Figure 9-10 presents a version of the Future Value app that accepts a total investment amount and number of years from the user and simulates getting the interest rate from a service provided by an external server. If the server is down, the app displays a message like the one shown by the second screen in this figure.

The HTML shows that the form includes three text boxes, two buttons, and <span> and <p> elements for messages. You can also see that this form uses HTML attributes for data validation. For instance, the first two text boxes have a required attribute, and the first text box has an autofocus attribute.

In addition, the first two text boxes use the number type, so up and down arrows appear when the text box has focus as shown by the first screen in this figure. The min and max attributes set the minimum and maximum values for the up and down arrows, and the step attribute sets the increment for the arrows.

If the user presses the up and down arrow keys, the current value of the text box increases or decreases by the amount in the step attribute, and stops when it reaches the value in the min or max attribute. However, if the user types in a value, they can enter a value that's out of the acceptable range as shown by the first screen in this figure.

The third text box displays the future value. This text box has a disabled attribute to make the text box read-only and to skip over it if the user tabs from the years text box.

After the form, the HTML defines <script> elements for two JavaScript files. The first JavaScript file contains functions that calculate a future value and the second file contains code that calls these functions. Because of that, the <script> element for the first file must be coded above the <script> element for the second file.

The Future Value app with error messages

The Future Value Calculator

Total investment: `-1`   Value must be greater than or equal to 0.

Number of years: `100`   Value must be less than or equal to 10.

Future value:

[Calculate]   [Clear]

The Future Value Calculator

Total investment: `100`   *

Number of years: `10`   *

Future value:

[Calculate]   [Clear]

Error: Unable to calculate future value. Interest Rate API is down.

The HTML for the <body> element

```html
<body>
    <form action="#" method="post">
        <h1>The Future Value Calculator</h1>

        <label for="investment">Total investment:</label>
        <input type="number" id="investment"
            min="0" max="1000" step="100" required autofocus>
        <span>*</span><br>

        <label for="years">Number of years:</label>
        <input type="number" id="years" min="0" max="10" step="1" required>
        <span>*</span><br>

        <label>Future value:</label>
        <input type="text" id="future_value" disabled><br>

        <label></label>
        <input type="submit" id="calculate" value="Calculate">
        <input type="reset" id="clear" value="Clear">

        <p id="message"></p>
    </form>

    <script src="calc_future_value.js"></script>
    <script src="future_value.js"></script>
</body>
```

Figure 9-10   The Future Value app (part 1)

Part 2 of figure 9-10 presents the JavaScript that's stored in the calc_future_value.js file. For demonstration purposes, this file has a function named getCurrentInterestRate() that simulates a call to an external server that occasionally fails. To do that, this function generates a random number between 1 and 10. When the number is 1, the function creates and throws an error indicating that the server is down. Otherwise, it returns an interest rate value of 3.9.

The calcFutureValue() function defines parameters for an investment amount and a number of years. This function starts by converting its parameters to numeric values. Then, it checks that the converted values are valid numbers greater than zero. If either is not, the function throws an exception.

If the function receives valid data from the user, it calls the getCurrentInterestRate() function to get the interest rate. However, since that function may fail, the code calls it from within the try block of a try-catch statement. Then, if an exception occurs, the catch block creates and throws a new Error object.

If all the data is valid, the code calculates and returns the future value. To do that, it uses the toFixed() method to round the future value to two decimal places, and it uses the Number() function to convert the resulting string back to a number.

The calc_future_value.js file

```javascript
// function that simulates an external service that is sometimes down
function getCurrentInterestRate() {
    const random = Math.ceil(Math.random() * 10);
    if (random === 1) {
        throw new Error("Interest Rate server is down.");
    } else {
        return 3.9;
    }
};

function calcFutureValue(investment, years) {
    // convert to numeric values
    investment = parseFloat(investment);
    years = parseInt(years);

    // throw error if investment or years aren't numbers greater than zero
    if (isNaN(investment) || investment <= 0) {
        throw new Error("Investment must be a number greater than zero.");
    }
    if (isNaN(years) || years <= 0) {
        throw new Error("Years must be a number greater than zero.");
    }

    // get interest rate - throw error if service returns an error
    let rate = 0;
    try {
        rate = getCurrentInterestRate();
    } catch(e) {
        throw new Error("Unable to calculate future value. " + e.message);
    }

    // if no errors, calculate and return future value
    let futureValue = investment;
    for (let i = 1; i <= years; i++) {
        futureValue += futureValue * rate / 100;
    }
    return Number(futureValue.toFixed(2));
};
```

Figure 9-10   The Future Value app (part 2)

Part 3 of figure 9-10 presents the future_value.js file. This code starts with the getElement() helper function that gets the specified HTML element. Then, it defines the clearMessages() helper function that resets the text of the <span> elements to an asterisk and also sets the text of the <p> element that displays messages to an empty string.

The DOMContentLoaded event handler begins by getting the <form> element and setting its noValidate property to true. Then, it attaches an event handler for the invalid event to each element. This event handler displays the value of the element's validationMessage property in the associated <span> element. Then, the code attaches the submit event handler of the form and the click event handler of the Clear button.

The submit event handler of the form starts by clearing any previous validation messages. Then, it prevents the form from being submitted to the server. That's because this app isn't designed to submit data. However, HTML data validation only works when a form is submitted. As a result, this app submits the form to activate the HTML data validation. Then, it cancels the submission.

After preventing the form from being submitted, the code gets the future value text box and clears any previous future value by setting the text of that element to an empty string. Then, it calls the checkValidity() method of the form to make sure the user entered valid data for the total investment and number of years. It does this even though the calcFutureValue() function throws exceptions if this data is invalid. That's because it's considered a best practice to prevent exceptions from occurring whenever possible instead of catching them. As a result, you should only need to catch exceptions in truly exceptional situations such as when a server is down.

One reason to prevent exceptions instead of catching them is that it tends to lead to better performance. Another reason is that it can improve the user experience. For example, with this app, if the user leaves both text boxes blank, the data validation displays the requirements for both text boxes. However, if the code handled the exceptions thrown by the calcFutureValue() function, it would have to notify the user one text box at a time, which many users find annoying. In addition, preventing exceptions allows you to provide more user-friendly error messages.

If the checkValidity() method determines that the user entries are valid, the code gets the values entered by the user and passes them to the calcFuture-Value() function. Because that function throws an exception if the interest rate service is down, the call to it is coded in a try-catch statement. By contrast, if the calcFutureValue() function only threw exceptions for invalid data, the call wouldn't need to be in a try-catch statement since the invalid event handlers display messages for these exceptions.

The click event handler for the Clear button clears any validation messages. Then it sets the focus on the investment text box.

The future_value.js file

```javascript
const getElement = selector => document.querySelector(selector);

const clearMessages = () => {
    getElement("#investment").nextElementSibling.textContent = "*";
    getElement("#years").nextElementSibling.textContent = "*";
    getElement("#message").textContent = "";
}

document.addEventListener("DOMContentLoaded", () => {
    const form = getElement("form");

    // turn off default HTML validation messages
    form.noValidate = true;

    // attach invalid event handler for form controls
    for (let element of form.elements) {
        element.addEventListener("invalid", evt => {
            const elem = evt.currentTarget;
            const span = elem.nextElementSibling;
            if (span) span.textContent = elem.validationMessage;
        });
    }

    form.addEventListener("submit", evt => {
        clearMessages();
        evt.preventDefault();   // prevent form submission

        // get future value text box and clear any previous value
        const fv = getElement("#future_value");
        fv.value = "";

        // if form is valid, display future value or error message
        if (form.checkValidity()) {
            try {
                const investment = getElement("#investment").value;
                const years = getElement("#years").value;
                fv.value = calcFutureValue(investment, years);
            } catch(e) {
                const msg = `${e.name}: ${e.message}`;
                getElement("#message").textContent = msg;
            }
        }
    });

    getElement("#clear").addEventListener("click", () => {
        clearMessages();
        getElement("#investment").focus();
    });
});
```

Figure 9-10   The Future Value app (part 3)

Perspective

Now that you've completed this chapter, you should have most of the skills you need to write code that performs client-side data validation on HTML forms. That's important because validating form data is a common use of JavaScript. In addition, you now know when and how to handle exceptions. That's important because it allows you to write professional-quality code that gracefully handles exceptions in a user-friendly way.

Terms

data validation	exception
regular expression	exception handling
regex	try-catch statement
pattern	try block
escape character	catch block
subpattern	finally block
quantifier	throw statement
Constraint Validation API	

Exercise 9-1   The Credit Card app

This exercise has you customize the HTML data validation for an app. When you're done, it should display error messages like this:

Credit Card

Name:	[ ]	Please fill out this field.
Card Number:	[ ]	Must be 16 digits.
Expiration Date (MM/YY):	[ ]	Must be a future date in MM/YY format.
Security Code:	[ ]	Must be 3 digits.
	[Save]	

Review the starting code

1. View the files in this folder:

   `exercises\ch09\creditcard`

2. Open the index.html file and review its code. Note that it defines a form with four text boxes where each text box has a <span> element immediately after it.

3. Open the creditcard.js file and review its code. Note that it defines an event handler for the submit event of the form but that this event handler doesn't contain any code.

4. Run the app and test it. Note that it uses HTML data validation for the first three text boxes but doesn't validate the text box for the security code.

Modify the HTML validation

5. Open the index.html file and modify the HTML so the security code is required and must be 3-digits.

6. Run the app and test it to make sure it works correctly.

Customize the HTML validation

7. Open the JavaScript file. In the DOMContentLoaded event handler, add code that turns off the default HTML validation.

8. Add code that attaches the invalid event handler to all four text boxes. This event handler should set the text for the <span> element that follows each text box to the corresponding HTML data validation message.

9. In the submit event listener, remove any existing messages from the <span> elements and check the validity of the form. If it is not valid, prevent the form from being submitted.

10. Run the app and test it. It should display the HTML data validation messages in the <span> elements that follow the text boxes.

11. Open the index.html file and set the title attribute for the last three text boxes to these messages:

    Card number: "Must be 16 digits."

    Expiration date: "Must be a future date in the MM/YY format."

    Security code: "Must be 3 digits."

12. Run the app and test it. It should display the HTML data validation message for the name text box, but it should display the error message specified by the title attribute for the three other text boxes.

13. Add custom validation that only allows an expiration date that's in the future.

14. Run the app and make sure it works correctly.

Exercise 9-2   The Guess the Number app

This exercise has you add exception handling to the Guess the Number app. This isn't the best way to validate the data for this app, but it's a good way to practice working with exceptions. Here's what the app looks like when an error message is displayed.

```
Guess the Number

It's between 1 and 10.

[                    ]  [ Guess ]  [ Play again ]

Not a valid number. Please enter a valid number.
```

Open and test the app

1. View the files in this folder:

   `exercises\ch09\exceptions`

2. Review the code. Note that the guess.js file contains a function named getGuess() that throws two exceptions and that the code that calls this function doesn't catch these exceptions.

3. Run the app and enter valid numbers. The app should work correctly.

4. Run the app and enter an invalid number. Then, use the developer tools to view the console. This should display information about the exception.

Add exception handling

5. In the guessButtonClick() event handler, use a try-catch statement to catch the exceptions that are thrown by the getGuess() function.

6. In the catch block, use the Error object to display the error message for the exception in the HTML element that has an id of "error_message".

7. Run the app and test it. It should display error messages in red, and it should display the rest of its messages in black.

10

How to work with web storage

JavaScript provides two ways to store data in the browser: cookies and web storage. To start, this chapter introduces you to both techniques and explains why web storage works better for most JavaScript apps. Then, it presents the skills you need to work with web storage.

An introduction to cookies and web storage

Before learning how to use web storage to store data in a browser, it's helpful to learn a little about how cookies can also store data in a browser.

An introduction to cookies

A *cookie* is a short text string that's stored in a browser as a name/value pair. When a browser requests a web page, the server can return a cookie as part of the HTTP response. If it does, the browser stores the cookie. Then, when the browser loads another page from the server, it sends any cookies for that server back to it as part of the HTTP request. Figure 10-1 shows how this works.

A cookie must start with a *name/value pair* where a name and its value are connected by an equal sign. For instance, the first example in this figure specifies a name/value pair with a name of username and a value of ghopper. This pair can be followed by attributes such as the two attributes listed in the table. In the cookie string, these name/value pairs must be separated by a semicolon and a space.

If a cookie includes a max-age attribute with a positive value, it's called a *persistent cookie*. The browser stores this type of cookie until the number of seconds in this attribute elapses. For instance, the first cookie example creates a persistent cookie by setting the max-age attribute to 21 days (21 days * 24 hours * 60 minutes * 60 seconds = 1,814,400 seconds).

On the other hand, if a cookie doesn't include a max-age attribute, it's called a *session cookie*. The browser deletes this type of cookie when the user closes the browser. For instance, the second cookie example creates a session cookie since it doesn't specify the max-age attribute.

Typically, the path attribute for a cookie is set to the root folder of the website as shown in both examples. That way, every page in the website has access to the cookie.

The second example shows how to use JavaScript to set the cookies specified by the first example in a browser. To do that, this example sets the string for each cookie in the document.cookie object. When you use JavaScript to set cookies, the browser treats them the same as cookies received from the web server.

The third example shows how to use JavaScript to get both cookies set by the second example. This returns a string that contains the first name/value pair for each cookie available from the current path. This string can be difficult to parse, which is one of the problems of using JavaScript to work with cookies.

The server typically sets a cookie as part of an HTTP response

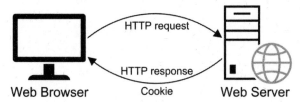

A browser sends the cookie back to the server with each HTTP request

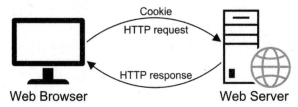

Two attributes of a cookie

Attribute	Description
max-age	The lifetime of the cookie in seconds
path	The path that can see the cookie

Cookie examples

```
username=ghopper; max-age=1814400; path=/
temp_id=12345; path=/
```

Set two cookies in the browser

```
document.cookie = "username=ghopper; max-age=1814400; path=/";
document.cookie = "temp_id=12345; path=/";
```

Get all cookies from the browser

```
const cookies = document.cookie;
```

Description

- A *cookie* is a small text string that is stored by a web browser. A cookie consists of *name/value pairs* where each name and its value are separated by an equal sign and multiple name value pairs are separated by a semicolon and a space.

- A cookie must start with a name/value pair that names the cookie and provides a value for the cookie.

- The browser usually gets a cookie from a web server as part of an HTTP response. Then, the browser sends the cookie back to the server as part of each HTTP request.

- A *session cookie* is deleted by the web browser when the browser is closed.

- A *persistent cookie* is saved by the web browser and remains available even after the browser is closed. This type of cookie has an expiration date that is after the current date.

- In JavaScript, you can use the document.cookie object to work with cookies.

Figure 10-1   An introduction to cookies

How cookies compare to web storage

Web storage provides another way for JavaScript to store data in the browser. Prior to the introduction of web storage, cookies were the only option for storing data in the user's browser. However, cookies have several disadvantages. First, since cookies were designed to work with server-side code, the browser passes them to the server with each HTTP request, which isn't efficient. In addition, cookies can only store about 4 kilobytes of data. This makes sense when you consider that cookies were designed to pass identifying information to a server, but some web apps need more storage than that. Third, the JavaScript code for working with cookies is often long and difficult to understand.

Fortunately, all modern browsers support *web storage*. Web storage provides several advantages over cookies. First, since web storage was designed to be accessed by client-side code, the browser doesn't pass web storage data to the server with each HTTP request. Second, web storage can store much more data than cookies, up to 10 megabytes in some cases. Third, the JavaScript for working with web storage is shorter and easier to understand than the comparable JavaScript for working with cookies.

Web storage includes both *local storage* and *session storage*. To work with these types of web storage, you can use the localStorage and sessionStorage objects shown in figure 10-2. An item in local storage persists between browser sessions, like a persistent cookie, and can store up to 10MB of data. On the other hand, like a session cookie, an item in session storage is removed when the browser session ends.

Both cookies and web storage can be exploited by cross-site scripting (XSS) attacks. As a result, you should avoid storing sensitive information in web storage. This includes data like user passwords, credit card numbers, and so on. Even though web storage data is only accessible by the same origin (same domain, protocol, and port), this data can be accessed by an XSS attack.

If you must store sensitive data in web storage, you can encrypt the data before you store it. Then, you can decrypt the data when you retrieve it. That way, if an attacker manages to access this data, it will be encrypted, so it won't be easy for the attacker to read it.

Two objects for storing data in the browser

Object	Description
localStorage	Never expires. Can store up to 10MB of data.
sessionStorage	Expires when the browser is closed. Can store up to 5MB of data.

Web storage

- Was designed to be accessed by client-side code.
- Doesn't send its data to the server with each HTTP request.
- Can store up to 10MB of data.

Cookies

- Were designed to be accessed by server-side code.
- Send their data to the server with each HTTP request.
- Can only store up to 4KB of data.

Description

- *Web storage* allows JavaScript to store data in the browser. This feature is supported by every modern browser.
- Of the two types of web storage, *local storage* retains its data indefinitely, and *session storage* loses its data when the user ends the session by closing the browser tab or by exiting the browser.
- Prior to the introduction of web storage, cookies were the only option for storing data in the user's browser.
- Both cookies and web storage can be exploited by cross-site scripting (XSS) attacks.

Figure 10-2   How cookies compare to web storage

How to get started with web storage

Now that you understand the differences between cookies and web storage, you're ready to learn how to work with the two types of web storage: local storage and session storage. Since the skills for working with local storage and session storage are the same, this chapter starts by showing how to work with local storage.

How to work with local storage

Figure 10-3 presents six examples that use the localStorage object. This object stores its items in *key/value pairs* and provides methods and a shortcut syntax to work with the key and the value for each item.

The first example shows how to set and get an item in the localStorage object. Here, the first statement sets an item by passing the key and value for the item to the setItem() method. Then, the second statement gets the value of that item by passing its key to the getItem() method.

To make this code more concise, the second example uses the shortcut syntax to set and get the same item. Here, the first statement specifies a key of email and assigns a value of "grace@hopper.com". Then, the second statement uses the key of email to get the value of that item.

The third and fourth examples show how to remove one or more items from storage. Here, the third example uses the removeItem() method to remove the item with a key of email, and the fourth example uses the clear() method to remove all items from local storage.

When you use web storage, it automatically converts the value to a string. Then, to get the original value, you must convert the string back to the original data type. For instance, in the fifth example, the first statement automatically converts a number to a string when it sets the number in local storage. Then, the second statement uses the Number() function to convert the string back to a number.

Similarly, in the sixth example, the first statement automatically converts a Date object to a string when it sets the date in local storage. Then, the second statement uses skills described in chapter 8 to convert the string back to a Date object. This is shown by the third statement, which calls the getFullYear() method from the Date object.

How to work with session storage

To get the examples in figure 10-3 to work with session storage instead of local storage, you use the sessionStorage object instead of the localStorage object. For instance, the seventh example works like the second example, but it uses session storage instead of local storage. As a result, when the user ends the session by closing the browser tab or by exiting the browser, the item stored by the seventh example is automatically removed from session storage.

Four methods for working with a web storage object

Method	Description
setItem(*key, value*)	Sets the specified value at the specified key.
getItem(*key*)	Gets the value at the specified key. If no item exists at the specified key, this method returns null.
removeItem(*key*)	Removes the value at the specified key.
clear()	Removes all items.

The shortcut syntax

Key	Description
key	Allows you to set or get a value at the specified key.

Set and get an item with methods

```
localStorage.setItem("email", "grace@hopper.com");
const email = localStorage.getItem("email");   // email is "grace@hopper.com"
```

Set and get the same item with the shortcut syntax

```
localStorage.email = "grace@hopper.com";
const email = localStorage.email;               // email is "grace@hopper.com"
```

Remove the specified item from storage

```
localStorage.removeItem("email");
```

Remove all items from storage

```
localStorage.clear();
```

Set and get an item that's a number

```
localStorage.score = 100;
const score = Number(localStorage.score);       // score is 100
```

Set and get an item that's a date

```
localStorage.startDate = new Date("5/1/2024");
const startDate = new Date(localStorage.startDate);
const year = startDate.getFullYear();           // year is 2024
```

Set and get an item in session storage

```
sessionStorage.email = "grace@hopper.com";
const email = sessionStorage.email;             // email is "grace@hopper.com"
```

Description

- Web storage stores *key/value pairs*.
- Web storage automatically converts values to strings before storing them.
- To get values from web storage in the original data type, you need to know the original type and convert the strings after you retrieve them.

Figure 10-3   How to work with local and session storage

How to use the nullish coalescing operator

If you attempt to get an item from web storage and no item exists for the specified key, JavaScript returns a null value. Figure 10-4 shows how to use the *nullish coalescing operator* (??) to provide a default value when a property or function returns null or undefined. This operator is often used to provide a default value when getting the value of an item from web storage.

The first example shows how to use an if statement to provide a default value when getting an email address from web storage. Here, the code begins by defining a variable named email and setting it to a default value of an empty string. Then, the code uses an if statement to check whether an email address has already been set in web storage. If so, it sets the email variable to the email address that's available from web storage. Otherwise, it leaves the email address at its default value of an empty string. So, after this code executes, the email variable holds either the email address that's available from web storage or an empty string.

The second example shows how to use the nullish coalescing operator to get the same result as the first example. This shows that the nullish coalescing operator provides a more concise way to write certain types of if statements.

The third example uses local and session storage for hit counters. To do that, it uses the nullish coalescing operator to check whether the hits item exists in local storage and session storage. If so, it gets the stored value for the hits. Otherwise, it assigns a default value of "0" to the hits. Then, it converts the value in that item to a number and adds 1 to it. Next, it sets the incremented value to hits in storage. Finally, the code displays the value of the hits item in both local and session storage in the console.

The fourth example shows the message that's displayed if the user views the page three times, closes the browser, and views the page two more times. This shows that local storage persists indefinitely while session storage ends when the browser is closed.

Provide a default value with an if statement

```
let email = "";
if (localStorage.email) {
    email = localStorage.email;
}
```

Provide a default value with the nullish coalescing operator

```
const email = localStorage.email ?? "";
```

Use local and session storage for hit counters

```
let localHits = localStorage.hits ?? "0";      // get hits
localHits = Number(localHits) + 1;             // increment by 1
localStorage.hits = localHits;                 // set hits to new value

let sessionHits = sessionStorage.hits ?? "0";
sessionHits = Number(sessionHits) + 1;
sessionStorage.hits = sessionHits;

console.log("Hits for this browser: " + localStorage.hits);
console.log("Hits for this session: " + sessionStorage.hits);
```

Possible values for the hit counters when displayed on the console

```
Hits for this browser: 5
Hits for this session: 2
```

Description

- The *nullish coalescing operator* (**??**) returns the specified value if the expression evaluates to null or undefined, eliminating the need for an if statement.

Figure 10-4   How to use the nullish coalescing operator

The Future Value app

Figure 10-5 presents a version of the Future Value app that "remembers" the user's previous entries. As a result, when a user starts the Future Value app with a browser that they've used before, the Future Value app reads the user's entries from web storage and displays them in the first three text boxes.

The DOMContentLoaded event handler contains the code that loads the user entries from web storage. To do that, this code begins by using the null coalescing operator to check if values for the investment, interest rate, and years have been saved in local storage. If so, the code gets each value from storage and sets it in its corresponding text box. Otherwise, it sets an empty string in the corresponding text box.

Conversely, the click event handler of the Calculate button contains the code that saves the user's entries in local storage. Although it isn't shown in this figure, this event handler begins by getting the three entries, converting them from strings to numbers, and checking whether the three entries are valid. If they are, the errorMsg variable is equal to an empty string. In that case, the code saves all three user entries by setting each value in web storage. Then, it calculates and displays the future value.

On the other hand, if the user entries aren't valid, the code doesn't store them. Instead, it displays the error message. That way, the user can fix the entries and click the Calculate button again.

An app that remembers the user's previous entries

The Future Value Calculator

Total investment: `10000`

Annual interest rate: `3.5`

Number of years `10`

Future value:

[Calculate]

The event handler for the DOMContentLoaded event

```
document.addEventListener("DOMContentLoaded", () => {
    // load user entries
    getElement("#investment").value = localStorage.investment ?? "";
    getElement("#rate").value = localStorage.rate ?? "";
    getElement("#years").value = localStorage.years ?? "";

    // attach the event handler
    getElement("#calculate").addEventListener("click", calcButtonClick);

    // set focus on first text box on initial load
    getElement("#investment").focus();
});
```

Some code in the event handler for the click event of the Calculate button

```
// if user entries are valid
if (errorMsg == "") {
    // save user entries
    localStorage.investment = investment;
    localStorage.rate = rate;
    localStorage.years = years;

    // calculate and display future value
    const futureValue = calcFutureValue(investment, rate, years);
    getElement("#future_value").value = futureValue.toFixed(2);
} else {
    // display error message
    alert(errorMsg);
}
```

Description

- This version of the Future Value app uses local storage to "remember" any valid values entered by a user the last time the Calculate button was clicked and loads the text boxes with those values.

Figure 10-5   The Future Value app

More skills for working with web storage

Now that you know the basic skills for storing strings and numbers in web storage, you're ready to learn some more skills for working with web storage. These skills include how to store more complex objects such as arrays in web storage, and how to use Chrome's developer tools to work with stored items.

How to convert an object to JSON and back

When working with a complex object like an array, you need to convert it to a string before you can set it in web storage. Later, when you get the string from web storage, you typically need to convert it back into an object so you can work with it. In the early days of JavaScript, developers typically had to write their own code to perform these types of conversions. Fortunately, modern JavaScript provides ways to make these conversions easier.

Figure 10-6 shows how you can use two methods of the JSON object to convert most types of objects, including arrays, to strings and then convert them back to objects again. To do that, the JSON.stringify() method provides a way to convert an object into *JSON (JavaScript Object Notation)*, a format designed for using a string to store the data for an object. Then, the JSON.parse() method provides a way to convert the JSON string back into an object.

The first example in this figure shows how to use the JSON.stringify() method to convert an Array object to a JSON string and store that string in web storage. To start, this code creates an array named tasks that stores two strings. Then, it uses the JSON.stringify() method to convert the array to a JSON string. Next, it stores that string in local storage.

The second example shows the JSON string that's stored in web storage. To start, the brackets identify the Array object for the tasks array. Then, the quotation marks identify the strings for the two elements of the array, and a comma separates these elements.

The third example shows how to use the JSON.parse() method to convert the JSON string back into an array. To start, this code gets the JSON string for the tasks array from local web storage. Then, it uses the JSON.parse() method to convert the JSON string back into an array.

Although this figure shows how to use the JSON methods to work with an Array object, you can use these methods with most types of native JavaScript objects. However, these methods don't work with Date objects. As a result, you can use the skills presented in chapter 8 to convert Date objects to strings and back, as shown in figure 10-3. In addition, you can use the JSON methods with user-defined objects like the ones presented in chapter 12.

Although the JS in JSON stands for JavaScript, many programming languages provide a way to convert objects to JSON and back. As a result, it's a useful data format for sharing object data across languages and apps.

Two methods of the JSON object

Method	Description
stringify(*object*)	Returns a JSON string for the specified object or array.
parse(*json*)	Returns an object or array that contains the data in the specified JSON string.

Convert an array to a JSON string

```
// create an array that contains two items
const tasks = [];
tasks.push("Finish current project");
tasks.push("Get specs for next project");

const tasksJson = JSON.stringify(tasks);   // convert array to JSON
localStorage.tasks = tasksJson;            // save JSON to web storage
```

The JSON string

```
["Finish current project","Get specs for next project"]
```

Convert a JSON string to an array

```
const tasksJson = localStorage.tasks;      // get JSON from web storage
const tasks = JSON.parse(tasksJson);       // convert JSON to array
console.log(tasks[0]);                     // "Finish current project"
console.log(tasks[1]);                     // "Get specs for next project"
```

Description

- *JSON (JavaScript Object Notation)* is a format that uses text to store and transmit the data for an object such as an array.

- The JSON format was originally based on the notation for objects that was used by JavaScript, but most programming languages now provide a way to generate and parse JSON.

- You can use the JSON.stringify() and JSON.parse() methods to work with most types of native JavaScript objects such as arrays.

Figure 10-6   How to convert an object to JSON and back

How to use Chrome to work with stored items

As you test and debug an app that uses web storage, it can sometimes be helpful to view the values of the items that are currently stored. That's why the first procedure in figure 10-7 shows how to use the Application panel of the Chrome browser to do just that.

When you view stored items, the Application panel displays their keys and values. This can be useful not only for testing your own apps, but for seeing what items other websites are storing in your browser. For example, you can navigate to google.com and open the Application panel to view what Google is storing on your computer, which can be an interesting exercise.

In addition to viewing stored items, the Application panel lets you delete, edit, and add stored items. This can be useful when testing and debugging your own apps. However, be careful when doing this for other websites, since it might cause the website to no longer work correctly for you.

Although this figure presents skills for working with web storage, most of these skills also apply to cookies. For example, to view the cookies being stored in your browser, you can display the Application panel and expand the Cookies node.

The local storage items for an app in the Application panel

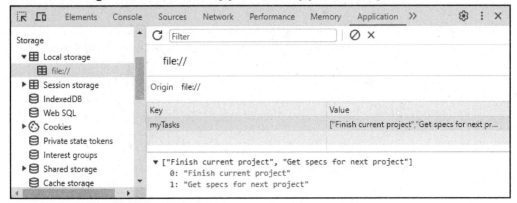

How to view stored items

1. Press F12 to open the developer tools.
2. Click the Application tab at the top of the tools window. If you don't see it, click the double arrow to see a list of tabs.
3. Find the Storage section in the pane on the left-hand side.
4. Expand "Local storage" or "Session storage".
5. Click the appropriate URL to display the stored values in a grid.

How to delete, edit, or add stored items

- To delete an item, right-click the item and select Delete.
- To change the name of a key, right-click the key and select Edit Key. Then, edit the text for the key.
- To edit a value, right-click the value and select Edit Value. Then, edit the text for the value.
- To add a key/value pair, right click the empty entry at the bottom of the list and click Add New. Then, type in the name of the key in the first column and the value in the second column.
- To apply your changes, reload the page.

Description

- You can use the Application panel in Chrome's developer tools to work with items in local and session storage.

Figure 10-7   How to use Chrome to work with stored items

The Task List app

To show you how web storage can make an app more useful, figure 10-8 presents a Task List app. This app saves the items in the task list in local storage. That way, the task list is available to the user each time the user accesses the page. However, because only the user's current browser stores the task list, this list isn't available if the user switches to a different browser.

The HTML for this app includes a text box and two buttons that let the user add and delete tasks. In addition, it includes a text area on the right side of the page that displays the task list.

In the <body> element of the HTML, the first <div> element contains the text area that displays the list of tasks. Then, the CSS floats this <div> element to the right of the <div> elements that contain the text box and buttons.

The Task List app

Task List

Task

Task List
Finish current project
Meet with Joel
Get specs for new project

Add Task

Clear Tasks

The HTML for the <body> element

```
<body>
  <h1>Task List</h1>
  <div id="tasks">
      <label for="task_list">Task List</label><br>
      <textarea id="task_list" rows="6" cols="50"></textarea>
  </div>
  <div>
      <label for="task">Task</label><br>
      <input type="text" id="task">
  </div>
  <div>
      <input type="button" id="add_task" value="Add Task"><br>
      <input type="button" id="clear_tasks" value="Clear Tasks">
  </div>
  <script src="task_list.js"></script>
</body>
```

The CSS for the <div> element with "tasks" as its id

```
#tasks {
    margin-top: 0;
    float: right;
}
```

Figure 10-8   The Task List app (part 1)

Part 2 of figure 10-8 presents the JavaScript for this app. This code begins by defining getElement() and getDisplayString() helper functions. Here, the getDisplayString() function accepts an array of tasks as its parameter. Then, if the array is empty, it returns an empty string. Otherwise, it returns a string with each item in the array separated by a new line character. This makes it easy to display each task on a separate line within the text area.

The DOMContentLoaded event handler begins by getting the JSON string for the tasks array from web storage. To do that, this code uses the nullish coalescing operator (??) to set a default value of null. As a result, if the tasks haven't yet been set in web storage, this sets the tasksStr constant to null. That way, the next statement can use the JSON.parse() method to convert the string to an array. Or, if the string is null, it provides a default value of an empty array.

Next, the DOMContentLoaded event handler displays the tasks, if any. To do that, it passes the tasks array to the getDisplayString() function and assigns the string it returns to the value property of the text area. Then, it sets the focus on the text box. As a result, when the app first loads, it displays any tasks that are already stored in local storage and moves the focus to the text box so the app is ready for the user to enter another task. Finally, this event handler attaches click event handlers for the Add Task and Clear Tasks buttons.

The click event handler for the Add Task button starts by getting the task text box element and assigning it to a constant named textbox. Then, it retrieves the text the user entered in that text box and assigns it to a constant named task. After that, it checks whether the task is an empty string. If so, the code displays an error message and sets the focus on the text box so the user can try entering a task again.

If the user has entered some text, the code adds the text to the tasks array and uses the JSON.stringify() method to store the updated array in local storage. Then, the code clears the tasks text box and refreshes the tasks list by assigning the string that's returned by the getDisplayString() function to the value property of the text area. Finally, it sets the focus back on the task text box so the app is ready for the user to enter another task.

The click event handler for the Clear Tasks button begins by clearing the array and web storage. To do that, it removes all tasks from the array by setting its length to zero, and it uses the removeItem() method to remove the array of tasks from local storage. Then, it clears the tasks displayed in the text area and sets the focus on the text box. At this point, the app is ready for the user to enter a new task.

The JavaScript

```javascript
const getElement = selector => document.querySelector(selector);

const getDisplayString = tasks => {
    if (tasks.length === 0) {
        return "";
    } else {
        return tasks.join("\n");
    }
};

document.addEventListener("DOMContentLoaded", () => {
    // get tasks array from web storage
    const tasksStr = localStorage.myTasks ?? null;
    const tasks = JSON.parse(tasksStr) ?? [];

    // display tasks on initial load
    getElement("#task_list").value = getDisplayString(tasks);
    getElement("#task").focus();

    getElement("#add_task").addEventListener("click", () => {
        const textbox = getElement("#task");
        const task = textbox.value;
        if (task === "") {
            alert("Please enter a task.");
            textbox.focus();
        } else {
            // add task to web storage
            tasks.push(task);
            localStorage.myTasks = JSON.stringify(tasks);

            // clear task text box and re-display tasks
            textbox.value = "";
            getElement("#task_list").value = getDisplayString(tasks);
            textbox.focus();
        }
    });

    getElement("#clear_tasks").addEventListener("click", () => {
        // clear tasks array and web storage
        tasks.length = 0;
        localStorage.removeItem("myTasks");

        getElement("#task_list").value = "";
        getElement("#task").focus();
    });
});
```

Figure 10-8   The Task List app (part 2)

Perspective

Now that you've finished this chapter, you should know what cookies are and why it typically makes sense to use web storage instead of cookies to store data in a user's browser. In addition, you should have the skills you need to work with web storage. This opens many possibilities that can make your apps more fun and easier to use.

Terms

cookie
name/value pair
session cookie
persistent cookie
web storage
session storage
local storage
key/value pair
nullish coalescing operator
JSON (JavaScript Object Notation)

Exercise 10-1   The Countdown app

This exercise has you enhance the Countdown app to save your event name and date in web storage when you enter an event successfully.

Countdown To...

Event Name: [Thanksgiving]

Event Date: [11/28/2024]

[Countdown!]

323 day(s) until Thanksgiving! (Thu Nov 28 2024)

Review the starting code

1. View the files in this folder:

    `exercises\ch10\countdown`

2. Run the app and test it. It should work correctly. However, if you refresh the browser, the app loses the data for the event name and date.

Use session storage

3. Open the count_down.js file.

4. In the DOMContentLoaded event handler, add code that gets the event name and date from session storage if they exist or empty strings if they do not. Then, put this data in the event name and date text boxes.

5. After the validation code in the click event handler for the Countdown button, add code that sets the event name and date in session storage.

6. Run the app and enter a valid event. If you refresh the browser, it should still display the event name and date.

7. Close the browser. Then, run the app again. When it starts, it should not display the event name and date.

Use local storage

8. Modify the JavaScript code so it uses local storage, not session storage.

9. Run the app and enter a valid event.

10. Close the browser. Then, run the app again. When it starts, it should display the event name and date.

11. Open the browser's developer tools and use them to view the items in local storage. You should be able to view the items for the event name and date.

11

More skills for working with arrays

In chapter 4, you learned the basics of working with arrays, including how to use some of the methods available from an array. Now, this chapter presents more skills for working with arrays. This includes using more of the methods available from an array, working with arrays of arrays, and making a copy of an array.

More methods of an array

In chapter 4, you learned how to use some of the methods available from an array. In the figures that follow, you'll learn to use even more of these methods.

How to inspect an array

The first table in figure 11-1 presents the isArray() method of the Array object. This method checks whether the object that's passed to it is an array. Developers typically use it to check that an object is an array before attempting to call any properties or methods from the array.

The second table summarizes some of the methods of an array that inspect the elements of an array. All of these methods accept a function as a parameter. Since these methods call this function to complete their tasks, this function is known as a *callback function*. Callback functions aren't just used with arrays. Any function passed as an argument to another function or method can be referred to as a callback function.

When you create a callback function to use with the methods for inspecting an array, you can include up to three parameters as shown by the syntax after the second table. The first parameter specifies the current element in the array and is required. In the examples in this figure, this parameter is named elem. The next two parameters are optional. They specify the index of the current element and the array itself. In this figure, these parameters are named i and arr respectively.

After the syntax of the callback function, this figure shows how to define a callback function named isEvenNumber(). This function uses the modulus operator to check whether the element passed to it is an even number.

The next example shows two techniques for passing a callback function to another function or method. The first technique passes the isEvenNumber() function defined by the previous example to the find() method. This returns either the value of the first even number or undefined if no number in the array is even. With this technique, the name of the function makes the code easier to understand. The second technique passes an anonymous function that performs the same task. This technique is a little harder to read, but it requires less code.

The findIndex() method works much like the find() method. However, it returns the index of the first element that meets the condition tested by the callback function. If no element meets the condition, it returns -1.

The some() and every() methods check whether some elements or every element in the array meet the condition tested by the callback function. This figure includes an example that shows how these methods work. This example reuses the isEvenNumber() function defined earlier in the figure.

When coding a callback function, you may need to compare the current element with other elements. When that happens, you can use the current-index and array parameters as shown by the last example. This example uses the some() method to check whether the array contains any repeating elements. To do that, the callback function uses all three parameters to check whether the array contains any repeating elements. The callback function gets the index for the previous element by subtracting 1 from the current index. Then, it checks

A method of the Array object for checking an array

Method	Description
`isArray(object)`	Returns a Boolean value that indicates whether the specified object is an array.

An array that's used by the examples in this figure

```
const numbers = [1, 2, 3, 4, 5, 6, 7, 8, 9, 10];
```

Check that an object is an array before working with it

```
if (Array.isArray(numbers)) {
    console.log("The numbers array has " + numbers.length + " elements.");
}
```

Methods for inspecting an array

Method	Description
`find(function)`	Returns the value of the first element that meets the condition of the function, or undefined if no element meets the condition.
`findIndex(function)`	Returns the index of the first element that meets the condition of the function, or -1 if no element meets the condition.
`every(function)`	Returns a Boolean value indicating whether all elements meet the condition of the function.
`some(function)`	Returns a Boolean value that indicates whether at least one element meets the condition of the function.

The syntax of a callback function for these methods

```
function(current-element, [current-index], [array])
```

A named callback function that checks if a number is even

```
const isEvenNumber = elem => elem % 2 === 0;
```

Two ways to pass a callback function

Pass a named function

```
const val = numbers.find(isEvenNumber);                // val is 2
```

Pass an anonymous function

```
const val = numbers.find(elem => elem % 2 === 0);      // val is 2
```

Get the index for the first even number

```
const i = numbers.findIndex(elem => elem % 2 === 0);   // i is 1
```

Check if all or some of the elements are even numbers

```
const allEven = numbers.every(isEvenNumber);           // allEven is false
const someEven = numbers.some(isEvenNumber);           // someEven is true
```

Check if the array contains any repeating elements

```
const isRepeatNumber = (elem, i, arr) => elem === arr[i-1];
let hasRepeats = numbers.some(isRepeatNumber);      // hasRepeats is false
numbers.push(10);
hasRepeats = numbers.some(isRepeatNumber);          // hasRepeats is true
```

Figure 11-1   How to inspect an array

whether the current element is equal to the previous element and returns true or false accordingly.

How to sort elements

Figure 11-2 begins by summarizing the sort() method of an array. If you don't pass any parameters, this method sorts the elements in the array into ascending alphanumeric sequence. By default, it sorts all elements as if they were strings. Because of this, it might not sort numbers in numeric sequence. For instance, the number 100 would appear before the number 25. In addition, the sort() method is case-sensitive and sorts any undefined elements last.

If that's not what you want, you can pass a callback function to the sort() function that controls how the elements are sorted. The syntax and return values for this function are presented below the first table.

A callback function used with sort() should receive two parameters, the first element to compare and the second element to compare. Then, it should return a positive number, zero, or a negative number based on a comparison of these two elements. If the first element should be before the second element, the function should return a negative value. If the first should be after the second, the function should return a positive value. And, if the first and second should be sorted at the same level, the function should return zero. Then, the sort() method uses these return values to sort the array elements.

The last table in this figure presents the localeCompare() method that's available from a string. You can use this method for case-insensitive sorts.

The first example after the tables shows how to perform a case-sensitive sort of an array of strings. To sort in ascending sequence, it calls the sort() method with no parameters. This causes the name that starts with a lowercase b to be sorted after the names that start with uppercase letters. To sort in descending sequence, it chains a call to the reverse() method to the call to the sort() method.

The second example shows how to use a callback function to perform a case-insensitive sort of an array of strings. To sort in ascending sequence, it calls the localeCompare() method on the first parameter of the callback function and passes it the second parameter. To sort in descending sequence, it reverses that and calls the localeCompare() method on the second parameter.

The third example shows how to sort numbers. First, this example calls the sort() method with no parameters to show that this doesn't always work the way you would expect with numbers. Then, the second and third statements use a callback function to sort the numbers. To sort in ascending sequence, the second statement subtracts the second parameter from the first parameter. So, if the first is greater than the second, it returns a positive value. If they are equal, it returns zero. And, if the first is less than the second, it returns a negative value. This causes the numbers in the array to be sorted in ascending numeric sequence. To sort in descending sequence, the third statement reverses that and subtracts the first parameter from the second.

The fourth example shows how to sort dates. As with numbers, to sort in ascending sequence, this example subtracts the second parameter from the first. To sort in descending sequence, it reverses that.

A method that sorts the elements of an array

Method	Description
`sort()`	Sorts the elements into ascending alphanumeric sequence (case-sensitive). If an element is not a string, it is sorted according to its value when converted to a string. As a result, numbers may not sort as expected.
`sort(function)`	Sorts the elements based on the numeric value returned by the specified callback function.

The syntax of a callback function for this method

```
function(first-element-to-compare, second-element-to-compare)
```

The possible return values for this callback function

Return value	Indicates
Less than zero	First value is less than second value.
Greater than zero	First value is greater than second value.
Zero	The values are equal.

A method of a string for comparing two strings

Method	Description
`localeCompare(string)`	Returns a numeric value that can be used to compare the calling string with the passed string (not case-sensitive).

Sort strings without a callback function (case-sensitive)

```
const names = ["Grace", "Ada", "bell", "Betsy"];

names.sort();                                    // ascending sequence
// names is ['Ada', 'Betsy', 'Grace', 'bell']

names.sort().reverse();                          // descending sequence
// names is ['bell', 'Grace', 'Betsy', 'Ada']
```

Sort strings with a callback function (case-insensitive)

```
names.sort((a, b) => a.localeCompare(b));        // ascending sequence
// names is ['Ada', 'bell', 'Betsy', 'Grace']

names.sort((a, b) => b.localeCompare(a));        // descending sequence
// names is ['Grace', 'Betsy', 'bell', 'Ada']
```

Sort numbers

```
const nums = [7, 6, 25, 1, 3, 100];
nums.sort();                       // unexpected - nums is [1, 100, 25, 3, 6, 7]
nums.sort((a, b) => a - b);        // ascending  - nums is [1, 3, 6, 7, 25, 100]
nums.sort((a, b) => b - a);        // descending - nums is [100, 25, 7, 6, 3, 1]
```

Sort dates

```
const dates = [new Date("7/4/2024"), new Date("1/1/2019")];
dates.sort((a, b) => a - b);    // ascending  - dates is [1/1/2019, 7/4/2024]
names.sort((a, b) => b - a);    // descending - dates is [7/4/2024, 1/1/2019]
```

Figure 11-2   How to sort elements

How to work with each element in an array

Figure 11-3 begins by summarizing the forEach() method that you can use to apply a callback function to each element in an array. Then, it summarizes the syntax of a callback function that you can pass to this method. Next, the first example defines an array that's used by the other examples.

The second example shows two ways to loop through each element in an array and create a string that contains each element. This string adds the # character before each element and a space after each element. To start, this example uses a for-of loop to create the string. Then, it uses the forEach() method to create the same string. Since this example doesn't modify the array or need to access more than one element at a time, it only needs to specify the first parameter of the callback function that it passes to the forEach() method.

The third example shows how to modify the array by multiplying each element by two. To start, this example uses a for-in loop to modify each element in the array. Then, it uses the forEach() method to perform the same task. To do that, it uses both of the optional parameters of the callback function. This allows the callback function to assign a new value that's equal to the current element multiplied by two to the current index of the array. This modifies the array.

Using a for loop to work with each element in an array often results in code that's easier to understand. However, using the forEach() method typically results in code that's more concise. As a result, you can choose the technique that works best for you.

A method for working with each element in an array

Method	Description
forEach(*function*)	Executes the specified callback function once for each element and returns a value of undefined.

The syntax of a callback function for this method

```
function(current-element, [current-index], [array])
```

An array that's used by the examples in this figure

```
const numbers = [1, 2, 3, 4, 5, 6, 7, 8, 9, 10];
```

Two ways to loop through each element

With a for-of loop

```
let numberString = "";
for (let elem of numbers) {
    numberString += "#" + elem + " ";
}
// numberString = "#1 #2 #3 #4 #5 #6 #7 #8 #9 #10 "
```

With the forEach() method

```
let numberString = "";
numbers.forEach(elem => numberString += "#" + elem + " ");
// numberString = "#1 #2 #3 #4 #5 #6 #7 #8 #9 #10 "
```

Two ways to modify each element

With a for-in loop

```
for (let i in numbers) {
    numbers[i] = numbers[i] * 2;
}
// numbers is [2, 4, 6, 8, 10, 12, 14, 16, 18, 20]
```

With the forEach() method

```
numbers.forEach((elem, i, arr) => arr[i] = elem * 2);
// numbers is [2, 4, 6, 8, 10, 12, 14, 16, 18, 20]
```

Figure 11-3   How to work with each element in an array

How to filter, map, and reduce elements

The table at the top of figure 11-4 summarizes three methods available from an array that you can use to filter, map, and reduce elements. All three of these methods return a new array and leave the original array unchanged.

The filter() and map() methods use the same callback function syntax as the forEach() method presented in the previous figure, but the reduce() method uses the callback function syntax presented in this figure. This syntax adds a total parameter that tracks the state of the value the reduce() method returns.

The filter() method searches for elements that meet the condition tested by the callback function and returns an array that contains all of the elements that meet that condition. The second example shows how this works. Here, the code creates an array that contains the even numbers in the numbers array created by the first example.

The map() method returns an array that contains the results of executing the callback function on each item of the array. The third example shows how to use this method to create a new array that contains each element of the original array after it has been multiplied by 2. This is similar to the second forEach() example in the previous figure, but it doesn't change the original array.

The reduce() method returns all the elements in the array, reduced to a single value. It accepts a callback function with the syntax described above. In addition, it accepts an optional second parameter that sets the initial value of the total parameter of the callback function. The fourth example shows how to use the reduce() method to create a string that contains the element values. Note that this code specifies an initial value of an empty string. Then, for each element, it adds the # character, the element, and a space to the string. This is similar to the first forEach() example in the previous figure, but it's more concise.

The last example shows how to use the reduce() method to total all of the element values. To do that, it specifies an initial value of 0. Then, the callback function adds each element to the total.

Methods that filter, map, and reduce array elements

Method	Description
filter(*function*)	Returns an array containing all the elements that meet the condition of the specified callback function. Original array is unchanged.
map(*function*)	Executes the specified callback function once for each element and returns an array that contains the results. Original array is unchanged.
reduce(*function*, *init*)	Executes the specified callback function that returns all the elements reduced to one value, processed in ascending sequence. The optional second parameter sets an initial value for the function. Original array is unchanged.

The syntax of a callback function for the reduce() method

```
function(total, current-element, [current-index], [array])
```

An array that's used by the examples in this figure

```
const numbers = [1, 2, 3, 4, 5, 6, 7, 8, 9, 10];
```

Create a new array with only even numbers

```
const evenNumbers = numbers.filter(elem => elem % 2 === 0);
// evenNumbers is [2, 4, 6, 8, 10]
```

Create a new array with each element multiplied by 2

```
const doubled = numbers.map(elem => elem * 2);
// doubled is [2, 4, 6, 8, 10, 12, 14, 16, 18, 20]
```

Create a string that contains the element values

```
const str = numbers.reduce((total, elem) => total + "#" + elem + " ", "");
// str is "#1 #2 #3 #4 #5 #6 #7 #8 #9 #10 "
```

Sum the element values

```
const sum = numbers.reduce((total, elem) => total + elem, 0);
// sum is 55
```

Description

- The callback function syntax for the filter() and map() methods is the same as the callback function syntax for the forEach() method.

Figure 11-4   How to filter, map, and reduce elements

The Test Scores app

Figure 11-5 presents another version of the Test Scores app that you saw in chapter 4. This version of the app shows how to use some of the skills presented in this chapter to work with an array. To start, it allows users to enter a score into the text box. Then, when the user clicks the Add Score button, the app adds the score to an array and displays all of the scores as well as the average score. In addition, it displays the letter grade that corresponds to each score, and it displays the scores ordered from highest to lowest.

Part 1 of this figure shows the HTML for this app. Unlike some earlier apps that were similar, this HTML uses labels, not disabled text boxes, to display score values.

As you review this code, note how this version of the Test Scores app combines skills that you learned in chapter 4, like using the join() method, with the skills from this chapter. This is a good moment to pause and recognize how much you've already learned even as your skills continue to grow.

The Test Scores app

My Test Scores

All scores:	89, 100, 95, 85, 79, 91, 67, 83
Letter grades:	B, A, A, B, C, A, D, B
Average score:	86.13
Highest to lowest:	100, 95, 91, 89, 85, 83, 79, 67
Enter new score:	[ ] [Add Score]

The HTML for the <body> element

```
<body>
    <h1>My Test Scores</h1>
    <div>
        <label>All scores:</label>
        <label id="all"></label>
    </div>
    <div>
        <label>Letter grades:</label>
        <label id="grades"></label>
    </div>
    <div>
        <label>Average score:</label>
        <label id="avg"></label>
    </div>
    <div>
        <label>Highest to lowest:</label>
        <label id="sort"></label>
    </div>
    <div>
        <label for="score">Enter new score:</label>
        <input type="text" id="score">
        <button id="add_score">Add Score</button><span></span>
    </div>

    <script src="test_scores.js"></script>
</body>
```

Figure 11-5   The Test Scores app (part 1)

Part 2 of figure 11-5 presents the JavaScript for this app. It starts with the getElement() helper method that returns the specified HTML element.

Next is the event handler for the DOMContentLoaded event. Within this event handler, the first statement creates an array named scores to hold the scores entered by the user. After this statement, the code adds an event handler for the click event of the Add Score button. This event handler contains most of the code for this app. After the click event handler, the DOMContentLoaded event handler ends by setting the focus on the score text box.

The click event handler starts by clearing any previous error messages in the span element that follows the Add Score button. Next, it gets the value the user entered in the score text box and converts it to a decimal value. Then, it validates that value by checking that it's a number from 0 to 100. If it isn't, it displays an error message in the span element that follows the Add Score button.

However, if the score is valid, the click event handler continues by using the push() method to add the score to the end of the scores array. After that, it uses the join() method to format the elements as a string of numbers separated by a comma and a space. Next, it assigns the formatted string to the label with an id of "all".

After displaying all the scores, this code displays the letter grades that correspond to the scores. To do that, it uses the map() method to get an array of letter grades. The callback function passed to the map() method uses an if/else statement to determine the letter grade for each score. Then, it uses the join() method to assign a formatted string to the label with an id of "grades".

After displaying the letter grades, this code calculates the average score. To do that, it uses the reduce() method to get the sum of the scores in the array. Here, the callback function for this method defines two parameters. The parameter named total represents the total of the elements that have already been processed, and the parameter named elem represents the value of the current element. Then, the callback function adds the value of the current element to the total.

Since this code passes an initial value of 0 as the second parameter of the reduce() function, the total parameter is initialized to zero, which is usually what you want. The sum of the elements is then divided by the length of the array to get the average, which is then rounded to two decimal places and assigned to the label with an id of "avg".

After calculating the total, this code displays the scores in descending order. First, though, it uses the slice() method to make a copy of the scores array. That way, the order of the scores array isn't changed. It uses a callback function to sort the scores in the copy in descending order, Then, it uses the join() method to format those scores and display them in the label with an id of "sort".

The last two statements in the click event handler prepare for the next user entry. The first statement sets the value of the text box to an empty string, and the second statement moves the focus to that text box.

The JavaScript

```javascript
const getElement = selector => document.querySelector(selector);

document.addEventListener("DOMContentLoaded", () => {
    const scores = [];

    getElement("#add_score").addEventListener("click", () => {
        // clear any previous error message
        getElement("#add_score").nextElementSibling.textContent = "";

        // get score entered by user and validate
        const score = parseFloat(getElement("#score").value);
        if (isNaN(score) || score < 0 || score > 100) {
            getElement("#add_score").nextElementSibling.textContent =
                "Score must be from 0 to 100.";
        }
        else { // score is valid

            // add score to scores array
            scores.push(score);

            // display all scores
            getElement("#all").textContent = scores.join(", ");

            // display letter grades for scores
            const grades = scores.map(elem => {
                if (elem >= 90) return "A";
                else if (elem >= 80) return "B";
                else if (elem >= 70) return "C";
                else if (elem >= 60) return "D";
                else return "F";
            });
            getElement("#grades").textContent = grades.join(", ");

            // calculate and display average score
            const sum = scores.reduce((total, elem) => total + elem, 0);
            const avg = sum/scores.length;
            getElement("#avg").textContent = avg.toFixed(2);

            // display the scores sorted in descending order
            const sortedScores = scores.slice();  // make a copy
            sortedScores.sort((a, b) => b - a);
            getElement("#sort").textContent = sortedScores.join(", ");
        }

        // get text box ready for next entry
        getElement("#score").value = "";
        getElement("#score").focus();
    });

    // set focus on initial load
    getElement("#score").focus();
});
```

Figure 11-5   The Test Scores app (part 2)

Advanced skills for working with arrays

So far, this book has presented most of the basic skills that you need for working with arrays. Now, you're ready to learn some advanced skills that will elevate your coding skills and allow you to create more complex apps.

How to destructure an array

So far, this book has used indexes to assign individual elements in an array to constants or variables. However, JavaScript also allows you to assign multiple array elements to multiple constants or variables in a single statement without using indexes. This is called *destructuring* an array.

To start, figure 11-6 presents the syntax for destructuring an array. To do that, you code the *const* or *let* keyword depending on whether you want to assign the elements of the array to constants or variables. Then, you code the names of the constants or variables within brackets. Next, you code the assignment operator followed by the name of the array whose elements are being destructured.

The examples show how this syntax works. After the first example defines two arrays, the second example assigns the first three elements in the totals array to constants named total1, total2, and total3. This is equivalent to these statements:

```
const total1 = totals[0];
const total2 = totals[1];
const total3 = totals[2];
```

The third example shows how you can skip the assignment of an element. To do that, you code a comma as a placeholder.

The fourth example shows how you can code a default value that's assigned if the corresponding element in an array doesn't exist. In this case, the fullName array only has three elements. As a result, this code assigns the default value to the fourth constant.

The fifth example shows how to use the rest operator (**. . .**) to assign elements in an array to a new array. To use the rest operator, you prepend it to the name of the new array. Then, after assigning any other elements, JavaScript assigns the rest of the elements to the new array. In this example, the code assigns the first two elements to the total1 and total2 constants, and it assigns the rest of the elements to an array named remainingTotals.

If you use the rest operator, you can only use it once per destructuring statement. In addition, you can only use it with the last constant or variable in the list.

The last example shows that you can also destructure strings. This makes sense because a string works much like an array of characters. When you destructure a string, JavaScript assigns the individual characters of the string to the variables or constants within the brackets. As with arrays, you can use commas to skip characters, you can provide default values, and you can use the rest operator to create an array of the remaining characters.

The syntax to destructure an array

```
const|let [identifier-1, identifier-2, ...] = arrayName;
```

Two arrays that are used by the following examples

```
const totals = [141.95, 76, 312.80, 9.99];
const fullName = ["Grace", "M", "Hopper"];
```

Assign the first three elements in an array

```
const [total1, total2, total3] = totals;
// total1 is 141.95, total2 is 76, total3 is 312.80
```

Skip an array element

```
const [firstName, , lastName] = fullName;
// firstName is "Grace", lastName is "Hopper"
```

Use a default value

```
const [first, middle, last, suffix = "none"] = fullName;
// first is "Grace", middle is "M", last is "Hopper", suffix is "none"
```

Use the rest operator to assign some elements to a new array

```
const[total1, total2, ...remainingTotals] = totals;
// total1 is 141.95, total2 is 76, remainingTotals is [312.80, 9.99]
```

Destructure a string

```
const [first, second, third] = "USA";
// first is "U", second is "S", third is "A"
```

Description

- *Destructuring an array* allows you to assign multiple array elements to multiple constants or variables in a single statement without using indexes.

- To destructure an array, code the *const* or *let* keyword followed by a list of variable or constant names enclosed in brackets ([]), an equal sign, and the name of the array.

- When you destructure an array, you can skip elements by coding commas as placeholders. You can also specify default values that are assigned if an element doesn't exist.

- When you destructure an array, you can use the *rest operator* (...) to assign the rest of the elements in an array to another array.

- You can also destructure the individual characters of a string.

- When you destructure an array or a string, the original array or string isn't changed.

Figure 11-6   How to destructure an array

How to create and use an array of arrays

An *array of arrays* is an array where each element stores another array. This can also be referred to as a *two-dimensional array*, and you can think of the data as columns within rows.

The first example in figure 11-7 shows how to create and use an array of arrays. First, it creates an empty array named students. This array represents the test scores for four students. To add the first two arrays of test scores, this code uses an index value to add each array of test scores directly. To add the next two arrays, this code uses the push() method.

After creating the students array, this example also shows how to access its elements. Here, the first statement displays the value that's at index 0 of the students array and index 1 of the nested test scores array. In other words, it displays the first student's second test score. The second statement displays the value that's at index 2 of the students array and index 3 of the test scores array. In other words, the third student's fourth test score.

The last statement in the first example shows what happens if you specify only one index when referencing the students array. This statement displays the element at index 1 of the students array, which is the nested array of test scores for the second student.

The second example shows how to create an array of arrays with mixed data types. As you can see, it uses the same skills as in the first example. Here, the first statement creates an array named invoice. Then, this example creates two more arrays that represent a line item in an invoice, and it uses the push() method to add these line item arrays to the invoice array. This array represents two line items in an invoice.

After creating the invoice array, the last two statements show how to access the elements of the nested arrays. Here, the first statement displays the first column of the first line item in the invoice. This displays "Duct Tape". Then, the second statement displays the second column of the second line item in the invoice. This displays "3.99".

Create an array of arrays

```
// create an empty students array
const students = [];

// add two arrays of scores to the students array directly
students[0] = [80, 82, 90, 87, 85];
students[1] = [79, 80, 74];

// add two more arrays to the students array with the push() method
students.push([93, 95, 89, 100]);
students.push([60, 72, 65, 71]);

// refer to elements in the nested arrays
console.log(students[0][1]);          // displays 82
console.log(students[2][3]);          // displays 100

// refer to an element in the outer array
console.log(students[1]);             // displays [79, 80, 74]
```

Create an array of arrays with mixed data types

```
const invoice = [];
const lineItem1 = ["Duct Tape", 5.99, 2];
const lineItem2 = ["12-Inch Zip Ties", 3.99, 5];
invoice.push(lineItem1);
invoice.push(lineItem2);

// refer to elements in the nested arrays
console.log(invoice[0][0]);           // displays "Duct Tape"
console.log(invoice[1][1]);           // displays 3.99
```

Description

- An *array of arrays* is an array where each element stores another array. This can also be referred to as a *two-dimensional array*, and you can think of the data as columns within rows.
- To refer to the elements in an array of arrays, you use two index values for each element. The first value is for an element in the outer array. The second value is for an element in the nested array.
- If necessary, you can nest arrays beyond two dimensions. In other words, you can create a three-dimensional array, a four-dimensional array, and so on.

Figure 11-7   How to create and use an array of arrays

How to loop through an array of arrays

The first example in figure 11-8 shows how to loop through the array of arrays named students from the last figure. To do that, it uses an outer loop for the students and an inner loop, also called a *nested loop*, for the test scores for each student.

The code starts by declaring a variable named str and initializing it to an empty string. Then it starts the outer loop. Note that this loop is a for-in loop rather than a for-of loop. That's because the code uses the index value to identify the students as Student 1, Student 2, and so on.

Within the outer loop, the code gets the array of scores for the current student. Then, it gets the index value, which it converts to a number and increments by one. As a result, the student at index 0 is identified as Student 1. Next, it appends the student id to the str variable.

The nested loop loops through the test scores for the current student. Within the nested loop, the code appends the current score and a pipe character to the str variable.

When the nested loop completes, the code in the outer loop continues by appending a new line character to the str variable. When the outer loop completes, the code displays the string that contains data about the students and their test scores in the console.

The second example in this figure shows how use a nested loop to loop through the invoice array from the previous figure. This works much like the first example. However, it begins by initializing a variable named str to the names for four columns followed by a new line character.

Within the nested loop, the code adds the current element followed by a pipe character to the str variable. After the nested loop, but still within the outer loop, the code calculates the total for each line item by multiplying the second line item element (price) by the third element (quantity). Then, it appends the total and a new line character to the str variable. When the outer loop completes, the code displays the string that contains data about the invoice and its line items in the console.

Loop through an array of arrays

```
let str = "";
for (let i in students) {                    // outer loop
    const scores = students[i];
    const id = Number(i) + 1;
    str += "Student " + id + ": ";

    for (let score of scores) {              // nested loop
        str += score + "|";
    }
    str += "\n";
}
console.log(str);
```

The string that's displayed in the console
```
Student 1: 80|82|90|87|85|
Student 2: 79|80|74|
Student 3: 93|95|89|100|
Student 4: 60|72|65|71|
```

Loop through another array of arrays

```
let str = "NAME|PRICE|QTY|TOTAL\n";
for (let lineItem of invoice) {              // outer loop
    for (let column of lineItem) {           // nested loop
        str += column + "|";
    }
    const total = lineItem[1] * lineItem[2];
    str += total.toFixed(2) + "\n";
}
console.log(str);
```

The string that's displayed in the console
```
NAME|PRICE|QTY|TOTAL
Duct Tape|5.99|2|11.98
12-Inch Zip Ties|3.99|5|19.95
```

Description

- A *nested loop* is a loop that's coded within another loop. You can use a nested loop to loop through every element in an array of arrays.

Figure 11-8   How to loop through an array of arrays

How to sort an array of arrays

Figure 11-9 starts by showing how to sort an array of arrays. To do this, you pass a callback function to the sort() method that compares the element or calculation that you want the sort to be based on. For instance, the first statement of the first example sorts the scores arrays by the first score in ascending order. When this statement completes, the scores arrays in the students array from the previous figures are sorted in the following order:

```
[[60,72,65,71], [79,80,74], [80,82,90,87,85], [93,95,89,100]]
```

The second statement in the first example sorts the scores arrays by average score in descending order. To do that, it uses the reduce() method and the length property of each nested array to calculate the average. Then, to sort in descending order, it subtracts the average of the first array parameter from the average of the second array parameter.

The second example shows how to sort the invoice array from the previous figures. This works much like the first example. Here, the first statement sorts the line item arrays by name, the second sorts them by price, and the third sorts them by the total for each line item. To calculate the total for a line item, this code multiplies the second element (price) by the third element (quantity). As you can see, you can sort arrays by almost any criteria you can think of by using callback functions.

How to flatten an array of arrays

After showing how to sort an array of arrays, this figure summarizes the flat() method of an array. You can use this method to convert a multi-dimensional array, such as a two-dimensional array, into a one-dimensional array (a regular array) as shown by the third example. Here, the first statement creates a two-dimensional array that stores three nested arrays that each have three elements. Then, the second statement calls the flat() method on the two-dimensional array. This returns a one-dimensional array with nine elements.

If you only want to flatten the array by one level, you don't need to pass a parameter to the flat() method. However, if you want to flatten an array by multiple levels, you can pass a parameter that specifies the number of levels you want to flatten. For example, if you wanted to flatten a three-dimensional array into a one-dimensional array, you can pass a value of 2 to the flat() method as shown in the last example.

Sort an array of arrays

```
// sort by the first score in ascending order
students.sort((a, b) => a[0] - b[0]);

// sort by the average score in descending order
students.sort((a, b) =>
    (b.reduce((total, elem) => total + elem, 0) / b.length) -
    (a.reduce((total, elem) => total + elem, 0) / a.length));
```

Sort another array of arrays

```
// sort by name in ascending sequence
invoice.sort((a, b) => a[0].localeCompare(b[0]));

// sort by price in ascending sequence
invoice.sort((a, b) => a[1] - b[1]);

// sort by total in ascending sequence
invoice.sort((a, b) => (a[1] * a[2]) - (b[1] * b[2]));
```

A method that flattens an array

Method	Description
`flat(depth)`	Returns a flattened array. The optional depth parameter specifies the number of levels to flatten. The default is 1. Original array is unchanged.

Flatten a two-dimensional array

```
const array2D = [[1, 2, 3], [4, 5, 6], [7, 8, 9]];

const array1D = array2D.flat();
// array1D is [1, 2, 3, 4, 5, 6, 7, 8, 9]
```

Flatten a three-dimensional array

```
const array3D = [["Math", [85, 70]], ["English", [92, 96]]]

const array2D = array3D.flat();
// array2D is ["Math", [85, 70], "English", [92, 96]]

const array1D = array3D.flat(2);
// array1D is ["Math", 85, 70, "English", 92, 96]
```

Description

- You can sort an array of arrays by comparing the value or values of specified elements of the nested arrays.
- When you flatten an array of arrays, you reduce its dimensions by one or more.

Figure 11-9   How to sort and flatten an array of arrays

The Task List app

To show how some of the skills you've just learned can be used in an app, figure 11-10 presents another version of the Task List app presented in the previous chapter. This version uses an array of arrays for the task list.

As before, this app displays the tasks in a textarea element on the right side of the page. Now, though, the tasks include a due date and are sorted by this date in ascending order.

The HTML for this app is shown in part 1 of this figure. This HTML is mostly the same as the Task List app presented in the previous chapter. However, the <body> element now includes a label and an input element for the due date as well as for the task description. Then, when the user clicks the Add Task button, the app adds a nested task array that includes the description and due date to the array of tasks.

The Task List app

The HTML for the <body> element

```
<body>
    <h1>Task List</h1>

    <div id="tasks">
        <label for="task_list">Task List</label><br>
        <textarea id="task_list" rows="6" cols="50"></textarea>
    </div>

    <div>
        <label for="task">Task:</label><br>
        <input type="text" name="task" id="task">
    </div>

    <div>
        <label for="due_date">Due Date:</label><br>
        <input type="text" name="due_date" id="due_date">
    </div>

    <div>
        <input type="button" id="add_task" value="Add Task"><br>
        <input type="button" id="clear_tasks" value="Clear Tasks">
    </div>

    <p id="message"></p>

    <script src="task_list.js"></script>
</body>
```

Figure 11-10   The Task List app (part 1)

Part 2 of figure 11-10 presents the JavaScript for this app. It starts with two helper functions. The first is the getElement() function you've seen throughout this book. And the second is a function named getDisplayString() that accepts an array of tasks and returns a formatted string of those tasks for display. To do that, this function starts by checking if the tasks array contains at least one element. If not, it returns an empty string.

If the tasks array contains any elements, the code passes a callback function to the map() method of the tasks array that converts the date string for each element to a Date object.

After the conversion, the code sorts the array of arrays by due date. It does this by passing a callback function to the sort() method of the tasks array. Since this is an array of arrays, the two elements being compared are arrays. The callback function gets the second element from each array, which is the date, and subtracts the second date from the first date. This sorts the tasks in ascending order by date.

After the sort, this function uses the reduce() method of the tasks array to create a single string to display all tasks, and returns that string value. Remember that a callback function for the reduce() method accepts a total parameter plus the value of the current element in the array. Since this is an array of arrays, that means the value of the current element is an array. So, the callback function formats the date element as a string and concatenates it with the description element, separated by a dash, and a new line character. The call to the reduce() method also sets the initial value of the total parameter to an empty string.

The event handler for the DOM content loaded event starts by retrieving the tasks JSON string from local storage. If there's no such value in local storage, null is assigned to the taskString constant. Then, the code calls the JSON.parse() method to convert the JSON string to an array and assign it to the tasks constant. If the JSON string value is null, it assigns an empty array to that constant.

Next, it codes click event handlers for the Add Task and Clear Tasks buttons. After that, it passes the tasks array to the getDisplayString() function and assigns the result to the Task List text area. This formats and displays the tasks in the text area when the app initially loads. Finally, it sets the focus on the Task text box.

The click event handler for the Add Task button starts by getting the two values the user entered and converting the date string to a Date object. Then, it checks that the user entered a task and date and that the date is valid. If so, this code creates a new task array and adds it to the tasks array, converts the tasks array to a JSON string, and stores that JSON string in local storage.

After that, it clears the Task and Due Date text boxes to prepare for the next entry and displays the updated tasks in the Task List text area. To do that, it passes the tasks array to the getDisplayString() function and assigns the resulting string to the text area. Finally, it sets the focus on the Task text box so the user can make another entry. If the user doesn't make valid entries for both text boxes, the app displays an error message. Then, it selects the Task text box so the user can change it if necessary.

The click event handler for the Clear Tasks button clears all the tasks. To do that, it sets the length of the tasks array to zero, removes the tasks from local storage, clears the text area, and sets the focus to prepare for the next entry.

The JavaScript

```javascript
const getElement = selector => document.querySelector(selector);

const getDisplayString = tasks => {
    if (tasks.length === 0) {
        return "";
    } else {
        // convert stored date string (second element) to Date object
        tasks = tasks.map(task => [task[0], new Date(task[1])]);

        // sort by date (second element)
        tasks.sort((task1, task2) => task1[1] - task2[1]);

        // return display string - concat date and event
        return tasks.reduce((str, task) =>
            str += task[1].toDateString() + " - " + task[0] + "\n", "");
    }
};

document.addEventListener("DOMContentLoaded", () => {
    const taskString = localStorage.tasks ?? null;
    const tasks = JSON.parse(taskString) ?? [];

    getElement("#add_task").addEventListener("click", () => {
        getElement("#message").textContent = ""; // clear previous message

        const task = getElement("#task").value;
        const dateString = getElement("#due_date").value;
        const dueDate = new Date(dateString);

        if (task && dateString && dueDate.toString() !== "Invalid Date") {
            tasks.push([task, dueDate]);
            localStorage.tasks = JSON.stringify(tasks);

            getElement("#task").value = "";
            getElement("#due_date").value = "";
            getElement("#task_list").value = getDisplayString(tasks);
            getElement("#task").focus();
        } else {
            getElement("#message").textContent =
                "Please enter a task and valid due date.";
            getElement("#task").select();
        }
    });

    getElement("#clear_tasks").addEventListener("click", () => {
        tasks.length = 0;
        localStorage.removeItem("tasks");
        getElement("#task_list").value = "";
        getElement("#task").focus();
    });

    getElement("#task_list").value = getDisplayString(tasks);
    getElement("#task").focus();
});
```

Figure 11-10   The Task List app (part 2)

How to copy an array

Sometimes you need to make a copy of an array. You might think that you could do this by assigning an existing array to another constant or variable as shown in the first example of figure 11-11. However, this doesn't work. This is because the constant named names doesn't store the array of names. It stores a *reference* to the location where the array's values are stored. When names2 is assigned the value of names, it copies the reference and only the reference. This means both names and names2 refer to the same array values.

As a result, if you change the value of an element in the array referred to by names, it's changed for names2 as well. Usually, this isn't what you want.

To copy an array, you need to create a new array and copy the value of each element from the original array into the new array. You can use a loop to do that, but JavaScript provides several other ways to copy an array that are less verbose than using a loop. In the figures that follow, you'll learn some of the common ways to copy an array.

How to make a shallow copy

Figure 11-11 presents two ways to make a copy of an array. Note that these techniques produce a *shallow copy*, which is an array that has copies of the top-level elements but any elements that are nested arrays or objects refer to the elements in the original array. In the next figure, you'll see how this can affect your code and what to do about it.

The first technique uses the slice() method of an array. If you don't pass any values to this method, it creates a new array and copies the elements of the original array to it as shown here.

The second technique uses the spread operator (...) to make a copy of an array. This operator takes the elements of an array and spreads them out into a comma-separated list that you can use as an initialization list with an array literal. In the example shown here, the spread operator spreads the elements in the names array into a list that the array literal uses to create a new array. This is functionally the same as the following code:

```
const namesCopy2 = [names[0], names[1], names[2]];
```

Another way to make a shallow copy of an array is with the Array.from() method that's presented here. This method accepts an array and returns a copy of the array. However, it can also accept some other types of objects, as long as it's possible to loop through the elements of that object with a for loop.

In the example shown here, the querySelectorAll() method of a document object returns a NodeList object with a collection of HTML element objects that you can loop through with a for loop. But, a NodeList object isn't an Array object, so you can't use some methods available from an array to work with it. However, if you pass the NodeList object to the Array.from() method, it returns an Array object that contains the HTML element objects in the NodeList. Then, you can use all of the methods available from an array to work with the copy.

Code that fails to copy an array

```
const names = ["Grace", "Charles", "Ada"];
const names2 = names;      // This doesn't copy the array!
names2[1] = "Brendan";
// names and names2 are ["Grace", "Brendan", "Ada"]
```

Two ways to make a shallow copy of an array

- Call the slice() method of the array.
- Use an array literal with a spread operator and the array.

Code that copies an array

```
const names = ["Grace", "Charles", "Ada"];
const namesCopy1 = names.slice();      // slice() method
const namesCopy2 = [...names];         // array literal and spread operator
// namesCopy1 and namesCopy2 are ["Grace", "Charles", "Ada"]
```

A method of the Array object for copying an array

Method	Description
`from(array)`	Returns a copy of the specified Array object. This method can also convert some other types of objects such as a NodeList object into an Array object.

Code that attempts to call an array method from a NodeList object

```
const items = document.querySelectorAll("li");
const text = items.reduce((tot, el) => tot + el.textContent + " ", "");
// TypeError - items is a NodeList object, reduce() not available
```

Code that gets an Array object from a NodeList object

```
const itemsArr = Array.from(items);  // copies above NodeList as an Array
const text = itemsArr.reduce((tot, el) => tot + el.textContent + " ", "");
// works - itemsArr is an Array object, reduce() is available
```

Code that gets an Array object from a NodeList object in one statement

```
const items = Array.from(document.querySelectorAll("li"));
```

Description

- A constant or variable doesn't actually store an array, but instead stores a *reference* to where an array is stored.
- A *shallow copy* of an array copies only the top-level elements in an array. Elements that are nested arrays or objects still refer to the same elements as the original array.
- Two common ways to make a shallow copy are the slice() method and using an array literal with the spread operator.
- The spread operator (`...`) spreads the elements of an array into a list separated by commas. Then, you can use that list in an array literal that initializes a new array.
- You can use the Array.from() method to copy a non-Array object into an Array object. This works as long as JavaScript can use a for loop to loop through the non-Array object.

Figure 11-11   How to make a shallow copy of an array

How to make a deep copy

In the last figure, you learned how to make a shallow copy of an array. Figure 11-12 starts by showing you what this can mean for your code.

The first example in this figure declares an array named nested with four elements. These are top-level elements, which means that they're available from the outer array. The second element, however, is a nested array. More accurately, it is a reference to the location of the nested array's values. So even though the reference to the array is a top-level element, the elements in the array that it points to are second-level elements.

The second example in this figure makes a shallow copy of the nested array named shallowCopy. Because the top-level elements are copied, you can change them in the copy without affecting the original array. You can see that in this example, which changes the value of the first element in the copy from 1 to 10. The code that displays the first element for each array shows that the copy is changed but the original is not. Note that this is true for the nested array, too. That is, if you execute the following code:

```
shallowCopy[1] = "changed!";
```

the second element in the copy is changed from a reference to an array to a string, but the original is unchanged.

However, if you change the value of one of the elements in the nested array in the copy, the original is changed, too. You can see that in the second example as well. Here, the value of the first element in the nested array in the copy is changed from 2 to 20. The code that displays this element for each array shows that both the copy and the original are changed. That's because the elements in the nested array aren't top-level elements.

To fix this, you can make a *deep copy* of a nested array. In a deep copy, none of the elements refer to any element in the original. In other words, all the element values are copied.

The third example in this figure shows a simple way to make a deep copy. To do that, you use the JSON.parse() and JSON.stringify() methods. When you pass the array to the JSON.stringify() method, it converts the array to a JSON string. So, this string doesn't refer to any element in the original array. Then, when you pass the string to the JSON.parse() method, it creates all new elements, including any nested arrays or objects.

One problem with the technique presented here is that it doesn't work with objects that need to have their constructors called again, such as Date objects. In that case, you may need to write some code that makes sure these types of elements are converted to the correct data types.

A two-dimensional array that's used in the following examples

```
const numbers = [1, [2, 3, 4], 5, 6];
```

What happens when you make a shallow copy

```
const shallowCopy = [...numbers];

// change a top-level value in the copy - only copy changes
shallowCopy[0] = 10;

console.log(shallowCopy[0]);      // displays 10
console.log(numbers[0]);          // displays 1

// change a nested value in the copy - copy and original change
shallowCopy[1][0] = 20;

console.log(shallowCopy[1][0]);   // displays 20
console.log(numbers[1][0]);       // displays 20
```

How to make a deep copy

```
const deepCopy = JSON.parse(JSON.stringify(numbers));

// change a nested value in the copy - only copy changes
deepCopy[1][0] = 20;

console.log(deepCopy[1][0]);      // displays 20
console.log(numbers[1][0]);       // displays 2
```

Description

- When you make a shallow copy of an array of arrays, you copy references to each nested array, not the values in those arrays.
- Changing the value of a nested element in a shallow copy of an array will change the value for the original array as well and vice versa.
- A *deep copy* of an array copies the value of every element in the array regardless of how deeply it is nested.
- You can use the JSON.stringify() and JSON.parse() methods to make a deep copy of a nested array.
- Because this technique converts values to JSON strings, you may lose some data when using this technique with an array of objects, such as Dates objects. In that case, you may need to create a custom function that loops through the array.

Figure 11-12   How to make a deep copy of an array

Perspective

In chapter 4, you learned the basics of working with arrays. In this chapter, you learned more skills for working with arrays, including how to work with arrays of arrays. If you understand the skills presented in these two chapters, you have a solid foundation for working with arrays.

Arrays are usually the optimal data structure to use if you want to keep a collection of elements in a sequence and use numbered indexes to quickly access and modify the elements. However, JavaScript provides other data structures that are optimal for other situations. For example, a set can be optimal if you need to store a unique set of values. And a map can be optimal if you need to store key/value pairs that you can access with a unique key that's a string. Either way, knowing how to work with arrays provides a good foundation for learning more about other data structures like sets and maps.

Terms

callback function	nested loop
destructuring an array	reference
rest operator	shallow copy
array of arrays	deep copy
two-dimensional array	

Exercise 11-1   The Shopping Cart app

In this exercise, you'll use an array of arrays to store the data for a shopping cart, and you'll use this data to display a shopping cart on a web page.

Shopping Cart

Item Description	Price	Quantity	Total
1984	$15	1	$15
Dune	$20	3	$60
HTML	$54.5	5	$272.5
Python Data Analysis	$59.5	2	$119
TOTAL		11	466.5

Review the starting code

1. View the files in this folder:

    `exercises\ch11\cart`

2. Open the index.html file. Note that it defines the elements for a table and its header row but doesn't define any other rows.

3. Open the cart.js file.

4. Examine the getLineItems() function. Note that it returns an array of arrays where each nested array represents an item in a shopping cart.

5. Run the app. Note that it displays the correct number of rows but doesn't display the correct data for the Total column or the summary row.

Fix the code so it displays the correct values

6. Fix the addRow() function so it calculates the value for the Total column. To do that, you can multiply the price by the quantity.

7. Fix the addSummaryRow() function so it totals the Quantity and Total columns. To do that, you can use a for-of loop to loop through each line item.

8. Run the app to make sure it works correctly.

Use methods to work with the array of arrays

9. In the DOMContentLoaded event handler, modify the code so it uses the forEach() method of the lineItems array instead of a for-of loop.

10. Still in the DOMContentLoaded event handler, add code that sorts the line items by their descriptions.

11. Run the app to make sure it works correctly.

Exercise 11-2   The Invoices app

The Invoices app uses an array of arrays to store invoices and display them in a table as shown below. It also allows the user to filter the invoices based on the Due Date and Paid columns.

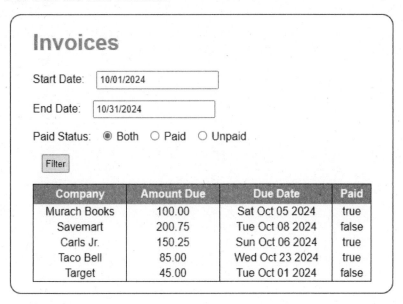

Review the starting code

1. View the files in this folder:

    `exercises\ch11\invoices`

2.   Open the index.html file. Note that it defines the HTML elements for this page.

3.   Open the invoice.js file. Note that it already contains invoice data and some code for working with the HTML elements, including a custom createCol() function.

4.   Run the app and click the Filter button. Note that the app doesn't display any invoices and the Filter button doesn't do anything.

Write the code that displays the invoices

5.   In the displayInvoices() function, add one row for each invoice. To do that, you can loop through the invoices and append one <tr> element for each invoice to the table. Hint: You can use the createCol() function to create a <td> element for each column in the table.

6.   Run the app and make sure that your code is working correctly. It should now display the invoices when the app starts.

Write code that filters the invoices

7.   In the filterInvoices() function, finish writing the code that filters the invoices by the date. To do that, you need to add an if statement that returns a Boolean value that indicates whether the invoice is within the specified date range.

8.   Run the app and make sure that your code is working correctly. It should now allow you to filter invoices by date range.

9.   In the filterInvoices() function, add code that filters the invoices by paid status. Hint: You can use the checked property of a radio button element to get a Boolean value that indicates whether it is selected.

10. Run the app and make sure that your code is working correctly. It should now allow you to filter invoices by date range and paid status.

12

How to work with objects

So far, the code in this book has been using native JavaScript object types like the Number, String, Date, and Array types. Now, this chapter shows how to create and use your own objects. This provides a way to group related data and functions, and that makes it easier to maintain and reuse the code that you create.

How to get started with objects

This topic presents the basic skills for creating and using objects. That includes how to create and use libraries that store your objects.

How to use an object literal to define an object

The simplest way to create your own object is by assigning an *object literal* to a variable or constant. To code an object literal, you enclose it in a pair of braces. Then, you code the *properties* and *methods* of the object within the braces.

The first example in figure 12-1 shows how this works. Here, an object literal with two properties and one method is assigned to a constant named invoice. You should notice four things about this example.

First, each property name is followed by a colon and the value. Second, the getTotal() method doesn't include the *function* keyword. Instead, the name of the function is followed by a set of parentheses. Then, within the parentheses, you can code any parameters for the function. Third, the properties and methods for this object are separated by commas. Fourth, the code in the getTotal() method uses the *this* keyword to get the values of the subtotal and taxRate properties. This works because the *this* keyword in this method refers to the object itself.

Although it's not shown here, you should know that you can also create an object without any properties and methods by coding just a pair of brackets. Then, you can add properties and methods to the object that's created as shown in figure 12-3.

After you create an object, you can work with its properties and methods the same way you work with the properties and methods of other objects you've seen in this book such as Date and Array objects. That means you can use the dot operator to refer to the properties and methods as shown by the second example. Here, the values assigned to the two properties and the value returned by the method are displayed in the console.

You can also use brackets to refer to an object's properties and methods, as shown in the third example. This is useful if you want to use a Symbol type as a property name as shown later in this chapter. Most of the time, though, you'll use the dot operator with objects.

Note that when you use an object literal to create an object, you are creating an instance of the Object type. If you want to create a custom object type, you can define a class as shown in the next figure.

Code an object literal with two properties and one method

```
const invoice = {                                      // object
    taxRate: 0.0875,                                   // property
    subtotal: 100,                                     // another property
    getTotal() {                                       // method
        return this.subtotal + (this.subtotal * this.taxRate);
                                                       // this = the object

    }
};
```

Use the dot operator to refer to an object's properties and methods

```
console.log(invoice.taxRate);                          // displays 0.0875
console.log(invoice.subtotal);                         // displays 100
console.log(invoice.getTotal());                       // displays 108.75
```

Use brackets to refer to an object's properties and methods

```
console.log(invoice["taxRate"]);                       // displays 0.0875
console.log(invoice["subtotal"]);                      // displays 100
console.log(invoice["getTotal"]());                    // displays 108.75
```

Description

- You can create a new object by coding a pair of braces (`{}`) with or without property and method assignments. This is known as an *object literal*.

- To code a *property* within an object literal, you code the property name, a colon, and the property value.

- To code a *method* within an object literal, you code a method name followed by a set of parentheses and a set of braces. Within the parentheses, you can code the parameters for the method. Within the braces, you code the statements for the method.

- Inside a method, the value of the *this* keyword typically refers to the object itself.

- To access a property or method, you can use the dot operator or brackets.

Figure 12-1   How to use an object literal to define an object

How to use a class to define an object

If you've worked in other programming languages, you're probably familiar with classes. You can think of a *class* as a template that defines the properties and methods of an object but isn't an object itself. Instead, you can create an object from the class. Languages that use classes to define and create objects are called *class-based* or *classical languages*.

By contrast, JavaScript is a *prototypal language* that uses prototypes to create objects. Nevertheless, modern JavaScript provides a syntax that's similar to class-based languages. This syntax is more concise than the syntax for working with prototypes. In addition, it's familiar to programmers who have experience with class-based languages. As a result, it's generally considered a best practice to use this syntax for new development.

Figure 12-2 shows how to use a class to define an Invoice type. By convention, class names start with an uppercase letter and object names start with a lowercase letter. That's why this figure uses Invoice as the name of the class and invoice or something similar for the objects created from the class.

In the first example, the Invoice class begins by defining the *constructor* that creates, or constructs, an object of type Invoice. To do that, this class defines the constructor() function. Within the constructor, the code defines the properties that store the data for the class, called *data properties*. Here, the code uses the *this* keyword to define data properties named subtotal and taxRate, and it initializes both properties to null. After the constructor, this class defines a method named getTotal() that gets the total for the invoice based on the values of the subtotal and taxRate properties.

After defining the Invoice type, the code in the second example uses the *new* keyword to create a new Invoice object named invoice. This is known as creating an *instance* of the class. Then, this code sets the subtotal and taxRate properties of the Invoice object. This is necessary because these properties are set to null for a new Invoice object. Next, this code calls the getTotal() method of the Invoice object to get the total for the invoice. To refer to the properties and method, this code uses the dot operator. However, it could also use brackets as shown in the previous figure.

Note that when you create an Invoice object, you must use the *new* keyword to call the constructor. If you don't, JavaScript throws a TypeError exception as shown in the third example.

In the fourth example, the constructor for the Invoice class includes two parameters that provide the values for its two properties. As a result, the code that uses this class can use a single statement to create an Invoice object and set its two properties. This makes it easier to create multiple Invoice objects. In the last example, for instance, the code creates Invoice objects named invoice1 and invoice2.

At this point, you may be wondering when to use a class to define an object and when to use an object literal. If you only need a single instance of an object, an object literal is often acceptable. However, if you need to create more than one instance of an object, you can use a class to define an object type and then create multiple instances of it. In addition, you may choose to use a class if you

A class that defines an Invoice type

```
class Invoice {
    constructor() {
        this.subtotal = null;
        this.taxRate = null;
    }
    getTotal() {
        return this.subtotal + (this.subtotal * this.taxRate);
    }
}
```

Create an object from the Invoice class

```
const invoice = new Invoice();
invoice.subtotal = 100;
invoice.taxRate = 0.0875;
console.log(invoice.getTotal());          // displays 108.75
```

What happens if you don't use the new keyword

```
const invoice = Invoice();                // throws a TypeError exception
```

Add parameters to the constructor

```
class Invoice {
    constructor(subtotal, taxRate) {
        this.subtotal = subtotal;
        this.taxRate = taxRate;
    }
    getTotal() {
        return this.subtotal + (this.subtotal * this.taxRate);
    }
}
```

Create two Invoice objects

```
const invoice1 = new Invoice(100, 0.0875);
const invoice2 = new Invoice(1000, 0.07);

console.log(invoice1.getTotal());      // displays 108.75
console.log(invoice2.getTotal());      // displays 1070
```

Description

- You can use a JavaScript *class* to define a *constructor* that allows you to create, or construct, an object from the class. This is also known as creating an *instance* of the class. To do that, you must use the *new* keyword.

- You code the properties that store the data for a class inside the constructor() function. These can be referred to *data properties*.

- You code the methods for your class outside the constructor() function. All instances of the object type share these methods.

- By convention, class names start with an uppercase letter.

Figure 12-2   How to use a class to define an object

want the convenience of using a constructor to set initial property values, you want to define a new type like Invoice or Person, or you want to use some of the encapsulation techniques described later in this chapter.

How to work with objects

Now that you know how to define objects and refer to their properties and methods, you need to learn some basic skills for working with objects. Figure 12-3 presents these skills.

The first example in this figure shows how to add a property to the invoice object that was created in figures 12-1 and 12-2. To do that, you refer to the property through the object using the dot operator. Then, you assign a value to a property. You can add a method using a similar technique, except you assign a function expression to a method as shown in the second example.

In the previous figure, you saw how to change the value of that's assigned to a property of an object. But you can also change the function that's assigned to an object's method. To do that, you just assign a new function expression to the method as shown in the third example. Here, the code for the getTotal() method is changed so it uses the getSalesTax() method that was added in the second example.

You can also remove a property or method from an object. To do that, you use the *delete operator* as shown in the third example. Here, the delete operator removes the taxRate property from the invoice object. Once deleted, the property has a value of undefined, just as if it had never been created.

When you create an object and assign it to a constant or variable, JavaScript stores a *reference* to the object in the constant or variable. To illustrate, the last code example starts by creating a new Invoice object and assigning it to the invoice1 constant. At that point, the invoice1 constant stores a reference to the Invoice object. Then, the code assigns the invoice1 constant to the invoice2 constant. Now, both constants refer to the same object, as shown by the diagram in this figure.

Because both constants refer to the same object, a change to the object through either of the constants applies to the other constant. In this example, the code changes the value of the taxRate property of the invoice2 constant to 0.07. Since the invoice1 constant refers to the same Invoice object, this change causes the taxRate property of the invoice1 constant to return 0.07.

Add a property to an existing object

```
invoice.customerId = 156;
```

Add a method to an existing object

```
invoice.getSalesTax = function() {
    return this.subtotal * this.taxRate;
};
```

Modify a method of an object

```
invoice.getTotal = function() {
    return this.subtotal + this.getSalesTax();
};
```

Remove a property from an object

```
delete invoice.taxRate;
```

Create two references to the same object

```
const invoice1 = new Invoice(100, 0.0875);
const invoice2 = invoice1;                      // reference to same object

invoice2.taxRate = 0.07;
console.log(invoice1.taxRate);                   // displays 0.07
```

Two references to the same object

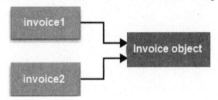

Description

- Once an object is created, you can add new properties and methods to it. This is true for object literals and objects that are instances of a class.
- To add a property to an object, code the object name, the dot operator, the property name, and assign a value.
- To add a method to an object, code the object name, the dot operator, the method name, and assign a function expression.
- You can also change the value of an existing property by assigning a new value to it, and you can change an existing method by assigning a new function expression to it.
- To delete a property or method, you can use the *delete* operator.
- A variable or constant stores a *reference* to an object, not the object itself.

Figure 12-3   How work with objects

How to create and use JavaScript libraries

A *library* is a file that contains a group of related functions, objects, or classes. Often, you'll write your own libraries, but you can also use third-party libraries like jQuery and jQuery UI. Figure 12-4 begins by listing some of the benefits of organizing your code in libraries.

One of the main benefits of libraries is code re-use. This is because you can write a function or object once, and then use it from several different places in your code or among several apps.

Another benefit of libraries is that they help you keep your JavaScript files smaller, which makes them easier to understand and reuse. For example, you can write a library that provides functionality for working with web storage. Since that's all it does, it should be small. Then, you can include that file with any apps that need to use web storage.

Finally, organizing your JavaScript code in libraries encourages you to group code that has related functionality. This, in turn, encourages *separation of concerns*. For example, one library might focus on web storage, another might focus on data validation, and another might focus on working with dates and times. When you group your code in libraries like this, your app becomes easier to maintain and the code becomes easier to re-use in other apps or libraries.

The first example in this figure shows a simple library file named lib_invoice.js. As its name suggests, it contains code for working with an invoice. Specifically, it contains a class named Invoice with properties and methods for calculating an invoice amount.

The second example shows how to include this JavaScript library in an app and use it in another JavaScript file. Since a JavaScript library is just a JavaScript file, you use a <script> element to include a library as shown throughout this book. In the index.html file shown here, the first <script> element refers to the invoice library and the second refers to the main JavaScript file for the app that uses this library.

When you include library files in this way, the JavaScript works as if all of the code is in the same file. However, you need to think about the sequence in which you include the files. Specifically, if one file depends on the functionality in another file, you need to include the files in the proper sequence. For example, the jQuery UI library uses the functionality in the jQuery library. So when you use jQuery UI, you need to make sure that the <script> element for jQuery UI comes after the <script> element for jQuery.

The same goes for working with your own libraries. In this figure, for instance, the main JavaScript file depends on the invoice library. As a result, its <script> element needs to be coded after the <script> element for the library.

The benefits of JavaScript libraries

- They let you group related functionality in a single file.
- They make your code easier to understand, maintain, and reuse.
- They encourage the separation of concerns.

The lib_invoice.js file

```
"use strict";

class Invoice {
    constructor(subtotal, taxRate) {
        this.subtotal = subtotal;
        this.taxRate = taxRate;
    }
    getSalesTax() {
        return this.subtotal * this.taxRate;
    }
    getTotal() {
        return this.subtotal + this.getSalesTax();
    }
}
```

The index.html file

```
...
<body>
    ...
    <script src="lib_invoice.js"></script>
    <script src="invoice.js"></script>
</body>
...
```

The invoice.js file

```
...
const subtotal = parseFloat(getElement("#subtotal").value);
const taxRate = parseFloat(getElement("#tax_rate").value);

const invoice = new Invoice(subtotal, taxRate);
getElement("#total").value = invoice.getTotal();
...
```

Description

- A *library* is an external file that contains related functions, objects, or classes.
- JavaScript libraries range from simple collections of functions and objects that you write yourself to extensive third-party libraries like jQuery.
- A library contains normal JavaScript, so you create a library by grouping related functions, objects, and classes in a single file. You should also name your JavaScript libraries so it's clear what they do.
- You include JavaScript libraries in your apps by using <script> elements. If a JavaScript file depends on a library, you must make sure that the <script> element for the required library precedes the one for the file that depends on it.

Figure 12-4   How to create and use JavaScript libraries

The Invoice app

Figure 12-5 presents the Invoice app that uses a class and a library file to organize its code. This makes it easier to understand the code that works with invoices. In addition, it makes it easier to reuse this code on other pages or in other apps or libraries.

The first <script> element at the end of the body section identifies the JavaScript library used by this app, which is the invoice library that you saw in the previous figure. Then, the second <script> element identifies the main JavaScript file that uses this library.

The HTML for the <body> element contains a text box that allows the user to enter a subtotal amount. Then, it contains two text boxes that display the calculated sales tax and total. These text boxes include the disabled attribute. That way, they can display the calculated values but the user can't change those values. Finally, the HTML defines the button that calculates the sales tax and total.

Next, this figure presents the invoice.js file, which is the main JavaScript file for this app. It starts by defining the getElement() helper method and an event handler for the DOMContentLoaded event. This event handler, in turn, defines a click event handler for the Calculate button. This handler begins by setting a tax rate constant and getting the subtotal value entered by the user. Then, it uses the *new* keyword to create a new Invoice object, passing the tax rate and subtotal values to the constructor.

Next, the code calls the getSalesTax() method of the Invoice object and assigns the return value to the value of the SalesTax text box. After that, it calls the getTotal() method of the Invoice object and assigns the return value to the value of the Total text box.

Since this app only needs a single instance of an Invoice object, it could use an object literal instead of a class. This would eliminate the need to create an instance with the *new* keyword. However, using a class makes it possible to pass the initial values to the class constructor. Ultimately, whether you use an object literal or a class with a simple app like this is mostly a matter of personal preference.

The Invoice app

The HTML of the \<body\> element

```html
<body>
    <h1>Invoice</h1>
    <div>
        <label for="subtotal">Subtotal:</label>
        <input type="text" id="subtotal">
    </div>
    <div>
        <label for="tax_amount">Sales Tax:</label>
        <input type="text" id="tax_amount" disabled>
    </div>
    <div>
        <label for="total">Total</label>
        <input type="text" id="total" disabled>
    </div>
    <div>
        <label></label>
        <input type="button" id="calculate" value="Calculate">
    </div>

    <script src="lib_invoice.js"></script>
    <script src="invoice.js"></script>
</body>
```

The invoice.js file

```javascript
"use strict";

const getElement = selector => document.querySelector(selector);

document.addEventListener("DOMContentLoaded", () => {
    getElement("#calculate").addEventListener("click", () => {
        const taxRate = 0.0875;
        const subtotal = parseFloat(getElement("#subtotal").value);

        const invoice = new Invoice(subtotal, taxRate);

        getElement("#tax_amount").value = invoice.getSalesTax();
        getElement("#total").value = invoice.getTotal();
    });
});
```

Figure 12-5   The Invoice app

How to work with encapsulation

A fundamental concept in working with classes is *encapsulation*, also known as *data hiding*. Encapsulation allows you to shield the implementation details of a class from outside code. This protects the data or functions your class needs from being overwritten.

How to work with private properties and methods

Early versions of JavaScript didn't provide an easy way to encapsulate data. However, modern JavaScript allows you to define *private* properties and methods that can't be called by outside code. Figure 12-6 shows how this works.

The first example in this figure defines an Invoice class that has a private subtotal property. To identify the property as private, it prefixes the property name with the hash character (#). It also has a private validateSubtotal() method. Once again, it prefixes the name of the method with the hash character (#).

The public methods of this class are then able to call this private property and method. To do that, they use the *this* keyword and the hash (#) prefix, like this:

```
return this.#subtotal;
```

Since the subtotal property of an Invoice object is private, a user can't set or get it directly. To set the value of the subtotal property, a user must pass a value to the constructor function or the setSubtotal() method. In both cases, the private validateSubtotal() method is called to make sure the subtotal value that's passed is greater than zero. This ensures that the class receives an appropriate value. Notice that both the subtotal property and the mechanism for validating it are hidden. All a user of this class knows is that they can set a subtotal amount and that if it's not greater than zero they'll get an error.

The last two examples in this figure demonstrate this in more detail. In the second example, a new Invoice object is created with a subtotal value of 100 passed to the constructor. Since this value is greater than zero, the code executes without error and the second statement can use the public getSubtotal() method to get the value of the private subtotal property. The third statement uses the public setSubtotal() method to change the value of the subtotal amount. Since this new value is also greater than zero, the code executes and the fourth statement is able to get the new subtotal amount. By contrast, the fifth statement attempts to pass a value that's less than zero to the setSubtotal() method. In this case, the private method that validates the subtotal amount throws an Error and the value of the private subtotal property isn't changed.

In the third example, two statements try to directly access the private property and method of the Invoice object. The code that tries to access the private property returns undefined, while the code that tries to call the private method throws a TypeError.

You can only code private properties and methods with classes. In the next chapter, you'll learn some techniques for hiding data with other types of objects.

An Invoice class with a private property and a private method

```
class Invoice {
    #subtotal = null;                    // private property
    constructor(subtotal, taxRate) {
        this.taxRate = taxRate;
        this.#subtotal = this.#validateSubtotal(subtotal);
    }
    #validateSubtotal(subtotal) {        // private method
        if (subtotal <= 0) {
            throw new Error("Subtotal must be greater than 0.");
        } else {
            return subtotal;
        }
    }
    setSubtotal(subtotal) {
        this.#subtotal = this.#validateSubtotal(subtotal);
    }
    getSubtotal() {
        return this.#subtotal;
    }
    getSalesTax() {
        return this.#subtotal * this.taxRate;
    }
    getTotal() {
        return this.getSubtotal() + this.getSalesTax();
    }
}
```

Use public methods to access private fields and methods

```
const invoice = new Invoice(100, 0.0875);
console.log(invoice.getSubtotal());        // displays 100

invoice.setSubtotal(500);
console.log(invoice.getSubtotal());        // displays 500

invoice.setSubtotal(-100);                 // throws error
```

What happens if you try to call a private property or method

```
console.log(invoice.subtotal);             // displays undefined
console.log(invoice.validateSubtotal()); // TypeError: not a function
```

Description

- *Encapsulation* allows you to hide the properties or methods of an object from other code that uses the object. This is also known as *data hiding*.

- In JavaScript, you can provide encapsulation by declaring *private* properties and methods. To do that, code the member name with the hash (#) prefix.

- Private properties and methods are available to all the other members of a class, but aren't available outside the class.

- Private properties and methods are only available with classes. In chapter 13, you'll learn how to use modules to provide encapsulation for other types of objects.

Figure 12-6   How to work with private properties and methods

How to work with accessor properties

So far, this chapter has shown how to work with properties that store a specific item of data in memory, sometimes called *data properties*. Now, figure 12-7 shows how to use *accessors*, sometimes called *accessor properties*. Unlike data properties, accessors don't store any data in memory. Instead, an accessor can refer to data that's stored in another property, constant, or variable. Or, it can refer to a computed value.

The first example shows how this works. Here, the Invoice class defines properties that store the subtotal and tax rate of an invoice. Then, the code uses the *set* keyword to define an accessor that sets the value of the private subtotal property. To do that, the *set* keyword is followed by a method that calls the private validateSubtotal() method to check whether the subtotal value is greater than zero. If it is, it stores the value in the subtotal property. Otherwise, this code throws a TypeError that includes an appropriate message. Since this accessor uses the *set* keyword to set a value, it's known as a *setter*.

After the setter, the code uses the *get* keyword to define an accessor that gets the value of the subtotal property. To do that, the *get* keyword is followed by a method that returns the value of the private subtotal property. Since this accessor uses the *get* keyword to get a value, it's known as a *getter*.

Although the subtotal property in this figure has a getter and a setter, you can create a *read-only property* by only coding a getter. Conversely, you can code a *write-only property* by only coding a setter. For instance, the next two methods of this Invoice class are read-only properties that return calculated values.

You call an accessor property just like you do a data property. In other words, you don't include the parentheses like you do for a normal method call. In the second example, for instance, the second statement uses the getter for the subtotal property to display the value in the private subtotal property. Then, the third statement uses the setter for the subtotal property to set a new subtotal amount. Finally, the last statement calls the read-only total property to display the calculated value.

Accessors can make your code easier to call. For example, you could code a regular method named getSubtotal() to get the subtotal amount, as you saw in the previous figure. However, coding a getter instead makes the calling code shorter since you don't need to code "get" or the parentheses after the method name. Accessors also allow you to perform tasks like transforming a value before returning it or validating a value before storing it.

Unlike private properties and methods, accessors are available to object literals as well as classes. For instance, you could code an invoice object literal that looks like this:

```
const invoice = {
    taxRate: 0.0875,
    subtotal: 100,
    get total() { ... }
};
```

An Invoice class with accessor properties

```
class Invoice {
    #subtotal = null;                            // private subtotal
    constructor(subtotal, taxRate) {
        this.taxRate = taxRate;
        this.#subtotal = this.#validateSubtotal(subtotal);
    }
    #validateSubtotal(subtotal) {
        if (subtotal <= 0) {
            throw new Error("Subtotal must be greater than 0.");
        } else {
            return subtotal;
        }
    }
    set subtotal(subtotal) {                     // subtotal setter
        this.#subtotal = this.#validateSubtotal(subtotal);
    }
    get subtotal() {                             // subtotal getter
        return this.#subtotal;
    }
    get salesTax() {                             // read-only property
        return this.#subtotal * this.taxRate;
    }
    get total() {                                // read-only property
        return this.subtotal + this.salesTax;
    }
}
```

Use accessor properties to access private fields and methods

```
const invoice = new Invoice(100, 0.0875);

console.log(invoice.subtotal);      // displays 100
invoice.subtotal = 200;             // use setter
console.log(invoice.total);         // displays 217.5
```

Description

- A *data property* stores a specific item of data in memory.
- An *accessor*, or *accessor property*, doesn't store data in memory. Instead, it refers to data that's stored in another property, constant, or variable. Or, it refers to a computed value.
- To code an accessor, you code the *get* or *set* keyword followed by a method. The resulting accessors are called *getters* and *setters*.
- A property with only an accessor that gets data is known as a *read-only property*, and a property with only an accessor that sets data is known as a *write-only property*.
- You call an accessor like any other property. Even though an accessor includes a method with parentheses, you don't include the parentheses like you do for a normal method call.
- Accessors can make your code easier to call, and they allow you to perform tasks like transforming a value before returning it or validating a value before storing it.

Figure 12-7   How to work with accessor properties

How to work with inheritance and object composition

When working with objects, it's common to create complex types based on simpler types. One way to do that is to use *inheritance* to create a new object that has all the properties and methods of an existing object. Another way is to use *object composition* to combine simple objects into more complex data structures.

How to work with inheritance

JavaScript has a hierarchy of *native object types* that's shown by the chart in figure 12-8. The first level consists of the Object type. The second level consists of other native object types like the String, Number, Boolean, Date, and Array types that you've already learned about. In addition, this hierarchy shows the Function type that's used to represent functions.

This hierarchy means that all of the object types at the second level *inherit* the properties and methods of the Object type. This also means that every object type can use the properties and methods of the Object type. For instance, the Object type defines a toString() method that converts an object to a string.

When you define a class, it inherits the Object type by default. For instance, the Person class in the first example inherits the Object type. As a result, you can call the toString() method from an object created from the Person class. In addition, you can call the firstName, lastName, and fullName properties defined by this class. Here, the last two statements use the instanceof operator to show that the Person object is an instance of both the Object type and the Person type.

When working with classes, you may sometimes want to use inheritance to create a new class based on an existing class. Then, the new class inherits the properties and methods of the existing class. For instance, the second example defines a class named Employee that uses the *extends* keyword to inherit the Person class. As a result, you can call all of the properties and methods of the Person class from an object created from the Employee class. In addition, you can call the hireDate property that's added to the Employee class as shown by the code below the Employee class.

In this figure, the Employee class is a *subclass* of the Person class. Conversely, the Person class is the *superclass* of the Employee class. For a subclass to work correctly, it sometimes needs to call constructors or methods of the superclass. To do that, it can use the *super* keyword. In this figure, the constructor of the Employee class uses the *super* keyword to pass the first and last name to the constructor of the Person class, which is necessary for the Employee class to work correctly.

Although it's not shown here, a class can *override* methods it inherits from another class. For example, instead of including the fullName accessor, the Person class could be coded to override the toString() method of the Object type so it returns the firstName and lastName properties. A method that overrides an inherited method must have the same *signature* as that method, which includes the method name, return type, parameters, and parameter types.

The JavaScript object hierarchy

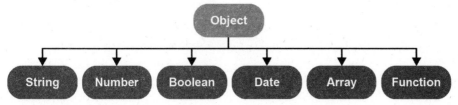

The Person class

```
class Person {
    constructor(fname, lname) {
        this.firstName = fname;
        this.lastName = lname;
    }
    get fullName() {
        return `${this.firstName} ${this.lastName}`;
    }
}
```

How to create and use a Person object

```
const p = new Person("Grace", "Hopper");   // create Person object
console.log(p.fullName);                    // displays "Grace Hopper"
console.log(p instanceof Object);           // displays true
console.log(p instanceof Person);           // displays true
```

An Employee class that inherits the Person class

```
class Employee extends Person {
    constructor(fname, lname, hireDate) {
        super(fname, lname);
        this.hireDate = hireDate;
    }
}
```

How to create and use an Employee object

```
const emp = new Employee("Bjarne", "Stroustrup", new Date("1/1/1979"));
console.log(emp.fullName);                  // displays "Bjarne Stroustrup"
console.log(emp.hireDate.toDateString());   // displays "Mon Jan 01 1979"
console.log(emp instanceof Person);         // displays true
console.log(emp instanceof Employee);       // displays true
```

Description

- JavaScript provides a two-level hierarchy of *native object types*. The first level consists of the Object type. The second level consists of other types that inherit the Object type.

- *Inheritance* lets you create a new class based on an existing class. Then, the new class *inherits* the properties and methods of the existing class.

- When you define a class, you can use the *extends* keyword to inherit the specified class.

- A *subclass* is a class that inherits another class that's known as a *superclass*.

- When you define a subclass, you can use the *super* keyword to call constructors and methods of the superclass.

- When you work with objects, you can use the instanceof operator to check whether an object is an instance of the specified class.

Figure 12-8   How to work with inheritance

When to use inheritance

Figure 12-9 begins by presenting a NumberArray class that inherits JavaScript's native Array type. This class defines a new property named lastNumber.

In addition, it overrides the push() method of the Array class so this method can only add a number, not any other type of data. This push() method begins by using the typeof operator to check whether the parameter value named num is a number. If it is, this code calls the push() method of the Array superclass to add the number to the array, and it sets the lastNumber property to the new number. Otherwise, this code throws an exception with an appropriate error message.

The code below the NumberArray class shows how to create and use a NumberArray object. Here, the first statement creates a NumberArray object. Then, the next three statements use the push() method to add three numbers. The next statement is commented out because it attempts to add a string, which would throw an exception. The next three statements show how to call the lastNumber property, the length property, and the toString() method from the NumberArray object. This shows that the NumberArray object can access properties and methods from the NumberArray, Array, and Object types. Finally, the last statement shows that you can use the unshift() method to add a string to a NumberArray object, which you probably don't want to allow.

This figure ends with guidelines for when it makes sense to use inheritance in your programs. First, it makes sense to use inheritance when the subclass *is a* type of the superclass. In this case, the NumberArray object *is a* type of Array object, just a more specialized type of array.

Second, it makes sense to use inheritance when both classes are part of the same logical domain. For example, the Person and Employee objects shown in the last figure are both in the same domain. In other words, they're both part of a domain that's attempting to define the different types of people for a system. Similarly, the NumberArray object is in the same domain as the Array object since they're both attempting to define a general-purpose array, though the NumberArray object is more specialized than the Array object.

Third, it makes sense to use inheritance when the subclass primarily adds features to the superclass. In other words, it makes sense when a subclass adds new properties or methods to the superclass that are only needed in the subclass. For example, the NumberArray object adds the lastNumber property and could add a getTotal() method that gets the total of all numbers in the array. In addition, a subclass may override some properties and methods to change the behavior of those properties and methods in the subclass. However, if the subclass needs to override many properties and methods, you may be better off using object composition as described in the next figure.

A NumberArray class that uses inheritance

```
class NumberArray extends Array {
    constructor() {
        super();
        this.lastNumber = null;              // defines a new property
    }

    push(num) {                              // overrides an existing method
        if(typeof num === "number") {
            super.push(num);
            this.lastNumber = num;
        } else {
            throw new TypeError("NumberArray can only store numbers");
        }
    }
}
```

Code that uses a NumberArray object

```
const arr = new NumberArray();
arr.push(1.07);
arr.push(2.21);
arr.push(3.14);

// arr.push("Grace");                     // Would throw TypeError
console.log(arr.lastNumber);              // displays 3.14
console.log(arr.length);                  // displays 3
console.log(arr.toString());             // displays 1.07,2.21,3.14
arr.unshift("Grace");                     // PROBLEM! stores invalid value
```

A problem with this NumberArray class

- Not all inherited methods that add elements to the array check to make sure the element is a number. As a result, it's possible to add invalid data to the NumberArray object.

It makes sense to use inheritance when...

- One object *is a* type of another object.
- Both classes are part of the same logical domain.
- The subclass primarily adds features to the superclass.

Description

- To change how a property or method of a superclass works in a subclass, you *override* it in the subclass by coding a new property or method with the same *signature*.
- When working with objects, you can use the typeof operator to check whether an object is an instance of the specified type.

Figure 12-9   When to use inheritance

When to use object composition

Figure 12-10 shows how to use object composition, which is often a good alternative to inheritance. That's why this figure shows the NumberArray class from the previous figure coded to use object composition instead of inheritance.

The NumberArray class begins by defining a private property named #numbers. Then, the constructor initializes that private property as an array and defines the lastNumber property.

After the constructor, the NumberArray class defines a read-only length property that returns the length of the #numbers array. Then, it defines push() and toString() methods that use the push() and toString() methods of the #numbers array. As a result, a NumberArray object only provides the lastNumber and length properties along with the push() and toString() methods.

This limits the options that other programmers have for working with a NumberArray object, which can make it easier to understand and use. For example, you can't use the unshift() method to add an element to a NumberArray object because this object doesn't define the unshift() method.

This figure ends with guidelines for when it makes sense to use object composition in your apps. First, it makes sense when one object *has a* type of another object. For example, the NumberArray object *has an* Array object as one of its properties, although outside code can't access this property because it's private.

Second, it makes sense to use object composition when the subclass primarily restricts access to features of the superclass. In other words, if you want to create a subclass that provides fewer properties and methods than the superclass, you should use object composition. For example, this figure shows how to use object composition to code a NumberArray class that provides far fewer properties and methods than are available from the Array class.

A NumberArray class that uses object composition

```
class NumberArray {
    #numbers = null;                        // a private property

    constructor() {
        this.#numbers = [];                 // initialize private array
        this.lastNumber = null;
    }

    get length() {                          // a read-only property
        return this.#numbers.length;
    }

    push(num) {                             // a method
        if(typeof num === "number") {
            this.#numbers.push(num);
            this.lastNumber = num;
        } else {
            throw new TypeError("NumberArray can only store numbers");
        }
    }

    toString() {                            // a method
        return this.#numbers.toString();
    }
}
```

Code that uses a NumberArray object

```
const arr = new NumberArray();
arr.push(1.07);
arr.push(2.21);
arr.push(3.14);

// arr.push("Grace");                  // Would throw TypeError
console.log(arr.lastNumber);           // displays 3.14
console.log(arr.length);               // displays 3
console.log(arr.toString());           // displays 1.07,2.21,3.14
// arr.unshift("Grace");               // Would throw TypeError
                                       // because method isn't defined
```

It makes sense to use object composition when...

- One object *has a* type of another object.
- The object restricts access to features of the internal object.

Description

- *Object composition* is a way to combine simple objects into more complex ones.

Figure 12-10   When to use object composition

The Trips app

The Trips app presented in figure 12-11 logs the destination, miles driven, and miles per gallon for several trips. Because of that, this app uses a separate Trip object for each trip, and it uses a Trips object to store multiple Trip objects. As a result, it's a good example of object composition.

The Trips app includes <script> elements at the end of the body section that identify the custom trips library and the main JavaScript file that uses this library. Since the main JavaScript file depends on the trips library, it's coded last.

The HTML in the <body> element contains text boxes for user input about a trip. It also contains a button that calculates miles per gallon and adds that trip to the display. If any values the user enters aren't valid, though, the code for the button displays an error message in the <span> element within the last <div> element. The HTML also contains a <div> element with an id of "trips" that contains a <textarea> element that displays data about each trip as well as the MPG calculation for all trips.

The CSS snippet below the HTML shows the style rule for the "trips" element. This style rule floats the <div> element that contains the text area to the right of the <div> elements that get the data for each trip.

The Trips app

The HTML of the <body> element

```html
<body>
    <h1>Trips Log</h1>
    <div id="trips">
        <textarea id="trip_list" rows="8" cols="42"></textarea>
    </div>
    <div>
        <label for="destination">Destination:</label>
        <input type="text" id="destination">
    </div>
    <div>
        <label for="miles">Miles Driven:</label>
        <input type="text" id="miles">
    </div>
    <div>
        <label for="gallons">Gallons of Gas Used:</label>
        <input type="text" id="gallons">
    </div>
    <div>
        <label></label>
        <input type="button" id="add_trip" value="Add Trip">
    </div>
    <div>
        <span id="msg"></span>
    </div>

    <script src="lib_trips.js"></script>
    <script src="trips.js"></script>
</body>
```

Some of the CSS for the app

```css
#trips {
    float: right;
}
```

Figure 12-11   The Trips app (part 1)

Part 2 of this figure begins by presenting the lib_trips.js file. This library file uses two classes to define the Trip and Trips types.

The Trip class begins by defining a constructor for the Trip object. This constructor accepts three parameters that it uses to set the initial values of the destination, miles, and gallons properties. Within the body of the constructor, the *this* keyword refers to the new object that the constructor creates.

After the constructor, the Trip class defines a read-only property named mpg and a method named toString(). The mpg property uses the data from the user to calculate and return the miles per gallon. And the toString() method overrides the toString() method of the Object type to create a string that contains data about the trip.

The Trips class begins by defining a private trips property. Then, it defines a constructor for the Trips object that doesn't accept any arguments. Within its body, it initializes the private trips property to an empty array. After the constructor, the Trips class defines two methods and a read-only property.

The push() method adds a Trip object to the private trips array. To start, this method checks whether the trip parameter is a Trip object. If it is, this method passes it to the push() method of the private trips array. Otherwise, it throws an exception with an appropriate error message.

The read-only property named averageMpg declares variables for the total miles and total gallons for all trips. Then, it loops through all the Trip objects in the private trips array and adds the miles and gallons to these variables. Finally, it calculates and returns the average MPG for all trips.

The toString() method of the Trips class overrides the toString() method of the Object class to return a string that summarizes all the trips. To do that, it initializes a string variable named str and then loops through all the Trip objects in the private trips array. Within that loop, the code appends the Trip object to the str variable, which calls the toString() method of the Trip object to get the string with data for that trip. After the loop, the code appends a string that contains the average miles per gallon for all trips and then returns the str variable. Note that the loop adds a new line character at the end of the data for each trip so each one is displayed on its own line.

The lib_trips.js file

```javascript
"use strict";

class Trip {
    constructor(destination, miles, gallons) {
        this.destination = destination;
        this.miles = parseFloat(miles);
        this.gallons = parseFloat(gallons);
    }

    get mpg() {                          // a read-only property
        return this.miles / this.gallons;
    }

    toString() {                         // override existing method
        const mpg = this.mpg.toFixed(1);
        return `${this.destination}: Miles - ${this.miles}; MPG - ${mpg}`;
    }
}

class Trips {
    #trips = null;                       // a private field

    constructor() {
        this.#trips = [];
    }

    push(trip) {
        if (trip instanceof Trip) {  // only add valid Trip objects
            this.#trips.push(trip);
        } else {
            throw new Error("Must be a Trip object.");
        }
    }

    get averageMpg() {                   // a read-only property
        let totalMiles = 0;
        let totalGallons = 0;
        for (let trip of this.#trips) {
            totalMiles += trip.miles;
            totalGallons += trip.gallons;
        }
        return totalMiles / totalGallons;
    }

    toString() {                         // override existing method
        let str = "";
        for (let trip of this.#trips) {
            str += trip + "\n";
        }
        str += "\nAverage MPG: " + this.averageMpg.toFixed(1);
        return str;
    }
}
```

Figure 12-11   The Trips app (part 2)

Part 3 of this figure presents the trips.js file, which is the main JavaScript file for this app. It starts with the getElement() helper method and an event handler for the DOMContentLoaded event.

The DOMContentLoaded event handler starts by creating a Trips object. Next, it defines a click event handler for the Add Trip button. After that, the code moves the focus to the text box for the destination. This makes it easy for the user to enter a trip when the page finishes loading.

The event handler for the Add Trip button creates a new instance of a Trip object by passing the values entered by the user to its constructor. Then, it validates the data to check whether the user entered valid data. If not, the code alerts the user.

However, if the data is valid, this code adds the Trip object to the Trips object. Then, it assigns the Trips object as the value of the <textarea> element, which calls the toString() method of the Trips object and displays the data for all the trips. Next, the code clears all three text boxes and moves the focus to the text box for the destination. This makes it easy for the user to start entering another trip.

The trips.js file

```javascript
"use strict";

const getElement = selector => document.querySelector(selector);

document.addEventListener("DOMContentLoaded", () => {
    const trips = new Trips();

    getElement("#add_trip").addEventListener("click", () => {
        const msgElement = getElement("#msg");
        msgElement.textContent = "";   // clear any previous message

        const destination = getElement("#destination").value;
        const miles = getElement("#miles").value;
        const gallons = getElement("#gallons").value;
        const trip = new Trip(destination, miles, gallons);

        if (destination == "" || miles == "" || gallons == "") {
            msgElement.textContent = "All fields are required.";
            getElement("#destination").focus();
        } else if (isNaN(trip.miles) || trip.miles < 0) {
            msgElement.textContent =
                "Miles must be a valid number greater than zero.";
            getElement("#miles").select();
        } else if (isNaN(trip.gallons) || trip.gallons < 0) {
            msgElement.textContent =
                "Gallons must be a valid number greater than zero.";
            getElement("#gallons").select();
        } else {
            trips.push(trip);
            getElement("#trip_list").value = trips;

            getElement("#destination").value = "";
            getElement("#miles").value = "";
            getElement("#gallons").value = "";
            getElement("#destination").focus();
        }

    });

    getElement("#destination").focus();
});
```

Figure 12-11   The Trips app (part 3)

More skills for working with objects

At this point, you have the basic skills you need for working with objects. Now, this chapter presents more skills that you may need.

How to create cascading methods

A *cascading method* is a method of an object that can be chained with other methods of that object. To do that, the method must return a reference to the original object as shown in figure 12-12. In most cases, a method can use the *this* keyword to return a reference to the original object.

Code that uses cascading methods is sometimes called *fluent*. That's because a line of code like

```
taskList.load().add(task);
```

reads like a sentence. This type of code is also known as *method chaining* because the method calls are chained together.

The first example presents an object literal named taskList with two methods: load() and add(). Since neither of these methods returns a reference to the taskList object, they can't be chained. If you try to chain the methods, a runtime error occurs because the load() method doesn't return an object that has an add() method. Thus, you must use separate statements to call these methods, as shown here.

The second example presents these same methods, but now they each end with this statement:

```
return this;
```

This returns a reference to the taskList object so the methods can be chained.

Since method chaining is common, it's a good practice to provide for chaining by returning the object at the end of a method. Of course, if you're returning something else, like a Boolean value or a string, you can't return the object too. But whenever you can return the object, you should.

Two methods that modify an object but don't return the object

```
const taskList = {
    tasks: [],
    load() {
        this.tasks = storage.retrieve();
    },
    add(task) {
        this.tasks.push(task);
    }
};
```

The methods must be called one at a time

```
taskList.load();
taskList.add(task);
```

Chaining these method calls doesn't work

```
taskList.load().add(task);
// TypeError: Cannot read property 'add' of undefined
```

Two methods that modify an object and then return the object

```
const taskList = {
    tasks: [],
    load() {
        this.tasks = storage.retrieve();
        return this;
    },
    add(task) {
        this.tasks.push(task);
        return this;
    }
};
```

Chaining these method calls works

```
taskList.load().add(task);
```

Description

- A *cascading method* is a method of an object that can be chained with other methods of that object. This style of coding is sometimes called *fluent* because of the way the code reads. This is also known as *method chaining*.

- To support cascading methods, a method must return the object represented by the *this* keyword.

Figure 12-12   How to create cascading methods

How to work with static properties and methods

In the class examples you've seen so far, the data properties for each instance of the class store different data. These are called *instance properties*.

Sometimes, though, you don't need each instance of a class to have its own data. For example, if every instance of an Invoice object will have the same tax rate, it might make sense to code a *static property* on the Invoice class itself. Then, you can access that property from the Invoice class rather than from each instance of that class.

Similarly, you might have a utility method that works with your class type but doesn't need access to the data that an instance of the class stores. In this case, you can code a *static method*. Figure 12-13 shows how this works.

The first example in this figure defines an Invoice class that has a static property and a static method. To define the static property and method, it codes each one with the *static* keyword. The static property and method of this class are then available to the other methods and properties of the class, as well as to outside code. To call them, you code the class name, the dot operator, and the property or method name, like this:

```
Invoice.taxRate;
```

The second example in this figure presents code that works with both static and instance properties and methods of the Invoice class. To start, it calls the Invoice constructor to create an instance of the Invoice class. Then, it calls the static taxRate property with the name of the Invoice class, and the instance total property with the name of the object. In the third example, you can see that you can't call a static property or method on an instance of a class.

The last example in this figure shows how to code a static property or method that's private. To do that, you simply add the hash prefix to the name of the property or method. Then, code within the class can access the private static method, as shown here. But, the method can't be called by code outside the class.

An Invoice class with a static property and a static method

```
class Invoice {
    static taxRate = .0875;            // static property

    static isInvoice(invoice) {        // static method
        return invoice instanceof Invoice;
    }

    constructor(subtotal) {
        this.subtotal = subtotal;
    }

    get total() {
        return this.subtotal + (this.subtotal * Invoice.taxRate);
    }
}
```

Call static methods

```
const inv = new Invoice(100);

if (Invoice.isInvoice(inv)) {
    console.log(Invoice.taxRate);      // displays 0.0875
    console.log(inv.total);            // displays 108.75
}
```

What happens if you try to call a static property or method on an instance of a class

```
console.log(inv.taxRate);              // displays undefined
console.log(inv.isInvoice(inv));       // TypeError: not a function
```

Code and use a private static property

```
class Invoice {
    static #taxRate = .0875;           // private static property
    ...
    get total() {
        return this.subtotal + (this.subtotal * Invoice.#taxRate);
    }
    ...
}
```

Description

- *Static* properties and methods are accessed on the class itself. They can't be accessed by an instance of a class.

- In JavaScript, you create static properties and methods by prefixing them with the *static* keyword. To make a static property or method private, add the hash prefix.

Figure 12-13   How to work with static properties and methods

How to nest objects

When you create custom objects, you should know that you can nest one object type within another. For example, an Invoice object might contain a Terms object that provides additional information for the invoice. Figure 12-14 shows how this works.

The first example in this figure shows how to create nested objects using object literals. To do that, you assign an object literal as the value of a property of another object. In this case, an object literal that includes two properties named taxRate and dueDays is assigned to the terms property of an object named invoice.

You can also nest objects created from classes, as shown in the second example. This example shows a class named Terms that includes two properties named taxRate and dueDays. Then, it shows a class named Invoice that includes two properties named subtotal and terms. In this case, the constructor of each class accepts the values of its properties.

The two statements that follow show how to create Terms and Invoice objects from these classes. Like other examples you've seen in this chapter, the first statement creates a Terms object by passing literal values to the constructor. The second statement is similar, except it passes the Terms object created by the first statement to the constructor of the Invoice object. This nests the Terms object within the Invoice object.

This example shows just one way to assign an object to the value of a property of another object. You can also use the other techniques shown in this chapter to assign a value to a property. For example, if the constructor for the Invoice class in this figure didn't accept parameters, you could set the value of the terms property after creating an Invoice object. Or, you could set the value of the terms property within a method of the class. You can also use these techniques with object literals.

The last example shows how to refer to a property of a nested object from an instance of the outer object. To do that, you refer to the nested object through the outer object. Here, the statement changes the value of the dueDays property of the object named terms that's nested within the object named invoice.

You can also refer to a property of a nested object from within the outer object. To do that, you use the *this* keyword to refer to the outer object. This is shown by the getTotal() method in the object literal for an invoice in the first example and the Invoice class in the second example.

Create nested objects with object literals

```
const invoice = {
    subtotal: 100,
    terms: {                                    // nested object
        taxRate: 0.0875,
        dueDays: 30
    },
    getTotal() {
        return this.subtotal + (this.subtotal * this.terms.taxRate);
    }
};
```

Create nested objects with classes

The Terms class

```
class Terms {
    constructor(taxRate, dueDays) {
        this.taxRate = taxRate;
        this.dueDays = dueDays;
    }
}
```

The Invoice class

```
class Invoice {
    constructor(subtotal, terms) {
        this.subtotal = subtotal;
        this.terms = terms;
    }
    getTotal() {
        return this.subtotal + (this.subtotal * this.terms.taxRate);
    }
}
```

Code that creates nested objects from the classes

```
const terms = new Terms(0.0875, 30);
const invoice = new Invoice(100, terms); // pass terms object to constructor
```

Refer to a property of a nested object from an instance of the outer object

```
invoice.terms.dueDays = 45;
```

Description

- To nest objects, you assign an object to the value of a property of another object.
- To refer to a property of a nested object, you code the name of the outer object, a dot operator, the name of the property that stores the inner object, another dot operator, and the name of the property.

Figure 12-14   How to nest objects

How to destructure an object

Figure 12-15 shows how to use the *destructuring* syntax to assign the values of object properties to individual constants or variables in a single statement. To start, the first example defines a person object that has firstName, lastName, and dob properties with values of "Grace", "Hopper", and null. Although this object is created using an object literal, you can use destructuring with objects created from classes as well.

To destructure this object, you code one or more constant or variable names within braces, separated by commas. Then, you code the assignment operator and the object. The second example shows how this works.

Here, the first statement specifies two constants (firstName and lastName) that have the same names as the properties of the person object. As a result, this code assigns "Grace" to the firstName constant and "Hopper" to the lastName constant.

The second statement assigns the same two properties to constants with names that are different from the property name. To do that, it maps the constant names to the property names by including a colon after each property name followed by the constant name. As a result, this code assigns "Grace" to the fname constant and "Hopper" to the lname constant.

The third example shows how to provide a default value for a property. To do that, you just code the name of the property followed by an equal sign and the default value. Here, the first statement provides a default value of "unknown" for properties named dob and age. When this statement runs, it assigns "Grace" to the firstName constant. Then, because JavaScript considers null to be a valid value, it assigns null rather than the default value to the dob constant. Finally, because the person object in this figure doesn't define a property named age, it assigns the default value "unknown" to the age constant.

The fourth example shows how to destructure an object in the parameter list of a function. Here, the code defines a function named displayGreeting() that uses destructuring to assign values to the firstName and lastName parameters. As a result, when the first statement calls this function and passes it the person object, it displays a greeting of "Hello, Grace Hopper". However, when the second statement calls this function without passing a person object, it causes a type error.

The fifth example shows how to use the destructuring syntax to work with the properties of the nested objects you saw in the previous figure. Here, the value of the subtotal property of an invoice object, along with the value of the taxRate property of the terms object that's nested within the invoice object, are assigned to constants named subtotal and taxRate. As you can see, to refer to properties of a nested object, you code the name of the object, followed by a colon, followed by a list of comma-separated properties within brackets. Although it's not shown here, you can also assign a nested property to a constant or variable with a name that's different from the property name by mapping the constant name to the property name.

A person object with three properties that have values

```
const person = {
    firstName: "Grace",
    lastName: "Hopper",
    dob: null
};
```

How to assign property values to variables or constants

```
// using the same names
const {firstName, lastName} = person;

// using different names
const {firstName: fname, lastName: lname} = person;
```

How to provide a default value for an assignment

```
const {firstName, dob = "unknown", age = "unknown"} = person;

console.log(dob);    // displays null
console.log(age);    // displays "unknown"
```

How to destructure an object in the parameter list of a function

```
const displayGreeting = ({firstName, lastName}) => {
    console.log("Hello, " + firstName + " " + lastName);
};
```

Code that calls the function

```
displayGreeting(person);    // displays "Hello, Grace Hopper"
displayGreeting();          // TypeError: Cannot destructure property
```

How to assign property values of a nested object

```
const {subtotal, terms: {taxRate}} = invoice;
```

Description

- The *destructuring* syntax provides a way to assign the values of object properties to multiple constants or variables in a single statement.
- To destructure an object, you code one or more constant or variable names within braces, separated by commas. Then, you code the assignment operator and the object.
- You can use destructuring with objects created using object literals or classes.
- You can assign a property to a constant or variable with the same name as the property, or you can map a constant or variable to a property with a different name.
- You can include default values for the individual constants or variables.
- You can destructure an object in the parameter list of a function.
- You can destructure an object that's nested within another object.

Figure 12-15   How to destructure an object

How to work with generator functions

JavaScript provides several ways to loop through, or *iterate*, the items in a collection such as an array or a string. For instance, you can use a for-of loop or the spread operator.

When you define a custom object that contains a collection of items, you often want to provide a way to iterate through the items. In other words, you want to make your custom object *iterable*. To do that, you can use a *generator function*. Figure 12-16 shows how that works.

The two tables at the top of this figure present a symbol and a keyword that you use to create a generator function. The first table presents Symbol.iterator, which is one of the *well-known symbols*. These are static properties of the Symbol type that are used as names for certain methods of the Object type. You can customize the way an object behaves by coding a custom method with a well-known symbol as the name.

The second table presents the *yield* keyword, which is used to code a *yield statement*. A yield statement returns an IteratorResult object with a next() method and then pauses execution.

The examples after the tables show how to code a generator function. To do that, you code the * operator at the beginning of the function name, as shown in the taskList object in the first example. Or, you code it immediately after the *function* keyword, as shown in the Date object in the third example. Then you use the Symbol.iterator well-known symbol within brackets as the method name. In the body of the generator function, you code yield statements.

When the code in the body of a generator function executes, it runs until it reaches a yield statement. At that point, the code returns an IteratorResult object that contains the value returned by the current iteration and then pauses execution.

When the loop or destructuring statement that receives the IteratorResult object calls its next() method, the code in the generator function executes from where execution was paused and continues until it reaches another yield statement. Then, it executes that yield statement and pauses execution again. This continues until the last yield statement is reached. At that point, the generator function ends.

The examples in this figure also show code that calls these generator functions. The second example uses a for-of loop with the iterable taskList object, while the fourth example uses array destructuring with the iterable Date object. In this fourth example, the first three values returned by the generator function are assigned to constants, and the rest are not used.

When you work with generator functions, you need to keep two things in mind. First, a generator function must be a regular function, not an arrow function. Second, the *yield* keyword can't be used outside of a generator function.

One of the well-known symbols

Symbol	Method Description
`Symbol.iterator`	Defines how an object behaves when used with a for-of loop, a spread operator, or destructuring.

A keyword that's used with generator functions

Keyword	Description
`yield`	Returns an IteratorResult object with a next() method and pauses execution.

A taskList object that's iterable

```
const taskList = {
    tasks: [],
    // properties and methods of the taskList object go here
    *[Symbol.iterator]() {
        for (let task of this.tasks) {
            yield task;
        }
    }
};
```

A for-of loop that works with a taskList object

```
for (const task of taskList) {
    console.log(task.description)
}
```

A Date object that's iterable

```
const today = new Date("4/15/2024");
today[Symbol.iterator] = function*() {
    yield this.getFullYear();
    yield this.getMonth();
    yield this.getDate();
    yield this.getHours();
    yield this.getMinutes();
    yield this.getSeconds();
};
```

Use array destructuring syntax with the Date object

```
const [year, month, date] = today;
console.log(`${date}-${month + 1}-${year}`);    // displays 15-4-2024
```

Description

- The *well-known symbols* are used as names for certain methods of the Object type. You can customize how an object behaves by coding a custom method for a well-known symbol.

- Symbol.iterator is used with *generator functions* to make an object *iterable*.

- You can use the * operator to identify a generator function. A generator function must be a regular function, not an arrow function.

- The code in the body of a generator function executes until it comes to a *yield statement*. Then, that statement returns an IteratorResult object and pauses execution.

Figure 12-16   How to work with generator functions

The Task List app

The Task List app presented in figure 12-17 is another version of the app presented in earlier chapters. This version has a due date as well as a task description, and it allows the user to delete individual tasks. To do its work, this app uses objects and object libraries.

The <script> elements at the end of the <body> element identify the libraries used by this app: a task library, a storage library, and a task list library. The last <script> element is for the main JavaScript file that uses these libraries. The <script> elements are in this order because the storage library depends on the task library, the task list library depends on both the storage and task libraries, and the main JavaScript file depends on the task list and task libraries.

The HTML in the main element has two <div> elements with id attributes of "form" and "display". In the CSS snippet below the HTML, the style rules for these elements float the "form" <div> to the left and the "display" <div> to the right. That way, the two elements display side by side. Next is a third <div> element with no id attribute but a class attribute of "clear". The CSS style rule for this class sets the CSS clear property to "both". This clears the floating of the elements that precede it.

The <div> element with an id attribute of "display" contains a <select> element with an id attribute of "tasks". The JavaScript code adds individual tasks as <option> elements to this <select> element, as you'll see in a moment.

For the <select> element to display more than one <option> element at a time, it includes the multiple attribute. In addition, the CSS style rule for the <select> element adds scrolling for both the x and y axis. This allows the user to scroll up and down if there are more tasks than the element's height, and side to side if there are tasks that are longer than the element's width.

To delete an individual task, the user clicks on a task to select it and then clicks the Delete Task button. If the user doesn't select a task, the app displays a message notifying them to select a task to delete. If the user selects more than one task (which they can do by holding down the Control or Command button and clicking on multiple tasks), the app deletes the first selected task.

The Task List app

The HTML of the <body> element

```html
<body>
    <div id="form">
        <h1>Task List</h1>
        <div>
            <label for="task">Task:</label>
            <input type="text" name="task" id="task">
        </div>
        <div>
            <label for="due_date">Due Date:</label>
            <input type="text" name="due_date" id="due_date">
        </div>
        <button id="add_task">Add Task</button>
        <button id="clear_tasks">Clear Tasks</button>
    </div>

    <div id="display">
        <select name="tasks" id="tasks" multiple></select><br>
        <button id="delete_task">Delete Task</button>
    </div>
    <div class="clear"></div>
    <p id="msg"></p>

    <script src="lib_task.js"></script>
    <script src="lib_storage.js"></script>
    <script src="lib_task_list.js"></script>
    <script src="task_list.js"></script>
</body>
```

Some of the CSS for the app

```css
#form { float: left; }
#display { float: right; }
.clear { clear: both; }
select {
    overflow-x: scroll;
    overflow-y: scroll;
}
```

Description

* This version of the Task List app has a <select> element with a multiple attribute that displays the tasks. This allows users to select and delete a task.

Figure 12-17   The Task List app (part 1)

Part 2 of this figure presents two library files. The lib_task.js file is the library for working with individual tasks. It contains a class named Task that defines a constructor that accepts description and dueDate parameters.

Within the constructor, the first statement assigns the description parameter to the description property of the current object. Then, the constructor converts the value of the dueDate parameter to a Date object and assigns it to a property named dueDate.

After the constructor, the class defines two read-only accessors that check the state of the dueDate property. The first, hasInvalidDueDate, returns true if the toString() method of the dueDate property returns "Invalid Date". Otherwise, it returns false. The second, isPastDue, returns true if the date is not a future date. Otherwise, it returns false. These properties make it easy for code that uses Task objects to perform data validation.

Finally, the Task class defines a toString() method that returns a string that displays the dueDate and description properties.

The lib_storage.js file defines an object literal named storage that provides a way to get Task objects in and out of local web storage. To start, the storage object defines a retrieve() method that gets a JSON string from local storage and converts it into an array of zero or more Task objects. Then, it defines a store() method that accepts an array of Task objects, converts that array to a JSON string, and stores that string in local storage. Finally, it defines a clear() method that clears all task data from local storage.

The lib_task.js file

```
class Task {
    constructor(description, dueDate) {
        this.description = description;
        this.dueDate = new Date(dueDate);
    }

    get hasInvalidDueDate() {
        return this.dueDate.toString() === "Invalid Date";
    }

    get isPastDue() {
        const today = new Date();
        return this.dueDate.getTime() < today.getTime();
    }

    toString() {
        return `${this.dueDate.toDateString()} - ${this.description}`
    }
}
```

The lib_storage.js file

```
const storage = {
    retrieve() {
        const tasks = [];
        const json = localStorage.tasks;
        if(json) {
            const taskArray = JSON.parse(json);
            for (let obj of taskArray) {
                tasks.push(new Task(obj.description, obj.dueDate));
            }
        }
        return tasks;
    },
    store(tasks) {
        localStorage.tasks = JSON.stringify(tasks);
    },
    clear() {
        localStorage.tasks = "";
    }
};
```

Figure 12-17   The Task List app (part 2)

Part 3 of this figure shows the library for working with a collection of tasks. It contains a class named TaskList that creates objects that store, edit, and display Task objects. Because the app only needs one instance of this object, you could code it as an object literal. However, since it needs a private array property to store Task objects, it's coded as a class.

The load() method calls the retrieve() method of the storage object to retrieve tasks from local storage as an array of Task objects. Then, it assigns this array of Task objects to the private tasks array.

The save() method calls the store() method of the storage object and passes it the array of Task objects. This stores the tasks in local storage.

The sortByDueDate() method calls the sort() method of the private tasks array. It passes that method a function that sorts the Task objects in the array in ascending order by due date.

The add() method accepts a Task object as a parameter. Then, it uses the push() method of the private tasks array to add the Task object to the array.

The delete() method accepts an index as a parameter. It starts by calling the sortByDueDate() method to sort the tasks. It does this to make sure the tasks are in the same sort order as those displayed in the browser. Then, it removes the task at the specified index in the private tasks array using the splice() method of that array.

This delete() method works adequately for this app, but it would be better if it accepted an id that uniquely identified the Task object. Then, this code could find the matching Task object in the array and remove it. However, for that to work, the Task object needs to have a unique identifier, and the Task object defined by this app doesn't have such an identifier.

The clear() method calls the clear() method of the storage object. This removes all task data from local storage.

Note that all of these methods return the current TaskList object. That way, the code can use method chaining with this object, as you'll see in the code for the main JavaScript file.

The last method is a generator function that makes a TaskList object iterable. Within this method, the code uses a for-of statement to loop through all Task objects in the private tasks array. Within the loop, a yield statement returns the current Task object and pauses execution until the next iteration.

Part 3 of this figure also shows the start of the main JavaScript file for the app. It begins by defining the getElement() helper method. After that, it creates a TaskList object that's used by the other functions in this file.

Next, the code defines a function that displays the tasks in the TaskList object. To start, this method calls the sortByDueDate() method of the TaskList object. Then, it gets an object that represents the HTML <select> element and clears any previous tasks displayed in that element.

After that, the function loops through the tasks, creates an <option> element for each task, and adds that element to the <select> element. To do that, it uses a for-of loop, which is possible because the TaskList object is iterable. To create the text for the <option> element, it passes the Task object to the createTextNode() method. This works because that method calls the toString()

The lib_task_list.js file

```
class TaskList {
    #tasks = null;
    constructor() {
        this.#tasks = [];
    }
    load() {
        this.#tasks = storage.retrieve();
        return this;
    }
    save() {
        storage.store(this.#tasks);
        return this;
    }
    sortByDueDate() {
        this.#tasks.sort((a, b) => a.dueDate - b.dueDate);
        return this;
    }
    add(task) {
        this.#tasks.push(task);
        return this;
    }
    delete(i) {
        this.sortByDueDate(); // sort so in same order as page
        this.#tasks.splice(i, 1);
        return this;
    }
    clear() {
        this.#tasks.length = 0;
        storage.clear();
        return this;
    }
    *[Symbol.iterator]() {
        for (let task of this.#tasks) {
            yield task;
        }
    }
};
```

The task_list.js file

```
const getElement = selector => document.querySelector(selector);

const taskList = new TaskList();

const displayTasks = () => {
    taskList.sortByDueDate();
    const select = getElement("#tasks");
    select.textContent = "";  // clear previous tasks

    for (let task of taskList) {
        const opt = document.createElement("option");
        opt.appendChild(document.createTextNode(task));
        select.appendChild(opt);
    }
    getElement("#task").focus();
};
```

Figure 12-17   The Task List app (part 3)

method of the Task object, which displays the task description and due date. Finally, this code sets the focus on the Task text box to prepare for the next user entry.

Part 4 of this figure shows the rest of the main JavaScript file. The event handler for the DOMContentLoaded event starts by defining the click event handler for the Add Task button. This event handler first clears any previous error messages that might have been displayed to the user. Then, it creates a new Task object by passing the values entered by the user to the constructor of the Task class.

After creating the Task object, this code uses its properties to check whether the user entered valid data. First, it initializes a message variable with an empty string. Then, it checks whether the description property has a value. If not, it assigns an appropriate message to the message variable. Then, it checks if the hasInvalidDueDate or isPastDue properties return true. If either one does, the code appends an appropriate error message to the message variable.

After validating the data, the code checks the value of the message variable. If it's an empty string, that means the user entered valid data. In this case, the code uses method chaining to call methods of the TaskList object that load the tasks from local storage, add the new task, and save the updated tasks back to local storage. Then, the function displays the new list of tasks and clears both text boxes.

If the value of the message variable isn't an empty string, it means that the task isn't valid. In this case, the code displays a message to the user. In either case, the function ends by selecting the Task text box.

The click event handler for the Clear Tasks button starts by calling the clear() method of the TaskList object to remove all tasks from local storage. Then, it clears the text from the <select> element that displays the tasks, as well as the two text boxes and the <p> element that displays messages. Finally, it sets the focus on the Task text box.

The click event handler for the Delete Task button starts by clearing any previous error messages that might have been displayed. Then, it calls the selectedIndex property of the <select> element to get the index of the <option> element the user selected. If no <option> elements are selected, this property returns -1. If more than one <option> element is selected, this property returns the index of the first element.

Next, the code checks to see if the user selected a task to delete. If not, the code notifies the user to select a task. Otherwise, it uses method chaining to call methods of the TaskList object that load the tasks from local storage, delete the selected task, and save the updated tasks back to local storage. Then, the function displays the new list of tasks and sets the focus on the Task text box.

After the click event handlers, this code loads and displays any tasks that are in local storage when the page loads.

The task_list.js file (continued)

```javascript
document.addEventListener("DOMContentLoaded", () => {
    getElement("#add_task").addEventListener("click", () => {
        getElement("#msg").textContent = "";

        const newTask = new Task(
            getElement("#task").value,
            getElement("#due_date").value);

        let message = "";
        if (newTask.description === "") {
            message = "Task is required. ";
        }
        if (newTask.hasInvalidDueDate || newTask.isPastDue) {
            message += "Due Date must be a valid date in the future."
        }

        if (message === "") {
            taskList.load().add(newTask).save();
            displayTasks();
            getElement("#task").value = "";
            getElement("#due_date").value = "";
        } else {
            getElement("#msg").textContent = message;
        }
        getElement("#task").select();
    });

    getElement("#clear_tasks").addEventListener("click", () => {
        taskList.clear();
        getElement("#tasks").textContent = "";
        getElement("#task").value = "";
        getElement("#due_date").value = "";
        getElement("#msg").textContent = "";
        getElement("#task").focus();
    });

    getElement("#delete_task").addEventListener("click", () => {
        getElement("#msg").textContent = "";

        const index = getElement("#tasks").selectedIndex;
        if (index === -1) {
            getElement("#msg").textContent =
                "Please select a task to delete.";
        } else {
            taskList.load().delete(index).save();
            displayTasks();
            getElement("#task").focus();
        }
    });

    taskList.load();
    displayTasks();
});
```

Figure 12-17   The Task List app (part 4)

Perspective

Now that you've finished this chapter, you should be able to define custom objects that you can use in your apps. That should make your apps easier to maintain and your code easier to reuse. That's especially true for apps that are large or complex.

Terms

object literal	getter
property	setter
method	read-only property
this keyword	write-only property
class	inheritance
class-based language	object composition
classical language	native object types
prototypal language	subclass
constructor	superclass
data property	override
new keyword	signature
instance	cascading method
delete operator	fluent coding
object reference	method chaining
library	static property
separation of concerns	static method
encapsulation	destructure
data hiding	iterate
private property	iterable
private method	generator function
accessor	well-known symbol
accessor property	yield statement

Exercise 12-1   Enhance the Countdown app to use a class

This exercise guides you through the process of changing a Countdown app that uses functions to organize its code to an object-oriented app that uses a class to organize its code.

Open, test, and review the app

1. View the files in this folder:

    `exercises\ch12\countdown\`

2. Run the app in Chrome and test it. To do that, enter an event name and an event date and click the Countdown button.

3. Review the code in the click event handler for the Countdown button. Note that this event handler contains most of the code for this app. As a result, the only way to reuse this code is to copy it, which isn't a good practice.

Add a JavaScript library file

4. Add a JavaScript file to the app named lib_event.js.

5. In the index.html file, add a <script> element to include this new file. Since the main JavaScript file will use this file, be sure to code the <script> element for the library file before the <script> element for the main file.

Use a class to define an Event object

6. In the event library file, code a class named Event that has a constructor that accepts two parameters: name and dateString.

7. Assign the value of the name parameter to a property of the same name.

8. Pass the dateString parameter to the Date constructor and assign the Date object it returns to a property named date.

9. Assign the value of the dateString parameter to a private property of the same name.

10. Create three read-only accessor properties that check the state of the event data. The hasName property returns true if the length of the name property is greater than zero. The hasDate property returns true if the length of the private dateString property is greater than zero. And the isValidDate property returns true if the toString() method of the date property does not return "Invalid Date". Otherwise, these properties return false.

11. Switch to the click event handler for the Countdown button. Then, find the code that gets the event name and date from the user and modify it to create an Event object from the Event class. To do that, pass the event name and date string entered by the user to the constructor of the Event class.

12. Find the code that validates the user's entry and modify it to use the read-only accessor properties of the Event object.

13. Find the code that calculates the days and builds and displays a message and modify it to use the name and date properties of the Event object.

14. Test the app to make sure it still works correctly.

15. In the Event class, add a read-only accessor property named days. Then, move the code that calculates the number of days from the click event handler to this property, and make sure the property returns the calculated number of days.

16. In the click event handler, modify the code so it uses the days property of the Event object instead of a variable.

17. Test the app to make sure it still works correctly.

18. In the Event class, add a read-only accessor property named message. Then, move the code that displays the countdown message from the click event handler into this property. Be sure to return a string that contains the count-down message.

19. In the click event handler, modify the code so it uses the message property of the Event object to get the countdown message. Then, display the countdown message on the web page.

20. Test the app to make sure these changes work correctly.

Exercise 12-2   Enhance the Test Scores app to use a class and an object literal

This exercise guides you through the process of changing a Test Scores app that uses functions to organize its code to an object-oriented app that uses a class and an object literal to organize its code.

My Test Scores

All scores: 90, 89, 95, 79

Letter grades: A, B, A, C

Average score: 88.25

Highest to lowest: 95, 90, 89, 79

Enter new score: [   ] [Add Score]   Score must be from 0 to 100.

Open, test, and review the app

1. View the files in this folder:

    `exercises\ch12\test_scores\`

2. Run the app in Chrome and test it. To do that, enter four or more scores and note that the app displays the scores, letter grades for the scores, the average score, and the scores in descending order.

3. Review the code in the click event handler for the Add Score button. Note that it contains most of the code for this app. As a result, the only way to reuse this code is to copy it, which isn't a good practice.

Add a JavaScript library file

4. Add a JavaScript file named lib_test_scores.js to the app.

5. In the index.html file, add a <script> element that includes this new file. Since the main JavaScript file will use this file, be sure to code the <script> element for the library file before the <script> element for the main file.

Use a class to define a TestScores object

Note: to code some of the following methods and properties, you can copy and paste code from the click event handler of the Add Scores button as needed.

6. In the test scores library file, code a class named TestScores with a constructor that doesn't accept any parameters.

7. Code a private property to hold test scores, and initialize the private property to an empty array in the constructor.

8. Code a method named add() that accepts a score and adds it to the private array.

9. Code a read-only accessor property named avg that returns the average of all the test scores in the private array.

10. Code a method named toString() that returns a string that contains the test scores in the private array with each score separated by a comma and a space.

11. Code a method named toLetterString() that returns a string that contains a letter grade for the test scores in the private array with each letter separated by a comma and a space.

12. Code a method named toSortedString() that returns a string that contains the test scores in the private array sorted in descending order with each score separated by a comma and a space. Make sure the order of the private array isn't changed.

13. Switch to the event handler for the DOMContentLoaded event and replace the existing scores array with a TestScores object.

14. In the click event handler for the Add score button, find the code that adds the score entered by the user to the test scores and modify it to use the add() method of the TestScores object.

15. Find the code that displays the average grade and modify it to use the avg

property of the TestScores object.

16. Find the code that displays the test scores, the letter grades for the test scores, and the test scores in descending order and modify it to use the string methods of the TestScores object.

17. Test the app to make sure it still works correctly.

Add another JavaScript library file

18. Add a JavaScript file named lib_validation.js to the app.

19. In the index.html file, add a <script> element that includes this new file. Since the main JavaScript file will use this file, be sure to code the <script> element for the library file before the <script> element for the main file.

Use an object literal to define a validation object

20. In the validation library file, code an object literal and assign it to a constant named validation.

21. Code a method named isNumeric() within the object literal that accepts a value and returns false if that value is not a number and true otherwise.

22. Code a method named isInRange() within the object literal that accepts a value to check, a minimum value, and a maximum value. The method should return true if the value to check is greater than or equal to the minimum value and less than or equal to the maximum value. Otherwise, it should return false. The method should also use the isNumeric() method to make sure the value to check is numeric.

23. Switch to the click event handler for the Add score button, find the code that validates the scores entered by the user, and modify it to use the isInRange() method of the validation object.

24. Test the app to make sure the validation still works correctly.

13

How work with modules

In the last chapter, you learned how to use objects to organize your code, and you learned how to use classes to create objects with private state. Another way to organize your code and create private state is to use modules. That's what you'll learn in this chapter.

How to work with ES modules

Instead of using objects to organize your code and classes to create objects with private state, you can use *ES modules*, or *ECMAScript modules*. A module is a JavaScript file that can contain variables, constants, functions, objects, and classes.

How to export and import module items

Before you can use the variables, constants, functions, objects, and classes coded in a module, you must export them from that module. Then, you can use these items from another module. To do that, you must import them into that module. Figure 13-1 shows how this works.

The first example shows a module for working with test scores that exports three functions. This file begins by defining a constant named scores and initializing it with an empty array. Then, it defines three functions, each preceded by the *export* keyword. As a result, these three functions are public and can be imported by other modules. However, the constant isn't exported. As a result, it's private and can't be imported by other modules.

Although you can code export statements like these for each item you want to export, it's sometimes more convenient to specify all the items you want to export at once. To do that, you can code an export statement with a list of the items you want to export as shown in the second example.

Once you've exported items from a module, you can use an import statement to import them into another module as shown by the third example. Here, the import statement imports the functions named addTestScore() and getScoreDisplayString() from the file named lib_test_scores.js. To specify a path to this file that's relative to the root directory for the app, this code starts the string for the path with "./".

After it imports the two functions, this code uses them to add a test score and then display all the test scores. Note that this code doesn't import all the functions available from the module. Instead, it only imports what it needs. Also note that, since the scores constant in the module file is private, this code would throw a ReferenceError exception if it tried to access it.

When you import items from a module, they're available in the file as read-only views of the exported items. Because of that, you can't change the value of an imported variable or constant, but you can modify its properties. This is similar to how a constant that's assigned an object like an array works. For example, if the module file shown here exported the scores constant and you imported it, you wouldn't be able to assign a new value to it. However, you would be able to call its push() method to add test scores to it.

A module that exports three functions

```
const scores = [];                          // private variable

export function addTestScore(score) {
    scores.push(score);
}

export function getAverageScore() {
    let total = 0;
    for (let score of scores) {
        total += score;
    }
    return total / scores.length;
}

export function getScoreDisplayString(separator = ", ") {
    return scores.join(separator);
}
```

Another way to export the three functions

```
export {addTestScore, getAverageScore, getScoreDisplayString};
```

A module that uses two of the exported functions

```
import {addTestScore, getScoreDisplayString} from "./lib_test_scores.js";

const getElement = selector => document.querySelector(selector);

getElement("#add_score").addEventListener("click", () => {
    const score = parseFloat(getElement("#score").value);
    addTestScore(score);
    getElement("#all").textContent = getScoreDisplayString();
    // const len = scores.length;    // ReferenceError: scores is not defined
});
```

Description

- *Modules* are JavaScript files that let you break up your code and protect private state.
- To export items, you use the export statement. To export a single item, you code the *export* keyword before the declaration for the item. To export multiple items, you code the export keyword followed by a comma-separated list of items enclosed in braces.
- You can't code an export statement inside a function. As a result, you can only export top-level items.
- To import items, code an import statement at the beginning of a JavaScript file. After the *import* keyword, code braces that contain a comma-separated list of items to import, the *from* keyword, and a path to the module file.
- To code a path that's relative to the root directory for the app, start the path with "./". To code a path to a folder that's in the same directory as the root directory for the app, start the path with "../".
- When you import items, they are available in the file as read-only views of the exported items. Because of that, you can't change the value of a variable or constant that's imported, but you can modify its properties.

Figure 13-1   How to export and import module items

How to declare a script as a module

To be able to import or export items from a JavaScript file, you must declare the script as a module. That way, JavaScript can use the ES module system to work with the script.

To declare a script as a module, you add a type attribute with a value of "module" to the <script> element as shown in figure 13-2. In the first example, the first <script> element sets the type attribute for the lib_test_scores.js file that exports the functions for working with test scores. Then, the second <script> element sets the type attribute for the test_scores.js file that imports two of these functions.

The second example works like the first example, but it shows that you can also declare inline JavaScript as a module. Here, the second <script> element contains inline JavaScript that uses an import statement to import two functions.

When you use ES modules, you should know that the ES module system provides many features beyond creating private state. Many of these features provide for better security and performance, and they impact the way you develop the code.

To start, code that uses ES modules must be run from a server. If you try to run a module from the file system, JavaScript throws errors due to module security requirements. In addition, ES modules use strict mode and the defer attribute automatically. As a result, you don't need to code the "use strict" directive at the top of a module or code the defer attribute when loading a module. Similarly, an ES module is only executed once. That's true even if it's referenced by multiple <script> elements.

Finally, an ES module is imported into the scope of a single script. In other words, it isn't imported into global scope. As a result, you can only access imported items in a script they are imported into.

The ES module examples in this chapter use files that have a .js extension to indicate that they are JavaScript files. Then, these examples use the type attribute of the <script> element to indicate that these files are ES modules. This works well on most servers because they're typically configured to work with .js files.

However, it's also possible for a module file to have an .mjs extension to indicate that it's a JavaScript module. This allows some servers to automatically treat the file as a JavaScript module without having to code the <script> element's type attribute. Unfortunately, not all servers work correctly with .mjs files. That's why this chapter uses .js files for ES modules.

Two <script> elements that declare modules

```
<script src="lib_test_scores.js" type="module"></script>
<script src="test_scores.js" type="module"></script>
```

A <script> element that declares inline JavaScript as a module

```
<script src="lib_test_scores.js" type="module"></script>
<script type="module">

    import {addTestScore, getScoreDisplayString} from "./lib_test_scores.js"

    const getElement = selector => document.querySelector(selector);

    getElement("#add_score").addEventListener("click", () => {
        const score = parseFloat(getElement("#score").value);
        addTestScore(score);
        getElement("#all").textContent = getScoreDisplayString();
    });
</script>
```

A module...

- Keeps variables, constants, and functions out of global scope.
- Prevents name conflicts.
- Can create private state for an object.

A module...

- **Must be run from a server.** If you try to run a module from the file system, JavaScript throws errors due to module security requirements.
- **Uses strict mode automatically.** As a result, you don't need to code the "use strict" directive at the top of a module.
- **Uses the defer attribute of the <script> element automatically.** As a result, there's no need to code this attribute when loading a module.
- **Is only executed once.** That's true even if it is referred to by multiple <script> elements.
- **Is imported into the scope of a single script.** In other words, it isn't imported into global scope. As a result, you can only access imported items in a script they are imported into.

Description

- To declare JavaScript as a module, you can set the type attribute of its <script> element to "module". Otherwise, the JavaScript is not treated as a module.
- A file for a module can have a .js or .mjs extension. The .mjs extension makes it clear that the file is a module and allows servers and build tools to automatically treat the file as a module. However, some servers don't work correctly with .mjs files. As a result, it's still common to use .js for module files.

Figure 13-2   How to declare a script as a module

The Slide Show app

This chapter presents a version of the Slide Show app that uses modules. This provides private state for the variables, constants, and functions the app needs for its internal operations.

Figure 13-3 begins by showing some of the HTML for the Slide Show app. In the <body> element, you can see an <img> element whose id is "image" and an <h2> element whose id is "caption". These elements display the image and caption for the current slide.

In addition, this HTML includes a button whose id is "pause_resume". As its name suggests, this button allows a user to pause a slide show that's playing and resume a slide show that's paused.

At the end of the <body> element are three <script> elements that use the type attribute to identify the JavaScript files as modules. This is necessary because the two library files use export statements and the slide_show.js file uses import statements. As a result, JavaScript needs to use the ES module system to process these files.

Because this app uses the ES module system, it doesn't work correctly if you run it from the file system. Instead, you must deploy it to a web server and run it from that server. One way to do that is to run this app from a Node.js web server like the http-server module described in the appendix.

One thing to note about this version of the Slide Show app is that it doesn't code the images of the slide show in the HTML. Instead, it uses JavaScript to load information about the images in the slide show as shown by part 3 of this figure.

The Slide Show app

The HTML of the <body> element

```
<body>
    <h1>Fishing Slide Show</h1>
    <p><img id="image"></p>
    <h2 id="caption"></h2>
    <p><input type="button" id="pause_resume" value="Pause"></p>

    <script src="lib_slide_show.js" type="module"></script>
    <script src="lib_DOM.js" type="module"></script>
    <script src="slide_show.js" type="module"></script>
</body>
```

Description

- The Slide Show app displays a series of photos and captions at two second intervals on a continuous loop.

- The user can click the Pause button to pause the slide show on the current image. Then, the button becomes a Resume button, which the user can click to resume the slide show.

- The <script> elements in the HTML set the type attribute of the JavaScript files to "module" so the files can export and import module items.

Figure 13-3   The Slide Show app (part 1)

Part 2 of figure 13-3 presents the two library files this app uses. The lib_DOM.js module exports a single function named getElement() that uses the querySelector() method of the document object to get an object that represents an HTML element.

The lib_slide_show.js file starts by defining a timer variable, a Boolean running variable, a numeric speed variable, a nodes constant that's an object literal, and an img constant that's an object literal. Then, this code defines the stopSlideShow() and displayNextImage() functions, which contain code similar to the code presented in chapter 8. These variables, constants, and functions are used by the slide show for its internal operations and aren't exported by the module. In other words, they're private.

Next, the code defines three more functions: loadImages(), startSlideShow(), and getToggleHandler(). These are the methods that the module exports. In other words, they're public.

The loadImages() function has code that's similar to code presented in chapter 8. However, this version gets information about the images in the slide show from the slides parameter rather than from an element in the page. It assigns that information to the private img object.

The startSlideShow() function starts by checking if both arguments were sent to it. If they were, the function assigns information from those arguments to the private nodes object. This is how the slide show gets the <img> and <h2> elements that it displays the slides in. After that, this function calls the displayNextImage() function to start the slide show. Then, it passes the definition of the displayNextImage() function and the private speed variable to the setInterval() function to show the next image at the specified interval. Finally, it assigns the timer object to the private timer variable.

The getToggleHandler() function returns a function definition. That's because it's meant to attach an event handler to the Pause/Resume button. This function begins by checking whether the private running variable is true. If it is, it calls the private stopSlideShow() function to stop the slide show. Otherwise, it calls the startSlideShow() function to start the slide show.

After starting or stopping the slide show, the getToggleHandler() function uses the currentTarget property of the Event object to get a reference to the button. Then, it sets the value of the button based on the value of the private running variable. Finally, it toggles the value of the private running variable by setting it to the opposite of its current value.

The lib_slide_show.js file ends with an export statement that exports the three public functions.

The lib_DOM.js file

```
export function getElement(selector) {
    return document.querySelector(selector);
}
```

The lib_slide_show.js file

```
let timer = null;                        // private variables/constants
let running = true;
let speed = 2000;
const nodes = {image: null, caption: null};
const img = {cache: [], counter: 0};

function stopSlideShow() {               // private functions
    clearInterval(timer);
}

function displayNextImage() {
    img.counter = ++img.counter % img.cache.length;
    const image = img.cache[img.counter];
    nodes.image.src = image.src;
    nodes.image.alt = image.alt;
    nodes.caption.textContent = image.alt;
};

function loadImages(slides) {            // public functions
    for (let slide of slides) {
        const image = new Image();
        image.src = "images/" + slide.href;
        image.alt = slide.title;
        img.cache.push(image);
    }
}

function startSlideShow(image, caption) {
    if (image && caption) {
        nodes.image = image;
        nodes.caption = caption;
    }
    displayNextImage();
    timer = setInterval(displayNextImage, speed);
}

function getToggleHandler() {
    return evt => {
        if (running) {
            stopSlideShow();
        } else {
            startSlideShow();
        }
        const button = evt.currentTarget;
        button.value = (running) ? "Resume" : "Pause";
        running = !running;    // toggle running flag
    };
}

export {loadImages, startSlideShow, getToggleHandler};
```

Figure 13-3   The Slide Show app (part 2)

Part 3 of figure 13-3 presents the JavaScript in the slide_show.js file. It begins with an import statement that imports the getElement() function from the lib_DOM.js file. Next is an import statement that imports the three functions exported by the lib_slide_show.js file. Then, the slide_show.js file defines an event handler for the DOMContentLoaded event.

Within this event handler, the code starts by creating an array of slide objects with information about the images for the slide show. After that, it calls the getElement() function to get the Pause/Resume button and the getToggleHandler() function to set the click event handler for that button. This shows how easy it is to import and use items from different modules.

After that, the code calls the loadImages() function and passes it the array of slide objects. Finally, it calls the startSlideShow() function and passes it the elements that display the slide show.

The slide_show.js file

```javascript
import {getElement} from './lib_DOM.js';
import {getToggleHandler, loadImages,
    startSlideShow} from './lib_slide_show.js';

document.addEventListener("DOMContentLoaded", () => {
    // define the slides
    const slides = [
        {href:"release.jpg", title:"Catch and Release"},
        {href:"deer.jpg", title:"Deer at Play"},
        {href:"hero.jpg", title:"The Big One!"},
        {href:"bison.jpg", title:"Roaming Bison"}
    ];

    // attach the event handler for the Pause/Resume button
    getElement("#pause_resume").addEventListener(
        "click", getToggleHandler());

    // load the images and start the slide show
    loadImages(slides);
    startSlideShow(getElement("#image"), getElement("#caption"));
});
```

Description

- The Slide Show app uses modules to break up its code and to protect the private variables, constants, and functions it uses.
- The lib_DOM.js module is a general purpose module that can be reused by other apps.
- The lib_slide_show.js module is specific to the Slide Show app and is less likely to be reused.

Figure 13-3 The Slide Show app (part 3)

More skills for working with modules

The previous figures presented the basic skills that you need to get started with ES modules. Now, you'll learn even more skills.

How to rename exports and imports

The first two examples in figure 13-4 show how to rename a module item when you import or export it. To do that, you code the item's name in the import or export statement followed by the *as* keyword and a new name for the item.

For instance, the import statement in the first example renames two imported functions so that they both start with "slideShow". That way, it's clear that both of these functions are for working with a slide show, and it reduces the chance that these function names will conflict with other function names defined in this script or in another module.

Conversely, the export statement in the second example renames functions in the module so they're shorter. This may increase the chances of these function names conflicting with other function names. However, you can minimize the chance of conflict by importing these functions into a module object as shown in the third example.

When you import items into a module object, all of the items are imported. To refer to all the items, you code the * character on the import statement. Then, you code the *as* keyword and the name of the module object. In this example, the code imports the load(), start(), and getToggle() functions defined in the second example as the methods of a module object named slideShow. Because you don't have to name each function on the import statement, this simplifies the statement. However, this also means you can't rename the items from the import statement.

After you import items into a module object, you can use that module object to access the items of the module. Here, the code uses the slideShow object to call its load() and start() methods.

How to export and import classes

So far, the modules presented in this chapter have only used variables, constants, and functions. However, you can also use modules to work with object-oriented code that uses classes to define objects. You work with classes the same way you work with the other items in a module. In the fourth and fifth examples in figure 13-4, for instance, the export statement exports two classes named Trip and Trips that are stored in the lib_trips.js file. Then, the import statement imports these two classes into the trips.js file so the code in this file can create Trip and Trips objects. Finally, the two <script> elements in the last example use the type attribute to identify both JavaScript files as ES modules.

How to rename imports

```
import {loadImages as slideShowLoadImages,
        startSlideShow as slideShowStart} from './lib_slide_show.js';
```

How to rename exports

```
export {loadImages as load,
        startSlideShow as start,
        getToggleHandler as getToggle};
```

How to create and use a module object

```
import * as slideShow from './lib_slide_show.js';
...
const slides = [...];
slideShow.load(slides);
slideShow.start($("#image"), $("#caption"));
...
```

How to export classes

```
export {Trip, Trips};

class Trip {...}
class Trips {...}
```

How to import classes

```
import {Trip, Trips} from './lib_trips.js';
...
const trips = new Trips();
const trip = new Trip("Seattle", 100, 3.5);
...
```

Code that declares the two files that use the classes as modules

```
<script src="lib_trips.js" type="module"></script>
<script src="trips.js" type="module"></script>
```

Description

- You can rename a module item when you import or export it, import all module items into a module object, or use a class as a module. These techniques are sometimes helpful for avoiding name conflicts.
- To rename an item, code the item's name in the import or export statement followed by the *as* keyword and a new name for the item.
- If you need to use most or all of the items of a module, you can simplify the import statement by importing all items of a module into a module object. To do that, you use the * character to indicate that you want to import all items, followed by the *as* keyword and the name of the module object. Then, you can use the module object to access the items of the module.
- To import or export a class, code the name of the class or classes within the braces of an import or export statement.

Figure 13-4   How to rename exports and imports and work with classes

How to create a default export

So far, this chapter has shown how to work with *named exports*. As you've seen, you can have as many named exports in a module file as you want. And, when you import named exports, you code the exact names of the items within braces separated by commas, unless you create a module object.

You can also include a *default export* in a module file. To do that, you include the *default* keyword in the export statement. This is shown by the module file in the first example in figure 13-5. This module contains a function named getElement() that's the default export. Unlike named exports, you can only have one default export per file.

When you import a default export into another module, you can give it any name you want, and you don't code that name within braces. This is shown by the import statement in the second example that imports the default export in the first example. When you import a default export into a module object, it's given the name default.

Since a default export is named by the statement that imports it, you don't have to name it in the module file. For instance, the default export in the third example is an anonymous function. Then, when it's imported in the fourth example, it's given the name addScore().

The fourth example also shows how to import the default export and named exports from the same file. To do that, you code the default export first, followed by a comma, followed by a comma-separated list of named exports enclosed in braces.

The use of default exports is mostly a matter of personal preference. Some programmers use them only when a module exports one item. Others use them for the item that provides the main use for a module. But some programmers prefer to always use named exports for consistency.

How to work with import maps

So far, the import statements in this chapter include the path, name, and file extension of the module file. However, suppose that you import from a module file throughout your app, and you later need to change that file's location or change its extension from .js to .mjs. In that case, you'd need to find and change every import statement in your app!

Fortunately, you can use an *import map* in your HTML to associate a text value called a *module specifier* with the module file name and path. Then, you can use the module specifier in your import statements. That way, if the module file ever changes, all you need to update is the import map.

An import map is a JSON object that's coded within the opening and closing tags of a <script> element with a type attribute of "importmap". For instance, the fifth example in figure 13-5 presents a <script> element with a JSON object that maps three module files to the module specifiers "dom", "trip", and "dayjs". Then, the import statement in the sixth example only needs to use the "trip" specifier. As you can see, an import map makes it simple to use module files in different directories as well as third party modules on the web.

A module file with a default export

```
export default function getElement(selector) {
    return document.querySelector(selector);
}
```

Import the default export

```
import get from './lib_DOM.js';        // no braces, different name
```

A module file with a default export that's an anonymous function and two named exports

```
const scores = [];

export default (score) => scores.push(score);

export function getAverageScore() {...}

export function getScoreDisplayString(separator = ", ") {...}
```

Import the default export and a named export

```
import addScore, {getAverageScore} from './lib_test_scores.js';
```

A <script> element with an import map

```
<script type="importmap">
  {
    "imports": {
      "dom": "../general_modules/DOM.js",
      "trip":"./modules/trip.js",
      "dayjs": "https://cdn.skypack.dev/dayjs@1.10.7",
    }
  }
</script>
```

An import statement that uses a module specifier from the import map

```
import {Trip} from 'trip';
```

Description

- The module file shown in figure 13-1 has *named exports*. To import a named export, you must code the exact name of the export within braces.

- You can also code a *default export* using the *default* keyword. To import a default export, you code whatever name you want and you don't use braces.

- You can have only one default export per module file. By contrast, you can have as many named exports as you want.

- To import both default and named exports, code the default export first, followed by a comma, followed by one or more named exports in a comma-separated list within braces.

- An *import map* is a JSON object that provides *module specifiers* that are text values rather than paths to the module files. This can make your code more flexible and easier to maintain.

- To create an import map, you code a <script> element with a type attribute that has a value of "importmap" and the JSON object between the opening and closing tags.

Figure 13-5   How to create a default export and use an import map

The Task List app

Figure 13-6 shows a version of the Task List app that uses modules. This version is similar to the one in chapter 12. However, it uses ES modules to protect its private state. Because of that, this app doesn't work correctly if you run it from the file system. Instead, like the Slide Show app you saw earlier, you must deploy this app to a web server and run it from that server to get it to work correctly.

The HTML for this version of the Task List app uses a <script> element with the type attribute "importmap" to create an import map. The JSON object within this element maps five module files to module specifiers. The first two module files are in a directory named general_modules that's in the root directory of the web server that contains the Task List app. That's why the file paths start with "../".

The next three module files are in a directory named modules that's in the root directory of the Task List app. Finally, the <script> element after the import map uses a type attribute with the value "module" to identify the task_list.js file as an ES module.

The Task List app

HTML of the <body> element

```html
<body>
    <div id="form">
        <h1>Task List</h1>
        <div>
            <label for="task">Task:</label>
            <input type="text" name="task" id="task">
        </div>
        <div>
            <label for="due_date">Due Date:</label>
            <input type="text" name="due_date" id="due_date">
        </div>
        <button id="add_task">Add Task</button>
        <button id="clear_tasks">Clear Tasks</button>
    </div>

    <div id="display">
        <select name="tasks" id="tasks" multiple></select><br>
        <button id="delete_task">Delete Task</button>
    </div>
    <div class="clear"></div>
    <p id="msg"></p>

    <script type="importmap">
        {
            "imports": {
                "storage": "../general_modules/storage.js",
                "DOM": "../general_modules/DOM.js",
                "task":"./modules/task.js",
                "task_storage":"./modules/task_storage.js",
                "task_list":"./modules/task_list.js"
            }
        }
    </script>
    <script src="task_list.js" type="module"></script>
</body>
```

Description

- The Task List app has its own modules in a folder named modules. In addition, it uses shared modules that are on the web server in a folder named general_modules.

Figure 13-6   The Task List app (part 1)

Part 2 of figure 13-6 presents two module files that contain general purpose functions for working with local storage and the DOM. Since these functions could be used by many different web apps, they're stored in a directory named general_modules in the root directory of the web server. That way, the functions in these modules can be imported and used by any web app on the same web server.

The storage.js file contains three functions for working with items in local storage. The retrieve() function accepts a key value and uses it to retrieve the value in local storage associated with that key. If a value is retrieved, the code passes it to the JSON.parse() method and returns the result. If there's no value in local storage for the specified key, the function returns null.

The store() function accepts a key value and a data value and passes them to the setItem() method to store them in local storage. First, though, it passes the data value to the JSON.stringify() method to make sure any objects or arrays are stored as strings.

The remove() function accepts a key value and uses it to remove any value in local storage that's associated with that key. The module file ends with an export statement that exports all three functions as named exports.

The DOM.js file contains nine functions for working with the DOM. The get() function accepts a selector and returns an object that represents the specified DOM element. Most of the other functions in this module use this get() function.

The setText() function accepts a selector and a text string and assigns the text string to the textContent property of the selected element. The setValue() function works similarly, but it sets the selected element's value property.

The clear() function accepts a selector and checks whether the selected element has a value property. If it does, the function sets that value property to an empty string. Otherwise, it sets the textContent property of the element to an empty string.

The focus() function accepts a selector and sets the focus on the selected element. The select() function works similarly, but it sets the focus and selects the value.

The load() function accepts a function definition and attaches it as the event handler for the DOMContentLoaded event. The addClick() function accepts a selector and a function definition and attaches the function as the event handler for the click event of the selected element.

The module file ends with an export statement that exports all nine functions as named exports.

The general_modules/storage.js file

```javascript
function retrieve(key) {
    const json = localStorage.getItem(key);
    if(json) {
        return JSON.parse(json);
    } else {
        return null;
    }
}
function store(key, data) {
    localStorage.setItem(key, JSON.stringify(data));
}
function remove(key) {
    localStorage.removeItem(key);
}

export {retrieve, store, remove};
```

The general_modules/DOM.js file

```javascript
function get(selector) {
    return document.querySelector(selector);
}
function setText(selector, text) {
    get(selector).textContent = text;
}
function setValue(selector, value) {
    get(selector).value = value;
}
function getValue(selector) {
    return get(selector).value;
}
function clear(selector) {
    const elem = get(selector);
    if (elem.value) elem.value = "";
    else elem.textContent = "";
}
function focus(selector) {
    get(selector).focus();
}
function select(selector) {
    get(selector).select();
}
function load(func) {
    document.addEventListener("DOMContentLoaded", func);
}
function addClick(selector, func) {
    get(selector).addEventListener("click", func);
}

export {get, setText, setValue, getValue, clear,
    focus, select, load, addClick};
```

Description

- These two modules are general purpose and are stored on the web server so they can be shared by all the apps on the same web server.

Figure 13-6   The Task List app (part 2)

Parts 3 and 4 of figure 13-6 present three module files that contain classes and objects that are specific to the Task List app. Because of that, they're stored in a directory named modules in the root directory of the app.

The task.js file contains a class named Task. Its constructor accepts description and dueDate parameters that it uses to initialize the description and dueDate properties of the class. Notice that it initializes the dueDate property as a Date object by passing the value of the dueDate parameter to the Date() constructor.

The Task class has two read-only accessor properties that return Boolean values that describe the state of the dueDate property. The hasInvalidDueDate property returns true if the toString() method of the dueDate property returns "Invalid Date". Otherwise, it returns false. Similarly, the isPastDue property returns true if the dueDate property is a date in the past. Otherwise, it returns false.

The last method in the Task class is a toString() method that overrides the toString() method that the Task class inherits from the Object type. It returns a string that consists of the values of the dueDate and description properties separated by a dash.

The file ends with an export statement that exports the Trip class as the default export of the module.

The task_storage.js file contains an object literal for working with Task objects in local storage. The file starts by importing the module items it needs to do its work. Specifically, it imports the functions in the general purpose storage module into a module object named storage. And, it imports the default Task class from the task module. Notice that these import statements use the module specifiers that are defined in the import map in the HTML.

The taskStorage object literal has three methods for working with Task objects in local storage. The retrieve() method uses the retrieve() method of the storage module object to get task data from local storage that's associated with the key "tasks". This data is returned as an array of objects, but not specifically an array of Task objects. To convert the data to Task objects, the method declares an empty tasks array, loops the array returned from local storage, uses the object data to create a new Task object, and adds that new Task object to the tasks array. When the loop completes, the method returns the array of Task objects.

The store() function accepts an array of Task objects and passes it to the store() method of the storage module object along with the key "tasks". This stores the task data in local storage with the associated key.

The remove() function calls the remove() method of the storage module object and passes it the key "tasks". This removes any value in local storage that's associated with that key.

The file ends with an export statement that exports the taskStorage object as the default export of the module.

The modules/task.js file

```
class Task {
    constructor(description, dueDate) {
        this.description = description;
        this.dueDate = new Date(dueDate);
    }

    get hasInvalidDueDate() {
        return this.dueDate.toString() === "Invalid Date";
    }
    get isPastDue() {
        const today = new Date();
        return this.dueDate.getTime() < today.getTime();
    }

    toString() {
        return `${this.dueDate.toDateString()} - ${this.description}`;
    }
}

export default Task;
```

The modules/task_storage.js file

```
import * as storage from 'storage';
import Task from 'task';

const taskStorage = {
    retrieve() {
        const tasks = [];
        const taskArray = storage.retrieve("tasks");
        if(taskArray) {
            for(let obj of taskArray) {
                tasks.push(new Task(obj.description, obj.dueDate));
            }
        }
        return tasks;
    },
    store(tasks) {
        storage.store("tasks", tasks);
    },
    remove() {
        storage.remove("tasks");
    }
};

export default taskStorage;
```

Figure 13-6   The Task List app (part 3)

The task_list.js file contains an object literal for working with the Task objects in the app. The file starts by importing the module items it needs to do its work. Specifically, it imports the default taskStorage object from the task_storage module. Again, this import statement uses the module specifier that's defined in the import map in the HTML.

The module starts by defining an empty array named tasks. Since this array isn't exported, it's private.

Next, it defines a taskList object literal with seven methods for working with Task objects. The first six methods return the taskList object so they can be chained. The last method, by contrast, is a generator function. This enables the taskList object to be iterated in a for-of loop.

The load() method calls the retrieve() method of the taskStorage object to initialize the private tasks array with an array of Task objects. If there's no task data, the array is initialized to an empty array. The save() method calls the store() method of the taskStorage object and passes it the private tasks array to save the task data.

The add() method accepts a Task object and adds it to the private tasks array. Similarly, the delete() method accepts an index value and removes the item at the specified index from the private tasks array. First, though, it sorts the items in the array to make sure they're in the same order as the tasks displayed on the page.

The clear() method removes all the items in the private tasks array by setting its length property to zero. Then, it calls the remove() method of the taskStorage module object to remove the task data.

The sortByDueDate() method sorts the Task objects in the private tasks array. To do that, it passes an arrow function to the sort() method of the tasks array. This sorts the Task objects by due date in ascending order.

The file ends with an export statement that exports the taskList object as the default export of the module.

Part 4 of figure 13-6 also presents the beginning of the task_list.js file. It starts by importing the module items it needs to manage the task list. Specifically, it imports the default taskList object from the task_list module, the default Task class from the task module, and the functions of the general purpose DOM module into a module object named dom. Again, these import statements use the module specifiers that are defined in the import map in the HTML.

Next, the code defines a helper function named displayTasks(). It starts by calling the sortByDueDate() method of the taskList object. Then, it uses the get() method of the dom module object to get the <select> element that displays the task data and clears it.

After that, the code loops through the Task objects in the taskList object. This works because the generator function of the taskList object makes it iterable. Within the loop, the code creates a new <option> element for each Task object, sets its text, and adds it to the <select> element. Note that when the Task object is passed to the createTextNode() method, its toString() method is called. Finally, the code uses the focus() method of the dom module object to set the focus on the Task text box. This makes it convenient for the user to add a new task.

The modules/task_list.js file

```javascript
import taskStorage from 'task_storage';
let tasks = [];            // private variable

const taskList = {
    load() {
        tasks = taskStorage.retrieve();
        return this;
    },
    save() {
        taskStorage.store(tasks);
        return this;
    },
    add(task) {
        tasks.push(task);
        return this;
    },
    delete(i) {
        this.sortByDueDate();
        tasks.splice(i, 1);
        return this;
    },
    clear() {
        tasks.length = 0;
        taskStorage.remove();
        return this;
    },
    sortByDueDate() {
        tasks.sort((a, b) => a.dueDate - b.dueDate);
        return this;
    },
    *[Symbol.iterator]() {
        for (let task of tasks) {
            yield task;
        }
    }
};
export default taskList;
```

The task_list.js file

```javascript
import taskList from "task_list";
import Task from "task";
import * as dom from "DOM";

const displayTasks = () => {
    taskList.sortByDueDate();
    const select = dom.get("#tasks");
    select.textContent = "";

    for (let task of taskList) {
        const opt = document.createElement("option");
        opt.appendChild(document.createTextNode(task));
        select.appendChild(opt);
    }
    dom.focus("#task");
}
```

Figure 13-6   The Task List app (part 4)

Part 5 of figure 13-6 presents the rest of the task_list.js file, which consists of the event handler for the DOMContentLoaded event. To attach this event handler, the code calls the load() method of the dom module object and passes it an arrow function.

The load event handler attaches event handlers for the click events of the Add Task, Clear Task, and Delete Task buttons. To do this, it calls the addClick() method of the dom module object and passes it the id of the button and an arrow function. After that, the load event handler calls the load() method of the taskList object to load the tasks. Finally, it calls the displayTasks() helper function to display the tasks to the user.

The click event handler for the Add Task button calls the clear() method of the dom module object to clear the <p> element that displays messages to the user. Then, it uses the getValue() method of that object to get the description and due date values entered by the user and pass them to the Task constructor.

After a new Task object is created, the code uses the properties of the Task object to check if the user entered valid data. If so, it chains three methods of the taskList object to load the tasks, add the new task, and save the updated tasks. Then, the clear() method of the dom module object clears the text boxes and the displayTasks() helper function displays the update tasks.

If the user didn't enter valid data, the setText() method of the dom module object displays an error message to the user. Then, the select() method of that object sets the focus on the first text box and selects any text it contains. This makes it convenient for the user to correct the invalid entry.

The click event handler for the Clear Tasks button starts by calling the clear() method of the taskList object to remove the tasks. After that, it uses the clear() method of the dom module object to clear the text boxes, the <select> element that displays the tasks, and the <p> element that displays error messages. Finally, it calls the focus() method of the dom module object to set the focus on the first text box. This makes it convenient for the user to add a new task.

The click event handler for the Delete Task button starts by calling the clear() method of the dom module object to clear any previous error messages. Then, it uses the get() method of the dom module object to get the <select> element that displays task data and chains a call to the select element's selectedIndex property. This property returns the index of the <option> element that the user selected, or -1 if no <option> element is selected.

Next, the code uses an if statement to check the user's selection. If no task is selected, the code uses the setText() method of the dom module object to notify the user. Otherwise, it chains three methods of the taskList object to load the tasks, delete the task at the specified index, and save the updated tasks. Then, the displayTasks() helper function displays the updated tasks.

The task_list.js file (continued)

```
dom.load(() => {
    dom.addClick("#add_task", () => {
        dom.clear("#msg");

        const newTask = new Task(
            dom.getValue("#task"), dom.getValue("#due_date"));

        let message = "";
        if (newTask.description === "") {
            message = "Task is required. ";
        }
        if (newTask.hasInvalidDueDate || newTask.isPastDue) {
            message += "Due Date must be a valid date in the future."
        }

        if (message === "") {
            taskList.load().add(newTask).save();
            dom.clear("#task");
            dom.clear("#due_date");
            displayTasks();
        } else {
            dom.setText("#msg", message);
            dom.select("#task");
        }
    });

    dom.addClick("#clear_tasks", () => {
        taskList.clear();
        dom.clear("#tasks");
        dom.clear("#task");
        dom.clear("#due_date");
        dom.clear("#msg");
        dom.focus("#task");
    });

    dom.addClick("#delete_task", () => {
        dom.clear("#msg");

        const index = dom.get("#tasks").selectedIndex;
        if (index === -1) {
            dom.setText("#msg", "Please select a task to delete.");
        } else {
            taskList.load().delete(index).save();
            displayTasks();
        }
    });

    taskList.load();
    displayTasks();
});
```

Figure 13-6   The Task List app (part 5)

The Clock app

Figure 13-7 presents the Clock app. The HTML for this app uses an import map to map two module files to module specifiers.

The first module file is the same dom module that the Task List app uses. This works because the Clock app is on the same web server as the Task List app. So, these apps can share the general purpose modules that are in the general_modules directory on the web server.

The second module file is a third party module called dayjs that's available on the web. It provides a library that works with dates and times. The <script> element after the import map uses a type attribute with the value "module" to identify the clock.js files as an ES module.

The clock.js file begins by importing the module items it needs to do its work. Specifically, it imports the load() and setText() functions from the dom module and the default export from the dayjs module. These import statements use the module specifiers that are defined in the import map.

Next, the code defines a helper function named displayClock(). First, it chains calls to the dayjs() and format() methods to get the current time and date. You can use the URL in this figure to get more information about the format() method. Next, it uses the setText() method to display the time and date to the user.

Finally, the code calls the load() method and passes it an arrow function. This attaches the arrow function as the event handler for the DOMContentLoaded event. The event handler calls the displayClock() function to display the initial time and date. Then, it passes the definition of the displayClock() function to the setInterval() function so the time and date are updated at 1 second (1000 millisecond) intervals.

This Clock app shows how easy it is to create an app from the "building blocks" provided by local and online modules. It also shows that you only need to import the module items the app uses, even if a module provides extensive functionality. This helps keep your app size manageable.

The Clock app

11:32:07 AM

Wed August 30, 2023

The HTML of the <body> element

```html
<body>
    <h1 id="time"></h1>
    <p id="date"></p>

    <script type="importmap">
        {
          "imports": {
            "DOM": "../general_modules/DOM.js",
            "dayjs": "https://cdn.skypack.dev/dayjs@1.10.7"
          }
        }
    </script>
    <script src="clock.js" type="module"></script>
</body>
```

The clock.js file

```javascript
import {load, setText} from "DOM";
import dayjs from "dayjs";

const displayClock = () => {
    const time = dayjs().format('h:mm:ss A');
    const date = dayjs().format('ddd MMMM D, YYYY');
    setText("#time", time);
    setText("#date", date);
};

load(() => {
    displayClock();
    setInterval(displayClock, 1000);
});
```

The documentation for the format() method of the dayjs module

https://day.js.org/docs/en/display/format

Description

- The Clock app is on the same web server as the Task List app, so it can use the same general purpose DOM module that the Task List app uses.

- In addition, it uses the third party dayjs module. Because of this, its own code is minimal.

- The Clock app only imports the items it needs from each module.

Figure 13-7   The Clock app

Legacy skills for working with modules

ES modules became available in 2015. Before then, programmers often used closures and the module pattern to organize code and create private state. Closures are a powerful feature of the JavaScript language, but they can be hard to understand. The figures that follow describe what closures are and how they are used to create modules.

How closures work

In chapter 5, you learned about *scope*, which refers to the visibility of JavaScript objects. In brief, a variable, constant, function, or object that's defined outside a function and not in an ES module has *global scope*, so it can be seen and used by any other JavaScript object. By contrast, a variable, constant, function, or object that's defined inside a function has *local scope*, so it can only be seen and used inside that function.

To understand closures, you need to understand two more things about scope. First, an object has access to its own scope as well as to the scope of the object that contains it. This is called the *scope chain*.

Second, if something refers to an object in the scope chain, that object stays *in scope* even if the object that contains it is *out of scope*. The most common way to create such a reference is to code an outer function that returns an inner function that refers to something in the outer function's scope. This is a *closure*.

To illustrate, the first example in figure 13-8 presents a function named createSlideShow() that contains several variables, constants, and functions and returns an object with three methods. The code in the functions and methods isn't shown here. That way, the figure can focus on where the variables, constants, functions, and methods are placed in the code.

The variables and constants declared at the start of the function store data that the slide show needs. Similarly, the two inner functions perform actions that the slide show needs. Because these variables, constants, and functions are coded inside the outer function, they have local scope. This means they're available to the other objects within the outer function, but they can't be called by code outside that outer function. In other words, they're private.

Next, the function defines and returns an object literal that has three methods. These methods are inner functions that refer to the variables, constants, and functions of the outer function. In other words, they're closures. Returning an object with methods is a common way to return more than one inner function from an outer function.

The second example in this figure calls the createSlideShow() function and assigns the object it returns to a constant named slideShow. Then, it calls the loadImages() method and passes it an array of slides. As long as this slideShow constant is in scope, the variables, constants, and functions defined in the createSlideShow() function are also in scope, even though the createSlide-Show() function itself has completed and is out of scope.

In addition, there's no way to directly access the private variables, constants, and functions of the CreateSlideShow() function. You can only access them

A closure

```
const createSlideShow = function() {
    let timer = null;                           // private variables/constants
    let play = true;
    let speed = 2000;
    const nodes = {image: null, caption: null};
    const img = {cache: [], counter: 0};

    const stopSlideShow = () => { ... };        // private functions
    const displayNextImage = () => { ... };

    return {                                    // a public object
        loadImages(slides) { ... },             // public method #1
        startSlideShow(image, caption) { ... }, // public method #2
        getToggleHandler(){ ... }               // public method #3
    };
};
```

Create and use the slide show object returned by the function

```
const slideShow = createSlideShow();   // create the slideShow object
slideShow.loadImages(slides);          // call a public method from it
```

Description

- The *scope chain* in JavaScript refers to what can be seen and used by an object. An object that is created within another object has access to its own scope as well as the scope of the object that contains it.

- An object in the scope chain is *in scope*, as long as something is referring to it. This is true even if the object that contains it has finished executing and is *out of scope*.

- A *closure* is created when an inner function refers to one or more objects in the scope of the outer function that contains it.

Figure 13-8   How closures work

indirectly by calling the public methods of the object that's returned by this function.

The module pattern

Prior to ES modules, many developers and third-party libraries used the *module pattern* to create a single object that has private state. The module pattern uses an *immediately invoked function expression (IIFE)* to define a function expression and immediately call, or *invoke*, it. In conversation, an IIFE is commonly referred to as an "iffy."

Usually, you use one statement to define a function and a second statement to invoke it. With an IIFE, you use a single statement to define and invoke a function. This is illustrated by the first example in figure 13-9. Here, the function expression is coded inside parentheses and parentheses are coded after the expression to invoke it immediately.

The module pattern uses an IIFE to create a single instance of the object that's returned by a function that creates a closure. That way, you get a single instance of an object that has private state. This object can be referred to as a module, but it works differently than an ES module.

The second example shows how this works. Here, the code uses an IIFE to create a slideShow object that has private state. Since the function expression is immediately invoked, the global slideShow constant refers to the object that's returned by the IIFE as soon as the library file loads. Then, the third example shows code that uses the module object created by the IIFE.

Note that if an IIFE is coded within a statement as shown in the second example rather than at the beginning of the statement as shown in the first example, the JavaScript engine doesn't require the enclosing parentheses. Still, it's considered a best practice to use them because it helps other programmers recognize the code as an IIFE.

An immediately invoked function expression (IIFE)

```
(function() {                  // define and invoke function in one statement
    console.log("Hello");
})();
```

The module pattern

```
const slideShow = (function() {
    let timer = null;                         // private variables/constants
    let play = true;
    let speed = 2000;
    const nodes = { image: null, caption: null };
    const img = { cache: [], counter: 0 };

    const stopSlideShow = () => { ... }        // private functions
    const displayNextImage = () => { ... }

    return {                                   // public methods
        loadImages(slides) { ... },
        startSlideShow(image, caption) { ... },
        getToggleHandler(){ ... }
    };
})(); // creates the object
```

Use the slide show object defined by the module pattern

```
slideShow.loadImages(slides);          // call a public method from it
```

Description

- An *immediately invoked function expression (IIFE)* is a function that is defined and invoked in a single statement. To do that, you surround the function definition with parentheses and then code parentheses to call that function.

- If an IIFE is coded within a statement, you don't need to code parentheses around it. Even so, it's considered a best practice to code an IIFE within parentheses to help other programmers recognize that the code is an IIFE.

- The *module pattern* uses an IIFE to create a single instance of the object, or *module*, that's returned by the function. That way, you have a single object with private state.

Figure 13-9   How the module pattern works

Perspective

Now that you've completed this chapter, you have the skills you need to use the ES module system to organize your code and create private state. This chapter also showed how to use closures and the module pattern. These techniques have been around for a long time and are still commonly used. As a result, it's helpful to be familiar with them.

Terms

ECMAScript modules (ES modules)	scope chain
named export	in scope
default export	out of scope
import map	closure
module specifier	immediately invoked function
global scope	expression (IIFE)
local scope	module pattern

Exercise 13-1   Enhance the Countdown app to use a module

This exercise guides you through the process of changing a Countdown app to use a module to organize its code.

Since modules are in strict mode by default, you can delete the "strict mode" directive from files you convert to modules. However, this is optional.

Open, test, and review the app

1. View the files in this folder:

    `exercises\ch13\countdown\`

2. Run the app in Chrome and test it. To do that, enter an event name and an event date and click the Countdown button.

3. Review the code in the library file and note that it contains a class that defines an Event object. Review the code in the click event handler for the Countdown button and note that it uses an Event object.

Modify the app to use a module

4. In the index.html file, modify the <script> elements to include a type attribute that identifies the scripts as modules.

5. In the event library file, add a statement that exports the Event class as the default export.

6. In the count_down.js file, add a statement that imports the default Event class.

7. Test the app to make sure it still works correctly. To do that, you'll need to run the app from a local web server as described in the appendixes.

Exercise 13-2   Enhance the Trips app to use modules

This exercise guides you through the process of changing a Trips app to use modules to organize its code.

Trips Log

Destination:	Tahoe
Miles Driven:	400
Gallons of Gas Used:	ten

[Add Trip]

Gallons must be a valid number greater than zero.

```
Fresno: Miles - 500; MPG - 41.7
Las Vegas: Miles - 300; MPG - 42.9

Average MPG: 42.1
```

Open, test, and review the app

1. View the files in this folder:

   `exercises\ch13\trips\`

2. Run the app in Chrome and test it. To do that, enter one or more destinations, miles driven, and gallons used.

3. Review the library files and note that they contain classes that define Trip and Trips objects. Review the code in the trips.js file and note that the event handler for the DOMContentLoaded event uses a Trips object and the click event handler for the Add Trip button uses Trip objects.

Modify the app to use modules

4. In the index.html file, convert the <script> elements for the library files to an import map. Then, add a type attribute to the <script> element for the main file to identify it as a module.

5. In the trip library file, add a statement that exports the Trip class as the default export.

6. In the trips library file, add a statement that imports the default Trip class.

7. Although the app only needs one instance of the Trips class, it's coded as a class because it has a private property. Change it so the module uses a private constant for the array that stores Trip objects and exports an object literal as the default export.

8. In the count_down.js file, add a statement that imports the default Trip class and the default object literal that works with trips. Make sure the object literal that's imported from the trips module is named trips.

9. In the event handler for the DOMContentLoaded event, delete the statement that calls the Trips() constructor, as it's no longer needed.

10. Test the app to make sure it still works correctly. To do that, you'll need to run the app from a local web server as described in the appendixes.

Add a validation module

11. Add a JavaScript file named lib_validation.js to the app.

12. In the validation library file, code a function that checks if a string value is empty, a function that checks if any of a variable number of string values is empty, and a function that checks if a value is less than zero. This last function should also check that the value is numeric.

13. Add a statement that exports all three functions as named exports.

14. In the index.html file, add the validation library to the import map.

15. In the count_down.js file, add a statement that imports the functions from the validation module as a module object.

16. Modify the data validation code to use the functions in the validation module object.

17. Test the app to make sure the validation still works correctly.

Section 3

More skills as you need them

Sections 1 and 2 present the essential skills for building most client-side JavaScript apps. Now, section 3 presents some advanced skills that you can learn as you need them.

To start, chapter 14 shows how to use Ajax to asynchronously update your web pages with data from a web server without reloading the entire page. Then, chapter 15 shows to use JavaScript with Node.js to create a web-based API that provides access to some data on a server. Since these chapters contain some related information, it makes sense to read them in sequence.

Finally, chapter 16 shows how to use JavaScript with the Canvas API to create drawings and animations. Since this chapter doesn't depend on any information in chapters 14 or 15, you can skip directly to this chapter if you prefer.

14

How to work with Ajax

This chapter shows how to use Ajax to update a web page without reloading the entire web page. Since Ajax is commonly used to get data from web services, this chapter also shows how to work with two web services that provide data you can use for development and testing. In addition, it shows how to use asynchronous code in a module and how to make cross-origin requests.

Introduction to Ajax

This chapter begins by describing how Ajax works. Then, it describes two data formats commonly used with Ajax.

How Ajax works

Ajax (Asynchronous JavaScript and XML) is a set of techniques that allow a browser to update a web page with data from a web server without having to reload the entire page. Figure 14-1 begins by showing Google's Auto Suggest feature because it's a typical use of Ajax. As you type the start of a search entry, Google uses Ajax to get the terms and links of items that match the characters that you've typed so far. It does this without reloading the page, so the user doesn't experience any delays. This is sometimes called a "partial page refresh."

Because Ajax is so powerful, it's used by many popular websites. For instance, when you post a comment to most social media sites, the comment appears immediately. That's because the browser doesn't have to reload the entire page.

The two diagrams in this figure show how a normal HTTP request compares to an Ajax request. For a normal HTTP request, the browser makes an HTTP request for an entire page, the server returns an HTTP response for the page, and the browser loads the entire page.

By contrast, with an Ajax request, the browser uses JavaScript to send an HTTP request for some specific data, not a whole page. Then, the server returns an HTTP response that contains the requested data. Finally, the browser uses JavaScript to update only the part of the DOM affected by the new data. As a result, the browser doesn't need to reload the entire page or wait for data it doesn't need.

On the web server, an app or script that's written in a server-side language like PHP is typically used to return the data that's requested. Often, these apps or scripts are part of a *web service* that provides an *Application Programming Interface (API)* that developers can use to get data from a website. In this chapter, you'll learn how to use an API provided by a web service.

Broadly, an API is a set of rules that allows different applications or components to communicate with each other. For example, this book has already shown how to use several APIs like the DOM API that allow JavaScript to communicate with the browser. Now, this chapter shows how to use the *Fetch API*. This API provides methods and objects that allow a web app to work with data that's managed by another app that's running on a web server.

The Fetch API is the most modern way to send an Ajax request to a web server and to process the data that's returned from the server. There's an older way to make an Ajax request by using a browser object known as the *XMLHttpRequest (XHR) object*. However, it doesn't work as well, so you should avoid using it when possible.

Google's Auto Suggest uses Ajax

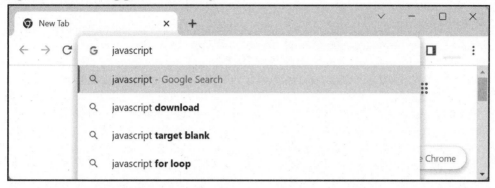

A normal HTTP request

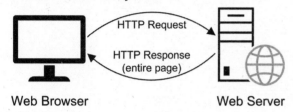

An Ajax request

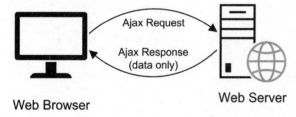

Description

- *Ajax* (*Asynchronous JavaScript and XML*) is a set of techniques for updating a web page with data from a web server without needing to reload the entire page. This is sometimes known as a "partial page refresh."
- When working with Ajax, JavaScript sends the request, processes the response, and updates the DOM with the new data. As a result, the browser doesn't need to reload the entire page.
- Ajax requests are often made to *web services* that provide *Application Programming Interfaces* (*APIs*) that developers can use to get data from a website.
- The modern way to make an Ajax request is to use the *Fetch API*.

Figure 14-1 How Ajax works

Two common data formats for Ajax

When the server returns the data for an Ajax request, it can use any data format that can be read by JavaScript. Figure 14-2 presents the two most common data formats for Ajax: XML and JSON. Ajax was originally designed to be used with *XML* (*Extensible Markup Language*). That's why XML is part of the Ajax name.

XML is a format that works well for exchanging data across the internet. In addition, XML is a markup language that works much like HTML. As a result, it's easy for programmers who have experience with HTML to understand. Because of that, XML was commonly used in the early days of Ajax.

Today, *JSON* (*JavaScript Object Notation*) is the most popular format for working with Ajax. JSON, pronounced "Jason", is similar to XML in that it's a format that works well for exchanging data across the internet. However, it's less verbose than XML.

In this figure, the XML and JSON examples store the same data about two management team members. However, the JSON example uses fewer characters. This makes it easier for humans to read. In addition, the JSON uses less memory when it's sent from the server to the client.

Most server-side languages provide functions for encoding data into JSON. For example, PHP provides the json_encode() function. That makes it easy for web services running on a server to include JSON in an HTTP response. Then, on the client side, JavaScript provides functions for parsing the JSON in the response into a JavaScript object.

These parsed JavaScript objects make it easy to work with JSON data. For example, after parsing the second example, each team member becomes an object in an array, and their information becomes properties of the corresponding object. So, to access the name of the first team member, you could code the following:

```
const username = teammembers[0].name;   //username is "Wilbur"
```

Although XML and JSON are the two most popular data formats for working with Ajax, they aren't the only ones that are supported. It's also possible for an HTTP response to store its data in plain text or other formats such as HTML, YAML, or CSV.

Two common data formats used with Ajax

Format	Description
XML	Extensible Markup Language
JSON	JavaScript Object Notation

Data formatted with XML

```
<?xml version="1.0" encoding="utf-8"?>
<management>
    <teammember>
        <name>Wilber</name>
        <title>Vice President of Accounting</title>
        <bio>With over 14 years of public accounting ... </bio>
    </teammember>
    <teammember>
        <name>Agnes</name>
        <title>Founder and CEO</title>
        <bio>While Agnes is the founder and CEO ... </bio>
    </teammember>
</management>
```

The same data formatted with JSON

```
{"teammembers":[
    {
        "name":"Wilbur",
        "title":"Vice President of Accounting",
        "bio":"With over 14 years of public accounting... "
    },
    {
        "name":"Agnes",
        "title":"Founder and CEO",
        "bio":"While Agnes is the founder and CEO ... "
    }
]}
```

Description

- The two most common data formats for working with Ajax are XML and JSON.

- Both *XML* (*Extensible Markup Language*) and *JSON* (*JavaScript Object Notation*) are formats that use text to store and transmit data.

- Most server-side languages provide methods for encoding data into JSON.

- JavaScript provides methods for parsing the JSON that's returned from a web service into a JavaScript object.

- JSON is less verbose than XML, so it uses less memory when being sent from the server to the client.

Figure 14-2   Two common data formats for Ajax

How to make an Ajax request

So far, this book has shown how to write *synchronous code*. Synchronous code waits for each statement to finish executing before executing the next one. As a result, if a statement takes a long time to execute, it blocks any other statements from executing. This can cause an app to appear unresponsive, especially if a synchronous statement needs to perform a time-consuming task such as retrieving data that's available from a web service.

Now, this chapter shows how to write *asynchronous code*. Asynchronous code allows multiple operations to be executed concurrently. This allows an app to continue executing the statements for one operation while waiting for another time-consuming operation to complete. In particular, this chapter shows how to use the Fetch API to make an Ajax request that works with data that's available from a web service. But first, it presents a simple web service that you can use for testing and development.

The JSON Placeholder API

Ajax requests typically get data from a web service. That's why figure 14-3 begins by presenting a web service named JSON Placeholder, which is an API that provides sample data in JSON format. This data mimics the kind of data that's typically returned by other web services. Using an API like this allows you to practice making Ajax calls without having to set up an account with a service or worry about other implementation details.

The table in this figure describes the sample data you can request from the JSON Placeholder web service. This data includes information about users, blog posts, comments, and so on. Most of the data is related to other data in the sample sets. For example, comments are related to a blog post, and photos are related to an album.

To get data from an API, you can make an HTTP GET request to the appropriate URL. For example, to get data for all of the users provided by the JSON Placeholder service, you can append /users to the URL for the API as shown in the first example. This returns the JSON shown in the second example. However, if you want to get the data for a single user, you can add the id for the user to the end of the URL like this:

```
https://jsonplaceholder.typicode.com/users/1
```

You can also use this API to simulate POST, PUT, and DELETE requests as described later in this chapter.

To view the data that's returned by a GET request to the JSON placeholder API, you can type the appropriate URL into a browser. This should return data that's formatted with JSON.

The JSON Placeholder web service

`https://jsonplaceholder.typicode.com`

The sample data that's available from this web service

Resource	Description
/users	10 users with data such as name, username, and email address.
/posts	100 blog posts with each one related to a specific user.
/comments	500 comments with each one related to a specific blog post.
/albums	100 photo albums with each one related to a specific user.
/photos	5000 simple photos of various colors with each one related to a specific album. This includes a photo that's 600x600 pixels and a thumbnail that's 150x150 pixels.
/todos	200 tasks with each one related to a specific user.

A URL that returns data for all users

`https://jsonplaceholder.typicode.com/users`

Some of the JSON that's returned

```
[
  {
    "id": 1,
    "name": "Leanne Graham",
    "username": "Bret",
    "email": "Sincere@april.biz",
    ...
  },
  ...
  {
    "id": 10,
    "name": "Clementina DuBuque",
    "username": "Moriah.Stanton",
    "email": "Rey.Padberg@karina.biz",
    ...
  }
]
```

Description

- *Synchronous code* executes statements in sequential order and waits for each statement to finish executing before it begins executing the next one.

- *Asynchronous code* allows an app to continue executing the statements for one operation while waiting for another operation to complete.

- The JSON Placeholder web service is an API that provides sample data in JSON format. This data mimics the kind of data that's typically returned by real web services.

- You can use the JSON Placeholder API to practice making Ajax calls without having to set up accounts or worry about other implementation details.

- You can view the data returned by the JSON Placeholder API by typing the appropriate URL into a browser.

Figure 14-3   The JSON Placeholder API

How to use the Fetch API for GET requests

The Fetch API provides methods and objects for making Ajax requests. The first table in figure 14-4 summarizes the fetch() method of the Fetch API. It accepts the URL for a request and returns a Promise object, which represents the eventual return value of the asynchronous request. In this case, that eventual return value, or result, is a Response object, which represents an HTTP response.

The fetch() method has an optional second parameter, which is an object that contains data about the request, including the type of HTTP request. If you omit this parameter, this method defaults to making a GET request.

A Promise object (or *promise*) has three states. When a Promise object is first created, it's *pending*. When the request returns its value, the promise is *fulfilled*. However, if an error occurs during the request, the promise is *rejected*.

When working with Promise objects, a promise that is no longer pending is considered *settled*. This is true whether the promise is fulfilled or rejected. In addition, a promise can be *resolved* without being fulfilled. For example, if a promise returns another promise, the original promise is resolved, even though the requested data isn't returned yet and so the promise isn't fulfilled.

The next two tables present methods you can use to work with the Fetch API. The then() method accepts a callback function that executes when the promise is resolved. In other words, it tells JavaScript to wait until the previous action has finished before executing its callback function. Then, after JavaScript executes the callback function, it wraps the return value in a new Promise object.

Because then() returns a Promise object, you can chain calls to as many then() methods as you like. This makes it easy to execute a series of functions without needing to know how long it will take any individual function to execute.

What if there's an error at some point in the chain? In that case, instead of executing their callbacks, each subsequent then() method returns the error wrapped in a promise. The error passes through the chain until it either reaches the end of the chain or a chained catch() method. Then, the callback function that's passed to the catch() method can process the error.

The example below the tables shows how to use these methods. To start, this code passes a URL for a GET request to the fetch() method. This returns a promise that will resolve when the HTTP response is received. After the fetch() method, this example chains calls to two then() methods and a catch() method, where each call is coded on its own line.

The first then() method waits until the promise from the fetch() method resolves. Its callback function accepts the Response object contained in the result of the promise and calls its json() method. This parses the JSON in the response into a JavaScript object.

The second then() method executes when the promise from the json() method called by the first then() method resolves. The second then() method's callback accepts a JavaScript object named json and displays that object in the console.

The catch() method accepts a callback that executes if the promise is rejected. This callback function displays an error message in the console.

One method of the Fetch API

Method	Description
`fetch(url, options)`	Makes an asynchronous request to the specified URL and returns a Promise object that eventually returns a Response object. If no options are included, this method makes a GET request.

Three states of a Promise object

- **Pending:** After a promise has been created but before the request returns its value.
- **Fulfilled:** When the request is successfully resolved.
- **Rejected:** If an error occurs during the request.

Two methods of the Promise object

Method	Description
`then(function)`	Registers the callback function to execute when the promise is resolved. The callback function receives a single parameter, which is the eventual return value of the asynchronous request. Returns a Promise object.
`catch(function)`	Registers the callback function to execute when the promise is rejected. The callback function receives a single parameter, which is usually an Error object. Returns a Promise object.

One method of the Response object

Method	Description
`json()`	Returns a Promise object that eventually resolves to a JavaScript object that's created from the JSON that's returned by the asynchronous request.

Use a GET request to display user data

```
const url = "https://jsonplaceholder.typicode.com/users";

fetch(url)                                // no options, so defaults to GET
    .then(response => response.json())
    .then(json => console.log(json))
    .catch(e => console.log(e.message));
```

The console

```
▼ Array(10) ⓘ
  ▶ 0: {id: 1, name: 'Leanne Graham', username: 'Bret', email: 'Sincere@april.biz', address: {…}, …}
  ▶ 1: {id: 2, name: 'Ervin Howell', username: 'Antonette', email: 'Shanna@melissa.tv', address: {…}, …}
  ▶ 2: {id: 3, name: 'Clementine Bauch', username: 'Samantha', email: 'Nathan@yesenia.net', address: {…}, …}
  ▶ 3: {id: 4, name: 'Patricia Lebsack', username: 'Karianne', email: 'Julianne.OConner@kory.org', address: {…}, …}
  ▶ 4: {id: 5, name: 'Chelsey Dietrich', username: 'Kamren', email: 'Lucio_Hettinger@annie.ca', address: {…}, …}
  ▶ 5: {id: 6, name: 'Mrs. Dennis Schulist', username: 'Leopoldo_Corkery', email: 'Karley_Dach@jasper.info', address: {…}, …}
  ▶ 6: {id: 7, name: 'Kurtis Weissnat', username: 'Elwyn.Skiles', email: 'Telly.Hoeger@billy.biz', address: {…}, …}
  ▶ 7: {id: 8, name: 'Nicholas Runolfsdottir V', username: 'Maxime_Nienow', email: 'Sherwood@rosamond.me', address: {…}, …}
  ▶ 8: {id: 9, name: 'Glenna Reichert', username: 'Delphine', email: 'Chaim_McDermott@dana.io', address: {…}, …}
  ▶ 9: {id: 10, name: 'Clementina DuBuque', username: 'Moriah.Stanton', email: 'Rey.Padberg@karina.biz', address: {…}, …}
```

Figure 14-4   How to use the Fetch API for GET requests

How to use the Fetch API for POST, PUT, and DELETE requests

Now that you know how to use the Fetch API to make GET requests, you're ready to learn how to use it to make other types of HTTP requests. Figure 14-5 starts by presenting three common HTTP request methods.

A POST request typically adds a new record, while a PUT request typically updates an existing record. Both requests send the data to be added or updated in the body of the HTTP request. In addition, a PUT request typically identifies the record to be updated in the URL.

A DELETE request, as the name suggests, typically deletes a record. In most cases, it identifies the record to be deleted in the URL. Because of that, a DELETE request doesn't usually need to store any data in the body of the request.

This figure uses the JSON Placeholder API to show how to make a POST request and a DELETE request with the Fetch API. This works because the JSON Placeholder API allows you to make sample POST, PUT, and DELETE requests. This doesn't actually add, update, or delete any data. However, the API accepts the requests and provides responses that are similar to what you'd see if the API were actually adding, updating, or deleting data.

The first example in this figure shows how to use Ajax to make a POST request to add a blog post. To do that, it creates an object to use as the options argument to the fetch() method. This object has properties that identify the request method as POST, set the request headers to identify the content type as JSON, and add the data entered by the user to the request body. You can copy and reuse most of this code for other POST requests. However, you need to supply the appropriate data in the body of the request.

Next, the code assigns the URL for the request to a constant. This isn't required, but it makes the example easier to read. Then, it passes that url and the options object to the fetch() method. After that, it uses the then() and catch() methods of the promise to process the HTTP response. This displays the object that's returned from the server in the console. In some cases, this object may include useful information such as an id that uniquely identifies the added data.

The second example shows how to use Ajax to make a DELETE request to delete a blog post. To do that, it gets the id of the blog post to delete and appends it to the URL for the request. Then, the code passes that URL and an options object to the fetch() method. This time, the options object doesn't need any properties other than the request method. As a result, this example doesn't define a constant named options. Instead, it creates the object for storing the options directly within the call to the fetch() method.

Next, the code uses the then() and catch() methods of the promise to process the HTTP response. This displays the object that's returned from the server in the console. When deleting data, it's common for the server to return an empty object.

Three common HTTP request methods

Method	Typical use
POST	Adds a new record. Data to be added is stored in the body of the request.
PUT	Updates an existing record. Data to be updated is stored in the body of the request. Data that identifies the record is stored in the URL.
DELETE	Deletes a record. Data that identifies the record is stored in the URL.

Use a POST request to add a new blog post

```
const title = getElement("#title").value;
const body = getElement("#body").value;
const userId = getElement("#user_id").value;

const options = {
    method: 'POST',
    headers: {
        'Content-type': 'application/json; charset=UTF-8',
    },
    body: JSON.stringify({title, body, userId})
};

const url = "https://jsonplaceholder.typicode.com/posts";

fetch(url, options)
    .then(response => response.json())
    .then(json => console.log(json))
    .catch(e => console.log(e.message));
```

Use a DELETE request to delete a blog post

```
const postId = getElement("#post_id").value;
const url = "https://jsonplaceholder.typicode.com/posts/" + postId

fetch(url, {method: 'DELETE'})
    .then(response => response.json())
    .then(json => console.log(json))
    .catch(e => console.log(e.message));
```

Description

- You can use Ajax and the Fetch API to make POST, PUT, and DELETE requests that add, update, and delete data. To do that, you include a second argument to the fetch() method that's an object containing data for the request.

- You can use the JSON Placeholder API to test POST, PUT, and DELETE requests. No data is actually changed on the server, but the JSON Placeholder API behaves as if it is so you can see if your code is working correctly.

Figure 14-5 How to use the Fetch API for POST, PUT, and DELETE requests

How to use the *async* and *await* keywords

So far, this chapter has shown how to use promises to create asynchronous code. However, most developers are used to synchronous code, and code that works directly with promises just *looks* different. This can make that code harder to read and understand. Fortunately, the *async* and *await* keywords make asynchronous code look more like synchronous code. This, in turn, makes working with promises easier.

When you define a function, you can use the *async* keyword to create an *asynchronous function* that automatically wraps the return value of that function in a Promise object. Then, within the asynchronous function, you can use the *await* keyword to tell JavaScript to wait until a promise is settled before returning its result.

To illustrate, the first example in figure 14-6 presents a function named loadPhoto(). It's defined with the *async* keyword, so it's an asynchronous function that can use the *await* keyword.

To start, the function uses the *await* keyword with the fetch() method to wait for the Response object that the promise resolves to. When the promise resolves, the code uses the *await* keyword again to wait for the json() method of the Response object to get the photo object that the promise resolves to.

After getting the photo object, the code uses similar code to get the album object that's related to the photo. Then, it assigns the album object as a property of the photo object. Finally, the function returns the photo object. Because it's an asynchronous function, this automatically wraps the photo object in a promise.

The second example shows how to create an asynchronous event handler. To do that, this code uses the *async* keyword to attach an asynchronous click event handler for a button. Then, it defines a try-catch statement. Within the try block, the first statement uses the *await* keyword to wait for the photo object the asynchronous loadPhoto() function eventually resolves to. This gets the photo object with the specified id. Then, the next two statements display properties of the photo object in the console. This example shows that when you use the *async* and *await* keywords you can use normal try-catch statements to handle errors.

If you compare the code in this figure with the code in the last two figures, you'll see that it looks more like the synchronous code that most programmers already understand. Because of that, it's easier to read and maintain.

This figure ends by presenting two static methods available from the Promise object. The resolve() and reject() methods return a Promise object that's already resolved or rejected. This can be useful to test your code to see how it handles a resolved promise, or to return a rejected promise when data validation fails, as shown in the last example.

An asynchronous function that uses await

```
async function loadPhoto(photoId) {     // declare function as asynchronous
    const domain = "https://jsonplaceholder.typicode.com";

    const photoResponse = await fetch(`${domain}/photos/${photoId}`);
    const photo = await photoResponse.json();

    const albumResponse = await fetch(`${domain}/albums/${photo.albumId}`)
    photo.album = await albumResponse.json();

    return photo;                  // automatically wraps value in a promise
}
```

An asynchronous event handler that calls the asynchronous function

```
getElement("#show_photo").addEventListener("click", async () => {
    try {
        const photo = await loadPhoto(1);
        console.log("Photo title: " + photo.title);
        console.log("Album title: " + photo.album.title);
    } catch(e) {
        console.log(e.message);
    }
});
```

Two static methods of the Promise object

Method	Description
resolve(value)	Returns a Promise object that's resolved with the specified value.
reject(value)	Returns a Promise object that's rejected with the specified value.

The asynchronous function updated to validate the data it receives

```
async function loadPhoto(photoId) {
    if (photoId < 0 || photoId > 5000) {
        const e = new Error("Photo id must be between 1 and 5000.");
        return Promise.reject(e);
    } else {
        // same as above
    }
}
```

Description

- The *async* keyword declares an *asynchronous function* that automatically wraps its return value in a Promise object.
- The *await* keyword tells JavaScript to wait until a promise is settled before returning its result. Unless you're coding a module, you can only use the *await* keyword within an asynchronous function.

Figure 14-6   How to use the *async* and *await* keywords

The Astronomy Picture of the Day app

Figure 14-7 presents the Astronomy Picture of the Day (APOD) app. It displays a NASA image or video for any date between June 16, 1995 and today. In addition, it displays some related data such as a title and explanation. To make this possible, the APOD app uses Ajax to asynchronously get data from an API that's available from NASA's APOD web service. Then, it updates some parts of its web page with that data. This improves the performance of the app and keeps the user interface responsive even when the app is retrieving data from the web service.

The Astronomy Picture of the Day app

Astronomy Picture Of the Day

Enter date: [2024-1-8]   [View]

The Phases of Venus

Venus goes through phases. Just like our Moon, Venus can appear as a full circular disk, a thin crescent, or anything in between. Venus, frequently the brightest object in the post-sunset or pre-sunrise sky, appears so small, however, that it usually requires binoculars or a small telescope to clearly see its current phase. The featured time-lapse sequence was taken over the course of six months in 2015 from Surgères, Charente-Maritime, France, and shows not only how Venus changes phase, but changes angular size as well. When Venus is on the far side of the Sun from the Earth, it appears angularly smallest and nearest to full phase, while when Venus and Earth are on the same side of the Sun, Venus appears larger, but as a crescent. This month Venus rises before dawn in waxing gibbous phases. Free APOD Lecture: January 9, 2024 to the Amateur Astronomers of Association of New York

Description

- The Astronomy Picture of the Day (APOD) app allows the user to enter a date and click the View button. Then, it displays a NASA image or video for the specified date. In addition, it displays some related data such as a title and explanation.
- The APOD app gets its data from an API that's available from NASA's APOD web service.
- When the APOD app loads, it displays the current date in the "Enter date" text box.

Figure 14-7   The Astronomy Picture of the Day app (part 1)

Part 2 of figure 14-7 begins by presenting some of the HTML and CSS for the app. To start, the HTML displays the title of the app as well as a text box and a View button that allow the user to enter a date. Here, the text box has an id of "date", and the View button has an id of "view_button". Below the View button, this HTML includes an <h3> element with an id of "title", a <div> element with an id of "display", and a <p> element with an id of "explanation". This is where the app displays the image or video and its related data if the Ajax request is fulfilled. Below these elements is a <p> element with an id of "msg". This is where the app displays any error messages.

The CSS aligns the label and input elements. In addition, it provides a class named error that the app uses to display error messages in red.

After the CSS, this figure shows the URL for NASA's APOD API. To use this API, you need to supply an api_key parameter as described in the table and shown by the example URL.

When you're first getting started, the api_key parameter can specify a value of DEMO_KEY. However, this key only supports 30 requests per hour or 50 requests per day. As a result, if you need to make more requests than that, you should get your own API key. To do that, you can visit this URL:

`https://api.nasa.gov/`

This URL also provides information about using the APOD API and other NASA APIs.

If you don't supply a date parameter, the APOD API returns the JSON data for the current date. However, the APOD app presented in this figure allows the user to specify a date. As a result, it must supply a date parameter as shown by the example URL.

The <body> element

```
<body>
    <h1>Astronomy Picture Of the Day</h1>
    <div>
        <label for="date">Enter date:</label>
        <input type="text" name="date" id="date">
        <input type="button" id="view_button" value="View">
    </div>
    <div>
        <h3 id="title"></h3>
        <div id="display"></div>
        <p id="explanation"></p>
        <p id="msg" class="error"></p>
    </div>

    <script src="apod.js"></script>
</body>
```

Some of the CSS

```
div {
    margin-bottom: 1em;
}
label {
    display: inline-block;
    width: 5em;
}
input {
    margin-right: 0.5em;
}
.error {
    color: red;
}
```

The URL for the APOD API

https://api.nasa.gov/planetary/apod

Parameters for the APOD API

Parameter	Description
api_key	An alphanumeric key that identifies the user of this API. You can specify a value of DEMO_KEY to explore this API. However, this key only supports 30 requests per IP address per hour or 50 requests per day. As a result, you should sign up for your own API key if you plan to use this API extensively.
date	The date of the image to retrieve. This date must be in YYYY-MM-DD format. If you don't specify this parameter, this API retrieves the image for today's date.

Example URL with two parameters

https://api.nasa.gov/planetary/apod?api_key=DEMO_KEY&date=2024-04-22

Figure 14-7   The Astronomy Picture of the Day app (part 2)

Part 3 of figure 14-7 shows the JavaScript for the APOD app. To start, this JavaScript defines the getElement() helper function and a helper function named getDateString(). This second helper function accepts a Date object and returns a corresponding date string in the YYYY-MM-DD format that's required by the APOD API. If no Date object is passed to it, it defaults to today's date.

The asynchronous function named getPicture() accepts a Date object. To start, it passes the Date object to the getDateString() function to get a date string in YYYY-MM-DD format. Then, the code builds the URL for the Ajax request. Here, the code uses an API key value of DEMO_KEY. This key is appropriate for testing, but a production app should have its own key, which would be a long string of letters and numbers. In addition, this code sets the date parameter of the request to the date string. After building the URL for the API request, the getPicture() function uses the *await* keyword with the methods of the Fetch API to make a GET request and return the object the Ajax request resolves to, wrapped in a promise.

The function named clear() sets the elements that display the API data and error message to an empty string. Since this function doesn't start with the *async* keyword, it's a synchronous function.

The function named displayPicture() displays the JSON data that's returned by the APOD API. To start, this code checks whether the data object it receives has an error property. If so, an error occurred. In that case, this code notifies the user by setting the text of the message element to the message in the error property.

After checking the error property, this code checks whether the data object has a code property. If so, the request succeeded but there's a problem with the data. In that case, the code notifies the user by setting the text of the message element to the message in the code property.

If the data object doesn't contain an error property or a code property, the Ajax request succeeded. In that case, the JavaScript gets data from the data object to set the title for the image or video, the image or video itself, and the explanation.

The JavaScript

```javascript
function getElement(selector) {
    return document.querySelector(selector);
}

function getDateString(dt = new Date()) {      // default to today's date
    return `${dt.getFullYear()}-${dt.getMonth() + 1}-${dt.getDate()}`;
}

async function getPicture(date) {
    const dateString = getDateString(date);
    const domain = `https://api.nasa.gov/planetary/apod`;
    const request = `?api_key=DEMO_KEY&date=${dateString}`;
    const response = await fetch(domain + request);
    return await response.json();
}

function clear() {
    getElement("#title").textContent = "";
    getElement("#display").textContent = "";
    getElement("#explanation").textContent = "";
    getElement("#msg").textContent = "";
}

function displayPicture(data) {
    if (data.error) {           // error
        getElement("#msg").textContent = data.error.message;
    }
    else if (data.code) {    // problem
        getElement("#msg").textContent = data.msg;
    }
    else {                      // success
        // heading
        getElement("#title").textContent = data.title;

        // image or video
        const displayDiv = getElement("#display");
        if (data.media_type === "image") {
            const img = document.createElement("img");
            img.src = data.url;
            img.alt = "NASA photo";
            img.width = 700;
            displayDiv.appendChild(img);
        }
        else if (data.media_type === "video") {
            const iframe = document.createElement("iframe");
            iframe.src = data.url;
            iframe.allowFullscreen = true;
            iframe.setAttribute("frameborder", "0");
            displayDiv.appendChild(iframe);
        }

        // text
        getElement("#explanation").textContent = data.explanation;
    }
}
```

Figure 14-7   The Astronomy Picture of the Day app (part 3)

Part 4 of figure 14-7 shows the event handler for the DOMContentLoaded event. To start, this event handler gets the "Enter date" text box. Then, it uses the getDateString() helper function to get today's date in YYYY-MM-DD format and set that date string as the value of the text box. This works because calling the getDateString() function with no argument returns a string for the current date. After that, it moves the focus to the text box. As a result, when the app loads, it displays the current date in the "Enter date" text box.

After setting up the "Enter date" text box, this code attaches an asynchronous event handler for the click event of the View button. Within this event handler, the code begins by calling the clear() method. This clears any API data or error messages that were previously displayed.

Next, it gets the date string from the text box, converts it to a Date object, and checks whether the Date object is invalid. If so, it notifies the user to enter a valid date.

Otherwise, the try block that follows uses the *await* keyword to call the asynchronous getPicture() function. When that function resolves, it passes the data that's returned to the displayPicture() method. If there's an error, the catch block displays the error message in the message element.

The last statement of the click event handler moves the focus to the "Enter date" text box. As a result, after the user clicks the View button, the focus is always moved to this text box, regardless of whether the app displays an error message or the NASA data.

The JavaScript (continued)

```javascript
document.addEventListener("DOMContentLoaded", () => {

    // set text box to today's date in YYYY-MM-DD format
    const dateTextbox = getElement("#date");
    dateTextbox.value = getDateString();
    dateTextbox.focus();

    getElement("#view_button").addEventListener("click", async () => {
        clear();  // clear any previous display

        const dateString = getElement("#date").value;
        const date = new Date(dateString);

        if (date.toString() === "Invalid Date") {
            const msg = "Please enter a valid date in YYYY-MM-DD format.";
            getElement("#msg").textContent = msg;
        } else {
            try {
                const data = await getPicture(date);
                displayPicture(data);
            } catch(e) {
                getElement("#msg").textContent = e.message;
            }
        }

        getElement("#date").focus();
    });
});
```

Figure 14-7   The Astronomy Picture of the Day app (part 4)

How to use asynchronous code in a module

In the last chapter, you learned how to work with modules. Now, you'll learn how to use asynchronous code in a module.

How to export an asynchronous function

The first example in figure 14-8 presents a module that exports a single asynchronous function named getUsers(). This module has a private constant that contains the URL for an API request. Then, the getUsers() function makes an asynchronous GET request to the URL and returns the requested data. Remember, an asynchronous function automatically wraps the return value in a promise.

The second example shows code that imports the asynchronous function and uses it in a click event handler. Since the getUsers() function returns a promise, this event handler uses the *await* keyword to call it. And to be able to use the *await* keyword, the event handler function is declared using the *async* keyword.

As you review this code, you can see that it looks the same as asynchronous code you saw earlier in this chapter. In other words, you can use the Fetch API and the *async* and *await* keywords in a module just like you can anywhere else.

How to use a top-level await

When you work with modules, you don't always want to return a function that retrieves data. Sometimes, you'd rather just return the data itself. To do this, you can use the *top-level await* feature. This allows you to use the *await* keyword without having to enclose it in an asynchronous function. The third and fourth examples in figure 14-8 show how this works.

In the third example, the module file simply uses the *await* keyword with the fetch() method and again with the json() method of the Response object. It no longer needs to wrap these calls in a function that's defined with the *async* keyword. The module ends by declaring the constant that's assigned the return value of the asynchronous request as the default export of the module.

The fourth example shows some code that imports the user data from the module and uses it in a click event handler. In this case, the event handler doesn't need to use the *async* or *await* keywords.

There are two things you should know when you use the top-level await feature. First, it's only available in modules. If you aren't using a module, you must use the *await* keyword within a function that's defined with the *async* keyword.

Second, code that imports a module with a top-level await waits for the module to load before evaluating it, but any synchronous code still runs. This can lead to unexpected results if, for example, the DOMContentLoaded event fires before a top-level await resolves.

A module that exports an asynchronous function

```
const url = "https://jsonplaceholder.typicode.com/users";

async function getUsers() {
    const response = await fetch(url);
    return await response.json();
}

export {getUsers};
```

Code that imports and uses the function

```
import {getUsers} from "./mod_example.js";

getElement("#get_users").addEventListener("click", async () => {
    const users = await getUsers();

    for (let user of users) {
        console.log(user);
    }
});
```

A module file with a top-level await

```
const url = "https://jsonplaceholder.typicode.com/users";

// no async function needed
const response = await fetch(url);
const users = await response.json();

export default users;
```

Code that imports and uses the data from the module

```
import users from "./mod_example.js";

// no async or await keywords needed
getElement("#get_users").addEventListener("click", () => {
    for (let user of users) {
        console.log(user);
    }
});
```

Description

- You can code asynchronous functions in modules just like you would anywhere else.

- The *top-level await* feature is only available with modules. It allows you to use the await keyword in a module without having to enclose it in an asynchronous function.

- Code that imports a module with a top-level await waits for that module to load before evaluating it.

- However, synchronous code still runs. For instance, an event handler for the DOMContentLoaded event might fire before the top-level module resolves.

Figure 14-8   How to use asynchronous code in a module

The User Directory app

Figure 14-9 presents the User Directory app. It uses a module to asynchronously get user data from the JSON Placeholder API. Then, it displays each user's name, phone number, and email address in a table. This allows the app to display the heading and table headers before it's done retrieving the user data from the web service.

The HTML for the app defines a <table> element with an id of "users". Within the <table> element is a <thead> element that defines a header row with header text for each table column. Next is a <tbody> element that's empty when the app loads. The app uses JavaScript to get the user data and add a row element for each user to this element.

The CSS shown here defines a style rule for all the rows in the head and the body of the table. This rule aligns the row content to the left.

The User Directory app

User Directory

Name	Phone	Email
Leanne Graham	1-770-736-8031 x56442	Sincere@april.biz
Ervin Howell	010-692-6593 x09125	Shanna@melissa.tv
Clementine Bauch	1-463-123-4447	Nathan@yesenia.net
Patricia Lebsack	493-170-9623 x156	Julianne.OConner@kory.org
Chelsey Dietrich	(254)954-1289	Lucio_Hettinger@annie.ca
Mrs. Dennis Schulist	1-477-935-8478 x6430	Karley_Dach@jasper.info
Kurtis Weissnat	210.067.6132	Telly.Hoeger@billy.biz
Nicholas Runolfsdottir V	586.493.6943 x140	Sherwood@rosamond.me
Glenna Reichert	(775)976-6794 x41206	Chaim_McDermott@dana.io
Clementina DuBuque	024-648-3804	Rey.Padberg@karina.biz

The HTML of the <body> element

```
<body>
    <h1>User Directory</h1>
    <table id="users">
        <thead>
            <tr>
                <th width="35%">Name</th>
                <th width="35%">Phone</th>
                <th width="30%">Email</th>
            </tr>
        </thead>
        <tbody></tbody>
    </table>

    <script src="mod_users.js" type="module"></script>
    <script src="user_directory.js" type="module"></script>
</body>
```

Some of the CSS

```
tr {
    text-align: left;
}
```

Description

- The User Directory app displays information about users in tabular format.
- It uses a module to retrieve user data from the JSON Placeholder API.

Figure 14-9   The User Directory app (part 1)

Part 2 of figure 14-9 presents the mod_users.js module file for the User Directory app. This file contains two top-level await statements that retrieve user data from the JSON Placeholder API. The module declares the constant that's assigned the user data as the default export of the module.

This figure also presents the user_directory.js file that imports the user data from the module. This file imports the default export from the module. Then, it gets the <tbody> HTML element and adds a table row with three columns of data for each user. This displays the user data in the browser. Note that this file doesn't need to use the *async* or *await* keyword to work with the module data because the promises were already resolved in the module code.

Since the DOMContentLoaded event could fire before the top-level awaits in the module resolve, the code in the user_directory.js file isn't coded within in an event handler for this event. That's OK, though, because, as you saw in part 1 of this figure, the <script> element for the user_directory.js file is coded at the end of the <body> element.

The mod_users.js file

```
const url = "https://jsonplaceholder.typicode.com/users";

// async not required because this is a module
const response = await fetch(url);
const users = await response.json();

export default users;
```

The user.directory.js file

```
import users from "./mod_users.js";

const tbody = document.querySelector("#users tbody");

for (let user of users) {
    const tr = document.createElement("tr");

    const td1 = document.createElement("td");
    td1.appendChild(document.createTextNode(user.name));
    tr.appendChild(td1);

    const td2 = document.createElement("td");
    td2.appendChild(document.createTextNode(user.phone));
    tr.appendChild(td2);

    const td3 = document.createElement("td");
    td3.appendChild(document.createTextNode(user.email));
    tr.appendChild(td3);

    tbody.appendChild(tr);
}
```

Description

- Since the DOMContentLoaded event could fire before the top-level awaits resolve, the user_directory.js file doesn't place its code within an event handler for this event.

Figure 14-9   The User Directory app (part 2)

How to make cross-origin requests

So far, the examples in this chapter work because they make requests to an API that allows *cross-origin requests*. However, many APIs don't allow cross-origin requests. If you make an Ajax request to an API that doesn't allow cross-origin requests, your request will fail with an error message like the one shown in figure 14-10. In that case, you can use the skills presented in this figure to make a cross-origin request.

For security, browsers enforce a *same-origin policy* for client-side code. This means JavaScript code from one *origin* (protocol, domain, and port) can't request a resource from another origin. For instance, JavaScript code at http://mysite.com can't request a resource from an API that's at https://yourapi.com.

Fortunately, browsers have a mechanism that allows exceptions to the same-origin policy. They use *Cross Origin Resource Sharing (CORS)* to check whether JavaScript is allowed to make cross-origin requests. To do that, CORS requires the server that's hosting the API to include an Access-Control-Allow-Origin header in the HTTP response that it returns. This figure shows two examples of this header. The first authorizes a cross-origin request from a specific website, and the second uses the wildcard (*) character to authorize requests from any website.

Unfortunately, if an API doesn't allow cross-origin requests, there's no way to fix this with client-side code. The error message in this figure mentions that you can use "no-cors" mode to get an *opaque response* to your request. However, this is a "black box" response that contains no headers or text and a status code of 0, regardless of whether the request succeeded or failed. Except in rare circumstances, such a response isn't useful.

To access an API that doesn't allow cross-origin requests, you must use server-side code. In the past, some developers used iframes or JSON with padding (JSON-P) to trick the API into thinking that the request was from a server. However, these techniques aren't recommended for modern development.

These days, it's generally considered a best practice to solve this issue by using a *server-side proxy*. If you want to develop a prototype or test an API, you can use a third-party proxy such as the CORS Anywhere proxy shown in this figure. However, this isn't recommended for a production app.

For a production app, you can use Node.js to create a server-side proxy as described in the next chapter. Such a proxy uses server-side code to request data from the API. Then, it makes that data available from an API that either has the same origin as your client-side app or adds CORS headers like the ones shown in this figure. As a result, your app can use an Ajax request to get the data from the API your proxy creates.

A CORS error in the console

```
⊗ Access to fetch at 'https://www.flickr.com/services/feeds/photos_public.gne' from   localhost/:1
  origin 'http://localhost:8080' has been blocked by CORS policy: No 'Access-Control-Allow-Origin'
  header is present on the requested resource. If an opaque response serves your needs, set the
  request's mode to 'no-cors' to fetch the resource with CORS disabled.
```

A CORS header that allows a specific cross-origin request

```
Access-Control-Allow-Origin: https://example.com
```

A CORS header that allows any cross-origin request

```
Access-Control-Allow-Origin: *
```

Ways to make a cross-origin request to an API that doesn't allow them

- Use a third-party, server-side proxy (only recommended for prototyping and testing).
- Create your own server-side proxy.

The URL for a third-party proxy named CORS Anywhere

```
https://cors-anywhere.herokuapp.com/
```

How to temporarily enable the CORS Anywhere proxy

- Navigate to the above URL in the browser you want to use.
- Click on the Request temporary access to the demo server button.

Code that uses the CORS Anywhere proxy to make a cross-origin request

```
const proxy = "https://cors-anywhere.herokuapp.com/";
const api = "https://www.flickr.com/services/feeds/photos_public.gne";
const url = proxy + api;  // prefix api URL with CORS Anywhere URL

const response = await fetch(url);
...
```

Description

- For security, browsers enforce a *same-origin policy*. This means JavaScript code from one *origin* (protocol, domain, and port) can't request a resource from another origin unless that server returns a response that contains the appropriate *Cross Origin Resource Sharing (CORS)* header.
- If the response from an API doesn't contain the correct CORS header, you can't use an Ajax request to access that API.
- To make a cross-origin request, you can use a *server-side proxy*. This is server-side code that requests the data from the API and makes it available as a web API. Then, you can use an Ajax request to get the data from the proxy.
- For testing and development, you can use a third-party , server-side proxy like CORS Anywhere.
- You must enable the CORS Anywhere proxy as described above before you can use it. If you don't, you'll get a 403 Forbidden response.

Figure 14-10   How to make cross-origin requests

Perspective

Now that you've completed this chapter, you should be able to use Ajax to get data from a web service, parse that data, and update a web page with that data without reloading the entire page. This is a powerful skill that's commonly used in modern websites. In addition, you should have a solid set of skills for working with asynchronous JavaScript. These skills are often useful when writing JavaScript that runs on a server as described in the next chapter.

Terms

Ajax (Asynchronous JavaScript and XML)	fulfilled
Fetch API	rejected
XMLHttpRequest (XHR) object	settled
web service	resolved
API (Application Programming Interface)	*async* keyword
XML (Extensible Markup Language)	*await* keyword
JSON (JavaScript Object Notation)	asynchronous function
synchronous code	cross-origin request
asynchronous code	same-origin policy
callback function	origin
promise	Cross Origin Resource Sharing (CORS)
pending	opaque response
	server-side proxy

Exercise 14-1   Finish the Email Manager app

This exercise has you finish an Email Manager app that makes Ajax GET, POST, and DELETE requests to an API that's running on your computer.

Email Manager

Name: [   ]

Email: [   ]

[Add Email]

Anne - anne@murach.com
Mike - mike@murach.com

[Delete Email]

Run the app

1. Review the files in this folder:

   `exercises\ch14\email_manager`

2. Run the app. Note that it displays a dialog that says "Failed to fetch". That's because the API that this app uses isn't running.

3. Start Command Prompt (Windows) or Terminal (macOS) and use the cd command to change to the following directory:

    ```
    Documents\murach\javascript\book_apps\ch15\email_list_api
    ```

    For details about using the cd command, check appendix A (Windows) or B (macOS).

4. To start the API, enter the node command like this:

    ```
    >node index.js
    ```

    This should display a message that says "API running on port 3000."

5. Run the Email Manager app again. It should now start and display a list of emails. However, if you try to add or delete an email, you'll get an error message.

Review and modify the code

6. Open the email_manager.js file. Note that the url constant at the top of the file specifies a URL for the API that includes a port number of 3000.

7. Find the displayEmails() function and review its code. Note that it loops through the JSON for the emails and creates an <option> element for each one. Note also that it assigns the id for each email to the value attribute of its <option> element.

8. Find the event handler for the DOMContentLoaded event. Note that it makes a GET request to the URL for the API.

9. Find the click event handler for the Add button. Note that it contains code that displays an error dialog but doesn't contain code that adds an email address to the list.

10. Add code that adds the email to the list. To do that, you can make an Ajax POST request to the URL for the API. In the body of this request, you must pass the JSON for an object that uses name and email properties to specify the name and email address.

11. If the email is added successfully, add code that makes an Ajax GET request to get and display the updated data.

12. Add a try-catch statement that handles any errors that occur when adding an email by catching the error and displaying its message in a dialog.

13. Find the click event handler for the Delete button. Note that it contains code that displays an error dialog but doesn't contain code that deletes the email address from the list.

14. Add code that deletes the email address from the list. To do that, you can identify the email to delete by getting the id value from the selected <option> element and appending it to the URL for the API. Then, you can make an Ajax DELETE request for that URL.

15. If the email is deleted successfully, add code that makes an Ajax GET request to get and display the updated data.

16. Add a try-catch statement that handles any errors that occur when deleting an email by catching the error and displaying its message in a dialog.

Exercise 14-2   Review and update the APOD app

This exercise has you review and update the Astronomy Picture of the Day (APOD) app that uses NASA's APOD API.

Run the app

1. View the files in this folder:

    `exercises\ch14\apod`

2. Run the app. Note that the text box contains today's date.

3. Click the View button and review the data that's displayed.

4. Experiment with other dates, including future dates, dates before June 16, 1995, dates not in the YYYY-MM-DD format the API requires, and invalid dates.

Review the code

5. Open the index.html file and review the HTML for the app. Note that the second <div> element is where the web page displays the data from the API.

6. Open the apod.js file.

7. Review the URL for the API and note that it includes an api_key parameter with a value of DEMO_KEY.

8. Visit the website for the NASA APIs (https://api.nasa.gov) to learn more about the limits of using the DEMO_KEY. If you want, you can get your own API key and replace the DEMO_KEY value with your own key. This removes most of the limits of using the DEMO_KEY.

9. On the website for the NASA APIs, review the documentation for the APOD API and explore any other APIs that you're interested in.

10. In the getPicture() function, review the code that makes the asynchronous request to the API. Note that it uses the fetch() method and the await keyword.

Modify the app to use modules

11. Add a new file for a module named lib_apod.js.

12. Move the getDateString() and getPicture() functions from the apod.js file to the lib_apod.js file. Make sure to export both functions.

13. In the apod.js file, add a statement that imports the functions from the module.

14. In the index.html file, make sure there are <script> elements for both JavaScript files with the type set to "module".

15. Run the http-server node module as described in appendix A (Windows) or B (macOS).

16. Use your browser to test the app by running it from the local web server. It should work the same as it did before.

15

How to work with Node.js

So far, this book has shown you how to use a web browser to run JavaScript. That's because JavaScript was originally developed to provide client-side scripting for browsers. In the early days of JavaScript, developers needed to use another language such as Java or PHP for server-side scripting. Today, however, you can use JavaScript for server-side scripting, too. The most common way to do that is to use Node.js.

How to use the node command

Node.js is an open-source, cross-platform runtime environment that executes JavaScript code outside a web browser. This provides a way to use JavaScript for server-side scripting.

There are a few scenarios in which you might want to use Node.js. First, Node.js provides a way to interactively test JavaScript expressions and statements without running them in a browser. Second, Node.js lets you write JavaScript apps that run outside of a web browser such as console apps and command-line tools. Third, Node.js provides libraries that contain APIs that let you work with the local file system or write networking apps such as web servers.

After you install Node.js as described in the appendixes, you can use the node command from your operating system's command line to interactively test code or to run a script that you've stored in a file. All of the examples in this chapter are shown using a Windows prompt, but these examples work similarly on a macOS or Linux system.

How to interactively test code

Node.js provides a *REPL* (*Read Eval Print Loop*) that interactively evaluates JavaScript code that you enter at the command line. To start the REPL, you enter the node command at the command prompt without any parameters as shown by the first example in figure 15-1. Then, the command line should show an empty prompt. At this prompt, you can interactively test JavaScript code by typing it and pressing Enter.

The second example shows how to test a JavaScript expression. To do that, you type the expression and press Enter. Then, the REPL evaluates the expression, displays the result below the prompt, and displays another command prompt so you can continue testing code.

As you type code at the command prompt, you may want to display code that you've already typed. To do that, you can press the Up and Down arrow keys to scroll through the command prompt history. If necessary, you can edit the code that's displayed. Then, you can press Enter to execute the code again.

The third example shows how to test one-line JavaScript statements. To do that, you type the statement. You don't need to type the semicolon that ends the statement. Then, you can press Enter to evaluate the statement. In this example, the first statement assigns a value of 200 to the constant named subtotal. But since this assignment doesn't return a value, the console displays "undefined". However, you can type the name of the constant at the prompt to display its value, or you can use it in another statement.

As you type code at the command prompt, it may suggest code completion possibilities. For example, when you type the start of a name, it may suggest the rest of the name. To accept the suggestion, you can press Tab.

The fourth example shows how to enter a multi-line statement. To do that, you end the first line with an opening brace (ƚ). Then, the Node.js command prompt displays three dots (**...**) and lets you type the rest of the multi-line state-

Start the Node.js command prompt

```
C:\Users\Joel>node
Welcome to Node.js v20.11.0
Type ".help" for more information.
>
```

Evaluate a JavaScript expression

```
> (3 + 4) * 5
35
>
```

Evaluate JavaScript statements

```
> const subtotal = 200
undefined
> subtotal
200
> const taxPercent = .05
undefined
> const taxAmount = subtotal * taxPercent
undefined
> taxAmount
10
```

Evaluate multi-line statements

```
> for (let i = 1; i < 4; i++) {
... console.log(i);
... }
1
2
3
undefined
```

Exit the Node.js command prompt

```
> .exit
C:\Users\Joel>
```

Description

- *Node.js* is an open-source, cross-platform runtime environment that executes JavaScript code outside a web browser. It provides a *REPL* (*Read Eval Print Loop*) that interactively evaluates the JavaScript code that the user enters at the command line.

- The examples in this chapter show Node.js on a Windows system. If you're using a macOS or Linux system, the prompt will look a little different.

- To evaluate JavaScript code, type it at the Node.js command prompt and press Enter.

- To display code that you've already entered, use the Up and Down arrow keys. If necessary, you can edit the code that's displayed. Then, you can press Enter to execute the code again.

- As you type, the Node.js command prompt may suggest code completion. To accept the code completion, press the Tab key.

- The Node.js command prompt lets you enter a multi-line statement if you end the first line with an opening brace ({).

Figure 15-1   How to interactively test code

ment. It doesn't evaluate the statement until you type the closing brace and press Enter.

The fifth example in figure 15-1 shows how to exit the Node.js command prompt and return to your operating system's command line. To do that, you enter the .exit command.

How to run a script

Figure 15-2 shows how you can use the node command to run a script. Here, the first example shows a script in a file named index.js that's in the book_apps/ch15/future_value directory. This script contains JavaScript that calculates a future value. When you use Node.js to run this script, it displays four lines containing the results in the command prompt.

The second example shows how to use Node.js to run the script in the first example. To start, this example uses the cd command to change the directory to the book_apps/ch15 directory. Then, it uses the node command to run the index.js file that's in the future_value directory. When it does, Node.js displays the four lines in the console. Note that if you're running the Node.js REPL, you'll need to exit it before changing the directory and using the node command to run a script.

The third example shows that you don't have to supply the entire filename of the JavaScript file when you use the node command. To start, if your file ends with an extension of .js, you don't have to supply the extension. Similarly, if your file has a name of index.js, you don't have to supply the filename at all. Instead, you can code the name of the directory that contains the file. This works because Node.js uses the index.js file as the default file for a directory.

The script in the future_value/index.js file

```
"use strict";

// set investment amount, interest rate, and years
const investment = 10000;
const rate = 7.5;
const years = 10;

// calulate future value
let futureValue = investment;
for (let i = 1; i <= years; i++) {
    futureValue += futureValue * rate / 100;
}

// display results
console.log(`Investment amount: ${investment}`);
console.log(`Interest rate: ${rate}`);
console.log(`Years: ${years}`);
console.log(`Future Value: ${futureValue.toFixed(2)}`);
```

Use the node command to execute the script

```
>cd Documents/murach/javascript/book_apps/ch15

>node future_value/index.js
Investment amount: 10000
Interest rate: 7.5
Years: 10
Future Value: 20610.32
```

Two more ways to execute this script

```
>node future_value/index
>node future_value
```

Description

- The console object is available to Node.js. You can use it within a script to display data on the command prompt.

- To run a script, use the cd command to change to the directory that contains the script. Then, enter the name of the script.

- If you are running the Node.js REPL, exit it before attempting to change the directory or use the node command to execute a script.

- If your script is in a file that has an extension of .js, you don't need to enter .js to run the file. That's because Node.js automatically adds the .js extension.

- If your script is in a file named index.js, you can enter the name of the directory that contains it instead of entering the filename. That's because Node.js uses the index.js file by default.

Figure 15-2   How to run a script

How to pass arguments to a script

In the previous figure, the script assigns hard-coded values for the investment amount, interest rate, and number of years to three constants. Typically, though, you would pass these arguments to the script. To do that, you can use the *process object* as described in figure 15-3.

The first example shows the script from the previous figure after it has been updated to accept three arguments. Here, the first three statements use the argv property of the process object to access these arguments. To understand this code, you need to know that the first two arguments of the argv property are for the path to the node command and the path to the script. As a result, the first argument that the user enters on the command line is actually the third argument, which has an index of 2. In turn, the second command line argument has an index of 3, and the third has an index of 4.

After getting the command line arguments, this code uses the parseFloat() and parseInt() functions to parse these arguments into numbers. This is necessary because the argv property stores all of its arguments as strings. Then, this code assigns these arguments to constants named investment, rate, and years.

After assigning the command line arguments to constants, this code uses an if statement with the isNaN() function to check whether any of these three arguments is not a valid number. If so, the code displays an error message in the console and calls the exit() method of the process object to exit the script. Here, the code passes a value of 1 to the exit() method to indicate that the script exited abnormally. By contrast, if you want to exit a script and indicate that the script exited normally, you can pass a value of 0.

After validating the user entries, the code calculates the future value and displays it in the console. This works just as it did in the previous example.

The second example shows how to use the node command to pass arguments to the script in the first example. To start, you use the node command to call the index.js script that's in the future_value directory. Then, you enter the three command line arguments, separating each argument with a space. In this example, the code passes arguments of 10000, 6.5, and 10.

The third example shows the array of arguments that are passed to the script. As described earlier, the first argument is the path to the node command, and the second argument is the path to the script. This is followed by the three arguments that are passed by the calling statement.

A script that accepts arguments

```
"use strict";

// set investment amount, interest rate, and years
const investment = parseFloat(process.argv[2]);
const rate = parseFloat(process.argv[3]);
const years = parseInt(process.argv[4]);

// validate command line arguments
if (isNaN(investment) || isNaN(rate) || isNaN(years)) {
    console.log("ERROR: Please pass valid numbers for all arguments.");
    process.exit(1);         // exit process with an error code of 1
}

// calulate future value
let futureValue = investment;
for (let i = 1; i <= years; i++) {
    futureValue += futureValue * rate / 100;
}

// display results
console.log(`Investment amount: ${investment}`);
console.log(`Interest rate: ${rate}`);
console.log(`Years: ${years}`);
console.log(`Future Value: ${futureValue.toFixed(2)}`);

process.exit(0);             // exit process normally
```

Use the node command to pass arguments to the script

```
>node future_value 10000 6.5 10
Investment amount: 10000
Interest rate: 6.5
Years: 10
Future Value: 18771.37
```

The array of five arguments passed to the script

```
[
  'C:\\Program Files\\nodejs\\node.exe',
  'C:\\...\\Documents\\murach\\javascript\\book_apps\\ch15\\future_value',
  '10000', '6.5', '10'
]
```

Description

- Node.js provides a *process object* that allows you to work with the process that runs the script.

- You can use the argv property of the process object to access arguments passed from the command line to the script. The first two arguments always specify the path to the node command and the path to the script.

- You can use the exit() method of the process object to exit a script. You can pass a value of 0 to indicate that the script exited normally. Or, you can pass other integer values to indicate that the script exited abnormally.

Figure 15-3   How to pass arguments to a script

How to work with Node.js modules

To make it possible for developers to share server-side scripts, Node.js includes two module systems, the ES (ECMAScript) module system described in chapter 13 and the older *CommonJS module* system. Since CommonJS modules were used widely before the ES module system became available, this section shows how to use both. However, most of the examples in this chapter use the more modern ES module system.

How to use ES and CommonJS modules

To start, figure 15-4 summarizes the two module systems available in Node.js. After that, it summarizes a built-in module that Node.js provides for working with the file system, including reading and writing files. However, Node.js also provides many other built-in modules that you can use for networking, cryptography, data streams, and other core functions.

To give you an idea of how you can use a built-in module, this figure shows how to use the fs module to read a file named email_list.txt. The first example shows the contents of this file.

The second example presents an ES module file named read.mjs that uses the fs module to read this text file. By default, Node.js expects ES module files to have an .mjs extension. In other words, an ES module file with a .js extension will fail by default. However, you can change the default to allow Node.js to work with an ES module file with a .js extension as shown in figure 15-8.

The read.mjs file begins with an import statement that imports the readFile() function from the fs module. This works just like the import statements presented in chapter 13. Then, the code calls the imported readFile() function to read the contents of the text file in the first example. This function accepts three arguments: the name or path of the text file, the encoding of the file, and a callback function. The callback function has two parameters. The first parameter is an Error object if an error occurs while attempting to execute this function. The second parameter is the contents of the text file if it's read successfully.

The third example shows how to call the script that's stored in the read.mjs file. To do that, it uses the cd command to change the current directory to the directory that contains the read.mjs file and the email_list.txt file. Then, it uses the node command to execute the read.mjs script. Note that this command must include the .mjs extension at the end of the file name.

The fourth example accomplishes the same task with the CommonJS module system. Here, a file named read.js uses the require() function to import the fs module into a module object named fs. To do that, the code passes a string that specifies the name of the module to the require() function. Then, the code uses the readFile() method of the fs module object to read the text file.

Finally, the fifth example uses the cd command to navigate to the correct directory and the node command to execute the read.js script. Although this example includes the .js extension, that isn't necessary because the node command uses that extension by default.

Two module systems available in Node.js

System	Description
ES	Newer module system. Can be used in Node.js and the browser. Module loading is asynchronous.
CommonJS	Older module system for Node.js. Module loading is synchronous.

A built-in module

Module	Description
`fs`	Contains functions for working with the local file system, including functions for reading and writing files.

The contents of a file named email_list.txt

```
mary@murach.com (Mary Delamater)
joel@murach.com (Joel Murach)
anne@murach.com (Anne Boehm)
```

A script named read.mjs that uses an ES module

```
import { readFile } from "fs";      // ES import statement

readFile("email_list.txt", "utf8", (error, text) => {
    if (error) console.log(error.message);
    else console.log(text);
});
```

Execute the script

```
>cd Documents/murach/javascript/book_apps/ch15/email_list
>node read.mjs
```

A script named read.js that uses a CommonJS module

```
const fs = require("fs");           // CommonJS import statement

fs.readFile("email_list.txt", "utf8", (error, text) => {
    if (error) console.log(error.message);
    else console.log(text);
});
```

Execute the script

```
>cd Documents/murach/javascript/book_apps/ch15/email_list
>node read.js
```

Description

- You can use either the ES (ECMAScript) or *CommonJS module* system with Node.js.
- It's generally considered a best practice to use ES modules. However, some modules are only available as a CommonJS module.
- By default, Node.js expects ES module files to have an .mjs extension.

Figure 15-4   How to use ES and CommonJS modules

How to use the built-in file system module with promises

In the previous chapter, you learned how to use promises to handle asynchronous calls. Fortunately, the file system module includes an API named fs.promises that provides an alternative set of asynchronous functions in which each function returns a promise instead of requiring that you code a callback function as shown in the previous figure. As a result, you can use this API to simplify code that makes asynchronous calls to the file system module.

The table in figure 15-5 presents the readFile() and writeFile() functions that are available from the fs.promises API. This shows that the fs.promises API provides functions with the same names as the regular fs API. However, a function that's available from the fs.promises API returns a promise and doesn't accept a callback function. As a result, you can use the *await* keyword.

The first example in this figure shows how to use the fs.promises API to read the contents of a file, add to the contents, and write the updated contents back to the file. To start, it uses an import statement to import the readFile() and writeFile() functions. After that, it defines constants that contain the name of the text file and the email address to add to it.

Next, the code uses a top-level await statement to call the readFile() function within the try block of a try-catch statement. This function reads the file and assigns its contents to a variable named list. After that, the code appends an email address to the list. Then, it uses another top-level await statement to call the writeFile() function. This overwrites the file with the contents of the list. Finally, it displays a message in the console indicating that the email was written to the file.

If either promise is rejected, the code in the catch block of the try-catch statement executes. This block of code displays an error message in the console.

If you compare the code in this figure with the code in the previous figure, you can see that the code that uses promises is easier to write and read than the code that uses callbacks. In general, you should use the fs.promises module for new development. However, the functions of the fs module that use callbacks were widely used before the introduction of promises, so you might see them in legacy code and online examples.

Finally, you should know that the fs module also provides synchronous versions of its functions. These versions have a suffix of Sync, such as readFileSync() and writeFileSync(). When these functions run, they block any other calls, which can cause frustrating delays in your app. For that reason, they're not widely used.

Two functions available from the fs.promises module

Function	Description
readFile(*fname*, *encoding*)	Reads the contents of the specified file, using the specified encoding, and returns a promise that resolves to the contents of the file after it has been read.
writeFile(*fname*, *contents*)	Writes the specified contents to the specified file and returns a promise that resolves when the contents have been successfully written to the file.

A module that uses the fs.promises module to read and write a file

```
import { readFile, writeFile } from "fs/promises";

const fname = "email_list.txt";
const email = "mike@murach.com (Mike Murach)";

try {
    // read the list from the file
    let list = await readFile(fname, "utf8");        // top-level await

    // append an email address to the list
    list += "\n" + email;

    // write the updated list to the file
    await writeFile(fname, list);                    // top-level await

    // display message in console
    console.log(email + " written to file.");
} catch (e) {
    console.log(e.message);
}
```

Description

- Node.js is designed for asynchronous programming. As a result, it's ideal for any server-side tasks that need to be asynchronous.

- The fs.promises module provides asynchronous functions where each function returns a promise.

- The fs module provides asynchronous functions that use callback functions instead of promises.

- It's generally considered a best practice to use fs.promises for new development.

Figure 15-5   How to use the built-in file system module with promises

How to create and use your own module

The previous two figures showed how to work with the built-in file system module. Now, figure 15-6 shows how to create and use your own module.

To create your own module, you can use the techniques described in chapter 13 to create an ES module. However, since Node.js expects ES module files to have an extension of .mjs by default, it's common to use this extension when creating modules for use with Node.js.

The first example in this figure presents an ES module that exports a single function. Then, the second example shows the filename that contains the code in the first example. By convention, this filename uses dashes instead of under-scores in its name. Also, since it's an ES module that's designed to be used with Node.js, it uses a file extension of .mjs.

The third example shows how to import the function from the ES module system. To do that, it uses the characters described in this figure to specify the path to the file that contains the module. In this example, the code uses the *./* characters to indicate that the module is in the same directory as the script that called it.

An ES module that exports a single function

```
export function calcFutureValue(investment, rate, years) {
    let futureValue = investment;
    for (let i = 1; i <= years; i++) {
        futureValue += futureValue * rate / 100;
    }
    return futureValue;
}
```

The name of the file that contains the function

```
murach-calc-future-value.mjs
```

Characters for specifying a path to a module

Characters	Description
/	The root directory for the file system.
./	The same directory as the current file.
../	One directory up from the current file.

Code that uses the module

```
import { calcFutureValue } from "./murach-calc-future-value.mjs";
...
const futureValue = calcFutureValue(investment, rate, years);
...
```

Description

- The ES module system presented in chapter 13 works the same with Node.js. However, by default, Node.js expects ES module files to have an .mjs extension.

Figure 15-6   How to create and use your own module

How to work with NPM modules

NPM (Node Package Manager) is a package manager for the JavaScript programming language. It's the default package manager for Node.js, and it's included when you install Node.js on your system.

A *package* is a module that's described by a package.json file, which is a file that provides all the data that NPM needs to share the package with other programmers. In other words, it's a module that's been "packaged" to be easy to share. As a result, all packages are modules, but not all modules are packages. For example, the murach-calc-future-value module in the last figure doesn't have a package.json file, so it's a module but not a package.

How to install NPM modules

Figure 15-7 provides an introduction to NPM. In broad terms, you can think of NPM as having two main components.

The first component is the *NPM registry*. This registry is an online database of packages that you can search via the NPM website. To do that, you can visit the URL shown at the top of this figure. Then, you can search for modules that provide many different types of server-side functionality. For example, the http-server module provides a simple web server that you can use to test web apps on a local server, and the express module provides a framework you can use to build web apps.

The NPM registry provides access to thousands of packages. Many of these packages provide high-quality code that extends the functionality that's available from the built-in packages of Node.js. As a result, it typically makes sense to use these packages instead of writing your own code whenever possible. However, the vetting process for the NPM registry relies on user reports to take down packages if they violate policies by being low quality, insecure, or malicious. As a result, you need to be careful when downloading and using these packages.

The second component of NPM is the npm command. You can use this command to install packages from the NPM registry. For instance, the first example in this figure shows how to use the npm install command to install the express module in the current directory.

With macOS (or Linux), you typically need to prefix the npm install command with the sudo (superuser do) command as shown by the second npm install command. Otherwise, you'll get an error that says "permission denied."

When you use the npm command, you often need to use flags to specify options. To do that, you can use a longer but more descriptive double-dash option or a shorter but less descriptive single-dash option. For instance, to use the global command presented here, you can use the `--global` flag or the `-g` flag. The third npm install command in this figure uses the single-dash flag.

When you install modules globally, npm installs them in a system directory. Conversely, when you don't use the global flag, npm installs the modules locally in the current directory. Typically, you install locally if you'll use the module only in your project, globally if you need to call the module from the command line, and locally and globally if you need to do both.

The NPM website

www.npmjs.com

Two modules available from NPM

Name	Description
http-server	A local web server that you can use for development and testing.
express	A routing and middleware framework for building web apps such as APIs.

Install the express module in the current directory

```
> npm install express
```

Solve a permissions problem in macOS

```
$sudo npm install express
```

A flag that's available with the install command

Flag	Alias	Description
--global	-g	Installs the module in a system directory rather than in the current directory.

Install the http-server module globally

```
> npm install http-server -g
```

How to decide whether to install an NPM module globally or locally

Install...	If you'll use the module...
locally	in your project with ES import statements or the CommonJS require() method
globally	from the command line
locally and globally	in your project and from the command line

Description

- *NPM (Node Package Manager)* is a package manager for the JavaScript programming language.
- NPM is the default package manager for Node.js, and it's included when you install Node.js on your system.
- A *package* is a module that is described by a package.json file. As a result, all packages are modules, but not all modules are packages.
- The *NPM registry* is an online database of packages that you can browse and search via the NPM website.
- To install packages from the NPM registry, use the npm install command. With macOS, you typically need to prefix this command with the sudo (superuser do) command. Otherwise, you'll get an error that says "permission denied."
- When you use the install command with no flags, the module is installed locally in your current directory in a subdirectory named node_modules.
- When you use the install command with the global flag, the module is installed in a system directory.

Figure 15-7   How to install NPM modules

How package.json files work

Figure 15-8 presents some excerpts from the package.json file for the express module to show how package.json files work. These excerpts show that the package.json file identifies important aspects of a package that are necessary to share it. For example, this file identifies the name, description, and version of the package.

When developers specify version numbers for packages, they should use *semantic versioning*. This versioning system uses three numbers separated by periods to indicate what kind of changes have been made in each new version. The first number indicates major changes. Incrementing this number usually means breaking changes have been made so the module is incompatible with previous versions. The middle number indicates minor changes that do not break API usage, and the last number indicates patches and bug fixes. When a number is incremented, numbers to the right are reset to zero.

The first package.json file shown in this figure also identifies the repository for the package, which is where the package can be downloaded from the web. It specifies *dependencies*, which are other packages that the package depends on. And it specifies that the package requires a Node.js engine of 0.10 or greater (0.10.0).

The dependencies for a package use special characters in front of a version number to indicate that the library can use a higher version under certain conditions. The caret character (^) indicates the library can use a higher version if that version is compatible with the specified version. Similarly, the tilde character (~) indicates the library can use a higher version if that version is approximately equal to the specified version.

If you have a module that you'd like to share on the NPM registry, you can use the npm init command to generate a package.json file for your module. The init command uses the command prompt to ask you to specify the data to include in the file. If you'd like to skip the prompts, you can include the **--yes** or **-y** flag as shown by the second example in this figure. This tells npm to use all default values when it generates the package.json file.

Once you've generated a package.json file, you can use a text editor to edit it. For example, after generating the default values for a package, you can edit the package.json file to change the default values. When editing these values, you can enable your module to allow the .js extension for ES module files by adding a type property with a value of "module" as shown by the third example. In this example, the type property is added at the end of the JSON generated by the init command, but you can add it anywhere.

When you have the package.json file for your module the way you want it, you can use the npm publish command to publish your package to the NPM registry. This makes your package available to the rest of the Node.js development community.

Excerpts from the express module's package.json file

```
{
  "name": "express",
  "description": "Fast, unopinionated, minimalist web framework",
  "version": "4.18.2",
  ...
  "repository": "expressjs/express",
  ...
  "dependencies": {
    "accepts": "~1.3.8",
    "array-flatten": "1.1.1",
    ...
  },
  ...
  "engines": {
    "node": ">= 0.10.0"
  },
  ...
  }
}
```

Command to generate a simple package.json file

```
> npm init -y
```

Allow ES module files to use the .js extension

```
{
  "name": "future_value",
  "version": "1.0.0",
  "description": "",
  "main": "index.js",
  "scripts": {
    "test": "echo \"Error: no test specified\" && exit 1"
  },
  "keywords": [],
  "author": "",
  "license": "ISC",
  "type": "module"
}
```

Description

- By convention, NPM packages use *semantic versioning*, a series of three numbers used to indicate if a new version contains major changes, minor changes, or bug fixes.

- The dependencies for a package use special characters to indicate whether the library can use a higher version under specified conditions.

- To package a module, you can use the npm init command to generate a package.json file for that module. If you include the **--yes** or **-y** flag, it generates the file with default values.

- To allow ES modules to use the .js extension, add a type property that's set to "module" to the package.json file.

- After you create a package.json file for a module, you can use the npm publish command to publish the package to the NPM registry.

Figure 15-8   How package.json files work

How to use Express to create a web-based API

This chapter has already shown how to use the npm command to install the express module. This module contains a framework known as Express that's designed for building web apps and web-based APIs. Now, this chapter shows how to use Express to create a web-based API. However, this just scratches the surface of what Express can do.

How to start an Express app for an API

If you want to use Express to create an API, and you want to allow the users of your API to make cross-origin requests, you should add CORS headers to the HTTP responses of your API. To do that, you can install the cors module as shown in the first example of figure 15-9.

Once you've installed the cors module, you can use the code shown in the second example as a starting point for a web-based API. Most of this code is boilerplate code that you can copy to get your API started. Here, the first two statements import the express and cors modules. Then, the third statement uses the express() function to create an object named app. By convention, this object is named app and is usually called the *Express app object*. It provides methods for working with HTTP requests and responses.

The fourth and fifth statements configure the app by adding *middleware*, which is software that performs a specific task after a request is received but before a response is returned. Here, the fourth statement adds the CORS middleware to the app. This adds CORS headers to all the HTTP responses for the app. Then, the fifth statement adds some JSON middleware to the app object. This converts the JSON in the body of a request to an object.

The middleware tasks are executed in the order that they're coded. For this app, the CORS middleware is executed before the JSON middleware.

The sixth statement adds a route for a GET request at the API root directory. This route just returns an HTTP response that contains some JSON for an object that has a property named info that's set to a message about the API.

The seventh statement uses the listen() method of the app object to begin listening for requests on port 3000. In addition, this statement uses a callback function to display a message in the console when the server starts listening. That way, you can tell that your API is up and running.

The third example shows how to start the API. To do that, you open a command prompt and use the cd command to change to the directory that contains the API script. In this case, that's the directory that contains the api.mjs file. Then, you use the node command to run the script. This displays a message in the console that shows the API is listening for requests on port 3000.

Once you start the API, it listens until you stop it. To do that, you can press Ctrl-C at the command prompt. Then, if you want to start the API again, you enter the node command again. For instance, if you make a change to the API code, you need to stop and re-start the API before the change takes effect.

Another module that's available from NPM

Name	Description
cors	Attaches CORS headers to an HTTP response.

Install the cors module

```
> npm install cors
```

Methods available from the Express app object

Method	Description
use(*middleware*)	Adds middleware to the app. Middleware is executed in the order it's coded.
listen(*port, funct*)	Binds the app to the specified port and listens for requests on that port. Optional callback function executes once the app starts listening.

The api.mjs file

```
import express from "express";
import cors from "cors";

const app = express();          // create the Express app object
app.use(cors());                // add CORS middleware
app.use(express.json());        // add JSON middleware

// route that handles GET requests to the API root
app.get("/", (request, response) => {
  response.json({info: "An API that includes CORS headers."});
});

// listen for requests on port 3000
app.listen(3000, () => {
  console.log("API listening on port 3000");
});
```

Start the API

```
> node api.mjs
API listening on port 3000
```

How the GET request looks in a browser

```
←  →  C  ⓘ localhost:3000                    ☆

{"info":"An API that includes CORS headers."}
```

Description

- *Middleware* is software that performs a specific task after a request is received but before a response is returned.
- To start an Express app for an API, you can add middleware that attaches CORS headers to your responses and makes it easier to process JSON that's stored in requests.

Figure 15-9   How to start an Express app for an API

Once the API is listening for requests, you can use a web browser to test it. To do that, just enter the URL for the root directory of the API in the web browser. This should display the JSON for the object that's returned by the HTTP request as shown at the end of figure 15-9.

How to set up a route for a GET request

A web-based API typically provides a way for a client app to submit HTTP requests to get and modify data that's stored on a server. Figure 15-10 begins by summarizing the get(), post(), put(), and delete() methods available from the Express app object. You can use these methods to set up the *routes*, or *endpoints*, for HTTP GET, POST, PUT, and DELETE requests.

The first parameter for these methods is the URL for the request. To include parameter values in this URL, you can add a colon prefix to a path segment. If you want the parameter to be optional, you can add a question mark suffix. The first example shows how this works.

The second parameter for these methods is a callback function that handles the request. This callback function must have two parameters for objects that represent the HTTP request and response. You can use these objects to get data about the request and to provide a response.

The second example in this figure creates a global array of names that the API uses as its sample data. This stores the array in memory. As a result, changes that are made to the array are lost each time you restart the API. In real life, an API typically gets its data from a file or a database. That way, any changes to the data aren't lost.

The third example shows how to set up a route for a GET request. This route specifies a URL with a path of /names followed by an optional parameter named index. Within the callback function, the first statement uses the params property of the request object to attempt to get the optional route parameter named index. If this parameter exists, the third statement uses the json() method of the response object to return an HTTP response that contains some simple JSON for the name at the specified index. Otherwise, it returns JSON for all of the names in the array. To do that, this code uses the nullish coalescing operator (??).

After the third example, this figure shows how you can enter URLs into a browser to test this route. The first URL requests the /names path with no parameter. This displays the names array in JSON format. Then, the second URL requests the /names path with an index parameter of 0. This displays the first element of the names array.

The last example shows how to use the API from a JavaScript app. To do that, this code makes an asynchronous request to the API like the asynchronous requests presented in chapter 14. Here, the code uses the fetch() method to make a GET request for the /names path with no parameter. As a result, it returns the JSON for the array of names.

More methods available from the Express app object

Method	Description
get(*url, function*)	Sets up a route for a GET request.
post(*url, function*)	Sets up a route for a POST request.
put(*url, function*)	Sets up a route for a PUT request.
delete(*url, function*)	Sets up a route for a DELETE request.

The syntax of a callback function for these methods

```
function(request, response)
```

How to work with route parameters

A required route parameter named index
```
/names/:index
```

An optional route parameter named index
```
/names/:index?
```

A global array that stores some data for the API

```
const names = ["Grace", "Ada", "Charles"];
```

Set up a route for a GET request

```
app.get("/names/:index?", (request, response) => {      // index is optional
  const i = request.params.index;
  response.json(names[i] ?? names);
});
```

How two GET requests look in the browser

An event handler that accesses the API

```
document.addEventListener("DOMContentLoaded", async () => {
    const response = await fetch("http://localhost:3000/names");
    const json = await response.json();
    console.log(json);    // displays ["Grace", "Ada", "Charles"]
});
```

Description

- In a URL, a path segment with a colon prefix represents a *route parameter*. A route parameter with a question mark suffix is optional.
- To access a route parameter, use the params property of the request object to specify the name of the route parameter.
- To return the JSON for the response, use the json() method of the response object.

Figure 15-10   How to set up a route for a GET request

How to set up routes for POST, PUT, and DELETE requests

Once you learn how to set up a route for a GET request as shown in the previous figure, you're ready to learn how to set up routes for POST, PUT, and DELETE requests as shown in figure 15-11. Most of the skills are the same as working with a GET request. However, you sometimes need to use the body property of the request object to get data that's stored in the body of a request.

The first example in this figure shows how to set up a route for a POST request. This example uses the post() method of the app object to specify a route with a URL path of /names. Within the callback function, the first statement uses the body property of the request object to get the name that's stored in the POST request. Then, the second statement uses the push() method to add this name to the global array of names. Finally, the third statement returns the name in the response. This indicates that the name was successfully added to the array.

The second example shows how to set up a route for a DELETE request. This example uses the delete() method of the app object to specify a route with a URL path of /names with a required route parameter named index. Within the callback function, the first statement gets the index from the route parameter. Then, the second statement uses the splice() method to delete the name at the specified index from the global array of names. This returns an array that contains a single element, the name that was deleted. Finally, the third statement returns the name in the response. This indicates that the name was successfully deleted from the array.

The third example shows how to set up a route for a PUT request. This is a slightly more complex operation than a POST or DELETE request. It starts by using the put() method of the app object to specify a route with a URL path of /names with a required route parameter named index. Within the callback function, the first statement gets the index from the route parameter. Then, the second statement gets the name from the body of the request. Next, the third statement sets the name at the specified index in the global names array. Finally, the fourth statement returns an object that has index and name properties for the element that was modified. This indicates that the array was successfully modified.

If you enter a URL in a browser, the browser makes a GET request. As a result, you can't enter a URL in a browser to test POST, PUT, and DELETE requests. Instead, you must use code as shown by the fourth example. Here, the code makes a POST request. To do that, this code makes an asynchronous request to the API like the asynchronous POST requests presented in chapter 14. Here, the code adds an object to the body property of the HTTP request. This object has a name property with its value set to the name to be added.

Set up a route for a POST request

```
app.post("/names", (request, response) => {
  const name = request.body.name;
  names.push(name);
  response.json(name);
});
```

Set up a route for a DELETE request

```
app.delete("/names/:index", (request, response) => {
  const i = request.params.index;
  const deletedNameArray = names.splice(i, 1);
  const name = deletedNameArray[0];
  response.json(name);
});
```

Set up a route for a PUT request

```
app.put("/names/:index", (request, response) => {
  const index = request.params.index;
  const name = request.body.name;
  names[index] = name;
  response.json({index, name});
});
```

An event handler that makes a POST request to the API

```
document.addEventListener("DOMContentLoaded", async () => {
    const name = "Guido";
    const options = {
        method: "POST",
        headers: {"Content-Type": "application/json"},
        body: JSON.stringify({name})
    }
    const response = await fetch("http://localhost:3000/names", options);
    const json = await response.json();
}
```

Description

- To access the JSON in the body of the request, use the body property of the request object.

- Since entering a URL in a browser makes a GET request, you can't enter a URL to in a browser to test POST, PUT, and DELETE requests. Instead, you must use code.

Figure 15-11   How to set up routes for POST, PUT, and DELETE requests

The Email List API

Figure 15-12 presents an API created with Node.js and Express that works with the data for an email list that's stored in a text file. Specifically, the API provides functionality to get all emails, add an email, and delete an email. To do this, it provides routes that handle HTTP GET, POST, and DELETE requests. To keep things simple, this API doesn't update any data. As a result, it doesn't handle HTTP PUT requests.

This figure starts by presenting some of the package.json file for the API. This file was generated with the npm init command described earlier in this chapter. Then, the file was edited to add a value to the description property and to add a type property that's set to "module" so the API can use ES module files with a .js extension.

The index.js file of the Email List API starts by importing the default exports of the express and cors modules. It also imports a custom module object that contains all the items of the module in the data.js file. This is an ES module that contains the code that works with the email address data in the text file. It's presented in part 2 of this figure.

Storing the data access code of an API in a separate module like this is generally considered a good practice. That way, the code that sets up your routes is simpler and easier to maintain. In addition, if your data access code ever changes, you don't need to make changes to your routing code. For instance, if you changed the data access code to store email data in a database rather than a text file, you wouldn't need to change any of the code in the index.js file, just the code in the data.js file.

After the import statements, the code creates the Express app object. Then, it sets up the middleware of the app to add CORS headers to the responses and to be able to parse the data in the body of a request as JSON.

After that, it sets up the routes for two GET requests, a POST request, and a DELETE request. The first route handles GET requests to the root URL of the API. This route returns a JSON object that describes the API.

The second and third routes handle GET and POST requests to the /emails path, and the fourth route handles DELETE requests to the /emails path with a required route parameter that contains the id of the data to delete. The code for these routes passes the definitions of methods of the data module object as the callback functions to the get(), post(), and delete() methods. Finally, the code starts the server.

Some of the package.json file for the API

```json
{
    "name": "email_list_api",
    "version": "1.0.0",
    "description": "A simple API for maintaining an email list.",
    "main": "index.js",
    ...
    "type": "module",
    "dependencies": {
        "cors": "^2.8.5",
        "express": "^4.18.2"
    }
}
```

The index.js file

```js
import express from "express";
import cors from "cors";
import * as data from "./data.js";

const app = express();          // create the Express app object

// set up middleware
app.use(cors());
app.use(express.json());

// set up API routes
app.get("/", (request, response) => {
    response.json({info: "A simple API for maintaining an email list. "})
});
app.get("/emails", data.getEmails);
app.post("/emails", data.addEmail);
app.delete("/emails/:id", data.deleteEmail);

// start the server
app.listen(3000, () => {
    console.log("API running on port 3000.")
});
```

Description

- The Email List API handles HTTP GET, POST, and DELETE requests to retrieve, add, and delete emails stored on the server in a text file.

- The API has a package.json file generated by the npm init command and modified to include a description and a type property with a value of "module" so the API can use ES module files with a file extension of .js.

- It's a good practice to keep the code that gets and saves data in a separate data module. That way, if your data storage changes, you don't need to change your routing code, only the code in the data module.

Figure 15-12   The Email List API (part 1)

Part 2 of figure 15-12 shows the code in the data module for the Email List API. This code is stored in a file named data.js that's in the same directory as the index.js file. This works because the package.json file for this API is configured so the ES module files in the API can have .js extensions.

The data module starts by importing the readFile() and writeFile() methods from the fs.promises module. Then, it defines a private constant that holds the name of the text file. Next, it defines two private helper functions.

The asynchronous readEmails() function uses the *await* keyword to call the readFile() method. Then, it uses the JSON.parse() method to convert the string returned from the file into a JavaScript object. That string looks like this:

```
[{"name":"Anne","email":"anne@murach.com","id":1},
 {"name":"Mike","email":"mike@murach.com","id":2}]
```

As a result, the code returns an array of objects where each object has name, email, and id properties.

The asynchronous writeEmails() function has a data parameter, which is the array of objects to save. The function uses the *await* keyword to call the writeFile() method, passing the data parameter to the JSON.stringify() method so the array of objects is written to the file as a string.

After the helper functions, the data module codes three named exports. These exports are asynchronous functions that have request and response parameters. In other words, they have the same signature as the callback function that's passed to the get(), post(), put(), and delete() methods of the Express app object.

In addition, all three functions contain a try-catch statement. Each catch block starts by writing the error to the console, which in this case is the command prompt window you used to start the API on the server. This is useful when you want to view the technical details of an error, but you don't want those details to be part of the response returned by your API.

Next, the catch block adds an object that provides information about the error to the response object in JSON format. This is a common way to pass error information to the web apps on the client that use your API.

The getEmails() function calls the asynchronous readEmails() helper function to get the array of objects from the text file. Then, it adds the array of objects to the response object in JSON format.

The addEmail() function gets an array of objects from the text file and computes the maximum value of the id property of the objects in the array. Then, it uses the body property of the POST request to get an object for the body. This works because the express.json() middleware converts the JSON in the body of the request to an object. After that, this code adds a new id property to the object and sets its value as the max id value plus one. Next, it adds the new object to the array and calls the asynchronous writeEmails() helper function to save the emails. Finally, it adds the new object to the response object in JSON format.

The deleteEmail() function gets an array of objects from the text file and the id route parameter from the URL. Then, it uses the id parameter to create a new array that contains all the objects except the one whose id property matches that parameter. Finally, it saves the emails and adds an empty object to the response object in JSON format. This is a common way to indicate that a delete operation has completed successfully.

The data module (data.js)

```
import {readFile, writeFile} from "fs/promises";

const fileName = "email_list.txt";

// private helper functions
async function readEmails() {
    const str = await readFile(fileName, "utf8");
    return JSON.parse(str);
}

async function writeEmails(data) {
    await writeFile(fileName, JSON.stringify(data));
}

// public named exports
export async function getEmails(request, response) {
    try {
        const data = await readEmails();
        response.json(data);
    } catch (e) {
        console.log(e);
        response.json({error:{message:"Unable to get emails."}});
    }
};

export async function addEmail(request, response) {
    try {
        const data = await readEmails();
        const maxId = data.reduce((prev, current) =>
            (prev.id > current.id) ? prev.id : current.id, 0);

        const newEmail = request.body;
        newEmail.id = maxId + 1;

        data.push(newEmail);
        await writeEmails(data);

        response.json(newEmail);
    } catch (e) {
        console.log(e);
        response.json({error:{message:"Unable to add email."}});
    }
};

export async function deleteEmail(request, response) {
    try {
        const data = await readEmails();
        const id = request.params.id;
        const newData = data.filter(e => e.id != id);
        await writeEmails(newData);
        response.json({});
    } catch (e) {
        console.log(e);
        response.json({error:{message:"Unable to delete email."}});
    }
};
```

Figure 15-12   The Email List API (part 2)

Part 3 of figure 15-12 presents some of the code from a JavaScript web app that uses the Email List API. This code includes a constant for the URL for the /emails path of the API and an asynchronous event handler for the DOMContentLoaded event.

Within the DOMContentLoaded event handler, the code starts with a try-catch statement that makes an asynchronous GET request to the specified URL. Then, the code asynchronously calls the json() method of the response object and checks if the object it returns has a property named error. If so, the call to the API did not succeed, and it added an error object to the response. In that case, the code uses the error object to display the error message in a dialog. Otherwise, it passes the object to the displayEmails() function, which isn't shown here to save space.

You should know that the try-catch statement here doesn't handle errors returned by the API. As you've seen, that's done by adding an error property to the object that the json() method returns. Instead, a try-catch statement like this handles errors such as the API being down or passing it an incorrect URL.

After the initial GET request, the DOMContentLoader event handler attaches event handlers for the click events of the Add and Delete buttons. The event handler for the Add button starts by getting a name and email from the user. To save space, there's no data validation here, but in real life you'd include that.

The click event handler for the Add button starts with a try-catch statement. Within the try block, the code begins by creating an options object for a POST request that includes the name and email in the body property. This data is stored in an object with a name and email property, and the code uses the JSON.stringify() method to convert this object to a string.

Then, the code makes an asynchronous call to the fetch() method, passing it the url constant and the options object. This makes a POST request to the specified URL with the user data in the body of the request.

Next, the code asynchronously calls the json() method of the response object and checks if the object it returns has a property named error. If so, the code displays the error message in a dialog. Otherwise, the code makes another asynchronous call to the fetch() method to get the updated list of emails and display them. To do that, it asynchronously calls the json() method of the response object and passes the return value to the displayEmails() function.

The click event handler for the Delete button gets the email to delete from the <select> element that displays the email data. This works because the displayEmails() function, not shown here, sets the id property of each email object as the value of each <option> element it adds to this <select> element. Then, if the user has selected an email, the code has a try-catch statement that makes a DELETE request to the specified URL for the specified id.

Next, the code asynchronously calls the json() method of the response object and checks if the object it returns has a property named error. If so, the code displays the error message in a dialog. Otherwise, the code makes asynchronous calls to get the updated list of emails and display them.

Some code that uses the Email List API

```javascript
const url = "http://127.0.0.1:3000/emails/";
...
document.addEventListener("DOMContentLoaded", async() => {
    try {
        const response = await fetch(url);
        const json = await response.json();
        if (json.error) {
            alert("Server error - " + json.error.message);
        } else {
            displayEmails(json);
        }
    } catch(e) {alert(e.message);}

    getElement("#add_email").addEventListener("click", async() => {
        const name = getElement("#name").value;
        const email = getElement("#email").value;
        try {
            const options = {
                method: "POST",
                headers: {"Content-Type": "application/json"},
                body: JSON.stringify({name, email})
            }
            let response = await fetch(url, options);
            const json = await response.json();

            if (json.error) {
                alert("Server error - " + json.error.message);
            } else {
                response = await fetch(url);
                displayEmails(await response.json());
            }
        } catch(e) {alert(e.message);}
    });

    getElement("#delete_email").addEventListener("click", async() => {
        const id = getElement("#emails").value;
        if (id == "") {
            alert ("Please select an email to delete.");
            return;
        }

        try {
            let response = await fetch(url + id, {method: "DELETE"});
            const json = await response.json();

            if (json.error) {
                alert("Server error - " + json.error.message);
            } else {
                response = await fetch(url);
                displayEmails(await response.json());
            }
        } catch(e) {
            alert(e.message);
        }
    });
});
```

Figure 15-12   The Email List API (part 3)

The CORS Proxy API

Figure 15-13 presents a server-side API for making cross-origin requests to third-party APIs that don't have CORS headers. This solves the problem described in the last chapter by creating a proxy server to request the third-party resource. A *proxy server* is an intermediary server between two servers.

If the response from an API doesn't contain the correct CORS headers, you can't use the Fetch API to access that API. However, you can access the API with server-side code. Then, the server-side code can make the data it gets from a third-party API available as a web API. Since you control the server-side code, you can make sure the web API has the correct CORS headers.

The table at the top of this figure summarizes the http-proxy-middleware module that's available from NPM. This module provides a framework for creating proxy requests. Then, the first example shows the npm command that installs the module.

The second example presents a module that contains code for creating a proxy server. To start, it imports the express and cors modules. In addition, it imports the createProxyMiddleware() function from the http-proxy-middleware module. Then, the code creates the Express app object and adds the cors middleware to it so all the responses from the API have CORS headers that allow cross-origin requests. Next, the code creates an options object with two properties named router and changeOrigin.

The router property specifies an arrow function that uses the path property of the request object to get the URL of the API that the proxy should target. The path property contains the portion of the URL that comes after the protocol, host, and port. For instance, to request data from a website named myapi.com, you can append its URL to the end of the URL for the proxy server like this:

```
http://localhost:8088/https://myapi.com/data
```

Then, the value of the path property is:

```
/https://myapi.com/data
```

As a result, the code uses the substring() method to remove the leading forward slash from the value in the path property.

The changeOrigin property specifies a value of true. This changes the origin of the host header from the proxy URL to the target URL.

After creating the options object, this code passes it to the createProxy-Middleware() function. Then, it uses the value that's returned by this function to finish setting up the proxy middleware.

The third example shows how to use the node command to start the proxy server created by the module. While your proxy server is running, you can use it to make cross-origin requests.

The fourth example shows how to use your proxy server to access a third-party API. This works the same as the CORS Anywhere example from the previous chapter. This time, though, you're using your own proxy server, which gives you more control over how it works.

Another module that's available from NPM

Name	Description
`http-proxy-middleware`	A framework for creating proxy requests.

Install the module

```
> npm install http-proxy-middleware
```

A module named proxy.mjs that uses the http-proxy-middleware module

```
import express from "express";
import cors from "cors";
import { createProxyMiddleware } from "http-proxy-middleware";

const app = express();              // create the Express app object
app.use(cors());                    // enable CORS

// create the proxy options
const options = {
  router: req => req.path.substring(1),  // get request URL, not proxy URL
  changeOrigin: true
};

// add the proxy middleware
app.use(createProxyMiddleware(options));

// start the server
app.listen(8088, () => {
  console.info("Proxy server is running on port 8088")
});
```

Start the proxy

```
>node proxy.mjs
[HPM] Proxy created: /  -> undefined
Proxy server is running on port 8088
```

Use the proxy to make a cross-origin request

```
document.addEventListener("DOMContentLoaded", async () => {
    const proxy = "http://localhost:8088/";
    const api = "https://www.flickr.com/services/feeds/photos_public.gne";
    const url = proxy + api;  // prefix api URL with proxy URL

    const response = await fetch(url);
    ...
});
```

Description

- The CORS Proxy API uses the NPM http-proxy-middleware module to create a server-side proxy that you can use to make cross-origin requests.

- The options object for the proxy has a router property that uses an arrow function to access the path of the combined URL, which is the URL for the cross-origin request. Then, this arrow function uses the substring() method to remove the leading forward slash from this URL.

Figure 15-13   The CORS Proxy API

Perspective

This chapter showed you how Node.js makes it possible to use JavaScript for server-side scripting. Because JavaScript is well-suited to asynchronous programming, and because servers often need to provide asynchronous code, using JavaScript on the server often makes sense. In addition, this chapter showed how you can use NPM to extend the server-side functionality that's built into Node.js.

However, Node.js and NPM are huge subjects, and there's much more to learn about both of them. For example, the built-in fs module alone provides dozens of functions for working with the file system. Similarly, the express and cors modules provide much more functionality than what's presented in this chapter. If you want to know more about these or any other modules, you can consult the online Node.js and NPM documentation.

Terms

Node.js	dependencies
REPL (Read Eval Print Loop)	Express app object
process object	middleware
CommonJS module	route
NPM (Node Package Manager)	endpoint
package	route parameter
NPM registry	proxy server
semantic versioning	

Exercise 15-1   Experiment with Node.js

This exercise guides you through using Node.js to evaluate JavaScript expressions and to run JavaScript scripts. If you followed the instructions in appendix A (Windows) or B (macOS), Node.js should already be installed on your system.

Use Node.js to evaluate JavaScript code

1. Start a Command Prompt (Windows) or Terminal (macOS) window.

2. Enter the node command without any options to start a Node.js command prompt.

3. At the Node.js command prompt, enter a statement that declares a constant named numbers that's an array literal. Then, enter a statement that uses the push() method to add a number to the array. When you do, the console should display the length of the array like this:

```
> numbers.push(4)
1
```

4. Press the Up arrow to redisplay the previous statement and edit it so the push() method adds a new value to the array. Then, press Enter to execute this edited statement.

5. Repeat the previous step to add another value.

6. Enter the numbers constant at the prompt. This should display the array of values. For example, if you added the numbers 4, 77, and 3.14, it would display like this:

```
> numbers
[ 4, 77, 3.14 ]
```

7. Use a for-of loop to loop through the array and write each array value to the console using the console.log() method. Code the for-of loop on multiple lines. As you do that, press Tab to accept any helpful code completion suggestions.

8. Enter the .exit command to exit the Node.js command prompt.

Use Node.js to run JavaScript code in script files

9. Use the following cd command to change to the specified directory:

```
cd Documents/murach/javascript/exercises/ch15
```

10. Run the index.js file for the test_scores app by entering the following command:

```
node test_scores
```

This should display three test scores and the average of those scores.

11. Start VS Code and open the index.js file. Then, update the code to accept arguments using the process object.

12. Enter the following command to pass three test scores to the index.js file.

```
node test_scores 97 88 92
```

This should display the three test scores and their average.

Use the fs.promises module to read a text file

13. View the files in this folder:

```
exercises\ch15\fs
```

14. Review the names.txt and read.mjs files in this directory. Note that the read.mjs file imports the readFile() function from the fs.promises module but contains no other code.

15. In the read.mjs file, add code that uses the readFile() method to display each name in the names.txt file.

16. From the command prompt, use the following command to change the directory to the fs directory of the ch15 exercises folder:

```
cd fs
```

17. Use the following command to execute the read.js file.

```
node read.mjs
```

This should display the names in the text file on the console.

Exercise 15-2   Work with a web-based API

This exercise guides you through using Node.js to use the Express framework to work with a web-based API.

Review the code for the Express app API

1. View the files in this folder:

```
exercises\ch15\task_list_api
```

2. Review the code in the data.mjs file. Note that it's a module with private functions that read and write a text file, and named exports that get all tasks, add a task, and delete all tasks.

3. Review the code in the index.mjs file. Note that it contains some boilerplate code for starting an API but doesn't set up the routes for that API.

4. Open the tasks.txt file. Note that it contains an array of two tasks.

Test the existing API

5. Start a command prompt and use the following cd command to change to the specified directory:

   `cd Documents/murach/javascript/exercises/ch15/task_list_api`

6. Use the command prompt to install the express and cors modules locally.

7. Use the node command to start the index.mjs file.

8. Open a browser and navigate to the following URL:

   `localhost:3000`

   This should display some information about the API.

9. Navigate to the following URL:

   `localhost:3000/tasks`

   This should display an error message since this route isn't set up yet.

Finish the API

10. Open the index.mjs file.

11. Add a statement that imports the data module from the data.mjs file.

12. Add code that sets up routes to handle GET, POST, and DELETE requests to the /tasks path. These routes can use the methods of the data.mjs module as the callback functions. Hint: None of them need to use route parameters.

13. To make these changes available from the API, switch to the command prompt and press Ctrl-C to stop the API. Then, use the node command to start the API again.

14. Open a browser and navigate to the following URL:

    `localhost:3000/tasks`

    This should display the two starting tasks.

Use the Task List app

15. View the files in this folder:

    `exercises\ch15\task_list`

16. Open the task_list.js file and review its code to see how it uses the API.

17. Run the Task List app and test it. You should be able to use it to add and clear tasks.

Create a package.json file for the API

18. Switch to the command prompt and press Ctrl-C to stop the API. Then, run the npm init command to create a simple package.json file.

19. Open the package.json file that was created for the API. Then, review this file and note that it has dependencies for the express and cors modules.

20. Update the package.json file to include a description of the API.

16

How to work with drawing and animation

In this chapter, you'll learn how to use the Canvas API to add shapes, colors, and animations to your apps. In addition, you'll learn how to use the HTML Drag and Drop API to drag elements from one location on a page to another. These skills will enable you to create apps with interesting functionality.

An introduction to the Canvas API

The *Canvas API* allows you to use JavaScript to add graphics and animations to your web apps. To use it, you add an HTML <canvas> element to your web page. This element is available in all modern browsers.

Although you can use the Canvas API to create both two-dimensional (2D) and three-dimensional (3D) graphics and animations, this chapter focuses on 2D graphics and animations. If you want to create 3D graphics and animation, you'll find some good tutorials online.

How the Canvas API works

Figure 16-1 presents the HTML for a web page that contains a <canvas> element for use with the Canvas API. Here, the <canvas> element includes id, width, and height attributes. It's a good idea to set the width and height this way rather than with CSS to avoid distortions when the element renders.

To place a graphic or animation within a <canvas> element, you use pixel coordinates. As the diagram in this figure shows, the coordinates start at zero at the upper left corner of the canvas and increase as you move from left to right along the x-axis and from top to bottom along the y-axis.

The first code example after the diagram shows how to get the drawing context object that you use to draw on a <canvas> element. First, the code gets the <canvas> element by id. Then, it calls the getContext() method of that element and passes it the string "2d". The resulting object provides methods for drawing 2D shapes and lines.

The second code example shows how to determine the location of the <canvas> element on the page, which you may occasionally need to do. To do that, you use the getBoundingClientRect() method. This method is available to all HTML elements and returns the smallest DOMRect object that contains the element. Then, you can use the x and y properties of that object to get the element position relative to the top left corner of the viewport, which is the area of the web page that's visible to the user. Note that the left and top properties of this object return the same values as the x and y properties.

How to provide for accessibility

When you use the <canvas> element, you should include *fallback text* within the opening and closing tags as shown in the last example. The fallback text provides for accessibility because it can be read by screen readers. Although the name implies that this is text, it can be any HTML element. For example, you could use an <img> element to include an image. In that case, a screen reader would read the text for the alt property of the <img> element.

If the <canvas> element provides content that is purely decorative, you can omit the fallback text. In that case, you should add a role attribute with the value "presentation".

A <canvas> element within an HTML document

```
<body>
    <h1>A canvas drawing</h1>
    <canvas id="drawing" width="200" height="200"></canvas>
    <!-- additional content -->
</body>
```

The x and y coordinates of a <canvas> element

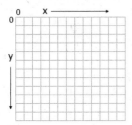

Get a 2D drawing context object for a <canvas> element

```
const canvas = document.querySelector("#drawing");
const ctx = canvas.getContext("2d");
```

Determine the location of the <canvas> element on the page

```
const rectangle = canvas.getBoundingClientRect();
const left = rectangle.x;
const top = rectangle.y;
```

A <canvas> element with fallback text

```
<canvas id="drawing" width="200" height="200">smiley face</canvas>
```

Description

- The *Canvas API* allows you to use JavaScript with an HTML <canvas> element to draw 2D and 3D graphics and animations.

- The <canvas> element uses pixel coordinates that start at zero at the upper left corner and increase as you move along the x-axis (left to right) and the y-axis (top to bottom).

- To draw graphics and animations, you use the getContext() method of the <canvas> element to get the drawing context it provides. This method accepts a parameter that specifies the types of objects you want to draw, such as "2d" for two-dimensional.

- It's a good practice to set the width and height of a <canvas> element using the HTML width and height attributes rather than the CSS width and height properties to avoid distortions.

- You can use the getBoundingClientRect() method of a <canvas> element to get a DOMRect object that specifies the size and position of the element. Then, you can use the x and y properties (or the left and top properties) of the DOMRect object to get the element's position relative to the top left corner of the viewport in pixels.

- For accessibility, you should provide *fallback text* within the opening and closing tags of the <canvas> element. If a <canvas> element is purely decorative, you can omit the fallback text and include the role="presentation" attribute instead.

Figure 16-1   An introduction to the Canvas API

How to draw rectangles and text

Now that you know how to get a drawing context object, it's time to draw something! In the topics that follow, you'll learn how to draw rectangles and text.

How to draw rectangles

Figure 16-2 presents three of the methods of the drawing context object that you can use to draw rectangles. All three methods have four parameters. The x and y parameters set the x and y coordinates for the upper left corner of the rectangle, and the width and height parameters set the width and height of the rectangle in pixels.

These three methods differ in the way the rectangle they produce is drawn. The strokeRect() method draws the outline of a rectangle. The fillRect() method draws a solid rectangle. And the clearRect() method draws a transparent rectangle.

The first code example gets the drawing context object of a <canvas> element by type. You'll typically use this technique if a page contains a single <canvas> element. If a page contains more than one element, you can select the element you want by id as shown in figure 16-1. The drawing context object that's returned is assigned to a constant named ctx. This constant is used by all the examples in this chapter.

The second code example uses this context object to draw three rectangles. The first statement draws the outline of a rectangle. Since the width and height values are the same, this produces a square. The second statement draws a solid square. It uses the x and y parameters to place this square within the first square. Finally, the third statement clears a rectangular portion of the solid square.

The third code example shows how to use the clearRect() method to clear all drawing from a <canvas> element. To do that, you pass the x and y coordinates for the top left corner of the element, which are always 0 and 0, along with the values of the width and height properties of the canvas.

How to draw text

Figure 16-2 also presents two methods and a property of the drawing context object that you can use to draw text. The methods have three parameters that specify the text to draw and the coordinates for the lower left corner of the text. These methods differ in the way the text they produce is drawn. The strokeText() method draws the outline of the letters of the text, while the fillText() method draws solid letters.

The font property sets or gets the font for the text. It uses the same syntax as the CSS font property. If you don't set the font property for a <canvas> element, it defaults to 10px sans-serif. Once you set this property, it's used for any text you draw until it's changed.

Three methods of the drawing context object for working with rectangles

Method	Description
strokeRect(*x*, *y*, *width*, *height*)	Draws a rectangular outline.
fillRect(*x*, *y*, *width*, *height*)	Draws a solid rectangle.
clearRect(*x*, *y*, *width*, *height*)	Clears a rectangular area, making it transparent.

Code used by the examples in this chapter

```
const canvas = document.querySelector("canvas");
const ctx = canvas.getContext("2d");
```

Draw three rectangles

```
ctx.strokeRect(10, 10, 130, 130);    // outer outline square
ctx.fillRect(30, 30, 90, 90);        // inner solid square
ctx.clearRect(40, 60, 70, 30);       // innermost clear rectangle
```

How it looks in the browser

Clear all drawing from a <canvas> element

```
ctx.clearRect(0, 0, canvas.width, canvas.height);
```

Two methods and a property for working with text

Method	Description
strokeText(*text*, *x*, *y*)	Draws the outline of the specified text.
fillText(*text*, *x*, *y*)	Draws the solid specified text.
Property	**Description**
font	Sets or gets the text font. The default is 10px sans-serif.

Draw two words

```
ctx.font = "48px serif";

ctx.strokeText("Hello", 10, 60);
ctx.fillText("World!", 120, 50);
```

How it looks in the browser

Figure 16-2   How to draw rectangles and text

The last code example in figure 16-2 shows how to draw some text. The first statement sets the font for the text. Then, the second statement draws a word with outlined letters, and the third statement draws a word with solid letters. Notice that the words aren't aligned at the bottom because their y-coordinates are different.

The Tic Tac Toe app

Figure 16-3 presents a simple Tic Tac Toe app. It displays a tic tac toe board and lets the user place X's and O's on the board by clicking on or touching a square. The HTML for the app consists of a heading, the canvas, and a <script> element for the external JavaScript file.

The JavaScript for the app attaches an event handler for the DOMContentLoaded event. This event handler starts by getting the <canvas> element and the context object for the canvas. Then, it sets the font property of the context object.

The event handler continues by declaring a constant named len that's set to 100, which represents the height and width of each square on the board in pixels. It also declares a variable named isX and assigns it an initial value of true. The code uses this variable to keep track of whether it's X's turn or O's turn.

Next, the event handler draws the tic tac toe board. To do that, it calls the strokeRect() method to draw a 100 by 100 pixel square at each corner of the canvas, plus a square in the middle. Then, it calls the strokeRect() method to draw an outer border on the canvas. Note that you could also add this outer border with CSS. In fact, you'll see an example of that later in the chapter.

Once the board is drawn, the code attaches an event handler for the click event of the <canvas> element. This event handler uses the isX variable to determine if it should draw an X or an O on the board. After that, it calls the fillText() method to draw the X or O at the position on the <canvas> element that the user clicked. To get the coordinates for that position, it uses the offsetX and offsetY properties of the PointerEvent object that's passed to the event handler. Finally, the code uses the NOT operator (!) to toggle the Boolean value in the isX variable. For example, if the value of the variable is true, this statement changes it to false.

To keep things simple, this app doesn't have the functionality that you'd expect from a real-life tic tac toe app. For instance, it allows you to draw text on a square that isn't empty, it doesn't center the X's and O's in the squares, and it doesn't identify a winner. However, this should be enough to get you started drawing rectangles and text.

The user interface

Tic Tac Toe

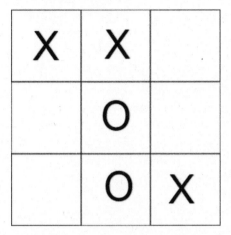

The HTML for the <body> element

```
<body>
    <h1>Tic Tac Toe</h1>
    <canvas width="300" height="300">
        Tic Tac Toe board
    </canvas>
    <script src="tic_tac_toe.js"></script>
</body>
```

The JavaScript

```
document.addEventListener("DOMContentLoaded", () => {
    const canvas = document.querySelector("canvas");
    const ctx = canvas.getContext("2d");
    ctx.font = "56px arial";              // set font

    const len = 100;
    let isX = true;

    // add squares at each corner and in the middle
    ctx.strokeRect(0, 0, len, len);        // upper left
    ctx.strokeRect(0, 200, len, len);      // lower left
    ctx.strokeRect(200, 0, len, len);      // upper right
    ctx.strokeRect(200, 200, len, len);    // lower right
    ctx.strokeRect(100, 100, len, len);    // middle

    // add outer border
    ctx.strokeRect(0, 0, canvas.width, canvas.height);

    // event handler for click event
    canvas.addEventListener("click", evt => {
        const text = isX ? "X" : "O";
        ctx.fillText(text, evt.offsetX, evt.offsetY);

        isX = !isX;  // toggle isX flag for next turn
    });
});
```

Figure 16-3   The Tic Tac Toe app

How to draw lines

In this section you'll learn how to create shapes by drawing lines. To do that, you need to know how to work with paths.

How to work with paths

A *path* is a list of points that defines one or more lines. You can use a path with multiple lines to draw various shapes. Figure 16-4 presents several methods of the drawing context object that you can use to create paths and draw the lines they contain.

The beginPath() method starts a new path. Then, the moveTo() method moves the "pen" for an existing path to the position specified by the x and y coordinates it receives.

The lineTo() method adds a line to the path from the current position to the position specified by the x and y coordinates it receives. If you call lineTo() immediately after beginPath(), it works the same as calling moveTo(). That is, it moves the "pen" to the position specified by x and y instead of adding a line.

The closePath() method adds a line to the path from the current position of the "pen" to the starting position of the path. You can use this method to finish a shape, such as drawing the last side of a triangle. It's not needed to fill a solid shape or to draw a path that doesn't close.

The stroke() and fill() methods actually draw the shape. The stroke() method draws an outline along the points of the path, while the fill() method fills the path so it's solid.

The first example shows how to draw two lines separated by a space. First, it calls the beginPath() method to start the path. Then, it calls the lineTo() method twice. The first call moves the "pen" to the specified position, and the second call adds a line to the right along the x-axis at the same y-coordinate. Next, it calls the moveTo() method to lift the "pen" and place it in a new position on the x-axis, and it calls the lineTo() method to add a second line. Finally, it calls the stroke() method to draw both lines.

The second example shows how to draw two triangles, one that's outlined and the other that's solid. To draw the outlined triangle, the code starts the path and moves the "pen" to the start position. The next two statements add two sides of the triangle to the path. Then, the closePath() method adds a line from the current position to the starting position, which adds the third side of the triangle to the path. Finally, the code calls the stroke() method to draw the triangle.

To draw the solid triangle, the code starts a new path, moves to the start position, and adds the lines for two sides of the triangle to the path. Because this code is going to fill in the path, it doesn't need to call the closePath() method. Instead, it calls the fill() method to draw the triangle, which fills in the path.

Note that you must start a new path for this second triangle. If you don't, the fill() method will also fill in the first triangle, since it's in the same path.

This figure also presents two properties of the drawing context object that you can use to configure the look of the lines that you draw. The lineWidth

Methods of the drawing context object for working with paths

Method	Description
beginPath()	Starts a new path.
moveTo(x, y)	Moves the "pen" to the specified x and y coordinates.
lineTo(x, y)	Adds a line to the path from the current position to the specified x and y coordinates. Can be called in place of moveTo() immediately after beginPath().
closePath()	Adds a line to the path from the current position to the start of the path. Not needed for solid shapes.
stroke()	Draws the outline of the shape.
fill()	Draws a solid shape.

Draw two lines

```
ctx.beginPath();
ctx.lineTo(25, 5);          // same as calling moveTo()
ctx.lineTo(75, 5);
ctx.moveTo(125, 5);         // lifts "pen" and places in new position
ctx.lineTo(175, 5);
ctx.stroke();
```

How it looks in the browser

Draw two triangles

```
ctx.beginPath();
ctx.lineTo(10, 10);
ctx.lineTo(60, 10);
ctx.lineTo(10, 50);
ctx.closePath();
ctx.stroke();               // triangle outline

ctx.beginPath();
ctx.lineTo(20, 50);
ctx.lineTo(70, 10);
ctx.lineTo(70, 50);
ctx.fill();                 // solid triangle - call to closePath() not needed
```

How it looks in the browser

Two properties of the drawing context object for working with lines

Property	Description
lineWidth	Sets or gets the width of the line in pixels. Default is 1 pixel.
lineCap	Sets or gets the style of the end caps for a line. Possible values are butt (ie, flat), rounded, or square. The default is butt.

Description

- A *path* is a list of points. You use paths to draw one or more lines.

Figure 16-4   How to work with paths

property sets or gets the width of the lines in pixels, and the lineCap property sets or gets the style of the end caps for the lines. Once you set these properties, the values persist until they're changed.

The Drawing app

Figure 16-5 presents the Drawing app, which allows a user to draw anything they want on the web page with their mouse, finger, or stylus. For instance, in this figure, a user has drawn a snowman. The app also has a Clear button so the user can clear the drawing and start again. The HTML for the app consists of a heading, the canvas, the Clear button, and a <script> element for the external JavaScript file.

This figure also presents the CSS for the <canvas> element. The first property adds a border to the element so the user can see the position of the drawing surface on the web page.

The second property makes touch work the same as the mouse when the user draws on the page. Without this property, mouse events will behave as you expect but touch events may not. That's because most browsers already have many touch events that fire at the browser level. When you set the touch-action property to none, you tell the browser to suppress those events for the <canvas> element and fire pointer events instead.

The user interface

Drawing App

Clear

The HTML for the \<body\> element

```
<body>
    <h1>Drawing App</h1>
    <canvas width="500" height="500">
        drawing surface
    </canvas><br>
    <button>Clear</button>

    <script src="drawing.js"></script>
</body>
```

Some of the CSS

```
canvas {
    border: 1px solid black;
    touch-action: none;
}
```

Description

- The Drawing app lets a user draw on the web page by clicking and moving the mouse. For touch-enabled devices, a user can also draw with a finger or a stylus.
- The CSS touch-action property makes sure that touch works the same as the mouse.

Figure 16-5   The Drawing app (part 1)

Part 2 of figure 16-5 presents the JavaScript for the Drawing app. It attaches an event handler for the DOMContentLoaded event. This event handler starts by getting the <canvas> element and the drawing context object for the canvas.

Then, it sets the lineWidth and lineCap properties of the drawing context object to configure how the lines in the app appear. Specifically, it sets the line width to 3 pixels and rounds the line ends.

Next, the code declares a variable named isDrawing that's used by the event handlers for the <canvas> element. Then, it attaches events handlers for the pointerdown, pointermove, pointerup, and pointerout events. These are pointer events that fire when a finger, stylus, or mouse interacts with the <canvas> element.

Until recently, if you wanted to handle both mouse and touch events for an element, you needed to write separate handlers for the mouse and touch events. That lead to redundant code that was difficult to maintain. Now, you can use pointer events instead, which are supported by all modern browsers.

The pointerdown event fires when a user touches the canvas with a finger or stylus or presses the mouse button. The event handler for this event sets the isDrawing flag to true and then calls the beginPath() method of the drawing context object.

The pointermove event fires when the user moves their finger, stylus, or the mouse. The event handler for this event first checks if the isDrawing flag is true. This makes sure that movements of the mouse only draw when the user is holding the mouse button down. Otherwise, this code would draw anytime the mouse moved over the <canvas> element, regardless of whether any buttons are pressed.

If the isDrawing flag is true, the code uses the lineTo() method to add a line to the path from the current position to the position of the mouse, finger, or stylus on the page. To get that position, the code uses the offsetX and offsetY properties of the PointerEvent object that the event handler receives. Then, it calls the stroke() method to draw the line.

Remember, though, that the first time the lineTo() method is called after the beginPath() method, it moves the "pen" to the position specified by x and y instead of adding a line to the path. In other words, the first time it's called, it's the same as calling the moveTo() method. After that, the call to lineTo() adds a line to the path.

The pointerup event fires when the user lifts their finger or stylus from the surface of the web page, or releases the mouse button. The pointerout event fires when the user moves their finger, stylus, or mouse outside the <canvas> element. In either case, the event handler sets the isDrawing flag to false. This stops the drawing until the user touches or clicks on the canvas again.

Finally, the DOMContentLoaded event handler attaches an event handler for the click event of the clear button. This event handler uses the clearRect() method of the drawing context object to remove any lines the user has drawn. To do that, it passes the x and y coordinates for the top left corner of the <canvas> element, along with the width and height of the <canvas> element.

The drawing.js file

```javascript
document.addEventListener("DOMContentLoaded", () => {
    // get canvas and context
    const canvas = document.querySelector("canvas");
    const ctx = canvas.getContext("2d");

    // configure line style
    ctx.lineWidth = 3;
    ctx.lineCap = "round";

    // flag to track state of drawing
    let isDrawing = false;

    // event handlers for mouse and touch
    canvas.addEventListener("pointerdown", () => {
        isDrawing = true;
        ctx.beginPath();
    });
    canvas.addEventListener("pointermove", evt => {
        if (isDrawing) {
            ctx.lineTo(evt.offsetX, evt.offsetY);
            ctx.stroke();
        }
    });
    canvas.addEventListener("pointerup", () => isDrawing = false);
    canvas.addEventListener("pointerout", () => isDrawing = false);

    // event handler for clear button
    const btn = document.querySelector("button");
    btn.addEventListener("click", () => {
        ctx.clearRect(0, 0, canvas.width, canvas.height)
    });
});
```

Description

- The Drawing app uses pointer events to handle both the movements of the mouse and the movements of a finger or stylus. Because of that, it doesn't need to code separate event handlers for mouse events and touch events.

Figure 16-5   The Drawing app (part 2)

How to draw circles and colors

At this point, you have the skills to draw some interesting shapes. Now, you'll learn how to draw circles and arcs and change the colors of the shapes that you draw.

How to draw circles and arcs

Figure 16-6 presents the arc() method of the drawing context object, which you can use to draw circles and arcs. It has five required parameters and a sixth optional parameter.

The first two parameters are the x and y coordinates for the center of the circle or arc. The third parameter is the radius of the circle or arc. The radius is the distance from the center point to the outside, or boundary, of a circle or arc.

The fourth parameter is the start angle for the circle or arc, and the fifth parameter is the end angle for the circle or arc. Both of these angles are measured in radians, where a value of 0 is at the 3 o'clock position. The easiest way to draw an entire circle, then, is to set the start angle to 0 and the end angle to $\pi * 2$. For a three-quarter circle, you can set the end angle to $\pi * 1.5$, for a half circle to π, and for a quarter circle to $\pi / 2$.

To understand how this works, you need to know how to convert degrees to radians. The formula for that is:

```
radians = pi / 180 x degrees
```

For example, if you substitute an approximate value of 3.1416 for pi and 360 for the degrees, which is the number of degrees in a circle, you get a value of 6.2832, or pi x 2.

The optional sixth parameter is a Boolean value that determines whether the arc is drawn in a counterclockwise direction. The default value for this parameter is false, which means that the arc is drawn in a clockwise direction.

The examples in this figure show how to use the arc() method to draw circles and arcs. The first example draws three circles, two that are outlined and one that's solid. To draw the outlined circles, the code starts the path and then calls the arc() method to add a circle to the path. Then, it calls the moveTo() method to move the "pen" to a new position, and it calls the arc() method again to add the second circle to the path. Finally, the code calls the stroke() method to draw the two outlined circles.

Next, the code starts a new path for the last circle so it can fill it in without filling in the other circles. Then, the code calls the arc() method to add a circle to the path. Finally, it calls the fill() method to draw the solid circle.

The second example draws two arcs, one that's a half circle and one that's a quarter circle. To do that, the code uses an end angle value of π for the half circle and $\pi / 2$ for the quarter circle. Both of these arcs are drawn in a clockwise direction, which is the default.

The last example shows how to draw an arc in a counterclockwise direction. To do that, the code sets the optional sixth parameter to true.

A method of the drawing context object for working with arcs

Method	Description
arc(*x, y, radius, startAngle,* *endAngle,* [*counterclockwise*])	Adds an arc to the path centered at x and y with the specified radius starting at startAngle and ending at endAngle. The optional counterclockwise parameter is a Boolean value that determines whether the arc is drawn in a counterclockwise direction. The default is false.

Draw three circles

```
ctx.beginPath();
ctx.arc(30, 50, 20, 0, Math.PI * 2);
ctx.moveTo(100, 50);                  // moves "pen" to new position
ctx.arc(80, 50, 20, 0, Math.PI * 2);
ctx.stroke();                         // draws both circle outlines

ctx.beginPath();
ctx.arc(130, 50, 20, 0, Math.PI * 2);
ctx.fill();                           // draws solid circle
```

How it looks in the browser

Draw two arcs

```
ctx.beginPath();
ctx.arc(30, 50, 20, 0, Math.PI);      // half circle
ctx.moveTo(100, 50);
ctx.arc(80, 50, 20, 0, Math.PI / 2);  // quarter circle
ctx.stroke();
```

How it looks in the browser

Draw a counterclockwise arc

```
ctx.beginPath();
ctx.arc(30, 50, 20, 0, Math.PI, true);
ctx.stroke();
```

How it looks in the browser

Description

- You can use the arc() method to draw circles and arcs.
- The start and end angles are specified in radians, where a value of 0 is at the 3 o'clock position.
- Arcs are drawn in a clockwise direction by default. To draw in a counterclockwise direction, you can set the optional counterclockwise parameter to true.

Figure 16-6   How to draw circles and arcs

How to draw colors

By default, the color that's used for lines and shapes is black. However, you can use the strokeStyle and fillStyle properties shown in figure 16-7 to change an outline or fill color. Once you set these properties, the values persist until they're changed.

You can use any valid CSS color value for these properties. For instance, the first example shows four different ways to set the strokeStyle property to the color blue. The first statement simply uses the string "blue". The second uses the hexadecimal value for blue, the third uses the rgb() function, and the fourth uses the rgba() function. The rgb() and rgba() functions specify the red, green, and blue values that make up the color. In addition, the rgba() function specifies the opacity of the color using a value from 0 to 1. A value of 1 indicates that the color is fully opaque, and a value of 0 indicates that it's fully transparent.

Although you can set the strokeStyle and fillStyle properties using any of the techniques shown here, a hexadecimal value is always returned when you get the value of one of these properties. If you set the strokeStyle property to "blue", for example, and then get the value of that property, the value is "#0000FF", not "blue". This is important to know when checking for a color value.

The second example shows how to draw a circle that has a lavender fill color and a purple outline color. This code starts by setting the fill and outline colors. In addition, it sets the lineWidth property so the outline is 5 pixels wide. Next, it begins the path and calls the arc() method to add the circle to the path.

Finally, the code calls the fill() method to fill in the circle and the stroke() method to draw the outline of the circle. The order of these statements is important. That's because if you call the fill() method after you call the stroke() method, the fill color might overwrite some of the outline. For instance, in the example here, if the order of these statements is reversed and the outline is drawn first, the fill color will overwrite part of the outline and make it 2.5 pixels wide rather than 5 pixels wide. In most cases, this isn't what you want.

Two properties of the drawing context object for working with colors

Property	Description
strokeStyle	Sets or gets the color of the shape outline. Default is black.
fillStyle	Sets or gets the color used to fill the shape. Default is black.

Valid CSS color values

```
ctx.strokeStyle = "blue";
ctx.strokeStyle = "#0000FF";              // same as "blue"
ctx.strokeStyle = "rgb(0,0,255)";         // same as "blue"
ctx.strokeStyle = "rgba(0,0,255,1)";      // same as "blue"
```

Draw a lavender circle with a purple outline

```
ctx.fillStyle = "lavender";
ctx.strokeStyle = "purple";
ctx.lineWidth = 5;                        // make outline 5 pixels wide

ctx.beginPath();
ctx.arc(70, 70, 50, 0, Math.PI * 2);
ctx.fill();                               // fill circle
ctx.stroke();                             // draw outline
```

How it looks in the browser

Description

- The value you use to set the strokeStyle or fillStyle property must be a valid CSS color value.
- When you use the rgba() function, the fourth value determines the opacity, with 1 being fully opaque and 0 being fully transparent.
- Once you set the strokeStyle or fillStyle properties, the values persist until changed.
- If you get the value of the strokeStyle or fillStyle property, it's returned as a hexadecimal value.
- When you use both the fill() and stroke() methods, you should call the fill() method before you call the stroke() method. Otherwise, the fill color might overwrite some of the outline.

Figure 16-7   How to draw colors

The Smiley Face app

Figure 16-8 presents the Smiley Face app. This app simply displays a smiley face on the web page. The HTML for the app consists of a heading, the canvas, and a <script> element for the external JavaScript file.

The JavaScript for the app starts by declaring a constant for the start and end angles of the circles in this app. Then it defines a helper function named drawSolidCircle(). This helper function has parameters for the x and y coordinates for the center of the circle, for the radius, and for the context object. It uses these values, plus the startAngle and endAngle constants, to start a path, add a circle to it, and draw a solid circle. Because it's called three times by the remaining code, it reduces code duplication.

Next, the code attaches an event handler for the DOMContentLoaded event. This event handler gets the <canvas> element and the drawing context object for the canvas. Then, it sets the fillStyle property to yellow and calls the drawSolidCircle() function. This draws the solid yellow circle of the smiley face.

Next, the event handler sets the fillStyle property to black, which is the color that will be used for the eyes. This is necessary because the yellow fill color the code previously set persists until it's changed. Then, the code calls the drawSolidCircle() method twice to draw the left and right eyes of the smiley face.

After that, the event handler starts a new path and adds a black outline to the yellow circle and a black half circle for the mouth to the path. This outline and half circle are black because the outline color hasn't been changed from its default. Then, this code calls the stroke() method to draw the circle outline and the mouth.

Because the outlines for the smiley face and mouth are both black, you can include them in the same path and draw them at the same time as shown here. By contrast, the smiley face and eyes have different fill colors. Because of that, they must be added to separate paths and drawn separately. That's the purpose of the drawSolidCircle() function.

The Smiley Face app

The HTML for the <body> element

```
<body>
    <h1>Have a nice day!</h1>
    <canvas width="200" height="200">
        smiley face
    </canvas>
    <script src="smiley.js"></script>
</body>
```

The JavaScript

```
const startAngle = 0, endAngle = Math.PI * 2;

function drawSolidCircle(x, y, radius, ctx) {
    ctx.beginPath();
    ctx.arc(x, y, radius, startAngle, endAngle);
    ctx.fill();
};

document.addEventListener("DOMContentLoaded", () => {
    const canvas = document.querySelector("canvas");
    const ctx = canvas.getContext("2d");

    ctx.fillStyle = "yellow";
    drawSolidCircle(100, 100, 75, ctx);         // draw yellow circle

    ctx.fillStyle = "black";
    drawSolidCircle(80, 70, 5, ctx);            // draw left eye
    drawSolidCircle(120, 70, 5, ctx);           // draw right eye

    ctx.beginPath();
    ctx.arc(100, 100, 75, startAngle, endAngle); // outer circle outline

    ctx.moveTo(135, 100);
    ctx.arc(100, 100, 35, startAngle, Math.PI);  // mouth (half circle)

    ctx.stroke();                                // draw outline and mouth
});
```

Figure 16-8   The Smiley Face app

How to create animations

So far, you've learned to create graphics that are static. Now, you'll learn how to create animations, which can take your web apps to the next level.

How to use the requestAnimationFrame() method

Figure 16-9 presents the requestAnimationFrame() method of the window object. It accepts a callback function that's executed prior to the next repaint of the browser, which typically happens at a rate of 60 times per second. In other words, the requestAnimationFrame() method usually produces an animation rate of 60 frames per second (FPS), which is considered optimal.

The requestAnimationFrame() method only fires once. Because of that, the callback function it receives must call the requestAnimationFrame() method to animate another frame.

The code example in this figure shows how this works. It creates a simple animation that moves a square from side to side of a <canvas> element.

The code starts by declaring variables named x and increment. The x variable holds the current value of the x-coordinate of the square, and the increment variable holds the number of pixels to move the square. Note that the numeric value of the increment variable doesn't change. Rather, the value changes from positive to negative or vice versa depending on the direction of the animation.

Next, the code defines a function named moveSquare(). This is the callback function that's passed to the requestAnimationFrame() method. It starts by deleting any previous drawing of the square. Then, it draws a new square using the value of the x variable for the x parameter of the fillRect() method, a value of 100 for the y parameter, and a value of 10 for the width and height parameters.

After drawing the square, the code checks its position. If it's at either side of the <canvas> element, the code changes the increment value from positive to negative or vice versa. This reverses the direction of the animation. For instance, if the increment value is positive, the square was being drawn with increasing x-coordinates to move the square from left to right. Then, when the increment value is changed to negative, the square will be drawn with decreasing x-coordinates to move the square from right to left.

Next, the callback function increments the value of the x variable by the value of the increment variable. This sets the value of the x-coordinate for the next drawing of the square. Finally, the callback function passes itself to the requestAnimationFrame() method to continue the animation.

After the moveSquare() function is defined, this code passes it as the callback function of the requestAnimationFrame() method. This starts the animation.

You may have noticed that the requestAnimationFrame() method is similar to the setTimeout() method you learned about in chapter 8. However, the requestAnimationFrame() method is preferred for animations because it's specifically designed for them. Animations created with the setTimeout() or setInterval() methods, by contrast, tend to be less smooth.

A method of the window object for working with animations

Method	Description
`requestAnimationFrame(function)`	Schedules the specified callback function to be executed prior to the next repaint of the browser.

Move a square from side to side

```
let x = 0;
let increment = 2;

const moveSquare = () => {
    // clear previous square (if any) and draw new one
    ctx.clearRect(0, 0, canvas.width, canvas.height);
    ctx.fillRect(x, 100, 10, 10);

    // reverse direction if at either side of canvas
    if (x < 0 || x > canvas.width - 10 ) {  // subtract width of square
        increment = -increment;
    }

    // calculate new x value
    x += increment;

    // continue animation
    requestAnimationFrame(moveSquare);
};

// start animation;
requestAnimationFrame(moveSquare);
```

How it looks in the browser

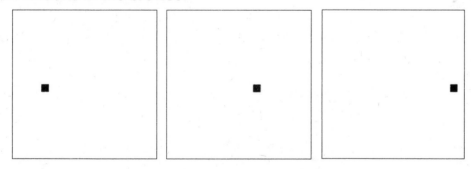

Description

- You can use the requestAnimationFrame() method of the window object to create animations. It executes a callback function at the next repaint of the browser.
- Most browsers have a constant repaint rate, typically 60 times per second. This produces an animation rate of 60 frames per second (FPS), which is considered optimal.
- The requestAnimationFrame() method only fires once. Because of that, you must call this method from within the callback function to continue an animation.
- Although you can use the setTimeout() and setInterval() methods for animation, they are less accurate and can lead to lags and hitches.

Figure 16-9   How to use the requestAnimationFrame() method

The Pong app

Figure 16-10 presents a single player Pong app, which lets a user play Pong against the computer. In the lower left corner, it displays the current number of consecutive times the user has hit the pong ball. In the lower right corner, it displays the user's highest number of consecutive hits. Since this data is displayed within the <canvas> element itself, the text is drawn. You could also use label or paragraph elements below the <canvas> element for this display.

The angle of the pong ball depends on where it hits in the paddle. If the ball hits near the center of the paddle, the angle is more up-and-down. The farther from the center that the ball hits, the angle is more side-to-side.

The HTML for the app consists of a heading, the canvas, and a <script> element for the external JavaScript file. The CSS for the canvas adds a black border.

The user interface

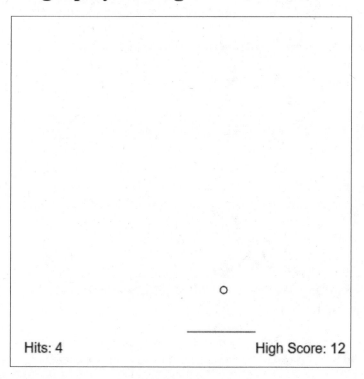

The HTML for the <body> element

```
<body>
    <h1>Single player Pong</h1>
    <canvas width="500px" height="500px">
        Pong game display
    </canvas>
    <script src="pong.js"></script>
</body>
```

Some of the CSS

```
canvas {
    border: 1px solid black;
}
```

Description

- The Pong app lets the user play against the computer.
- When the ball hits near the middle of the paddle, the angle of the bounce is more up-and-down. When the ball hits near the ends of the paddle, the angle is more side-to-side.
- The Pong app tracks and displays the number of consecutive hits and the user high score.

Figure 16-10   The Pong app (part 1)

Part 2 of figure 16-10 presents some of the JavaScript for the Pong app. It starts by attaching an event handler for the DOMContentLoaded event. This event handler begins by getting the <canvas> element and the drawing context object for the canvas. Then, it assigns the x-coordinate at the midpoint of the canvas to a constant named midX.

After that, the code declares three objects with starting values for the ball, the paddle, and the player. The hits and highScore properties of the player object are the values displayed at the bottom of the canvas and are initialized to 0.

The ball object is declared as a variable, since it is reset each time the player misses the ball. The x and y properties of this object set the initial position of the ball at the top middle of the canvas. The speedX property sets the ball to move along the x-axis from left to right at 1 pixel per frame. And the speedY property sets the ball to move along the y-axis from top to bottom at 5 pixels per frame.

The x and y properties of the paddle object set the initial position of the paddle at the bottom middle of the canvas. The direction property sets the number of pixels that the paddle moves along the x-axis to the left or right. The initial value of 0 means that, to start, the paddle isn't moving. As you'll see in part 3 of this figure, the direction value is set to 5 when the user presses the right arrow key so the paddle moves to the right. The value is set to -5 when the user presses the left arrow key so the paddle moves to the left. And the value is set to 0 when no key is pressed so the paddle stops moving.

Next, the code defines a function named render(), which is the callback function for the requestAnimationFrame() method. It starts by calculating the position of the paddle and ball. To calculate the paddle position, the code adds the paddle's direction to its current x-coordinate. To calculate the ball position, the code adds the x and y speeds to the current x and y coordinates.

The render() function continues by checking the position of the ball. If it's at the right or left border of the canvas, it reverses the x speed, which makes the ball reverse direction along the x-axis. This simulates the ball bouncing off the right or left border. Similarly, if the ball is at the top border of the canvas, it reverses the y speed to simulate the ball bouncing off the top border.

If the y-coordinate for the ball is greater than the y-coordinate for the paddle, the code needs to determine if the paddle hit the ball. To see if the ball is to the left of the paddle, the code compares the x-coordinate of the ball to the x-coordinate of the paddle. To see if the ball is to the right of the paddle, it compares the x-coordinate of the ball to the x-coordinate of the paddle plus the paddle length. If the ball is to the left or right, the paddle didn't hit the ball. In that case, the code resets the ball to its initial position and speed and sets the player hits to zero.

If the paddle hits the ball, the code reverses the speed of the ball along the y-axis to simulate the ball bouncing off the paddle. Then, it changes the speed of the ball along the x-axis based on where the ball hit the paddle. Because the speed indicates the pixels per frame that the ball moves, this determines the angle of the bounce. If the ball hits near the middle of the paddle, the result of the calculation is a smaller value and the angle is more up-and-down. On the other hand, if the ball hits toward the paddle ends, the result of the calculation is a larger value and the angle is more side-to-side. To make the angle more pronounced, you can change the literal value to more than .1.

The pong.js file

```javascript
document.addEventListener("DOMContentLoaded", () => {
    // get canvas and context
    const canvas = document.querySelector("canvas");
    const context = canvas.getContext("2d");

    // set constant for midpoint of x-axis
    const midX = canvas.width / 2;

    // define objects for ball, paddle, and player with starting values
    let ball = {x: midX, y: 0, speedX: 1, speedY: 5};
    const paddle = {x: midX - 50, y: canvas.height - 50, len: 100,
                    direction: 0};
    const player = {hits: 0, highScore: 0};

    // callback function for requestAnimationFrame()
    const render = () => {
        // calculate paddle position
        paddle.x = paddle.x + paddle.direction;

        // calculate ball position
        ball.x = ball.x + ball.speedX;
        ball.y = ball.y + ball.speedY;

        // if ball hits right/left border, reverse x speed to simulate bounce
        if (ball.x < 0 || ball.x > canvas.width)) {
            ball.speedX = -ball.speedX;
        }
        // if ball hits top border, reverse y speed to simulate bounce
        if (ball.y < 0) {
            ball.speedY = -ball.speedY;
        }
        // if ball is below paddle level...
        if (ball.y > paddle.y) {
            const isLeftOfPaddle = ball.x < paddle.x;
            const isRightOfPaddle = ball.x > paddle.x + paddle.len;
            if (isLeftOfPaddle || isRightOfPaddle) {
                // missed - start over
                ball = {x: midX, y: 0, speedX: 1, speedY: 5};
                player.hits = 0;
            } else {
                // hit - reverse y speed to simulate bounce
                ball.speedY = -ball.speedY;

                // Change x speed based on where ball hits paddle. If near
                // middle, angle of ball is more up-and-down. If near ends,
                // angle is more side-to-side.
                const midPaddle = paddle.x + (paddle.len / 2);
                ball.speedX = .1 * (ball.x - midPaddle);

                // increment hits and update high score if necessary
                player.hits++;

                if (player.hits > player.highScore) {
                    player.highScore = player.hits;
                }
            }
        }
    }
```

Figure 16-10   The Pong app (part 2)

Finally, the code increments the player hits. Then, if the number of hits is greater than the high score, it sets the new high score value to the number of hits.

Part 3 of figure 16-10 presents the rest of the render() callback function. This part of the function uses the earlier calculations to draw the ball, paddle, current hit count, and high score on the canvas.

To start, it clears any previous drawings. Then, it starts a path and uses the values in the ball object to add the ball to the path. Next, it uses the values in the paddle object to add the paddle to the path. At this point, it calls the stroke() method to draw the items in the path.

Next, the code sets the font property of the context object so the text is bigger than the default of 10 pixels. After that, it uses the values in the player object to draw the hits and high score text.

The render() callback function ends by calling the requestAnimationFrame() method and passing itself to this method. This continues the animation.

The event handler for the DOMContentLoaded event continues by attaching event handlers for the keydown and keyup events of the document. The keydown event handler checks the code property of the KeyboardEvent object it receives. If the value is "ArrowLeft", the code sets the direction property of the paddle object to -5. This moves the paddle along the x-axis 5 pixels to the left. Similarly, if the value of the code property is "ArrowRight", the code sets the direction property to 5, which moves the paddle 5 pixels to the right.

The keyup event handler simply sets the direction property of the paddle object to zero. This causes the paddle to stop moving when the user stops pressing the right or left arrow key.

The event handler for the DOMContentLoaded event ends by calling the requestAnimationFrame() method and passing it the render() callback function. This starts the animation.

The pong.js file (continued)

```
        // clear previous drawing and start new path
        context.clearRect(0, 0, canvas.width, canvas.height);
        context.beginPath();

        // ball
        context.arc(ball.x, ball.y, 5, 0, Math.PI * 2);

        // paddle
        context.moveTo(paddle.x, paddleY);
        context.lineTo(paddle.x + paddle.len, paddleY);

        // draw ball and paddle
        context.stroke();

        // draw hit count and high score text
        context.font = "20px sans-serif";
        context.fillText("Hits: " + player.hits, 20, paddle.y + 30);
        context.fillText("High Score: " + player.highScore,
            canvas.width - 140, paddle.y + 30);

        // continue animation
        requestAnimationFrame(render);
    };

    // event handlers
    document.addEventListener("keydown", e => {
        if (e.code == "ArrowLeft") paddle.direction = -5;
        if (e.code == "ArrowRight") paddle.direction = 5;
    });
    document.addEventListener("keyup", () => {
        paddle.direction = 0;
    });

    // start animation
    requestAnimationFrame(render);
});
```

Figure 16-10   The Pong app (part 3)

How to work with the HTML Drag and Drop API

In addition to the Canvas API, modern browsers also provide the *HTML Drag and Drop API*. It allows you to drag HTML elements from one location on a web page and drop them in another.

How to drag and drop an HTML element

Figure 16-11 presents three events available to HTML elements. The dragstart event fires when the user starts dragging an element. To make an HTML element draggable, you need to code an event handler for this event. In addition, you need to set the draggable attribute of that element to true.

The dragover event fires when an element is dragged over an element that's a drop target, and the drop event fires when an element is dropped onto an element that's a drop target. To make an HTML element a valid drop target, you need to code event handlers for these two events.

The examples in this figure show how this works. The first example presents two <div> elements whose ids are "left" and "right". In addition, the first <div> element contains a <p> element whose id is "dragme". As you can see, the draggable attribute of this element is set to true. You can also use JavaScript to set the draggable attribute, as you'll see in the next figure. The CSS for the two <div> elements is not shown here to save space, but it floats them side by side and outlines each with a border.

The second example presents code that allows the <p> element to be dragged and makes both <div> elements valid drop targets. To start, it gets each element. Then, it declares event handlers for the dragstart, dragover, and drop events.

Each event handler receives a DragEvent object that has a dataTransfer property that returns a DataTransfer object. You can use the setData() method of the DataTransfer object to store information about the element that's being dragged, and you can use its getData() method to retrieve that information.

The dragStartHandler() function stores the id of the dragged element in the dataTransfer property of the DragEvent object. To do that, it passes a key and a value to the setData() method. This associates the id value of the <p> element with the key value of "p".

The dragOverHandler() function simply calls the preventDefault() method of the DragEvent object. This is necessary to prevent the default behavior of not allowing drag and drop.

The dropHandler() function also calls the preventDefault() method of the DragEvent object. Then, it gets the id of the dragged element from the dataTransfer property of the DragEvent object. To do that, it passes a key value of "p" to the getData() method. Then, it uses the id it retrieves to get the dragged element and add it to the element that's the drop target.

Finally, the code in this example attaches the dragstartHandler function to the dragstart event handler. It also attaches the dragOverHandler and dropHandler functions to the dragover and drop events. That makes both <div>

Three common drag events

Event	Description
dragstart	Fires when the user starts dragging an element.
dragover	Fires when an element is being dragged over a valid drop target.
drop	Fires when an element is dropped onto a valid drop target.

The HTML for the following example

```
<div id="left">
    <p id="dragme" draggable="true">Drag me!</p></div>
<div id="right"></div>
```

Drag and drop <p> element to and from <div> elements

```
const dragme = document.querySelector("#dragme");   // <p> element
const left = document.querySelector("#left");       // left <div> element
const right = document.querySelector("#right");     // right <div> element

// event handlers for the drag events
const dragStartHandler = evt =>
    evt.dataTransfer.setData("p", evt.target.id);   // store element id

const dragOverHandler = evt => evt.preventDefault();

const dropHandler = evt => {
    evt.preventDefault();
    const id = evt.dataTransfer.getData("p");        // retrieve element id
    const p = document.querySelector("#" + id);
    evt.target.appendChild(p);
};

// make <p> element draggable
dragme.addEventListener("dragstart", dragStartHandler);

// make right <div> element a drop target
right.addEventListener("dragover", dragOverHandler);
right.addEventListener("drop", dropHandler);

// make left <div> element a drop target (so can drag element back)
left.addEventListener("dragover", dragOverHandler);
left.addEventListener("drop", dropHandler);
```

How it looks in the browser

During drag   ### After drop

Description

- To make an HTML element draggable, set its draggable attribute to true and handle its dragstart event. To make an element a drop target, handle its dragover and drop events.
- The DragEvent object of a drag event has a dataTransfer property to store data.

Figure 16-11   How to drag and drop an HTML element

elements drop targets so you can drag the <p> element back to the left <div> element after dropping it in the right <div> element.

The Movie List app

Figure 16-12 presents the Movie List app. This app displays a list of movie titles and allows the user to reorder the movies by dragging and dropping them. When the user drops a movie, it's placed above the movie that it's dropped on. For instance, in the example here, if the Wonder Woman movie that's being dragged is dropped on the Star Wars movie, it will display above the Star Wars movie in the list.

The HTML for the app consists of a heading, an unordered list that contains the movie titles, a paragraph that notifies the user to drag and drop to change the order, and a <script> element for the external JavaScript file. To keep things simple, the movie titles are hardcoded in the HTML. In real life, this data would come from a data store like a database or text file.

The JavaScript for the app starts by attaching an event handler for the DOMContentLoaded event. This event handler uses the querySelectorAll() method of the document object to get all the <li> elements that contain movie titles. Then, it loops through these elements to make each one both draggable and a valid drop target.

To make each <li> element draggable, the code sets its draggable property to true and attaches an event handler for its dragstart event. This event handler stores the id value of the element in the dataTransfer property of the DragEvent object.

To make each <li> element a valid drop target, the code attaches event handlers for its dragover and drop events. Both of these event handlers prevent the default behavior so drag and drop is allowed. In addition, the event handler for the drop event uses the id in the dataTransfer property of the DragEvent to get the <li> element that's being dragged. Then, it adds that element to the <ul> element before the <li> element that's the drop target.

The Movie List app

> # My Favorite Movies
>
> Barbie
> Oppenheimer
> Star Wars
> Casablanca
> Black Panther
> Some Like It Hot
> Lord of the Rings
> Wonder Woman
> Wizard of Oz
> Taxi Driver
>
> Drag and drop a movie to change the order

The HTML for the <body> element

```html
<body>
    <h1>My Favorite Movies</h1>
    <ul>
        <li id="barbie">Barbie</li>
        <li id="op">Oppenheimer</li>
        ...
        <li id="taxi">Taxi Driver</li>
    </ul>
    <p>Drag and drop a movie to change the order</p>
    <script src="movie_list.js"></script>
</body>
```

The JavaScript

```javascript
document.addEventListener("DOMContentLoaded", () => {
    const movies = document.querySelectorAll("li");

    // make movie list items draggable and droppable
    for (let movie of movies) {
        movie.draggable = true;

        movie.addEventListener("dragstart", evt =>
            evt.dataTransfer.setData("id", evt.target.id));

        movie.addEventListener("dragover", evt => evt.preventDefault());

        movie.addEventListener("drop", evt => {
            evt.preventDefault();
            const id = evt.dataTransfer.getData("id");
            const li = document.querySelector("#" + id);
            evt.currentTarget.parentNode.insertBefore(li, evt.target);
        });
    }
});
```

Figure 16-12   The Movie List app

Perspective

This chapter shows how to create 2D graphics and animations using the Canvas API. It also shows how to add drag and drop functionality to your web apps using the HTML Drag and Drop API.

Terms

Canvas API   path
fallback text   HTML Drag and Drop API

Exercise 16-1   Create a logo

In this exercise, you'll create a graphic to use as a logo for a pizza restaurant.

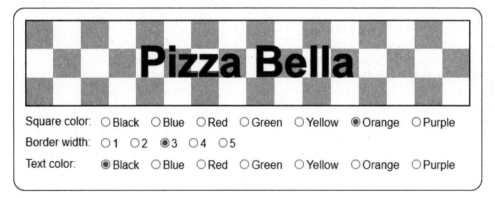

Open and review the app

1. View the files in this folder:

   `exercises\ch16\logo\`

2. Review the HTML in the index.html file. Note that the radio buttons are in groups named "square_color", "border_width", and "text_color".

3. Review the code in the logo.js file, and note the following:

   - It includes helper functions that set the default options for the radio buttons and draw the logo;

   - It uses a nested for loop to add the squares, with the outer loop tracking the x-coordinate and the inner loop tracking the y-coordinate;

   - It includes event handlers that set the specified color or width and redraw the logo when a radio button is clicked;

   - It sets the default options and draws the logo when the page loads.

Add code to draw the logo

4. Within the DrawLogo() function, set the fill color for the first square to the selected color.

5. Within the inner for loop, draw a solid square using the len constant to get the x and y coordinates and for the height and width of the square. Then, set the fill color for the next rectangle based on whether the current color is white.

6. Set the line width for the canvas to the selected border width, and then draw the rectangular border around the canvas.

7. Set the fill color for the text to the selected color, the line width to 1, and the font to bold 60px sans-serif.

8. Draw the name of the restaurant (Pizza Bella) with solid text and then with outline text. You may need to run the app and experiment with the x and y coordinates to position the text.

9. Run the app to be sure that it looks as shown above. Then, select different color and width options to be sure that the logo displays correctly.

Exercise 16-2   Create a screen saver animation

In this exercise, you'll create an animation that simulates an old-style screen saver.

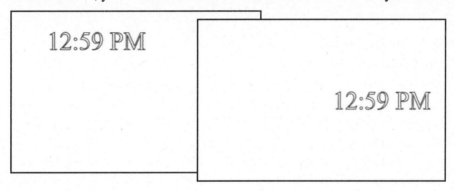

Open and review the app

1. View the files in this folder:

    `exercises\ch16\screen_saver\`

2. Review the code in the screen_saver.js file. Note that it contains a function that gets the current 12-hour time in string format. Also note that the DOMContentLoaded event handler sets some variables and constants for use in the animation.

Update the move() callback function

3. Clear any previous drawing, and then draw the text of the current time.

4. Check if the animation text is at either side of the canvas, and reverse the x increment value if it is. Then, check if the text is at the top or the bottom of the canvas, and reverse the y increment value if it is. Be sure to offset the text width and height as needed so the animation "bounces" correctly.

5. Use the increment values to calculate new x and y values for the next frame, and then continue the animation.

6. Run and test the app, adjusting the offsets in step 4 as needed.

Exercise 16-3   Create a drag and drop menu

In this exercise, you'll create a drag and drop menu to select the toppings on a pizza.

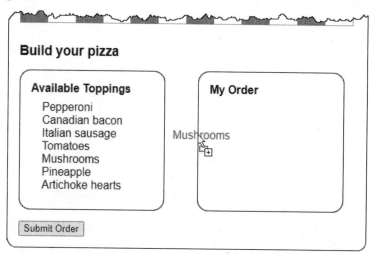

Open and review the app

1. View the files in this folder:

    `exercises\ch16\pizza_order\`

2. Review the HTML in the index.html file. Note the two <ul> elements within the two <div> elements with the ids "toppings" and "order".

3. Review the code in the pizza_order.js file, and note that it has three empty event handler functions for the drag events. Also note that the DOMContent-Loaded event handler gets the two <div> elements and all the <li> elements, and the Submit Order button displays any toppings that are in the <div> element with id "order".

Code the event handler functions

4. Code the dragStart() function to store the id of the element being dragged.

5. Code the dragOver() and drop() functions to prevent the default behavior of not allowing drag and drop.

6. Code the drop() function to get the stored id and use it to add the dragged element to the <ul> element in the drop target.

Configure the <div> and <li> elements to enable drag and drop

7. Make each <li> element draggable and attach a handler for the dragstart event.

8. Attach handlers for the dragover and drop events for the order and toppings <div> elements.

9. Run the app and drag toppings to the order area and back to the toppings area.

Appendix A

How to set up Windows for this book

This appendix shows how to set up a Windows computer so it's ready to be used with this book. This includes downloading the files for this book and installing the software that we recommend for developing JavaScript apps. When you're done setting up your computer, you'll be ready to edit and run the JavaScript apps presented in this book, and you'll be ready to do the exercises that are at the end of each chapter.

As you read these descriptions, please remember that most websites are continually upgraded. As a result, some of the procedures in this appendix may have changed since this book was published. Nevertheless, these procedures should still be good guides to installing the software. And if there are significant changes to these setup instructions, we will post updates on our website (www.murach.com).

How to download the files for this book

Figure A-1 shows how to download and set up the files for this book. This includes the code for the apps presented in this book. In addition, it includes the starting files for the exercises that are at the end of each chapter and the solutions to those exercises.

When you finish the procedure shown in this figure, the folders shown in this figure should contain the book apps, the starting points for the exercises, and the solutions to those exercises. Then, you can review the apps that are presented in this book, and you'll be ready to do the exercises.

The Murach website

`www.murach.com`

The folder that contains the files for this book

`Documents\murach\javascript`

The subfolders

Folder	Description
`book_apps`	The apps that are presented throughout this book.
`exercises`	The starting points for the exercises at the end of each chapter.
`solutions`	The solutions to the exercises.

How to download the files for this book

1. Go to www.murach.com.
2. Find the page for *Murach's Modern JavaScript*.
3. Scroll down to the "FREE downloads" tab and click it.
4. Click the Download Now button for the zip file. This should download a zip file.
5. Double-click the zip file to extract the files for this book into a folder named javascript.
6. Create the murach folder within the Documents folder.
7. Copy the javascript folder into the Documents\murach folder.

Description

*   We recommend that you store the files for this book in folders that start with Documents\murach\javascript. That way, they will match the book exactly.

Figure A-1 How to download the files for this book

How to install Chrome

When you develop JavaScript apps, you need to test them on the browsers that your users are likely to use. For a commercial app, that usually includes Chrome, Firefox, Edge, Safari, and Opera. Then, if an app doesn't work on one of those browsers, you need to debug it.

As you do the exercises and work with the apps in this book, though, you can test your apps on just Chrome. Then, if you need to debug an app, you can use Chrome's developer tools as described in chapter 7.

The first procedure in figure A-2 shows how to install Chrome. In addition, we recommend that you set Chrome as the default browser for Windows. To do that, you can use the second or third procedure shown in this figure.

Once you've got Chrome installed and your default browser set correctly, you can use the fourth procedure to make sure that your system is set up correctly. To do that, you can double-click on an HTML file to test the default browser. For this book, that's all you need to do.

However, if you want to test your web apps in other browsers, you can also right-click on an HTML file to test the other browsers on your system. Since the Edge browser is installed on most Windows systems, you should be able to test your web apps with Edge. If you want to test your web apps in browsers that aren't already on your system, you can install them. To do that, you should be able to use a procedure similar to the one in this figure to install Firefox, Opera, or Safari.

The Chrome website

https://www.google.com/chrome/

How to install Chrome

1. Go to the download page for Chrome. One easy way to find this page is to search the internet for "chrome download".
2. Locate the Download Chrome button, click it, and respond to the resulting dialogs.
3. If you're asked what you want to do with the installer file, click the Save File button. This should download an exe file to your computer.
4. When the exe file finishes downloading, double-click it to start the installation.
5. If you get a dialog that indicates that this app isn't a verified app from the Microsoft Store, click the Install Anyway button.
6. If you're asked if you want to allow the program to make changes to your computer, click the Yes button.

How to make Chrome the default browser (Windows 10)

1. Click the Windows Start button and type "default apps".
2. In the search results, select Default Apps.
3. Under Web Browser, click the current default browser.
4. Select Google Chrome from the list of browsers.

How to make Chrome the default browser (Windows 11)

1. Click the Windows Start button and type "default apps".
2. In the search results, select Default Apps.
3. Select Google Chrome from the list of apps.
4. Click the "Set default" button.

How to make sure your browsers are set up correctly

1. Start File Explorer and navigate to this folder:

    Documents\murach\javascript\book_apps\ch01\email_list

2. Double-click the index.html file. This should display that file in Chrome.
3. Right-click the index.html file and select Open With. This should display a list of all browsers that are installed on your system. From this list, select the browser you want to test. This should display the index.html file in that browser.

Description

- Because Chrome is a popular browser that has excellent tools for testing and debugging JavaScript code, we recommend testing all of the exercises for this book in this browser.
- Because Edge comes preinstalled on Windows systems, it should also be available for testing apps.
- Because Firefox, Safari, and Opera are also popular browsers, you may want to install them too. To do that, you can use a procedure similar to the one for installing Chrome.

Figure A-2   How to install Chrome

How to install Visual Studio Code

If you're already comfortable with a text editor that works for editing HTML, CSS, and JavaScript files, you can continue using it. Otherwise, we recommend using Visual Studio Code. It is a free text editor that offers many features and runs on Windows, macOS, and Linux.

The first procedure in figure A-3 shows how to install Visual Studio Code (VS Code). To do that, you download the installation file from the VS Code website. Then, you run the installation file that's downloaded.

The second procedure shows how to make sure Visual Studio Code is installed correctly. To do that, you can use VS Code to open the book_apps folder described in figure A-1. Then, you can use the Explorer window on the left side of the main VS Code window to expand and collapse the folders that contain the HTML, CSS, and JavaScript files for this book. To learn how to use VS Code to work with these files, you can start by reading chapter 1.

The VS Code website

`https://code.visualstudio.com/`

How to install VS Code

1. Go to the download page for Visual Studio Code (VS Code). One easy way to find this page is to search the internet for "vs code download".
2. Click the button for downloading the Windows version and respond to any dialogs.
3. If you're asked what you want to do with the installer file, click the Save File button. This should download an exe file to your computer.
4. When the exe file finishes downloading, double-click it to start the installation.
5. If you get a dialog that indicates that this app isn't a verified app from the Microsoft Store, click the Install Anyway button.
6. If you're asked if you want to allow the program to make changes to your computer, click the Yes button.

How to make sure VS Code is installed correctly

1. Start VS Code.
2. Select File→Open Folder from the menu system.
3. Use the resulting dialog to select this folder:
   `Documents\murach\javascript\book_apps`
4. This should open the folder that contains all the apps for this book in the Explorer window that's displayed on the left side of the main VS Code window.
5. Expand or collapse the folders in the Explorer window to view the files for the apps presented in this book. If you can view these files, VS Code is installed correctly.

Description

- Chapter 1 shows how to get started with Visual Studio Code (VS Code).

Figure A-3   How to install Visual Studio Code

How to install Node.js and the http-server module

Figure A-4 begins by showing how to install Node.js. To do that, you can use the first procedure in this figure. This is similar to the procedure for installing most apps.

After you install Node.js, you can make sure it's installed correctly by starting the Command Prompt app to get a prompt like this:

`C:\Users\`*YourUsername*`>`

At this prompt, you can enter the "node -v" command. This should display the version of Node.js that you just installed.

The third procedure shows how to use the npm install command to install the http-server module on your system. When you run this command, it should display messages that show that the http-server module was installed successfully. In this figure, you can see a message indicating that 44 packages were added.

The Node.js website

`www.nodejs.org`

How to install Node.js

1. Go to the download page for Node.js. One way to find this page is to search the internet for "node.js download".

2. Click the button for the installer file for the most current LTS (Long Term Support) release and respond to the resulting dialogs.

3. If you get any warning dialogs, choose to continue with the installation. This should download the installer file to your computer.

4. Double-click the installer file to start the installer.

5. Respond to the resulting dialogs by accepting the default options.

How to make sure Node.js is installed correctly

1. Start the Command Prompt app.

2. Enter the node command like this:

```
C:\Users\mike>node -v
v20.11.0
```

If this displays a version number, Node.js is set up correctly.

How to install the http-server module

1. Start the Command Prompt app.

2. Enter the npm install command like this:

```
C:\Users\mike>npm install -g http-server
added 44 packages in 4s
```

Description

- *Node.js* is an open-source, cross-platform, runtime environment that executes JavaScript code outside a web browser.

- *NPM (Node Package Manager)* is a package manager for the JavaScript programming language.

- NPM is the default package manager for Node.js, and it's included when you install Node.js on your system.

- The http-server module provides a way to test web apps on a local web server.

Figure A-4   How to install Node.js and the http-server module

How to test an app on a local web server

Figure A-5 shows how to use the http-server module to test web apps on a local web server. This is important because some of the apps presented in this book use features that only work if the app is run from a web server. For example, the Clock app presented in chapter 13 only works when you run it on a web server. To do that, you can use the http-server module.

After you install the http-server module, you can use the cd command to change the directory to the javascript directory that contains the web apps for this book as shown by the first example.

After changing the directory, you can start the http-server module by entering the http-server command as shown in the second example. Then, your firewall software may display a message that asks whether you want to allow Node.js to communicate on private networks. If you want the local server to work correctly, you must allow this.

When the http-server module starts, it should display messages that indicate that the web server is starting and where it's available. In this figure, these messages show that the web server is available from port 8080 of the IP address of 127.0.0.1. In addition, they show that you can stop the web server by pressing Ctrl-C.

Since the localhost keyword is a synonym for 127.0.0.1, you can run the web app in the current directory by starting a web browser and entering "localhost:8080" for the URL as shown in this figure. Here, because the current directory has already been set to the javascript directory, the browser displays three links that correspond to the book_apps, exercises, and solutions directories. You can click on these links to navigate to any of the apps presented in this book, including the Clock app presented in chapter 13.

The command for changing the directory

```
>cd Documents\murach\javascript
```

The command for starting the server

```
>http-server
Starting up http-server, serving ./
...
Available on:
  http://192.168.113.4:8080
  http://192.168.86.234:8080
  http://127.0.0.1:8080
Hit CTRL-C to stop the server
```

A URL you can use to view the server

```
http://localhost:8080
```

The browser displaying the server's root directory

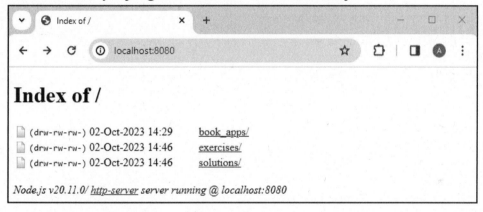

A book app from chapter 13 that must be run from a web server

11:02:13 AM

Fri January 26, 2024

The message that's displayed when you press Ctrl-C

```
http-server stopped.
```

Description

- Some of the apps presented in this book use features that only work if the app is run from a web server.
- You can use the http-server module to run a local web server on your computer.
- If your firewall software displays a message that asks whether you want to allow Node.js to communicate on private networks, you must allow it for the local web server to work.

Figure A-5   How to test an app on a local web server

Appendix B

How to set up macOS for this book

This appendix shows how to set up a macOS computer so it's ready to be used with this book. This includes downloading the files for this book and installing the software that we recommend for developing JavaScript apps. When you're done setting up your computer, you'll be ready to edit and run the JavaScript apps presented in this book, and you'll be ready to do the exercises that are at the end of each chapter.

As you read these descriptions, please remember that most websites are continually upgraded. As a result, some of the procedures in this appendix may have changed since this book was published. Nevertheless, these procedures should still be good guides to installing the software. And if there are significant changes to these setup instructions, we will post updates on our website (www.murach.com).

How to download the files for this book

Figure B-1 shows how to download the files for this book. This includes the code for the apps presented in this book. In addition, it includes the starting files for the exercises that are at the end of each chapter and the solutions to those exercises.

When you finish the procedure shown in this figure, the folders shown in this figure should contain the book apps, the starting files for the exercises, and the solutions to those exercises. Then, you can review the apps that are presented in this book, and you'll be ready to do the exercises.

The Murach website

`www.murach.com`

The folder that contains the files for this book

`Documents/murach/javascript`

The subfolders

Folder	Description
`book_apps`	The apps that are presented throughout this book.
`exercises`	The starting points for the exercises at the end of each chapter.
`solutions`	The solutions to the exercises.

How to install the files for this book

1. Go to www.murach.com.
2. Find the page for *Murach's Modern JavaScript*.
3. Scroll down to the "FREE downloads" tab and click it.
4. Click the Download Now button for the zip file. This should download a zip file.
5. Double-click the zip file to extract the files for this book into a folder named javascript.
6. Create the murach folder within the Documents folder.
7. Copy the javascript folder into the Documents/murach folder.

Description

- We recommend that you store the files for this book in folders that start with Documents/murach/javascript. That way, they will match the book exactly.
- This book sometimes instructs you to right-click, because that's common in Windows. On macOS, you can hold down the Ctrl key and click instead of right-clicking.

Figure B-1   How to download the files for this book

How to install Chrome

When you develop JavaScript applications, you need to test them on the browsers that your users are likely to use. For a commercial application, that usually includes Chrome, Firefox, Edge, Safari, and Opera. Then, if an application doesn't work on one of those browsers, you need to debug it.

As you do the exercises and work with the applications in this book, though, you can test your applications on just Chrome. Then, if you need to debug an application, you can use Chrome's developer tools as described in chapter 7.

The first procedure in figure B-2 shows how to install Chrome. In addition, we recommend that you set Chrome as the default browser. To do that, you can use the second procedure shown in this figure.

Once you've got Chrome installed and your default browser set correctly, you can use the third procedure to make sure that your system is set up correctly. To do that, you can double-click on an HTML file to test the default browser. For this book, that's all you need to do.

However, if you want to test your web apps in other browsers, you can also Ctrl-click on an HTML file to test the other browsers on your system. Since the Safari browser is installed on most macOS systems, you should be able to test your web apps with Safari. If you want to test your web apps in browsers that aren't already on your system, you can install them. To do that, you should be able to use a procedure similar to the one in this figure to install Firefox, Opera, or Edge.

The Chrome website

https://www.google.com/chrome/

How to install Chrome

1. Go to the download page for Chrome. One easy way to find this page is to search the internet for "chrome download".

2. Click the Download Chrome button and respond to the resulting dialog boxes. This should download an install file to your computer.

3. When the install file finishes downloading, double-click on it and respond to the resulting dialog boxes.

4. If you get a dialog that indicates that Google Chrome was downloaded from the internet and asks if you want to install it, click the Open button and respond the resulting dialog boxes.

5. In the sidebar, double click on the Google Chrome disk image and respond to the resulting dialog boxes. This should move Google Chrome to the Apps folder.

6. In the sidebar, click the eject icon that's to the right of the Google Chrome disk image.

How to make Chrome the default browser

1. Start Chrome.

2. Select Preferences from the Chrome menu.

3. If necessary, scroll to the bottom of the preferences.

4. Click the "Make default" button.

How to make sure your browsers are set up correctly

1. Start Finder and navigate to this folder:

   Documents/murach/javascript/book_apps/ch01/email_list

2. Double-click on the index.html file. This should display the index.html file in Chrome.

3. Ctrl-click the index.html file and click Open With. This should display a list of all browsers that are installed on your system. From this list, select the browser you want to test. This should display the index.html file in that browser.

Description

- Because Chrome is a popular browser that has excellent tools for testing and debugging JavaScript code, we recommend testing all of the exercises for this book in this browser.

- Because Safari comes preinstalled on macOS systems, it should also be available for testing apps.

- Because Firefox, Edge, and Opera are also popular browsers, you may want to install them too. To do that, you can use a procedure similar to the one for installing Chrome.

Figure B-2   How to install Chrome

How to install Visual Studio Code

If you're already comfortable with a text editor that works for editing HTML, CSS, and JavaScript files, you can continue using it. Otherwise, we recommend using Visual Studio Code. It is a free editor that offers many features and runs on Windows, macOS, and Linux.

The first procedure in figure B-3 shows how to install Visual Studio Code (VS Code). To do that, you download the app file from the VS Code website. Then, you move the app file into the Applications folder.

The second procedure shows how to make sure Visual Studio Code is installed correctly. To do that, you can use VS Code to open the book_apps folder described in figure B-1. Then, you can use the Explorer window on the left side of the main Visual Studio Code window to expand and collapse the folders that contain the HTML, CSS, and JavaScript files for this book. To learn how to use VS Code to work with these files, you can start by reading chapter 1.

The VS Code website

https://code.visualstudio.com/

How to install VS Code

1. Go to the download page for Visual Studio Code (VS Code). One easy way to find this page is to search the internet for "vs code download".
2. Click the button for downloading the macOS version and respond to any dialogs. This should download the app file for Visual Studio Code.
3. Move the app file for Visual Studio Code from the Downloads folder to the Applications folder.

How to make sure VS Code is installed correctly

1. Start VS Code.
2. Select File→Open from the menu system.
3. Use the resulting dialog to select this folder:
   Documents/murach/java_script/book_apps
4. This should open the folder that contains all the apps for this book in the Explorer window that's displayed on the left side of the main VS Code window.
5. Expand or collapse the folders in the Explorer window to view the files for the apps presented in this book. If you can view these files, VS Code is installed correctly.

Description

- Chapter 1 shows how to get started with Visual Studio Code (VS Code).

Figure B-3   How to install Visual Studio Code

How to install Node.js and the http-server module

Figure B-4 begins by showing how to install Node.js. To do that, you can use the first procedure in this figure. This is similar to the procedure for installing most apps.

After you install Node.js, you can make sure it's installed correctly by starting the Terminal app to get a prompt like this:

```
Your-Computer-Name:CurrentDirectory YourUsername$
```

At this prompt, you can enter the "node –v" command. This should display the version of Node.js that you just installed.

The third procedure shows how to use the npm install command to install the http-server module on your system. To get this command to run, you typically need to prefix it with the sudo (superuser do) command as shown in this figure. When you run the npm install command, it should display messages that show that the http-server module was installed successfully.

The Node.js website
`www.nodejs.org`

How to install Node.js

1. Go to the download page for Node.js. One way to find this page is to search the internet for "node.js download".

2. Click the button for the installer file for the most current LTS (Long Term Stable) release and respond to the resulting dialog boxes.

3. If you get any warning dialog boxes, choose to continue with the installation. This should download the installer file to your computer.

4. Double-click on the installer file to start the installer.

5. Respond to the resulting dialog boxes by accepting the default options.

How to make sure Node.js is installed correctly

1. Start the Terminal app.

2. Enter the node command like this:

   `$node -v`
   `V21.6.1`

   If this displays a version number, Node.js is set up correctly.

How to install the http-server module

1. Start the Terminal app.

2. Enter the npm install command like this:

   `$sudo npm install -g http-server`
   `added 40 packages in 4s`

Description

- *Node.js* is an open-source, cross-platform, runtime environment that executes JavaScript code outside a web browser.

- *NPM (Node Package Manager)* is a package manager for the JavaScript programming language.

- NPM is the default package manager for Node.js, and it's included when you install Node.js on your system.

- The http-server module provides a way to test web apps on a local web server.

Figure B-4   How to install Node.js and the http-server module

How to test an app on a local web server

Figure B-5 shows how to use the http-server module to test web applications on a local web server. This is important because some of the apps presented in this book use features that only work if the app is run from a web server. For example, the Clock app presented in chapter 13 only works when you run it from a web server. To do that, you can use the http-server module.

After you install the http-server module, you can use the cd command to change the directory to the javascript directory that contains the web apps for this book as shown by the first example.

After changing the directory, you can start the local web server by entering the http-server command as shown in the second example. Then, your firewall software may display a message that asks whether you want to allow Node.js to communicate on private networks. If you want the local web server to work correctly, you must allow this.

When the http-server module starts, it should display messages that indicate that the web server is starting and where it's available. In this figure, these messages show that the web server is available from port 8080 of the IP address of 127.0.0.1. In addition, they show that you can stop the web server by pressing Ctrl-C.

Since the localhost keyword is a synonym for 127.0.0.1, you can run the web app in the current directory by starting a web browser and entering "localhost:8080" for the URL as shown in this figure. Here, because the current directory has already been set to the javascript directory, the browser displays three links that correspond to the book_apps, exercises, and solutions directories. You can click on these links to navigate to any of the apps presented in this book, including the Clock app presented in chapter 13.

The command for changing the directory

```
$cd Documents/murach/javascript
```

The command for starting the server

```
$http-server
Starting up http-server, serving ./
...
Available on:
  http://127.0.0.1:8080
  http://10.0.0.218:8080
Hit CTRL-C to stop the server
```

A URL you can use to view the server

```
http://localhost:8080
```

The browser displaying the server's root directory

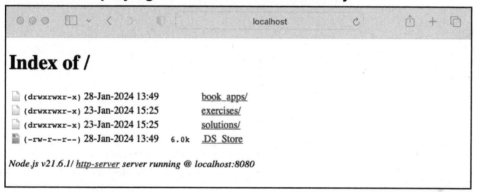

A book app from chapter 13 that must be run from a web server

```
1:58:43 PM

Sun January 28, 2024
```

The message that's displayed when you press Ctrl-C

```
http-server stopped.
```

Description

- Some of the apps presented in this book use features that only work if the app is run from a web server.
- You can use the http-server module to run a local web server on your computer.
- If your firewall software displays a message that asks whether you want to allow Node.js to communicate on private networks, you must allow it for the local web server to work.

Figure B-5   How to test an app on a local web server

Index

.. / character, 494-495
. / character, 494-495
.exit command, 484-485
.mjs file extension, 490-491, 494-495
/ character, 494-495
2D array, 348-351

A

Accessor property, 378-379
Accessor, 378-379
Ajax, 452-453
alert() method, 40-41, 242-243, 68-69
Anonymous function, 150-151
APOD API, 466-467
App
    APOD, 464-471
    Bio, 140-141, 162-163
    Clock, 268-269, 440-441
    Countdown, 260-263
    Drawing, 526-529
    Email Check, 138-139
    FAQ, 194-197
    Future Value, 106-107, 154-155
    Guess the Number, 90-91, 168-171
    Image Swap, 218-221
    Invoice, 374-375
    Magic Eight Ball, 98-99
    Miles to Kilometers, 72-73
    Movie List, 546-547
    Pong, 538-543
    Register, 206-209, 212-215, 288-289
    Slide Show, 272-275, 420-425
    Smiley Face, 534-535
    Task List, 326-329, 354-357
    Test Scores, 73-74, 122-123, 128-129
    Tic Tac Toe, 522-523
    Timer, 270-271
    Trips, 386-391
    Typewriter, 174-175
    User Directory, 474-477
appendChild() method, 210-211
Application Programming Interface, 452-453
Application server, 4-5

arc() method, 530-531
argv property, (process), 488-489
Arithmetic expression, 52-53
Arithmetic operator, 52-53
Array, 114-121
    add element, 116-117
    copy element, 124-125
    delete element, 116-117
    destructure, 346-347
    element, 114-115
    empty slot, 116-117
    filter, 340-341
    index, 114-115
    inspect, 126-127, 334-335
    length, 114-115
    literal, 114-115
    loop through, 338-339
    map, 340-341
    methods, 334-341
    modify element, 124-125, 338-339
    reduce, 340-341
    replace element, 116-117
    sort elements, 336-337
    transform element, 126-127
    with for loop, 118-119
Array of arrays, 348-351
Arrow function, 152-153
as keyword, 426-427
Assignment operator, 46-47
Assignment statement, 54-55
async keyword, 462-463, 472-473
Asynchronous code, 456-457
Asynchronous function, 462-463
at() method
    array, 126-127
    string, 130-131
Attribute, 284-285
Autocomplete attribute, 284-285
Autofocus attribute, 282-283
await keyword, 462-463, 472-473, 492-493

B

beginPath() method, 524-525
Binary operator, 94-95
Block scope, 156-157
blur event, 204-205
blur() method (form control), 204-205
book_apps folder, 552-553, 564-565

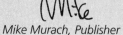
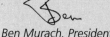

Web development books

Murach's HTML and CSS (5th Ed.)	$59.50
Murach's Modern JavaScript	59.50
Murach's JavaScript and jQuery (4th Ed.)	59.50
Murach's PHP and MySQL (4th Ed.)	59.50
Murach's ASP.NET Core MVC (2nd Ed.)	59.50

Books for data analysis

Murach's R for Data Analysis	$59.50
Murach's Python for Data Analysis	59.50

Programming language books

Murach's Python Programming (2nd Ed.)	$59.50
Murach's C++ Programming (2nd Ed.)	59.50
Murach's Java Programming (6th Ed.)	59.50
Murach's C# (8th Ed.)	59.50

Database/SQL books

Murach's MySQL (4th Ed.)	$59.50
Murach's Oracle SQL and PL/SQL for Developers (2nd Ed.)	54.50
Murach's SQL Server 2022 for Developers	59.50

Prices and availability are subject to change. Please visit our website or call for current information.

Have you mastered HTML and CSS?

The best web developers master HTML and CSS along with JavaScript. That's why *Murach's HTML and CSS* is the perfect companion to this book. Get it today and see for yourself!

We want to hear from you

Do you have any comments, questions, or compliments to pass on to us? It would be great to hear from you! Please share your feedback in whatever way works best.

 www.murach.com

 1-800-221-5528
(Weekdays, 8 am to 4 pm Pacific Time)

 murachbooks@murach.com

 twitter.com/murachbooks

 facebook.com/murachbooks

 linkedin.com/company/
mike-murach-&-associates

 instagram.com/murachbooks

What software you need for this book

- **Any text editor.** We recommend Visual Studio Code (VS Code) because it provides many excellent features.
- **At least one web browser.** We recommend Google Chrome because it provides excellent developer tools.
- **Node.js.** We recommend this runtime environment for learning how to run JavaScript on a server and for testing your web apps on a local web server.

All of this software can be downloaded from the internet for free.

To view step-by-step instructions for installing this software, please see appendix A (Windows) or B (macOS).

What the download includes

- The apps presented in this book.
- The starting files for the exercises at the end of each chapter.
- The solutions to those exercises.

How to download the files for this book

1. Go to murach.com.
2. Navigate to the page for *Murach's Modern JavaScript*.
3. Scroll down to the "FREE downloads" tab and click it.
4. Click the Download Now button for the zip file. This should download a zip file.
5. Double-click the zip file to extract the files for this book into a folder named javascript.
6. Create the murach folder within your Documents folder.
7. Copy the javascript folder into the murach folder.

For more details, please see appendix A (Windows) or B (macOS).

www.murach.com